Praise for *Reading Comics*

"Douglas Wolk has delivered what will surely be a cornerstone of comics criticism for years to come. . . . thoughtful and entertaining throughout."
 —*The Onion*

"Wolk's informed, readable assessment is lucid enough to serve as a primer for neophytes wondering what these 'graphic novels' are all about, yet even the most hardcore comics fans will garner considerable insight from it."
 —*Booklist*

"Wolk has established his credentials as a walking encyclopedia of comics and their most articulate watchdog. . . . Everything is here."
 —*Los Angeles Times*

"Wolk has found a niche for himself as a knowledgeable insider who knows how to talk to outsiders, a devotee who can communicate his passion to novices. . . . If comics are, as he says, in a golden age, Wolk is the right critic to memorialize the moment. "
 —*Toronto Globe and Mail*

"Wolk doesn't float in on word balloons with qualms about your intelligence. . . . He doesn't pull punches or apologize for his passion for comics books; he is, instead, inspired by their ambition and protective of their dignity."
 —*The Oregonian*

"For a relaxed overview that concentrates on reviews of specific works, you can't do better. . . . One of Wolk's great strengths is that he is as comfortable with mainstream commercial comics (including superheroes) as he is with 'art comics.'"
 —*Raleigh News & Observer*

"A perceptive and enlightening examination of the sudden rise of graphic novels and what they say about society."
 —*Seattle Post-Intelligencer*

"While most people have now warmed up to the idea of graphic novels as unique fusions of literature and art, nobody has so smartly written about them before."
 —*Portland Mercury*

"Critics in any artistic field could learn from Wolk's willingness to express not just appreciation but joy. . . . Intelligent, discerning, incisive, and terrifically engaging."
 —*The Irish Times*

DOUGLAS WOLK

READING COMICS

*How Graphic Novels Work
and What They Mean*

DA CAPO PRESS
A MEMBER OF THE PERSEUS BOOKS GROUP

Library of Congress Cataloging-in-Publication Data

Wolk, Douglas.
Reading comics : how graphic novels work and what they mean / Douglas Wolk.— 1st Da Capo Press ed.
    p. cm.
Includes index.
ISBN-13: 978-0-306-81509-6 (hardcover : alk. paper)
ISBN-10: 0-306-81509-5 (hardcover : alk. paper)
1. Comic books, strips, etc.—United States—History and criticism. I. Title.

PN6725.W65 2007
741.53—dc22

2007005232

HC: ISBN: 978-0-306-81509-6
PB: ISBN: 978-0-306-81616-1

Published by Da Capo Press
A Member of the Perseus Books Group
http://www.dacapopress.com

Parts of some chapters of this book have appeared in slightly or substantially different form in *The Believer, Salon, Comic Art, Ruminator, The Boston Phoenix*, and *The Village Voice*.

Da Capo Press books are available at special discounts for bulk purchases in the U.S. by corporations, institutions, and other organizations. For more information, please contact the Special Markets Department at the Perseus Books Group, 2300 Chestnut Street, Suite 200, Philadelphia, PA 19103, or call (800) 810-4145, ext. 5000, or e-mail special.markets@perseusbooks.com.

1 2 3 4 5 6 7 8 9

For Sterling

CONTENTS

ACKNOWLEDGMENTS

Thanks to Lisa Gidley, Jessica Bruder, Hillary Frey, Ed Park, James Schamus, Andras Szanto, Sarah Fan, Joe Gross, Calvin Reid, Heidi MacDonald, Todd Hignite, Sarah Lazin, and Ben Schafer for all their assistance and encouragement.

PART ONE

THEORY AND HISTORY

CHAPTER 1

What Comics Are and What They Aren't

The Golden Age Is Right Now

It's no longer news that comics have grown up. A form that was once solely the province of children's entertainment now fills bookshelves with mature, brilliant works by artists like Chris Ware, the Hernandez brothers, Dan Clowes, and Charles Burns, discussed in the sort of tone that was once reserved for exciting young prose novelists. Cartoonists' work is hung on the walls of galleries and museums; there's an annual anthology of *The Best American Comics*. A character in a 2004 *New Yorker* cartoon spoke for a lot of people: "Now I have to pretend to like graphic novels, too?"

For better and worse, though, the people who sustained the comics medium through its awkward childhood and difficult adolescence—and who have kept those aspects of comics alive if not always healthy, too—aren't just readers but collectors. To collect comic books is to treasure them as physical artifacts—not just vehicles for stories but primary documents that tell us something about our history as well as their own. So let's look closely at the covers of a handful of comics that will explain, in the broadest terms, how we got to where we are.

Carmine Infantino and Joe Kubert's cover for *Showcase* #4, the first Silver Age comic. "Showcase" #4, ©1954 DC Comics. All rights reserved. Used with permission.

The first one is *Showcase* #4, published in the summer of 1956. Its cover shows a strip of film, with a superhero called the Flash racing along on each of its frames and bursting bodily through the last one. As it turns out, this is a historically important comic: it's the first comic of the "Silver Age," which is what came after the "Golden Age" of comics. These are not references to foggy moments in the past; they're technical terms collectors use. The Golden Age began around 1937 or 1938, when the earliest regularly published ten-cent comic books appeared. (*Detective Comics* was launched in '37, and *Action Comics*, which introduced Superman in its first issue, in '38.) The age was dealt a mortal blow in 1954, with a public outcry about how comics caused juvenile delinquency, and arguably clung to life until that issue of *Showcase* showed up on newsstand and drugstore spinner racks.

Look again at the cover: it tells in miniature the early history of the understanding and misunderstanding of comics. The Flash is a new character with an old character's name, the first of endless recapitulations of the glories of the past. The artists, Carmine Infantino and Joe Kubert, aren't named, but it's easy enough for the trained eye to identify them (Infantino by his design sensibility, Kubert by his slightly feathered linework)—someone with a trained eye would consider their distinctive styles among the most important things about this cover, actually. In the upper right-hand corner, there's the seal of the Comics Code, which had been established a few years earlier. It's a sign that this comic book is meant for children and safe for them, and that if by chance it had struggled against being safe for children, its errors had been corrected. The cover's text and art reveal fumbling confusion over what exactly it is advertising. Is this comic a showcase for art, as in a museum? A series of frozen representations of reality or representations of something so unreal that a body moving at high speed leaves parallel lines of ink behind it? A movie that isn't really a movie, made out of individual images that the eye can see in or out of sequence or at the same time? Something that breaks destructively out of attempts to fix it in place?

Any art with a bygone golden age is doomed to try to repeat it, and to repeat its failings. The big problem with the idea of the Silver Age is that, by definition, the Golden Age it follows is lost, and the people who use that name for it are working from the assumption that the gold belongs to the past. The cartoonists of the '30s and '40s and early '50s were, for the most part, desperate, underpaid kids and sleazy entrepreneurs. Sometimes they managed to make crudely powerful imagination-bombs anyway, and a small handful of them were way ahead of their time. Most of the rest were simply *of* their time; they knew they could fob off any old thing on the children who were their audience—and did. All of them left their mark on the next generations of cartoonists, though, because they were the Ancients. For the next couple of decades, new comics either imitated the Golden Age's artistic and storytelling strategies, developed improvements on them, or (occasionally) rebelled against them.

On the following page is the cover from another comic book, *The Amazing Spider-Man* #31, cover-dated December 1965. The artist here is Steve Ditko, at the peak of his powers; the "spider" design is freakier than anything that would have been seen on a cover a few years earlier, and some of the inset images are unnerving on their own, especially the one with Spider-Man trapped in a lattice of thick black lines. The name of the publisher appears in the upper left-hand corner as "Marvel Pop Art Productions," the new name that writer and editor in chief Stan Lee gave the company for a few months. It reverted to "Marvel Comics Group" the month after this issue was published; somebody must have pointed out

Steve Ditko's cover for *The Amazing Spider-Man* #31, from Marvel's brief "Pop Art Productions" period. ©2007 Marvel Characters, Inc. Used with permission.

that the point of pop art was to recontextualize images and visual motifs from popular culture in a fine-art setting, and that if you're the producer of mass-produced popular culture that is generating those images and providing their initial context, you're ipso facto not recontextualizing them. Or maybe Lee just realized it sounded kind of pretentious and silly. What the "pop art" also evoked, though, was comics reaching for an effect that wasn't merely entertainment—although maybe not quite getting there.

Both text captions on the cover appear on "scroll" effects: a bit of self-deflating pomposity, suggesting both "something important is happening here" and "we're just kidding about the 'important' thing." And the bottom caption, "Dedicated to you, the great new Marvel breed of reader!"—well, that's a clue to the future: most obviously, Lee is setting up the idiotic brand rivalry between Marvel and its chief competitor, DC, that continues to this day. But he's also suggesting that he and Ditko are establishing something new that has more to do with a broader system (the "Marvel breed") than with the particular comic book at hand, and that what they're presenting is a kind of fan service—giving the "Marvel breed" exactly what they want.

The Comics Code seal is still up in the corner, as it was on virtually every comic published for the next decade, and many more after that: whatever else this issue of *Amazing Spider-Man* is, it's first and foremost a piece of entertainment for kids. At least as late as the mid-'70s, there were still universally understood rules for what a comic book looked like, how long it was, who it was for, and what kind of stories could be told in it. The few comics that didn't stay within the boundaries of those rules always seemed to be dancing frantically just outside them.

This next cover is a bit later: *Cerebus* #44, cover-dated November 1982 and drawn by the series' creator, Dave Sim. Its most obvious difference from our earlier examples is that it's a very design-conscious image, with its vertical bar, inset images, fancy typeface, decorative border, extensive use of negative space, and sideways logo. (In fact, the story inside the cover is sideways, too.) There's no Comics Code seal; children are simply not the intended audience for Sim's sprawling, satirical narrative about politics and religion in a medieval culture. The company publishing it is also something new: Aardvark-Vanaheim, a tiny Canadian concern started by Sim and his then wife, specifically to publish his series. There had been small publishers of black-and-white "underground" comics in the '60s, but Aardvark-Vanaheim didn't position itself as part of any kind

of counterculture: it was just independent, and this series had already lasted forty-four issues, far longer than any of the undergrounds. The issue's cover price is $1.50, two and a half times what was then the price of a new four-color superhero comic book. But this is something different—the cover's only explicit links to that visual aesthetic are the guy in the fuzzy parka with the antennae (a parody of the then popular superhero Moon Knight) and, of course, the size and shape of the cover itself.

Around the time *Cerebus* #44 was published, the rules of comics' style and substance were softening to conventions and norms. Breaking them was still a significant, conscious decision on a cartoonist's

Cerebus #44, drawn by Dave Sim: part of the independent-comics revolution of the '80s. ©2007 Dave Sim.

part, but it wasn't inconceivable or radical anymore. Over the course of the '80s, as independent comics companies sprang up all over, cartoonists took baby steps away from "the way we've always done things," figuring out which parts of their assumptions about the medium were just based on habit. For a while, it almost seemed that important or meaningful comics were, by definition, the ones that were dramatically different from all the others or somehow ruptured their conventions irreparably.

That's partly because, in 1986, three convention-rupturing comics appeared. Frank Miller and Klaus Janson's *The Dark Knight Returns* blew the dust off Batman's grim, gaudy subtext and made it the center of a brutal, smart, exquisitely drawn satire; Art Spiegelman's *Maus: A Survivor's Tale*, a shattering memoir of his father's experiences in the Holocaust and a formal triumph of cartooning, which was initially serialized in his magazine *RAW*, made waves beyond the comics world as a book; and Alan Moore and Dave Gibbons's *Watchmen*, a structurally magnificent superhero adventure that systematically demolished the entire idea of superhero adventures, galvanized mainstream comics. It was, it seemed, comics' annus mirabilis, the first year of a new era. From then until the turn of the millennium, those three books became the standard against which comics that wanted to be important or meaningful were measured and the standard to which too many cartoonists who wanted to create something important or meaningful (but didn't know how) aspired.

This brings us to our next comic: *Big Numbers* #1, published in the spring of 1990. The cover is at least as design intensive as that issue of *Cerebus* (this time, the price is exiled to the back cover, which looks classier, and is much higher: $4.50), and the publisher is another creator-owned independent company (Mad Love, formed by *Watchmen* writer Alan Moore). A few things are obviously different about this one, though. The first is its format: it's big and square. The second is that the image is a painting—not a pen-and-ink drawing—of a deliberately quotidian street scene. And the third is the most consequential: not only is the image signed by Bill Sienkiewicz, but Moore's and Sienkiewicz's names appear in huge letters. The creators, not the characters, are the selling point.

Over the course of the '90s and early 2000s, a neat thing happened as a result of all the convention-rupturing that went on in the '80s (as well as a bunch of economic shifts that I'll describe in chapter 2): the conventions about comics' form and content that had had a million holes poked in them, as well as a few that hadn't, stopped being normative. A lot of comics still adhere to the old standards of form and style and subject matter, but that's now a creative choice like any other, instead of a default. Comics no longer have to make a point of what they *aren't*.

Big Numbers #1, whose cover prominently features its creators' names.
©2007 Alan Moore and Bill Sienkiewicz.

Next, instead of another cover, you'll have to imagine a stack of ten books and comics: Bryan Lee O'Malley's *Scott Pilgrim and the Infinite Sadness*, Alison Bechdel's *Fun Home*, Grant Morrison and Frank Quitely's *All-Star Superman* #4, Kevin Huizenga's *Curses*, the *Kramers Ergot 6* anthology, Ed Brubaker and Michael Lark's *Daredevil* #86, Ellen Forney's *I Love Led Zeppelin*, David B.'s *Babel* #2, Lilli Carré's *Tales of Woodsman Pete*, and Megan Kelso's *The Squirrel Mother*. They couldn't be much more different from each other; they're all executed in radically different styles, and only two of them (*All-Star Superman* and *Daredevil*, the two superhero comics) even have the same physical dimensions. Half of them don't have "issue numbers" of any kind. They were published by nine different companies. What they all have in common, though, is being somewhere between ambitious-and-very-good and the sort of flat-out phenomenal work people will be recalling for years; featuring their creators' names prominently on their covers, which is now standard practice; and having been published during a period of about a month in the middle of 2006.

If there's such a thing as a golden age of comics, it's happening right now. As I write this, with that stack of new comics in front of me, it's obvious that there has never been as enormous a volume of extraordinary English-language comics published in a single year as there has been in the last twelve months. Long-awaited masterpieces like *Fun Home* and Charles Burns's *Black Hole* have appeared as hardcovers from large book-publishing companies. Cartoonists from the phenomenal French art-comics collective L'Association have found an audience for English translations of their work. The big companies that dominate the superhero genre are publishing some terrific, formally adventurous work (as well as a lot of by-the-numbers crap, but only the good stuff counts toward the Golden Age).

On top of all the new things worth getting excited about, publishers have finally learned that it's in their interest to keep the best comics of the past in print in book form—often printed much more nicely than they were when they originally appeared as ephemeral periodicals. Has something been lost in their shift from disposable pulp to acid-free archival paper? The jealous collector in me says "maybe"—but what's been lost is more cultural context than anything intrinsic to the work itself.

It's not that the average quality of new comics has improved. As always, there are hacks, no-talents, and bandwagon jumpers everywhere, and right now a lot of them smell money. But there are a lot more comics in print that reward close attention than there have ever been before. This book is possible to write now in a way it wouldn't have been even five years ago.

The best part is that it looks like the Golden Age is only beginning: the aesthetic development of comics has finally built up enough momentum to keep attracting more creators (and, thank God, more kinds of creators—women cartoonists aren't anomalous anymore), and to give them the time they need to get good and produce significant work. Nobody has ever gone into comics for the money, but with the audience and cultural prestige expanding, it is becoming more possible for good cartoonists to make a living. A very young generation of cartoonists has grown up on manga and animation as much as on American comics, and they're already publishing their own work or disseminating it on the Internet; the new kids are still mostly figuring out how to make the leap from pretty-picture-making to storytelling, but within ten years or so, they're going to be doing amazing things.

Finite Crisis

All this creative bounty and cultural power has brought comics to a moment of crisis. It's a "we should all have such crises" crisis, and a distinctly finite crisis, but a dilemma nonetheless. There have been so many interesting comics in the last few years that a worthwhile addition to the bookshelf isn't surprising. Over the last decade or so, the main format for narrative comics has been shifting from periodical pamphlets to books. Meanwhile, the schism between the two big American schools of comics—let's call them "the mainstream" and "art comics," and I'll explain what those terms mean later—is becoming wider and bitterer. And the big, awkward question hanging in the air is how to read and discuss comics now that they're very different from what they used to be.

There's a problem with the way a lot of people talk about comics: it's very hard to talk about them *as comics*. One numbingly common mistake in the way culture critics address them is to invoke "the comic book genre." As cartoonists and their longtime admirers are getting a little tired of explaining, comics are not a genre; they're a *medium*. Westerns, Regency romances, film noir: those are genres—kinds of stories with specific categories of subjects and conventions for their content and presentation. (Stories about superheroes are a genre, too.) Prose fiction, sculpture, video: those, like comics, are media—forms of expression that have few or no rules regarding their content other than the very broad ones imposed on them by their form.

Still, there's a reason people make that mistake. Until about twenty years ago, the way almost everybody experienced the medium was intimately tied to a handful of genres. That's what made money for the big pulp-comics companies: superhero stuff, mostly, but sometimes horror or romance or science fiction or crime comics, each of which has its own familiar codes and formulas.

The box of "genre"—it's easy to visualize as a long, white cardboard box, the kind collectors store plastic-bagged back issues inside—is easy to close, and hard to see out of, once you're inside it. Occasionally, comics-industry types assert that comics are good at telling stories in lots of different genres, which misses the big picture in the same way as a dairy-industry type insisting that milk can be made into lots of different flavors of ice cream. On the art-comics side of things, there's even a backlash now: readers and critics dismissing genre-based comics out of hand on the grounds that they *are* genre-based. This is also known as the "I'm so sick of superheroes I could scream" effect, and even though I don't subscribe to it, I'm kind of sympathetic to it.

Another common error is to assert that highbrow comics are, some-how, not really comics but something else (preferably with a fancier name, as I'll discuss in chapter 3)—different not just in breed but in species from their mass-cultural namesakes. There's a certain nose-in-the-air class consciousness inherent in this particular argument; it's evident, for instance, in a review by Gloria Emerson in the June 16, 2003, issue of *The Nation*. "It has never been a habit of mine to read comic books," she writes, "so I was, at first, slightly taken aback by *Persepolis: The Story of a Childhood*, by Marjane Satrapi. But she is such a talented artist and her black-and-white drawings are so captivat-ing, it seems wrong to call her memoir a comic book. Rather, it is a 'graphic memoir' in the tradition of *Maus*, Art Spiegelman's brilliant story of the Holocaust." If you don't see what's wrong with that pas-sage, imagine it beginning: "It has never been a habit of mine to watch movies . . . ," and ending by asserting that, say, *Syriana* is not actually a movie but a "cinematic narrative" in the tradition of *Saving Private Ryan*.

The genre/medium confusion is an error of ignorance, while the if-it's-deep-it's-not-really-comics gambit is just a case of snobbery (in the sense of wanting to make a distinction between one's own taste and the rabble's taste). But the most thoroughly ingrained error in the language used to discuss comics is treating them as if they were particularly weird, or failed, examples of another medium altogether. Good comics are sometimes described as being "cinematic" (if they have some kind of broad visual scope or imitate a familiar kind of movie) or "novelistic" (if they have keenly observed details, or simply take a long time to read). Those can be descriptive words when they're applied to comics. It's almost an insult, though, to treat them as compliments. Using them as praise implies that comics *as a form* aspire (more or less unsuccessfully) to being movies or novels.

When comics try to be *specific* movies or novels, they are indeed unsuccessful. Comics adaptations of movies are pointless cash-ins at best—movies that don't move, with inaccurate drawings of the actors and scenery. Why would anyone but an obsessive want to look at that? Likewise, comics adaptations of prose books are almost uniformly terrible, from the old *Classics Illustrated* pamphlets to the contemporary versions of *Black Beauty* and *The Hunchback of Notre Dame*; they don't run on the same current, basically, and they end up gutting the original work of a lot of its significant content. The one major exception to date—the only prose book I can think of that has been turned into first-rate comics—is Paul Auster's *City of Glass*, and David Mazzucchelli and Paul Karasik's 1994 variation on it works only because it extends Auster's metafictional games into a visual dimension.

I'm not trying to make the essentialist argument that the only good comics are the ones that avoid strategies from other media. A lot of great ones do use storytelling devices they've adapted from film, in particular. Think, for instance, of the deservedly famous opening sequence of *Watchmen*: six panels of identical size, starting with a close-up image of a smiley-face pin in a puddle of blood and zooming upward until the camera is looking out a window many stories above. "Close-up," "zooming," "camera": not only the concepts but the words belong to movies. As readers, we imagine a stable, continuous Steadicam motion upwards (and also visualize the sign carrier in the "shot" walking at a constant pace, perpendicular to the direction the "camera" is moving). Still, that's a great scene that *uses* a cinematic technique, not a great scene *because* the technique it uses is cinematic.

Other comics actually do aspire to being movies, mostly for economic reasons: license your story or characters to Hollywood and there's a lot of money to be made. (A few comics imprints, whether covertly or openly, exist mostly to create and publicize properties that can be pitched as movies. Their comics tend to be dreadful, of course.) Still, that aspiration has to do with content rather than form. And nobody has ever wanted to write a novel and settled for making their story into comics: for one thing, it just takes too damn long to draw something when you could write it instead.

I'm even going to take issue with Will Eisner, the late grandmaster of American comics, who liked to describe comics as a "literary form." They bear a strong resemblance to literature—they use words, they're printed in books, they have narrative content—but they're no more a literary form than movies or opera are literary forms. Scripts for comics are arguably a literary form in exactly the same way that film and theater scripts are literary forms, but a script is not the same thing as the finished work of art. I occasionally find it convenient to refer to some kinds of comics as "literary" (essentially, the ones that have the same sorts of thematic concerns as literary fiction), but that's still a dangerous convenience. Samuel R. Delany's term "paraliterary" is useful here, if clunky: comics are *sort of* literary. But that's not all they are.

Comics are not prose. Comics are not movies. They are not a text-driven medium with added pictures; they're not the visual equivalent of prose narrative or a static version of a film. They are their own thing: a medium with its own devices, its own innovators, its own clichés, its own genres and traps and liberties. The first step toward attentively reading and fully appreciating comics is acknowledging that.

French critics sometimes refer to comics as the "ninth art," a phrase that has slipped into Anglophone discussion. (I first encountered it as the name of a Web site that ran from 2001 to 2006.) The phrase is inspired by Ricciotto Canudo's 1923 manifesto *Reflections on the Seventh Art*—the seventh art being film, and the first six being architecture, mu-

The opening sequence of *Watchmen's* first issue, written by Alan Moore and drawn by Dave Gibbons. From *Watchmen,* ©DC Comics. All rights reserved. Used with permission.

sic, dance, sculpture, painting, and poetry. (The eighth? Photography, television, cuisine, or fireworks, depending on whom you ask.) The numbering's a little arbitrary, but giving comics-the-art a number is useful, because it suggests that it requires a vocabulary of its own to discuss and evaluate.

That said, it's not a bad idea, exactly, to talk about comics using some of the same language we use to talk about prose and film and nonnarrative visual art; sometimes it fits. (In fact, we have to, because the language of comics criticism is still young and scrawny—it's so un-derdeveloped that there's no good adjective that means "comics-ish.") It's just worth being careful about. Describing the viewer's perspective in a particular comics panel is entirely reasonable; talking about where the "camera" is, as I did a few paragraphs ago, has some loaded associa-tions. On the other hand, borrowed language is sometimes a fair trade-off for clarity. As Hedwig said to Tommy Gnosis, it's what we've got to work with.

Explaining Myself to a Straw Man

I've seen a handful of questions about the point, terms, and function of comics criticism raised in various places; some have been raised by cartoonists I admire (or don't), some by other critics, some by me. For the sake of convenience, I'm going to put them all in the mouth of a single impertinent straw man, and I will try to patiently explain myself to him.

> STRAW MAN: Why would criticism about comics be useful? They're such an immediate art: so seductive, so easy to sink into and get carried away by, so un-hungry for explanation. It's all there on the surface!

> ME: In ten years, I suspect, that question will sound sillier than it does now, but it deserves an answer in any case. It's true, Mr. Straw, that this particular visual, narrative medium can offer some very easy pleasure—but easy pleasure and simple pleasure aren't the same thing. It's worth thinking about how that immediacy and seduction you mention work, what makes good comics different from mediocre or bad ones, and even what virtues can be found in lesser ones. Critical analysis and strong opinions are a necessary response to any art—they're part of what helps it grow and change and what bonds its audience to it. And criticism is particularly valuable to an art coming into its Golden Age.

That's part of my mission with this book: to explore some of the ways it's possible to read comics, and to figure out where their power comes from. I'm not alone in that mission, either. There are magazines devoted to serious discussion of comics and the artists who make them (*The Comics Journal* is the longest running, while *Comic Art* is fairly new and pretty impressive so far), and there have been a handful of interesting books about the way comics work—Will Eisner's *Comics and Sequential Art* was the first, and Scott McCloud's *Understanding Comics* is the best known. But I'm most interested in the reader's side of the comics experience: figuring out how we experience them in general and looking carefully at particular artists and works.

STRAW MAN: Let's get started by defining terms, then. McCloud famously defined comics as "juxtaposed pictorial and other images in deliberate sequence, intended to convey information and/or to produce an aesthetic response in the viewer"; Dylan Horrocks affectionately picked apart that definition in an essay called "Inventing Comics" that can be read at www.hicksville.co.nz. What's *your* definition, Mr. Critic Guy?

ME: My reply is that I'm not going to define "comics" here, because if you have picked up this book and have not been spending the last century trapped inside a magic lantern, you already pretty much know what they are, and "pretty much" is good enough. That word I mentioned above that Samuel Delany coined, "paraliterary," is part of a terrific essay called "The Politics of Paraliterary Criticism" that's effectively scared me off trying to come up with a definition. If you try to draw a boundary that includes everything that counts as comics and excludes everything that doesn't, two things happen: first, the medium always wriggles across that boundary, and second, whatever politics are implicit in the definition always boomerang on the definer. (As Horrocks points out, although McCloud's definition counts photo-booth strips and

Scott McCloud presents his definition of comics in *Understanding Comics*.
©2007 Scott McCloud.

Hogarth's etchings as comics, it deliberately excludes single-panel cartoons like "Dennis the Menace," and McCloud has tried to distance himself from the idea that it includes illustrated children's books.)

STRAW MAN: Fine, then. I'll just have to be trickier and ask you what the hell the thing you're writing about is.

ME: A good way of putting it. What I'm going to be discussing in the rest of this book is actually a *subset* of comics—and please note that while I'll be covering a pretty broad range of material, I'm passing over a lot of perfectly legitimate comics, too. I'm mostly interested in sustained narrative, which means comic books and graphic novels, much more than newspaper comic strips or one-off cartoon illustrations. I'm basically going to avoid discussing manga—the enormous category of Japanese comics—and its international derivatives altogether, partly because manga seems to operate by a slightly different set of rules, but mostly because I simply don't have the taste for most of it, and I'm not going to go on about stuff I don't "get." I'm also going to deal here only with work published in English and available without much difficulty in the United States, which rules out most of the enormous body of European comics and a lot of worthy British material.

STRAW MAN: Have you noticed that that's mostly a description of what you're *not* writing about?

ME: I'm getting there. But before I get there, I should explain some of my central arguments and some of my major biases. If any of this seems vague or obvious or both, I apologize; the explanations and justifications will come later. First of all, what matters to me is mostly particular cartoonists and their work, rather than characters and series published by large companies, with stories written and drawn by interchangeable cartoonists.

STRAW MAN: You're saying you're an "indie" guy—you don't have much use for superhero comics. That's fair. I mean, I've noticed that you use "mainstream" in a slightly dismissive way.

ME: That's not what I'm saying! It's true that a lot of the comics that stick with me are owned by their creators and published by somebody other than DC or Marvel, but not a week goes by that I don't read, with pleasure, some glossy corporate superhero comics product from a writer or artist I really like. "Mainstream" is a useful piece of shorthand, even though it's a lot less literal than it was back when *Batman* and *The Fantastic Four* had much higher circulation and cultural potency, and black-and-white art comics had no hope of being seen by anyone who didn't frequent weird little grottos that specialized in them. Now "mainstream" basically means "superhero and other genre comics, serialized as pamphlets and then sometimes collected into books, and marketed mostly to comics stores," as opposed to "general-interest comics marketed outside the specialty comics industry." Weird, but there you go.

STRAW MAN: Okay. Let me rephrase that: you're an "indie" guy, but you don't want to break up your collection of *Green Lantern*.

ME: Don't get me started on collectors. (At least not yet—I'll get to that in chapter 3.) And, actually, I'm a lot less interested in, say, *Green Lantern* as an ongoing series or ongoing franchise than I am in the specific early-'70s issues of *Green Lantern* by Denny O'Neil and Neal Adams, or in the messy but ambitious *Green Lantern: Mosaic* project that Gerard Jones wrote in the late '80s. What tends to get my attention is *style*—a distinctive, coherent, and interesting aesthetic expressed in the way a comic's story is told. I'm also less interested in Green Lantern as a cultural icon, or in what Green Lantern the character is going to do next month, than I am in the way the cartoonists who contribute to the enormous body of stories about Green Lantern use that character and the metaphorical associations attached to him.

STRAW MAN: Metaphorical associations?

ME: Metaphors are the core of what I'm going to be talking about, because comics are particularly well suited to extended and large-scale metaphors, for reasons I'll get into shortly. When you look at a comic book, you're not seeing either the world or a direct representation of the world; what you're seeing is an interpretation or transformation of the world, with aspects that are exaggerated, adapted, or invented. It's not just unreal, it's deliberately constructed by a specific person or people. But because comics are a narrative and visual form, when you're reading them, you *do* believe that they're real on some level. (Cartoonists have lots of tricks to immerse the reader in invented environments.) So the meaning of the comics story within the world we see on the page is different from its meaning within the reader's world.

STRAW MAN: This is exactly what Susan Sontag was complaining about in "Against Interpretation," isn't it? You're saying that comics can't just be what they are—that they're actually always something other than what they appear to be.

ME: Well, they *are* always what they appear to be, at the very least. And I don't think that good comics *require* metaphors to be built into their structure, other than one very basic one: cartooning is, inescapably, a metaphor for the subjectivity of perception. No two people experience the world the same way; no two cartoonists draw it the same way, and the way they draw it is the closest a reader can come to experiencing it through their eyes.

Still, an awful lot of the comics that have stuck with me most seem to be built around metaphors. Some of them are blatant, like Art Spiegelman drawing Jews as mice and Nazis as cats in *Maus*; sometimes they operate at a level so deeply entrenched that they can be hard to notice or can be taken for granted. Genre comics, and especially superhero comics, involve concrete representations of abstract ideas in ways that have become so familiar it's easy to gloss over them.

STRAW MAN: You're saying your job as a comics critic is to say what those metaphors *really* mean, Mr. Arbiter of Meaning?

ME: It can be, in part; it can also be figuring out the mechanisms that make those metaphors function. But the way I experience and think about comics has a lot to do with the fact that I really *enjoy* them. I like figuring out how that pleasure works and describing it to other people so that they can enjoy them too, or at least enjoy them more fully than they would otherwise. And what I like (and want to pass along) about a particular comic can be the pleasure of pure spectacle, or of ingenious design, or of kinetic flow, or of characters' psychological depth, or of a story that's funny or engaging, or any number of other things.

I also think it's my responsibility as a critic to be harsh and demanding and to subject unambitious or botched work to public scorn, because I want *more good comics*: more cartoonists who challenge themselves to do better, and more readers who insist on the same. Here's a bit from one of my favorite critical manifestos, Rebecca West's 1914 essay, "The Duty of Harsh Criticism": "Just as it was the duty of the students of Kelvin the mathematician to correct his errors in arithmetic, so it is the duty of critics to rebuke these hastinesses of great writers, lest the blurred impressions weaken the surrounding mental fabric and their rough transmissions frustrate the mission of genius on earth."

STRAW MAN: All this "genius on earth" stuff sounds kind of po-faced—what about comics that are just cheap and vulgar and exciting?

ME: Cheap and vulgar and exciting is great. I love cheap and vulgar and exciting, and I don't think there's any contradiction between that and genius on earth. I just hate cheap and vulgar and boring. I probably hate expensive and refined and boring at least as much.

STRAW MAN: So what you're into is really just fun? Do you test comics on a fun-ometer or something? And do you really think you can have much to say about something if you're judging it on the basis of "I laughed; I cried"?

ME: Some of that intent to entertain, honestly, is coded into the DNA of comics: the medium was incubated in the marketplace, and for decades, cartoonists knew that their work had to *instantly* give pleasure if they wanted to eat. In the course of its development as a populist art, the comic book got really good at entertainment: thrills! chills! laughs! When the art-comics revolution came along, a lot of its point was that the medium was capable of *more* than being entertaining in a few overfamiliar, blatant ways. But one thing that's always entertaining is being caught up in a story, and since comics simultaneously feed the parts of the brain that make sense of written language and pictures, narrative seems natural or at least formally appropriate to them.

STRAW MAN: It's a little on the tautological side, maybe, to point out that comics tell stories, especially since you've already mentioned that you're mostly interested in "sustained narrative," I think the phrase was? Isn't this McCloud's "Dennis the Menace" problem again?

ME: Maybe, but it also illustrates my point. If you look at a block of text, you don't necessarily expect that it's going to be a story. If you look at a series of comics panels, you have the expectation that you're going to "find out what happens." (Even single-panel comics, "Dennis the Menace" and others, are almost always meant to be funny, and the humor usually comes from implying a story of which we're only seeing one moment.) I'm sure it's theoretically possible to come up with comics that would do the same sort of thing Laura Mulvey proposed as an avant-garde for movies, deliberately eliminating not just their narrative conventions but the pleasure of looking at them. That doesn't make it worth doing, though. For all the unsavory habits and formal clichés American capitalism has bred into comics, I think the tradition that they generally try to tell stories, and tell them in a compelling way, is pretty healthy.

STRAW MAN: To recap: you're into metaphors and stories. So comics criticism, as far as you're concerned, is basically literary criticism, except that the texts you're writing about happen to have drawings of Captain America attached to them?

ME: Do me a favor and say "Hopey Glass" sometimes instead of "Captain America," will you? Comics criticism actually works pretty differently from literary criticism—partly because what drawings do is very different from what words do (we'll get into that more in chapter 5) and partly because *style* is so important to the way comics work.

By style, I mean all the elements that go into a comic's "look and feel," to use the computer-design term: the things that affect the reading experience irrespective of the story's content. Some of that is linguistic tone, some of that is pacing and storytelling, but the biggest element of it is the idiomatic way a comic is drawn.

It's very easy to think of comics in terms of their plots and incidents—to slip from "what happens in this story" to "what this comic is about" to "what this comic *is*." And it's true that some comics are intended as not much more than vehicles for narrative: their stylistic gestures aren't supposed to count for nearly as much as what happens between the beginning and the end. Those are mostly mainstream comics meant to be read as having their publisher's and period's "house style." (Of course, there's no such thing as a genuinely neutral style: every stylistic decision, even if it's arrived at by default, means something.)

If you want to evaluate comics as a critic, or enjoy them fully as a reader, you have to be attentive to both their narrative substance and their style—and cartoonists' visual style is manifested in every image they draw on every page of every comic book.

"Only Inarticulate People Use Language"

Back, for a moment, to one of those comics I was waving around near the beginning, for a quick quote and another excuse. *Big Numbers #1* begins with a scene in which poet Christine Gathercole, sleeping on a train to her hometown, is awakened by a kid throwing a heavy bolt through her window, and yells "Shit!" "I don't think there's any need to use language," says the old man sitting across from her. "Only inarticulate people use language."

It's worth noting that what comics are closest to, in the way we physically experience them, are prose books. We watch a movie, we look at a photograph (or a single, wordless drawn image), but we *read* comics. That's the process: holding them in our hands, turning their pages, getting stories from them as we burrow from one end to the other.

Even so, the comparison is badly flawed, because comics aren't just more visual than prose; they're *less verbal*. Comics can get across the image of a physical setting or person or object or any other visual phenomenon much more easily than prose—they can just show it—but dialogue, or anything nonvisual that needs to be described or explained, takes up

Christine Gathercole questions her own medium in *Big Numbers* #1 (written by Alan Moore, drawn by Bill Sienkiewicz). ©2007 Alan Moore and Bill Sienkiewicz.

an awful lot of space very quickly in comics form. More than 150 words or
so on a six-panel page, and things start to look pretty crowded.

For that reason, and some others, the actual text in American comic
books was generally pretty impoverished until the '80s. It's always been
subordinate to plot and storytelling, out of necessity; narrative isn't the
same thing as language usage, and a lot of comics' best-loved writers were
ace storytellers but mediocre wordsmiths. Stan Lee revolutionized comics
writing in the '60s, but his dialogue and captions back then were oddly
stylized at best and cringeworthy at worst (let's not even get into his more
recent writing); in the '70s and early '80s, Chris Claremont's *X-Men*
scripts made their impact on the strength of his dexterous approach to
characterization, not the mannered eccentricities of dialogue that have
since hardened into almost unbearable tics. When Alan Moore earned
his stripes on *Swamp Thing* in the '80s, his precise, naturalistic dialogue
seemed shockingly good—better than it really was, probably, because it
was so far out of the league of anything around it. Moore was arguably the
first mainstream comics writer who seemed fully in command of his style,
but a few years later, other writers, mostly British, started to follow his example of sensitivity to language: Neil Gaiman, Warren Ellis, Garth Ennis, Grant Morrison, and a few others belonged to the first wave.

All of the writers I've just mentioned have a couple of things in
common: they made their name in mainstream genre comics, and
they write scripts for other people who draw them. The other thing
that was happening in the mid-'80s, while Moore and the "British Invasion" were raising the mainstream's standard for writing, was the independent comics revolution. Most of the notable comics that came
out of it were by cartoonists who both wrote and drew their work and
for whom "writing" and "drawing" sometimes didn't even seem like
separate activities.

As it turned out, a lot of the prominent cartoonists in the independent scene were good with language, too. Jaime and Gilbert Hernandez, Howard Chaykin, Dave Sim, and (although it took them a little
longer to get up to speed) Peter Bagge and Dan Clowes all made comics
with a unified force and grace that most writer/artist collaborations

lacked. They attracted the attention of readers who had grown bored of trying to scratch for pellets of genuinely original expression in the formula-bound world of genre comics.

But the big mainstream companies still had plenty going for them: the X-Men, Superman, and lots of other character names people recognize; devoted if slowly dwindling audiences; money enough to buy the services of some top-flight cartoonists who didn't mind not owning their work (and initiatives that allowed some of them to own their work); and deep if convoluted collective histories that would eventually become the focus of the way they intended their comics to be read. (I'll explain in chapter 4.)

Since the mid-'80s, both the mainstream (which has expanded beyond Marvel and DC to encompass a bunch of smaller companies that specialize in the same sorts of stuff) and the artists and publishers outside it have retrenched and concentrated on what they do best. The result is that American comics, which had seemed for a while like they fit on a continuum with convention on one side and expressiveness on the other, have become divided into two very different schools,* with almost no overlap between them—in fact, there's a distance between the two of them that sometimes turns into outright mutual contempt.

One school—the larger one, in terms of its market share—is mainstream comics: *Wolverine, Batman, Conan, Y: The Last Man*, and so on. Mainstream comics are genre-based and almost always serialized as monthly or quasi-monthly pamphlets, and they're generally written and drawn by different people—sometimes by mid-sized committees. They're story-driven and series-based, so there are always more stories to tell; they rely partly on readers' attachment to certain characters or franchises. The best ones are usually by writer/artist teams who plan the look and feel of their collaboration.

The other major school is art comics: *Love & Rockets, Ghost World, La Perdida, Palookaville*, and the like. Art comics avoid genre, unless

---

*American-produced manga-style comics are a smaller third category, which, as I mentioned earlier, I'm not going to go into here. I'll note, though, that they have very firmly set conventions of their own.

they can keep it at some kind of ironic remove. They are almost always written and drawn by a single cartoonist, and they tend to be conceived as self-contained books, even when they're initially serialized in pamphlets, which is becoming increasingly rare. Their visual style is usually outside, and sometimes far outside, the stylistic range of the mainstream, and the art carries a lot more of their storytelling and thematic weight. Art cartoonists often work much more slowly than mainstream cartoonists—it can take many years to finish a single substantial work. Still, they've collectively built up enough cultural capital to rival the mainstream; as we'll see in the next chapter, that happened very slowly, with the aid of the peculiar economic structure of the comics business.

CHAPTER 2

Auteurs, the History of Art Comics, and How to Look at Ugly Drawings

Auteurs, Authors, and Art

The comics form has a long and distinguished history, and I would like to propose temporarily ignoring a lot of it. A whole subculture of comics experts spend their time debating what the first comic was, trying to find earlier and earlier examples of the form. One school of thought holds that the nineteenth-century Swiss artist Rodolphe Töpffer was the first cartoonist in the modern sense. Scott McCloud argues in *Understanding Comics* that the Bayeux Tapestry, which was probably created in the eleventh century, is an example of sequential visual narrative and therefore counts as comics.

No matter how far back you go, though, there's always going to be something comicslike—if a bit less so with every step. There's not much to be gained from that kind of ancestor seeking, other than a kind of validation that salves nothing but insecurity. Better, perhaps, to wave vaguely at the past and say that, yes, comics have been around for a good long time, and a lot of the formal conventions associated with the medium's current state were solidified (although probably not created)

An early-'90s explo-
sion of expressive style
from Peter Bagge's
series *Hate*, now col-
lected in *Buddy Does
Seattle*. ©2007 Peter Bagge.

in the early twentieth century. No one genius gave birth to the form; it
just coalesced.

For my purposes, it's much more interesting to figure out how one
particular breed of comics—the kind I'm discussing in most of the second half of this book—got to be the way it is. Let's call it "art comics,"
noting that its development has happened on a very long and very steep
curve and is still happening.

Again, some explanation is necessary before we can go any further.
What's an art comic? As an art critic, I can (tautologically) describe it as
the kind of comic I find it most fruitful to discuss critically, but there are
actually a couple of other useful parameters I'd like to propose.

First of all, art comics' *style* is at least as important as the content of
their narrative, and always a direct expression of their creators' idiosyn-
crasies and work-specific intentions. "Expressiveness" is more the point
of art comics than characters or plot points; they privilege the distinctiveness of the creator's hand, rather than the pleasures of the tools of
genre and readerly expectations.

The content of art comics is also almost invariably *owned* by their creators—which means that most of the fundamental restrictions on what they look like and what happens in the course of their narratives are set by the creators alone.

I'd also like to clarify that "art comics" and "good comics" aren't the same thing: when I say that something is within the orbit of art comics, that isn't a value judgment, just a description. The two categories overlap, but there are lots of examples of each that don't fit the other. "Good comics"? There aren't many terms more loaded than "good," and when I use some form of it, it usually just means that I'm talking about something I like—the critic's prerogative! But comics I like enough to impute goodness to generally have a couple of more specific attributes. First, they're somehow *pleasing* to me—engaging and compelling, which is the way pleasure in narrative works, rather than necessarily amusing or entertaining, although being amusing and entertaining doesn't hurt—and, second, they're *resonant*, with images or ideas that linger with me after I've finished reading them. I apologize for spelling out all this potentially bone-obvious stuff, but I'd rather be too precise about it than too sloppy.

Here's where the overlap between "art" and "good" comes from. The style-first mandate for art comics means that their primary value for their readers is as the work of their creators' hands—an idea that tends to be called "auteurism," by which comics readers mean something rather different from what the film critics of the '50s and '60s meant when they referred to *"auteur* theory." The creator of a comic—the person who applies pen to drawing board or (lately) stylus to digital tablet—is its author, and comics produced under the sole or chief creative control of a single person of significant skill are more likely to be good (or at least novel enough to be compelling and resonant) than comics produced by a group of people assembly-line style—one writing, one penciling, one inking, one lettering, one coloring—under the aegis of an editor who hires them all individually. This naturally coincides with the observation that a comic owned by its creator is more likely to be stylistically adventurous than one produced on a work-made-for-hire basis for a publisher who owns all the copyrights.

Once again, I'm equivocating with those "more likelies." It's not impossible for ad hoc teams of creators doing work for hire to make wonderful comics; it's just fairly rare. But (given enough time) comics can be made soup-to-nuts by a single artist or a very small group of artists on a budget of next to nothing. Virtually the only writer/artist teams that have produced really first-rate comics are the ones that have worked together closely from the beginning of a project and are pulling very hard in the same direction. (One significant exception is *The Invisibles*, written by Grant Morrison and drawn by a host of artists, which really only worked because part of the point of *The Invisibles* is that it represents the points of view of a fragmented, many-bodied consciousness. We'll get to that later in the book. Another is *The Sandman*, written by Neil Gaiman and drawn by a series of artists with whom, once again, he worked very closely, tailoring his approach to their strengths.) Intense, fruitful collaborations are not often possible to pull off in mainstream comics, which are under constant deadline pressure. And outside the mainstream, virtually all American comics are inextricably linked to a particular creator or long-term creative collaboration.

It's worth contrasting comics auteurism with the film-critical auteur theory, for whose definition I'll quote the formulation that was devised by Andrew Sarris in his essay "Notes on the Auteur Theory in 1962" and subsequently eviscerated by Pauline Kael in her response "Circles and Squares: Joys and Sarris." "The first premise of the auteur theory," Sarris wrote, "is the technical competence of the director as a criterion of value." But, as Kael pointed out, technical competence is a slippery idea. If it means "making pretty pictures"—an equation that art comics has done its best to debunk, as we'll see—then the apex of technical competence in comics was probably the Image Comics of the early '90s, a set of studios whose artists made everything they drew look almost erotically delectable, even though they generally booted storytelling into the street. (Lots of readers found those cartoonists' work valuable; the note of gentle disparagement you may have noticed in my

The opening sequence from Gary Panter's magnificent postmodern elaboration on Dante, *Jimbo in Purgatory.* ©2007 Gary Panter.

tone is not accidental.) If storytelling and communication are the hallmarks of technical competence, then the standard-bearers of the criterion of value are the likes of Will Eisner and Steve Ditko and Keith Giffen; there's something to be said for that, too, and in fact that's where my sympathies tend to lie.

But there are also extraordinary cartoonists who don't fit either of those categories. Gary Panter, for instance, couldn't even begin to pull off a Wonder Woman or X-Men story, and I can't imagine him having any interest in trying; his drawings are vehemently unpretty, barbed and gnarled, and he has no aspirations to realism or hyperrealism or conventional narrative. Even so, *Jimbo in Purgatory*, his fantasia on the structure of Dante's "Purgatory," is a knockdown masterpiece of cartooning, so clever and complicated and beautifully executed that it takes ages to sink in fully. Shall we call him "technically competent," then, since he's able to realize his own vision? (How can we not?)

In that case, arguably anyone who is capable of getting paid for cartooning has to be technically competent. At one time that wasn't quite true—during the first few years of the comics boom in the late '30s and early '40s, there were a lot of artists whose work doesn't even look competent today—but that time is long gone. Beyond the point of simple communication, as Kael points out, the quasi-objective idea of competence slides into more subjective, taste-based criteria.

The second of Sarris's premises is "the distinguishable personality of the director as a criterion of value." If for "director" we substitute "cartoonist" (and for "personality" we substitute "style," since the idea is what their work is like rather than what they're like as people), this becomes something of a straw-man argument. It's true that every great cartoonist has a distinctive style, but the converse—that having a distinctive style is a sign of greatness—is ridiculous. Rob Liefeld, for instance, is a stylist above all else, and his drawing is instantly identifiable by its bursts of tiny marks, its hyper-exaggerated anatomy, its reptilian detail. (When he was growing into that style, in the late-'80s period when he was drawing X-Force, it was novel enough that he attracted a horde of fans and even some imitators and parodists.) He's also a god-awful hack with no tonal range at all, and his flailing attempts at storytelling are inevitably derailed by his inability to think beyond the next dramatic full-page shot. "Distinguishable personality" his work has plenty of, but that doesn't give it value.

The same goes for much better artists than Liefeld. The magnificent Jack Kirby's final years of cartooning were an embarrassing mess: his dynamic compositions and narrative eccentricities had devolved into a sludge of stylized, incoherent tics. Late Kirby projects like *Super Powers* and *Captain Victory and the Galactic Rangers* are disastrous, but you can't deny that his personality as an artist is front and center in every panel. For the people who still hold up those comics as a significant part of Kirby's career, that's apparently enough, although their only imaginable value is as a reminder of when he used to be good.

Sarris again: "The third and ultimate premise of the *auteur* theory is concerned with interior meaning, the ultimate glory of the cinema as an art. Interior meaning is extrapolated from the tension between a director's personality and his material." This is the part of Sarris's article that comes in for Kael's harshest and wittiest scorn: "If we have been puzzled because the *auteur* critics seemed so deeply involved, even dedicated, in becoming connoisseurs of trash, now we can see by this theoretical formulation that trash is indeed their chosen province of film," she writes. "Their ideal *auteur* is the man who signs a long-term contract, directs any script that's handed to him, and expresses himself by shoving bits of style up the crevasses of the plots. If his 'style' is in conflict with the story line or subject matter, so much the better—more chance for tension."

This is tough reading for someone who loves some—frankly—trashy comics and wants to understand what's meaningful about them and why they have the power they do. But *tension* between a cartoonist's "personality"—again, I'm pretty sure that "style" would be a better word—and material very rarely seems to yield anything that approaches "ultimate glory." (That sort of tension, in comics as well as in film, only really comes about through a studio system that hands assignments to artists.)

Again, auteurist comics are not quite the same thing as art comics, but the presence of an auteur is pretty much a prerequisite for art comics. To clarify the art/auteurism/ownership muddle a little bit with an example: Kyle Baker was the auteur of his 2004–2006 run on *Plastic Man*. With the exception of a couple of fill-ins, he wrote and drew the whole series himself, in the jokey, loopy style he'd developed many years before for his humor comics, and they're mostly very good and very funny. But they're not quite art comics, because he's playing with somebody else's toys: Plastic Man, created by Jack Cole in the '40s, is the property of DC Comics. There's no way to tell how much his work was circumscribed by working with a franchise he wouldn't have been allowed to damage in the long term; the point is that it *could* have been.

Anytime a French word comes into play in an English-language discussion, you can be sure there are some class dynamics going on, and it's worth mentioning that auteurists are trying to distinguish their (or perhaps "our") tastes from the tastes of the bulk of the American comics audience, as I'll discuss more in the next chapter. But the work I'm talking about hasn't been created in a vacuum either, and the art-comics revolution hasn't replaced the rest of what's happening in the medium.

The rise of art comics has happened in the context of a whole lot of mostly crappy (and occasionally inspired) assembly-line comic books, and it's happened roughly in tandem with the rise of star cartoonists in the mainstream.

The enormous majority of comic books, since the form's inception, have been constructed in a hurry, with nearly interchangeable writers and artists. The enormous majority of them are also not very good at all. (There is a causal relationship there.) Over the last fifteen years or so, though, the big American comics companies have realized that, to put it bluntly, Superman and Spider-Man don't really sell comics anymore: the likes of Brian Michael Bendis and Joss Whedon and Jim Lee do. Those star mainstream creators—some of them writers, some artists, not many both—have far more latitude than they once did, and virtually every mainstream comic now lists its creators' names on the cover, hoping to either capitalize on star power or build it. Art comics' insistence on stylistic expressiveness and the way they make the creator the center of attention have been creeping into the mainstream—within relatively narrow limits.

Where We Are and How We Got Here

As I mentioned above, the glide toward art comics starts in the prehistory of the medium, and there are examples and near misses throughout the twentieth century. But there have been a lot more examples in the last five years, say, than in the fifteen years or so before that, and a lot more in that period than there were earlier. The reason they've proliferated recently is that they've become commercially viable, as an almost accidental by-product of the long, twisted history of the comics industry. Here's a selectively myopic overview of their evolution in its economic context; bear in mind that there are exceptions to every generalization I make here.

First, I should emphasize that this is an economic history of art comics much more than an aesthetic history, because art comics don't really *have* much of a continuous line of aesthetics: since they lionize the individual cartoonist's voice, there aren't many identifiable schools within the field. The cartoonists who admire Jaime Hernandez, say, have generally tried to honor the spirit of his work by doing something that doesn't look or read anything like it. Also, if I seem to refer to independently published comics and art comics interchangeably, I don't mean to; the latter is more or less a subset of the former.

For the first half of the twentieth century, stylistic expressiveness in cartooning happened more in comic strips than in comic books. Newspaper readers cared at least as much about Winsor McCay as they did about "Little Nemo in Slumberland," at least as much about Milton Caniff as about "Terry and the Pirates." What newspaper strips had going against them, though, was that newspapers were meant to be totally disposable—outmoded and discarded the next day—and you had to be a fanatical clipper and collector to be exposed to the best comic strips over time. (McCay's classic "Little Nemo" strips from the early 1900s had, incredibly, *never* been reprinted at their intended size until the 2005 book *So Many Splendid Sundays!*)

Comic books had a slightly longer half-life, since they could be traded or passed around. They were also mostly meant to have a sort of neutral style: their selling point was characters, not creators, and they were often unsigned. As with so many things, Will Eisner was a pioneer here: his weekly comic book *The Spirit*, included with newspapers in lieu of a Sunday comics section in the '40s and early '50s, prominently featured both his signature and his visual experiments, and he owned the rights to the character.

By the '50s, a few comics started to win their audience on the strength of their artists' styles; they generally featured self-contained, one-off genre stories rather than ongoing serials or recurring characters. EC Comics was the most significant publisher of style-centered comics, and they encouraged their readers ("Fan-Addicts") to have an attachment to particular cartoonists' work rather than particular characters. But EC also specialized in shocking, lurid, button-pushing stories—for every little miracle of cartooning like Harvey Kurtzman's "The Big If" or Bernard Krigstein's "Master Race," they published half a dozen dumb gross-outs—and the same public backlash that created the Comics Code essentially wiped them out.

I mentioned the Comics Code briefly earlier, but it's worth explaining here, because it provided a set of rules for cartoonists to obey or rebel against. In 1954, Dr. Fredric Wertham's book *Seduction of the Innocent* claimed that morally suspect comic books were contributing to juvenile delinquency, and the subsequent public outcry led to congressional hearings later that year. To protect itself from legal regulation, the comics industry created the Comics Code Authority; the initial version of the Code it enforced featured clauses like: "Inclusion of stories dealing with evil shall be used or shall be published only where the intent is to illustrate a moral issue and in no case shall evil be presented alluringly, nor so as to injure the sensibilities of the reader."

By 1955, EC was reduced to publishing almost hilariously toothless, short-lived series like *M.D.* and *Psychoanalysis*. Only one title from their line survived, and only by becoming a black-and-white magazine: *MAD*. You can bet, though, that a lot of cartoonists started thinking a lot more deliberately about how to get away with "injuring the sensibilities of the reader."

An excerpt from "Howdy Dooit," drawn by Bill Elder—one of the smart, rowdy, subversive parodies from the early years of *MAD*. From *MAD* #18, ©E.C. Publications, Inc. All rights reserved. Used with permission.

Thanks to the Comics Code, a wave of enforced blandness swept over the mainstream comics of the late '50s and early '60s, although a few kids who had grown up on the rougher stuff (and held on to MAD for its subversion—this was back when cultural subversion was a big deal) were ignoring the weak tea on the stands and learning to draw on their own. In the meantime, Marvel Comics had started prominently crediting its writers and artists, partly as a marketing gesture to build followings for them, but also partly because de facto editor in chief Stan Lee encouraged the artists he worked with to stretch out stylistically. (Up to a point, anyway.)

Still, until the late '60s, virtually all American comic books were published by a handful of large companies, because that was the only way they could claw their way onto the limited rack space at newsstands; no matter how expressive and creative a comic book was, it also had to be broadly commercially viable or there was no sense in publishing it. The fact that unsold comics were returned to the publisher meant that a not-especially-successful issue could be a financial disaster. And a print run of five thousand or ten thousand copies of a comic was unthinkable— there would have been nowhere to sell it.

That began to change in the '60s, as the counterculture created an informal network of head shops and record stores that were prime outlets for selling "underground comix"—mostly black-and-white, artist-driven comics that mainly showed off their countercultural credentials by being as transgressive as possible. Artists like Robert Crumb and Gilbert Shelton were able to sell tens of thousands of copies of their comics without much help from big magazine cartels; their publishers also kept their work in print as long as it kept selling, which was a conceptual breakthrough for the medium. The underground cartoonists were interested in self-expression above all, although they tended to conflate self-expression with breaking taboos and, sometimes, with old issues of MAD. But the best of them were revelatory at the time, even if they haven't aged well, and beyond that they were *promising*—they hinted at the possibilities they didn't realize very often.

Early underground cartoonist Robert Crumb embraces ugliness, goofily.
From his story "Whiteman" in *Zap Comix* #1. ©Robert Crumb.

The early undergrounds broke one particular taboo by being some of
the first *deliberately* ugly comics (as opposed to just inept). Their lusty
indulgence of gross little details and unsavory subjects also had its roots
in *MAD* and old EC comics, but it was just as much a declaration of
their alienation from the cultural mainstream. When you look at an image and find it beautiful to the eye (rather than intellectually "beautiful"), you automatically imagine that everyone else will note its beauty
too; it gives you a sense of kinship with everyone else who might see it.
To look at an image you know is viscerally repulsive and find in it something pleasing, on the other hand, is *alienating*: you have the sense that
your experience is different from most people's and that that difference
sets you apart from them. And the meta-pleasure of enjoying experiences that would repel most people is, effectively, the experience of being a bohemian or counterculturalist.

The underground artists also flaunted the quirks of their drawing
style more than any comic book artists before them had; as with the
contemporary art scene around them, they presented their comics as artifacts of their artistic personae and creations of their hand, rather than
as specific pieces that they happened to have made. Crumb, and some
of his imitators, also made the small but significant gesture of drawing
their panel borders freehand, instead of with a straightedge. That could
make the borders look sloppier—and sometimes almost comically

slovenly—but it was also a way of declaring that everything on the page was the work of their hand, and that its borders were of a piece with the drawings surrounded by them. (A few cartoonists still make a point of using freehand borders, most notably the Hernandez brothers.)

At around the same time that undergrounds were taking off, comics fan culture started to be more than a tiny clique. Stan Lee's attempts to build cults of personality around Marvel Comics' creators, and to market their comics to college-age readers, led to more people collecting old comic books and looking for back issues. Stores that specialized in comics, often alongside the odd decorative glass pipe, sprang up everywhere there were students. Comics projects aimed somewhere between the underground and the mainstream—*Arcade, Star*Reach*, and others—started to appear.

In the mid-'70s, largely as a result of the efforts of a guy named Phil Seuling, comics' "direct market" came into being. Distributors made deals with comics publishers to sell comics to specialty stores earlier than newsstands got them and for a deeper discount than newsstands got, but on a nonreturnable basis. Newsstands and drugstores, the traditional venues for comics, had no use for old issues once the new ones came out, so they'd tear the covers off comics that didn't sell and return them to distributors for credit, as with any other magazine. Comics stores, which knew their market, could order exactly as many copies of each title as they figured they could use, and whatever didn't sell before the next issue appeared could always be sold later for a bit of a markup.

The direct market transformed the comics industry, although it took a few years before cartoonists figured out how to use it to their advantage. Eventually, though, small publishers, who dealt only with specialty stores, began to spring up. Since direct distribution meant that publishers got orders before they had to print their comics, they could print exactly as many copies of each issue as the market demanded (or a few more), without having to worry about paying for copies they would never sell or losing their shirts on returns. That meant that stranger, artier projects that wouldn't have stood a chance on newsstands could at least break even—especially if they were printed in black and white, which was much cheaper than color.

By the beginning of the '80s, there were a handful of successful, on-going, self-published black-and-white comics, Wendy and Richard Pini's fantasy series *Elfquest*, Dave Sim's *Cerebus*, and Harvey Pekar's autobiographical *American Splendor* among them. In 1980, Art Spiegelman and Françoise Mouly launched their magazine *RAW* (its title's similarity to *MAD* was not entirely an accident) as a showcase for full-on avant-garde cartooning, most famously the serialized version of Spiegelman's *Maus.*

RAW was considerably fancier than the other independent comics of its day: printed on better paper, larger than standard comic or even magazine size, more expensive. Its contents were unequivocally art comics, and Spiegelman and Mouly encouraged their contributors' embrace of style: not just resistance to the commercial-comics ideal of "good drawing" or "house style," but flamboyant, exaggerated stylistic gestures and jagged resistance to the idea that any *RAW* contributor's work could ever be mistaken for someone else's. *RAW* never sold in huge numbers and published its final volume in 1991, but many of its artists have gone on to artistic careers within and outside comics—Charles Burns, Mark Beyer, Richard McGuire, Drew Friedman, and others—and modern commercial illustration sometimes looks as if it grew up on a steady diet of Mouly and Spiegelman's favorite comics. (Mouly, incidentally, is now the cover editor for the *New Yorker,* and a lot of *RAW* contributors are now semi-regular illustrators there, which is as good a lesson as any in the way the avant-garde becomes the mainstream. I'll discuss Spiegelman and *RAW* more in chapter 21.)

After the first wave of black-and-white publishers came a wave of quasi-mainstream color comics publishers that operated entirely within the direct market: Pacific Comics, First Comics, Eclipse Comics, and more. In the early '80s, they signed up cartoonists who had done significant work with Marvel and DC in the past but wanted to own their own work or to publish things that wouldn't fly under the Comics Code. Again, most of what those companies published was more memorable for boundary pushing than for its actual content, but some of it was terrific, like Howard Chaykin's densely packed, scabrous science fiction political satire *American Flagg!* DC and Marvel even started publishing a few projects that they made available only through the direct market, without the Code's seal of approval: the likes of Marvel's *Moon Knight* (whose Bill Sienkiewicz artwork was too peculiar to succeed in the newsstand market) or DC's *Camelot 3000* (a science fiction series so out-there it featured an actual lesbian kiss). Around the same time, Fantagraphics, which had been publishing *The Comics Journal* for a few years, began to publish black-and-white comics, too, mostly in a larger "magazine-size" format; it helped that one of their first publishing projects was Jaime and Gilbert Hernandez's *Love and Rockets*, which became the flagship title of their line and didn't really fit into any genre paradigm.

The next big brainstorm in comics happened in the mid-'80s, when publishers small and large, from Aardvark-Vanaheim and Fantagraphics on up to DC Comics, realized that once stories had been serialized in individual pamphlets, they could be collected in books with a reasonably high profit margin that could be kept in print. There had been paperback collections of comics before, and Will Eisner had popularized the term "graphic novel" with his book *A Contract with God and Other Tenement Stories* in the '70s, but now the number of squarebound volumes of comics in print could no longer be counted on the fingers of one hand. (Dave Sim's *High Society*, which collected a five-hundred-page story line from *Cerebus*, was the first "phone book," as they were called—a huge collection of a single series.)

Gradually, books-of-comics became the province of bookstores and libraries—"respectable" places—as much as comic shops, which were still nasty little holes in the ground. For big comics publishers, trade paperbacks were a way to squeeze more profit out of successful projects; for independent publishers, book collections offered a lifeline that made the prospect of drawing art comics a little more feasible. Even if your small-press or self-published comic book couldn't sell enough copies month by month for you to live on the proceeds, if you finished enough issues to fill a squarebound paperback, it could stay in print and bring in money as long as new readers still became interested in your work.

Over the next few years, a few things happened that made art comics more viable than they'd been before, while aiming mainstream comics' spotlight at creators rather than characters for the first time. As I mentioned earlier, in 1986 and 1987, *Maus*, *The Dark Knight Returns*, and *Watchmen* were all collected as books that sold well enough to create a demand for more self-contained, artistically satisfying volumes of comics on library and bookstore shelves. Art cartoonists like Daniel Clowes, Seth, and Peter Bagge, who'd been drawing comics since the early '80s, worked most of the adolescent kinks out of their system and started producing work that was impressive rather than just promising. (Most of it took a while to come to fruition anyway; cartooning is slow.) And the idea of "creators' rights" became Topic A for discussion among cartoonists, for whom any way of doing business other than signing away everything to a corporate boss had until recently been almost unthinkable.

At the same time, the American comics business endured a combined blessing and curse—mostly a curse—as the result of a pop-culture fad that had started in the independent comics world. Kevin Eastman and Peter Laird had created *Teenage Mutant Ninja Turtles* in 1984 as a self-published, one-shot black-and-white parody of two Marvel superhero series, *New Mutants* and Frank Miller's *Daredevil*. By 1987, the Turtles had become a marketing phenomenon and a huge hit, commanding high prices from collectors; that set off a collecting bubble for independent black-and-white comics, which were fairly cheap to produce. Within months, comics stores' shelves were flooded with knockoffs and parodies and parodies of knockoffs— *Adolescent Radioactive Black-Belt Hamsters, Aristocratic Xtraterrestrial Time-Traveling Thieves, Pre-Teen Dirty-Gene Kung-Fu Kangaroos* (I swear I'm not making this up)—as well as a locust-invasion wave of random product from new publishers who would publish anything that looked vaguely like a comic book and was in black and white. It was almost all unreadable, and because it all went through the direct market, it was all nonreturnable; in short order, lots of stores went under.

(The Turtles' creators did try to give something back to the comics community, though. In 1990, Eastman founded Tundra Comics, a company dedicated to publishing handsome-looking comics by top-rank cartoonists; it burned through $14 million in three years, then folded. Laird founded the Xeric Foundation in 1992; it still awards grants twice a year to emerging cartoonists to help them with the costs of self-publishing their work.)

Despite the black-and-white bust and the crunch it put on the entire comics industry, the direct market remained a much better bet for big publishers than newsstands, where comic book sales were slipping precipitously. DC and Marvel all but gave up on selling new comics outside of specialty stores; they started playing to collectors and even speculators with enormous "event" comics (a new *Spider-Man* series drawn by fan-favorite artist Todd McFarlane, for instance), printed with multiple, variant covers. That led to a second speculation bubble, in the early '90s, which created demand for work by a few "hot" artists in superhero comics—and put the squeeze on smaller indies, whose comics were a lower priority for stores' limited ordering budgets.

Still, the idea of creators' rights and creative ownership had lingered from the black-and-white boom and spilled over into mainstream comics a few years later. When Marvel refused to give a group of star artists, including Todd McFarlane and Jim Lee, the rights to own and control their work, they quit and formed their own company, Image Comics. Over the next few years, the collapse of the second bubble killed more stores and strangled some independent publishers (as Marvel, DC, and Image fought for market share by pumping out series after series). Meanwhile, the direct market's network of distribution companies gradually consolidated until one company, Diamond Comic Distributors, effectively controlled almost all direct comics distribution in the United States by the end of the '90s.

The small comics publishers that survived the booms and busts, though, had managed to establish some kind of beachhead and to support a handful of art cartoonists until they'd built up a substantial catalogue. In the '90s, Fantagraphics Books became the gold standard of indiedom, publishing comics by the Hernandez brothers, Chris Ware, Dan Clowes, Peter Bagge, Roberta Gregory, Jim Woodring, and others—supported in part by an unutterably sleazy porn comics line, Eros, but any port in a storm. Drawn & Quarterly had a smaller roster of cartoonists, including Seth and Chester Brown, and a reputation for beautifully produced books. Dark Horse Comics published Frank Miller's various projects, notably *Sin City*, and paid for its artier, more creator-driven projects by publishing a line of *Star Wars* comics. Dave Sim weathered the storm by making his self-published *Cerebus* the only indie comic that reliably appeared every month and by keeping all of the series' book collections in print.

In fact, by the mid-'90s, every comics publisher of any importance was publishing squarebound book collections of its comics and keeping them in print. As it turned out, that was where the money was, and within a few years the economic engine of the industry had made a major conversion: instead of trade paperbacks being a way to capitalize further on successful comics, periodical comics became a way to amortize the cost of producing the books of which they were components.

After the second bust of the direct market, pretty much anyone still trying to draw independent comics was in it for the love of it—there wasn't a lot of money to be had. Gradually, a community of indie artists and tiny publishers came together. In the mid-'90s, they started having their own conventions, outside the mainstream comics convention circuit. Around the same time, indie cartoonists finished long-running serialized projects and saw them gain a second audience as books: Dan Clowes's *Ghost World*, Alan Moore and Eddie Campbell's *From Hell*, Seth's *It's a Good Life, If You Don't Weaken*. (The first two of those subsequently became movies—as did Harvey Pekar's *American Splendor*—which led to those movies' audiences discovering their source material.)

It's rarely been easy to make a living doing independent art comics, but in the last few years it's become nearly impossible for indie pamphlets to break even (aside from a few not-so-arty licensed nostalgia properties like *Red Sonja*, *Transformers*, and *G.I. Joe*). Carla Speed McNeil's *Finder*, once a bimonthly comic serializing stories that were collected as books once a year, has dropped its pamphlet incarnation in favor of page-by-page serialization on the Internet; Eric Shanower's acclaimed, award-winning *Age of Bronze* series is, as of this writing, barely sustainable as a periodical. Fortunately, serializing long stories in pamphlet comics has gone from art cartoonists' standard operating practice to a no-longer-mandatory option to a rare curiosity. Craig Thompson's very successful *Blankets* is a five-hundred-page graphic novel that couldn't possibly have made sense as a serial.

The last couple of years have seen traditional New York book publishers experimenting with publishing art cartoonists' work. A few ambitious comics projects appeared in the '80s from book publishers—*Maus*, *American Splendor*—but there simply wasn't a lot of first-rate non-genre work around then. Chris Ware's 2000 graphic novel *Jimmy Corrigan, the Smartest Kid on Earth*, published by Pantheon, was a critical and commercial success, though, and it was followed by a few more collections of long stories that had been serialized by independent publishers— Charles Burns's *Black Hole*, Jessica Abel's *La Perdida*, Jeff Smith's *Bone*. The popularity of the movies based on Frank Miller's *Sin City* series and Dan Clowes's *Ghost World* didn't hurt, either. By 2005, there was something like a feeding frenzy going on, with book publishers snapping up cartoonists who'd previously been affiliated with indie presses and sometimes starting their own comics imprints, notably Holtzbrinck's all-graphic-novel imprint First Second.

What's come out of all of this is that the American comics world, both as an artistic phenomenon and as an industry, has a few relatively discrete divisions. The first is the mainstream: the majority of comics from long-running superhero publishers DC and Marvel, both of which make a lot of their profits from characters and franchises rather than directly from particular creators' work. A handful of smaller companies like Image and Dark Horse also publish some comics with the tone and style that mark them as mainstream; in most cases, the particular cartoonists who work on projects like *Conan* and *Spawn* are, again, less important than their characters and concepts. And there's a weird dynamic going on in mainstream comics now, which is that their "ultimate form" has mostly switched from the disposable and therefore collectible form of pamphlet comics to the book form, which is designed for permanence—but they're still almost always serialized before they're collected as books, so they have to build to some kind of climax every twenty-two pages.

Beyond that, there's the "indie" scene (as with music, the independence of the nickname refers to the corporate structure around the work, rather than the work itself): artists whose work's selling points are their names and styles, rather than what their stories are about. As far as publishers go, Fantagraphics is still the eight-hundred-pound gorilla of the indie world, having skirted financial catastrophe for years until it started publishing a series of hardcovers reprinting Charles Schulz's complete *Peanuts* in chronological order. Others of note include Drawn & Quarterly, Top Shelf, and Buenaventura Press, but there are hundreds of indie comics companies, the majority of them run by the sole artist whose work they publish. (Self-publishing is a mark of mediocrity in the prose book world, but it's easy enough to do in comics—since there's only one distributor of note—that it's not just an acceptable first step but, in more than a few cases, a long-term career path.)

Finally, there's the manga phenomenon: Japanese comics in translation (and occasional American imitations of that style), whose American editions are mostly sold by a few companies, notably Viz and Tokyopop. Manga evolved almost entirely separately from American comics, it's sold more through bookstores than through comics stores, and its audience has relatively limited overlap with other American comics' audience; as I mentioned before, it's largely outside the scope of this book.

Style, Beauty, and Ugliness

Matt Madden's 2006 book 99 *Ways to Tell a Story* is a comics variation on the late French experimental writer Raymond Queneau's *Exercises de style*: the same barely-an-incident turned into ninety-nine different comics pages, each executed in a different style: horizontal panels, a

Excerpt from the "template" version of Matt Madden's story from *99 Ways to Tell a Story.* ©2005 Matt Madden and Chamberlain Brothers, an imprint of Penguin Group USA.

Excerpt from the "superhero comics" version of same.
©2005 Matt Madden and Chamberlain Brothers, an imprint of Penguin Group USA.

Western, flashbacks, a Jack Chick religious tract, chiaroscuro without outlines. (One is in the style of the Bayeux Tapestry, as a joke at the expense of that sort of snuffling around for roots.)

It's an amusing and enlightening book, but it also points out that "style" can mean a number of not-entirely-related things in comics: drawing technique, storytelling technique, linguistic technique, the illustrative quirks associated with a particular genre. Almost all of the book's examples look like Matt Madden drawings, with his characteristic line and visual tone; there are a few he's drawn in the style of specific artists (Jack Kirby, Hergé, Osamu Tezuka). And then there's the exercise called "Superhero," which he tries to draw in a *generic* style: both in the sense of being of its genre and in the sense of not looking like his own or any other particular artist's work.

As I've said, there isn't really a specific aesthetic through-line connecting art cartoonists, who mostly try not to draw like each other. (An art cartoonist's selling point, or one of them, is that he or she has a singular vision—not like anybody else's.) To the extent that there *is* a shared aesthetic, it's more of a negative phenomenon than a positive one: American art cartoonists generally try very hard to adopt a style that's far away from the default style of the superhero mainstream.

But what is that default style, exactly? You know it when you see it, but it's hard to pin down. Here's a stab at it: it's designed to read clearly and to provoke the strongest possible somatic response. You're supposed to react to it with your body before you think about it. Most of its characters, especially the heroic ones, are drawn to look as "sexy" as possible—wasp waists, big breasts, and flowing hair on women; rippling muscles on men. People and objects are partly abstracted and partly modeled, but always within a framework of representation. There's a lot of foreshortening, for the somatic excitement of seeing something right in front of your face. The style gives a sense of even the most everyday actions and interactions being charged with sex, power, and beauty. Most of all, generic mainstream drawing is doggedly quasi-realistic—or, rather, it's realism pumped up a little, into something whose every aspect is cooler and sexier than the reality we readers are stuck with. It's meant to provide an escape route into a more thrilling world than our own.

There is, actually, an identifiable ancestry behind the DNA of "generic mainstream comic," and it's mostly come into being since the mainstream comics of the '60s, when there was more room for stylistic quirks than there is now. Back then, a single cartoonist would be identified with a particular series for years—Carmine Infantino with *The Flash*, Jack Kirby with *The Fantastic Four* and *Thor*, Joe Kubert with *Sgt. Rock*—and could put a personal imprint on it. These days, *The*

Neal Adams's photorealist art from a circa-1970 horror story, "The Game."
From *Showcase Presents: House of Mystery, Vol. 1.* ©DC Comics. All rights reserved. Used with permission.

Flash looks like *The Fantastic Four* and *Justice League of America* and *Catwoman* and *X-Men* and almost everything else.

Part of that change came from the rise of "house style" in the '70s—the 1978 publication of *How to Draw Comics the Marvel Way* was its apex, creating a generation of cartoonists who learned that there was a right ("Marvel") way and wrong way to draw everything. But the way the standard style evolved came from the influence of a few particular artists. One of them is Neal Adams, whose early work, published between 1968 and 1974 or so, was shockingly original when it appeared. Adams was one of the first cartoonists to attempt anything like photorealism in the context of a comic book; it was a pumped-up sort of photorealism, full of very beautiful people, accurate or at least convincing anatomy that showed the ripples and wrinkles of everything, and freaky perspectives that heightened the drama of most of his images (worm's-eye views, extreme close-ups).

A lot of the major cartoonists of the '70s and early '80s were Adamsians; either they worked with him directly, or they were deeply influenced by him. Bill Sienkiewicz, Mike Grell, Howard Chaykin, and Frank Brunner all had some Adams in their inkwells—Sienkiewicz, in particular, was almost an Adams clone at the beginning of his career. John Byrne synthesized Adams's anatomical precision with Jack Kirby's broad, evocative distortions and smoother, bubblier textures than either of them had drawn, and he also became a huge influence on the next generation of mainstream cartoonists.

Very few mainstream cartoonists of the moment draw much like Adams or Byrne, aside from the immensely popular Jim Lee, who owes a lot directly to both of them. But a lot of cartoonists are the great-grand-disciples of both of them. The current "good" style isn't quite Adams's realism: most cartoonists don't have anything like his grasp on anatomy and perspective or his patience for minute details. It's more of a simplified realism, with its compositions inspired by the look of action movies and its perspectives chosen to give every panel exaggerated dramatic impact.

The response of art cartoonists to the slickly beautiful (or at least somatically provocative) look of mainstream comics, beginning in the mid-'70s, was a lot like the '60s underground cartoonists' response to the less slick but semi-realistic look of mainstream comics in their day: an embrace of ugliness, in style more than in content. And, similarly, they were going for the alienating effect of making readers find their artwork intellectually appealing rather than attractive. (An important clarification: when I talk about "ugly" cartooning here, I don't necessarily mean that it repels the eye—most of what I'm talking about is actually pretty compelling—or that it doesn't reward attention. I just mean that it's the result of a conscious choice to incorporate a lot of distortion and avoid conventional prettiness in style. I also don't want to argue that *all* art cartoonists have adopted an ugly style; a lot of them have, though.)

Again, the combination of a well-crafted narrative and heavily distorted images has the simultaneous effect of giving counterculturally

The look of superhero comics, circa 2007: a Steve McNiven–drawn panel from *Civil War* #5. ©2007 Marvel Characters, Inc. Used with permission.

minded readers pleasure, making them realize that their pleasure is not going to be shared by a lot of other people who look at it, and giving them an us-against-the-world sense of kinship with other people who *do* feel that pleasure. As almost all of the early art cartoonists emphasize in interviews, in the United States circa 1980, being serious about comics as something other than light entertainment for kids made you a freak—Fantagraphics's forthcoming book about the company's history is called *Comics As Art: We Told You So*—and if there's one thing freaks like to do, it's forming alliances with other freaks.

RAW's Mouly and Spiegelman created a genuine community of comics freaks. The stylistic extremes of the *RAW* cartoonists' work are almost all approaches to ugliness: the deliberate, monotonal flatness of

Jerry Moriarty's "Jack Survives"; the creepy-crawly patterns and barely recognizable geometric distortions of people and things in Mark Beyer's "Amy and Jordan"; the way Drew Friedman's early cartoons used a monomaniacally intensive pointillist technique that blew out Adams-style photorealism, like a botulism-bloated can, into clammy in-your-face distortions that overemphasized every horrible wart and mark on his subjects' flesh. Outside of that circle, other young art cartoonists played with grotesquerie, too. In *Neat Stuff* and *Hate*, Peter Bagge developed a variation on old *MAD* and *CARtoons* caricatures that made all of his characters sweaty, angry, flailing messes. William Messner-Loebs drew *Journey* with a wiry, uncertain line that constantly wobbled out of place. Charles Burns and Dan Clowes both warped the hip angularity of '50s and '60s illustration into twitchy, deadpan confections of slightly off-kilter line and shadow, hinting at something rotting beneath their crisp surfaces.

Chris Ware's work seemed like a revelation when his *Acme Novelty Library* started appearing as a comic book in the early '90s; he was the first major American art cartoonist since Jaime Hernandez a decade before to devote himself to an unironically beautiful, smooth, likeable visual style. The way Ware drew, even then, had nothing to do with the default style of mainstream comics—it was and still is symbolic and iconic, with only the faintest nod to "realism" or thrills or sexiness, and deliberate in a way that doesn't permit any accidents of composition or linework. Where he found his ugliness was in the content of his stories, which are endless, agonizing psychological nightmares. (The friction between the exquisite design and excruciating emotional tone of his work is its main point, as I'll discuss at greater length in the chapter about him.)

It's also possible to see a sort of ideological agenda in the rebellion against easy prettiness: the implication that mainstream work was suspect because the unchallenging likeability of its surface could let it get away with all kinds of nasty or reactionary subtexts. (That might not have been a *conscious* agenda, but it proceeded from the reasoning behind turning away from the mainstream and its technique.) An ugly style might still work as a mask for a story's content, but at least it wouldn't be sugarcoating anything, and readers would have to really look at the art in front of them, instead of letting it be an "invisible" vehicle for narrative. That ideology can turn into a kind of snobbery, too—suspiciousness about the Trojan horse of prettiness can become a reflexive opposition to anything that gives pleasure too easily.

There is, of course, the hurdle that the more stylized and unpretty art cartoonists' work is, the more it fights back against people who look at it. It can be tough to get into. So it's worth considering the way deliberately ugly comics are supposed to work: what unpretty pictures do for readers and how their audience is meant to respond to them. Please don't throw this book across the room, but I'm going to bring Immanuel Kant's *Critique of Aesthetic Judgement* in here, since he worked out how visual art works on the viewer's mind more clearly than pretty much anyone else.

One big distinction Kant draws is between the "agreeable," the "good," the "beautiful," and the "sublime." Agreeable things, he says, give pleasure for reasons having to do with "interest"; they gratify desires and specific tastes. Mainstream comics' default art style tries to be as agreeable as possible. A drawing that's *somatically* effective can be sexy or exciting—it's meant to work on the body, in a way that ducks around the brain, which can also mean it functions in an "invisible" sort of way.

"Good" things, Kant argues, give pleasure because they refer to something besides themselves that we find valuable or laudable. Political art with whose politics the viewer agrees, for instance, counts as "good"; so does art that we find heartwarming—and, in fact, any art that we can make an argument for on the basis of something other than its surface qualities.

Then there's the category of the "beautiful," which Kant says gives pleasure for reasons other than "interest"/gratification or "goodness." It also, he says, gives pleasure in consideration of the thing itself, without reference to something else. Kant doesn't cite too many examples of things that are "freely" beautiful—birds, music without words, and certain kinds of wallpaper are among his few examples—and notes that other kinds of beauty (like human beauty) are dependent on preexisting concepts of perfection. And he observes, as I mentioned earlier, that when you experience something beautiful, you imagine that your delight in it will be shared by everyone else.

(The idea of human beauty, even as a contingent kind of beauty, raises the question: Is a mainstream comic's drawing of an attractive, ultra-fit person in spandex meant to be beautiful or agreeable? I'd argue that the answer is mostly "agreeable"—a superman doesn't look like an approximation of the preexisting, culturally defined concept of human perfection but like an exaggeration that goes beyond the ideal and is meant to work on the reptile brain. Even people obsessed with "perfecting" their bodies' appearance don't generally want to look like the Hulk or Wonder Woman, and if they try, they look ridiculous.)

It's also possible to combine the various kinds of pleasure in one's reaction to a single thing—if most beauty isn't unalloyed, that doesn't mean it's not present at all. A panel of a comic book might, for instance, be an exquisitely composed and rendered image of a sexy-looking person demonstrating exercise techniques, which would make it agreeable, good, and beautiful at the same time.

Kant's fourth category, "sublime," works differently from the other three. Sublime things give a kind of pleasure that's also a kind of terror (and their viewers' reactions vacillate between the two, rather than being unalloyed pleasure)—they're too big to wrap one's brain around. "The sublime is that by comparison with which all else is small," Kant writes, and comics occasionally literalize that idea: they're a good medium for conveying a sense of physical hugeness, or even infinity. One of the defining moments of Stan Lee and Jack Kirby's *Fantastic Four* run is the arrival of Galactus, the inconceivably huge creature who's come to devour the world. ("We're like ants . . . just ants . . . ants!!" declares another character in his presence.) Unsurprisingly, enormous mainstream comics events have come to cite the infinite in their titles: *Infinite Crisis, Infinity Gauntlet*.

The way that nonmainstream comics try to create the effect of the sublime is more metaphorical: making the reader understand the crush

The Fantastic Four face Galactus, by comparison with whom all else is small. From *Fantastic Four* #50, written by Stan Lee and drawn by Jack Kirby and Joe Sinnott. ©2007 Marvel Characters, Inc. Used with permission.

of the infinite. (As filmmakers know too, a long-distance shot of a tiny figure against a gigantic background is such a powerful device for this that it's practically cheating.) You see it in the final zoom-out at the end of Gilbert Hernandez's *Love & Rockets* X, in the cosmic games of scale in the *Cerebus* volume *Minds*, in the fanatical level of detail in Frank Miller and Geof Darrow's *Hard Boiled*.

So what do these four categories have to do with how people are supposed to read comics with deliberately ugly cartooning styles? First of
all, ugly comics aren't "agreeable": they refuse outright to provide any
kind of pleasure that isn't mindful. They may have an immediate impact, but that impact isn't satisfying on its own, and it can't *by itself* sell
anyone a fantasy or an ideal. Unpretty drawing makes the fantasy of par-
ticipation or identification less easy and powerful; it calls us back to
what's really going on in the image and in the narrative it belongs to.
The viewer is forced to look beyond the image's surface for what it
might mean: what its lines' character and style have to say, how it's composed, what details might be significant, what its significance to a
greater metaphor might be. It makes you consider both what you're
looking at and what's wrong with it—anything from the drawing distortion that makes it something other than the "correctness" of a real or realistic image to some kind of moral significance that the artist means to
imply.

That leads us to a consideration of the place of the "good" in ugly
cartooning. If the early art cartoonists were rebelling against the look of
mainstream comics, they were also rebelling against those comics'
moral tone—the tone that was effectively dictated by the Comics Code,
in which the distinction between the just and the unjust (and the ultimate punishment of the unjust) was the most important thing. To draw
in a style that was one's own—rougher than the default style but self-
determined—could imply a more personally determined kind of morality. (And to draw in a fully developed style of one's own could be a victory of "goodness" by itself, in which the artwork becomes the symbol of
the goodness of its creation's circumstances.)

So where is the "beauty" in ugly cartoon images? It's the part that's
pleasing without reference to something else—their composition, their
psychological acuity, the force of their style, and most of all, the way
they function as part of a narrative. There is a pleasure, in fact, in giving
one's attention over to someone else's storytelling voice, and ugly cartooning also directs its reader to the *intentionality* of the cartoonist's

style: the sense that a particular person is in charge of determining what you're looking at.

Thesis, antithesis, synthesis: for decades, comics outside the mainstream were called first "underground" and then "alternative," which just underscored their sense of exile from and rebellion against the mainstream. In the last few years, though, American cartooning style outside the old mainstream has become more of a thing in itself, not just a reaction against the dominant style. That means that pretty (especially unconventionally pretty) and ugly styles are both options for developing cartoonists, and both extreme prettiness and extreme ugliness have started turning up in their work. I'll discuss some trends among the newest generation of cartoonists in the afterword.

CHAPTER 3

What's Good About Bad Comics and What's Bad About Good Comics

Names and How to Use Them

Comics' content and their social context are inextricably linked. Reading comics, or not reading them, often presents itself as taking some kind of stand; in picking up something with words and pictures to read, you become the sort of person who reads comics, and that can be a badge of pride or shame or both. That means that comics readers make up a subculture (the way that book readers and moviegoers and music listeners don't), and members of subcultures are very particular about what sub-subgroups they do and don't belong to.

As we've seen, the divergence of art comics from mainstream comics has led to a schism that looks a lot like class conflict, although it has more to do with class as expressed through taste than actual economics. But when people want to differentiate rather similar things from one another, there are always struggles over names, and where there's class tension over taste, there are always social climbers: people who want to make it very clear that what they like is a higher-status thing and not a lower-status thing. Those conflicts have been going on for a couple of decades in relation to the very basic question of what to call the things with panels and word balloons and so on that I'm discussing in this book. The cheap way of referring to them is "comics" or "comic books"; the fancy way is "graphic novels" (or "graphic narratives" or "sequential art").

Whatever you call them marks you as a product of an ideology, and that goes for me too, but I do have some reasons behind my preferences. In general, I tend to use "comics," because it's the word that people who actually make them use among themselves. The industry calls thin, saddle-stitched pamphlets "comic books" (or, more jokingly, "floppies" or "periodicals"), virtually any squarebound volume of comics sold on bookstore shelves a "graphic novel," and the form in the abstract "comics." That's how I generally use those terms, too. Consider, by analogy, the difference between "movies," "films," and "cinema."

Comics as a medium and comics as physical pamphlets have pretty much the same name, because for historical and economic reasons they're almost always tied together. American comics as we know them started out as pamphlets, and that's still how a lot of major projects first appear (aside from the eternal exception of manga): they're serialized in twenty- to forty-page installments, which are more or less economically foolproof (because, remember, the ones that go to comics stores are nonreturnable) and amortize the publishers' cost of producing them. Then, if they've proven to have enough of an audience, they're collected as books. (One reason the serial form has stuck around despite ever-dwindling sales: creative types are lazy, and having regular deadlines forces them to actually get work done.)

I don't much love *any* of the common words for comics, but that's what you get when a medium develops before it starts thinking of itself as an art form. "Comic book" is, as plenty of people have noted, a terrible name: "comic" implies that they're funny, and "book" suggests that they're not pamphlets and come in a single, concrete form. "Graphic novel" is even more problematic, though. The origins of the term are slightly murky—it seems to have been first used in the '60s as a name for a *potential* "higher" form of comics, and it was popularized by Will Eisner's 1978 book *A Contract with God and Other Tenement Stories*. (As its

From Will Eisner's *A Contract with God*: not the first graphic novel or the first to use the name, but the first major work to be called one. "Contract with God." ©1978, 1985, 1989, 1995, 1996 by Will Eisner, from *The Contract with God Trilogy: Life on Dropsie Avenue* by Will Eisner. Used by permission of W.W. Norton and Company, Inc.

name suggests, Eisner's volume is not so much a novel as a collection of four not-all-that-long stories linked by their setting.)

But the "novel" part of "graphic novel" blots out the idea of short fiction and nonfiction—it's odd to call, say, books of reportage in cartoon form by Joe Sacco and Ted Rall "novels," or to suggest that memoirs by Alison Bechdel and Harvey Pekar are fictional, or that a collection of short pieces by Ellen Forney or C. Tyler is actually an extended, unified story. Given how long it takes to draw comics, the idea that the "novel" is the default form for the ones with high aspirations is also pernicious, because it suggests that shorter stories can't be serious. (Working on short fiction or poetry carries about the same prestige as working on a novel, but if you're drawing comics, that's not the same thing as working on a graphic novel—which is why too many young cartoonists start in on novel-length pieces before they've developed storytelling skills.) "Graphic narrative" sounds like a euphemism twice removed from its source and still has the unfortunate resonance of "graphic" with the way it tends to be paired with "sexuality" or "violence." And "sequential art" sounds utterly arid.

(Dave Sim riffed on the name problem a bit in *Cerebus*, in which the upper classes have books and the lower classes have "reads"; comics are

Dandy Don Duffbeer shows Cerebus the joys of "graphic reads," from the *Cerebus* volume *Guys.* ©2007 Dave Sim and Gerhard.

called "graphic reads." Sim also called his 240-page comic *Melmoth* "a short story," based on how long it takes to read—as he noted, if word count is the criterion of a graphic novel, practically nothing deserves the name.)

The class implications of "graphic novel" almost instantly led to the term's thorough debasement. As a ten-dollar phrase, it implies that the graphic novel is serious in a way that the lowly comic book isn't. That, of course, leaves it open to being co-opted by anybody who wants to dress up their inept little drawings in a jacket and tie, which is why shitty forty-eight-page superhero stories started to be sold as "graphic novels" within a few years of the appearance of *A Contract with God*—1983's *Super Boxers* could have killed off the prestige of any term attached to the form.

Even so, to this day, people talk about "graphic novels" instead of comics when they're trying to be deferential or trying to imply that they're being serious. There's always a bit of a wince and stammer about the term; it plays into comics culture's slightly miserable striving for "acknowledgment" and "respect." It's hard to imagine what kind of cultural capital the American comics industry (and its readership) is convinced that it's due and doesn't already have. Perhaps the comics world has spent so long hating itself that it can't imagine it's not still an underdog. But demanding (or wishing for) a place at the table of high culture is an admission that you don't have one; the way you get a place at the table of high culture is to pull up a chair and say something interesting.

Why I Hate My Culture

The blessing and curse of comics as a medium is that there is such a thing as "comics culture." The core audience of comics is *really* into them: we know that Wednesdays are the day when new comics appear in the stores, we populate endless Web sites and message boards, we preserve our comics with some degree of care even if we think of ourselves as "readers" rather than "collectors." A few times a year, we congregate at conventions of one kind or another. (Alternative Press Expo, Small Press Expo, and the Museum of Comic and Cartoon Art Festival are our Sundances, where small-press and independent publishers display their wares; Wizard World Chicago is where the superhero buffs go; Comic-Con International is where *everybody* goes—around a hundred thousand attendees paralyze the entire city of San Diego for five days in July.) We gravitate to our kind.

That's part of the problem. Over the last half century, comics culture has developed as an insular, self-feeding, self-loathing, self-defeating flytrap. A lot of the people who hit their local comics store every Wednesday think of comics readers as some kind of secret, embattled fellowship: a group with its own private codes that mark its members as belonging and everybody else as not belonging. (That's why most comics stores are deeply unfriendly places: everything about them says, "You mean you don't *know*?" In some of them, even new pamphlets and books are sealed in plastic before they go out on the shelves; if you don't walk into the store knowing what you want, you're not going to find out.) It's a stupid and destructive mind-set for any number of reasons, the biggest one being that it means you have to buy into an entire culture, or at least come up with a reason that you're *not really* buying into it, to enjoy a comic book.

That incestuous relationship between audience and medium has been encouraged by the big comics publishers. As we'll see in the next chapter, mainstream comics pamphlets that are incomprehensible to anyone not already immersed in their culture aren't just the norm now; they're the point. If you pick up a story crammed full of inside references, and you're enough of an insider to catch them all, you're going to feel like it was made just for you, and it will intensify the sense of difference between you and non–comics readers.

The next step along that path of difference is the fetishization of the object that symbolizes it. The first wave of comics collectors were trying to preserve the past of their culture — to rescue the ephemeral pamphlets that made up comics' fragile history from the quick and sure destruction they were intended for. They wanted to hold on to the pleasure their favorite comics gave them and perhaps to understand how years' worth of stories about particular characters might fit together into a grander narrative than even those stories' creators imagined. There's something honorable about that.

The preservation impulse turned into a collector's impulse — what was once called "the nostalgia market." Uncommon issues, naturally, were worth a bit more, then a lot more, then became the object of speculation. Publishers started to play on the idea of collectibility (in 1965, Marvel launched a series reprinting comics that had been published less than four years earlier, *Marvel Collectors' Item Classics*); people started to hoard new comics with an eye to their future financial value, not the future pleasure to be had from owning them.

There was once a kind of nerdy charm to the collectors who sought out old comics in "pristine mint" condition — cover still glossy, no dings or dents on the spine — and valued them according to their historical importance as well as their condition. First appearances of favorite characters were in high demand, and so were issues with well-loved artists, and a few more specialized kinks. The *Overstreet Comic Book Price*

Guide, updated annually, singled out horror comics involving the "injury-to-eye motif," for instance.

Sometime in the '80s, though, there started to be collectors who cared only about the investment potential of their comics and didn't have any particular interest in reading them. I worked in a comic book store in the mid-'80s and loathed the customers who came up to the counter with their own plastic bags and acid-free cardboard backing boards to begin the process of preserving their investments right away. It was easy to spot the kids who would become those collectors, too: they'd look quizzically at the first issue of some new series, and ask, "What's this going to be worth?" (I always told them that if I knew what things were going to be worth, I probably wouldn't be working behind a counter.)

No one ever really made their fortune as a comics investor, but the legions of clueless speculators brought on the boom-and-bust cycles I described in chapter 2. The comics speculation game got a slightly disgusting twist in 2001, with the launch of Comic Guaranty LLC and "slabbing." CGC, as it's better known, grades collectible comics for condition on a ten-point scale, then seals them between hard plastic slabs, so that they can never risk being damaged—or read—again: perfect financial fetish objects, entirely severed from their original aesthetic purpose.

That's the sort of protective response that's arguably appropriate for a singular object whose meaning as art can be experienced through clear plastic—something with what Walter Benjamin called "aura." There's something almost parodically wrong about seeing a piece of mass-produced entertainment framed like an irreproducible original. (After a decade or so of avoiding blatantly courting collectors, mainstream comics publishers have started encouraging the comics-investment game again with one-in-ten or one-in-fifteen variant covers. The variants are still not singular or even rare, but there are fewer of them, and there are always suckers for that strategy.) Naturally, the art-comics world mostly thinks of CGC and comics investment as beneath contempt— one piece of industry slang is "FYOV," the "forty-year-old virgins" who fuel the collector market. (It was around long before the movie.)

At the same time, even within art comics, there's a longing for the medium to get more of something that's usually called "legitimacy." There's an element of comics culture, sometimes called (a little derisively) "Team Comics," that gets excited whenever anything that looks like that acknowledgment or respect I mentioned above turns up in the outside world—a college class on the graphic novel, a Hollywood movie based on a graphic novel, a newspaper or magazine article about a cartoonist, somebody reading a comic book on a TV show. Different segments of Team Comics take notice if a TV character is reading a new issue of *Aquaman* or Lynda Barry's *One!Hundred!Demons!*, but the principle is the same.

Both the "Team Comics" culture vultures and the alternate-cover-hoarding mavens are driven by the desire to turn their hobby into some kind of *success* or *validation*, whether through affluence or cultural power, and that impulse is directly connected to the class aspirations that afflict the entire medium. A lot of comics readers are unhealthily attached to the idea that everyone else thinks what they do is kind of trashy and disreputable, and that they have to prove their favorite leisure activity worthy of respect—to show the world that they were right all along.

It's probably time to let go of that strain of earnest defensiveness. The snobbery of the rest of American culture toward comics is, if not entirely gone, dissipating quickly. In late 2006, Gene Luen Yang's graphic novel *American Born Chinese* was nominated for a National Book Award (in the Young People's Literature category); when one commentator—Tony Long, a blogger at Wired News—opined that it shouldn't have been nominated because it wasn't prose, the comics world jumped down his throat. But it's not as if literary culture revolted as one: Long appears to have been the only voice of dissent, and as clueless as part of his argument was (he noted that, well, he hadn't actually read *American Born Chinese*), his point that Yang's book was the wrong medium for its award was at least debatable.

What's actually happening in culture at large is more like everyone trying to jump on the comics bandwagon—the "you mean I have to pretend to like graphic novels now, too?" effect. The medium's new enemies are internal: the much less casual snobbery of the commercial mainstream and the art-comics world toward each other, and cartoonists' nostalgic yearning for the badness of the bad old days.

To use yet another film analogy, reading only auteurist art comics is like being a filmgoer who watches only auteurist art cinema, but more than a few art-comics enthusiasts wouldn't dream of picking up a mainstream comic book, even as entertainment. In *The Comics Journal*, the largest magazine of comics criticism in America, coverage of superhero stuff is almost entirely exiled to Joe McCulloch's (very entertaining) occasional column "Cape Fear." Likewise, plenty of superhero buffs can't imagine being interested in some actionless black-and-white independent comic. In *Wizard*, the largest magazine of mainstream comics culture, there is very occasionally a don't-be-scared-of-this mention of *Bone* or *Blankets*.

Some comics criticism works from the assumption that comics with "serious" historical subject matter or "arty" presentation are *intrinsically* superior to monthly saddle-stitched genre stuff—or, rather, that seriousness and artiness confer goodness on a comic. Ridiculous: there are any number of arid, bludgeoning, stultifying art comics that don't have anything like the verve and inventiveness and life of resonant pop about superheroes and monsters. Likewise, there's an anti-genre argument that sometimes pops up, to the effect that stories about real-world types of people in real-world sorts of situations, especially if they're autobiographical, have an *intrinsic* edge over fantasy or science fiction or detective stories because it's "easier to relate to them." (That doesn't explain the readers who relate just fine to well-constructed characters in genre stories or who understand that the characters they're reading about don't have to have lives like their own as long as the characters are interesting.) The counterargument from the all-genre crew is that "slice-of-life" stories are prima facie boring—that the point of comics is escapism and intrigue with an unlimited special-effects budget. Which brings us back to the genre-versus-medium problem again.

The most frustrating effect of the art/pop divide in comics, though, is *nostalgie de la boue*. A lot of the best cartoonists of the moment have picked up their visual vocabulary from the crap and hackwork of the past, and they're fondly and unhealthily attached to it in a sentimental, self-loathing way, as a curdled by-product of the attachment they felt to it as children. You can find this fascination with the feeble, uninspired comics of the artists' youth in Chris Ware's *Rusty Brown*; in Dan Clowes's *Ice Haven* and *Like a Velvet Glove Cast in Iron*; in Seth's *It's a Good Life, If You Don't Weaken*; and in a lot of other art comics, and it's an utter drag. Robert Crumb is a particular offender: most of his early work riffed on the toothless pop culture of his youth, and his drawing and sense of humor still haven't entirely let go of fifty-year-old issues of *MAD*.

In mainstream comics, *nostalgie de la boue* manifests itself as stories whose main point is to trigger nostalgic responses in their older readers—forgotten Golden Age characters being trotted out again and integrated into the tapestry of continuity; "retcons," or "retroactive continuity," meant to explain apparent contradictions in old comics or draw connections where there hadn't been any intended in the first place. The inbred children of that approach are stories nostalgic for old retcons, attempts to recapture the past of attempting to recapture the past, even if it wasn't that good the first time and was even worse the second.

Nostalgia, especially nostalgia for childhood, is a heavy burden for a medium to bear, and comics have been carrying it since the culture around them began to coalesce. The comics collecting market was called the "nostalgia market" at first; *The Comics Journal* was renamed from *The Nostalgia Journal*. The earliest books of essays about comic books were collections like *All in Color for a Dime*—reminiscences of early childhood experiences with funnybooks. As far as thinking about what makes comics interesting, though, nostalgia is poison—not just because it makes people overvalue the stories that fueled their childhood fantasies but because it makes them misunderstand the reasons *why* the good stuff or even the resonant crap affected them so strongly, and what exactly might have been messed up about it, or the way it made them feel the first time around.

Internalized Sexism and the Fortress of Solitude

The world of comic book readers is an insular world, and it's also an annoyingly male world. The archetypal comics store employee—think of *The Simpsons'* Comic Book Guy—is a lonely, socially maladjusted man, and so are his archetypal customers. For a few decades, mainstream comics were so overwhelmingly male-dominated that the industry had not the faintest idea of how to connect with potential women customers. I remember seeing a Marvel sales plan, sometime in the early '90s—a huge document, several hundred pages long; near the back, a little section labeled "Female Readers" listed the two titles Marvel published for half of their potential audience: *Barbie* and *Barbie Fashion.*

Unsurprisingly, the maleness of comics culture has been self-perpetuating: if reading (or collecting) comics is understood as "something that guys do," then the woman in the comics store is an anomaly. If you'll forgive a little grad-school speak, either she's performing womanhood wrong, or she's performing comics reading wrong. When you factor in the self-definition as "the kind of person who reads comics" that the culture requires of its participants, it's pretty clear how the pattern got entrenched.

The surprising, and heartening, thing is that the pattern is actually changing—in part because the broader culture of creator-focused media fandom that has evolved over the last couple of decades has drawn young women into comics as a sort of side effect (if you watch *Buffy the Vampire Slayer* and listen to Tori Amos, there's a reasonable chance you read *The Sandman* and *Transmetropolitan* too). There are many, many more people coming to comics conventions now than there were ten years ago; there aren't figures on who those people are, but anecdotally, the influx sure seems to be mostly women. And the manga phenomenon in the United States is very much a teenage-girl-driven trend.

But all that has to do with comics' audience; there's also the problem that the best-known creators of comics are men pretty much all the way

Megan Kelso aims for the jugular in her short story "The Squirrel Mother," from the collection of the same name. ©2007 Megan Kelso.

down. The fifteen cartoonists included in the touring "Masters of American Comics" exhibit in 2006 were all men. The real question, though, isn't quite "why have there been no great women comics artists?" (to paraphrase Linda Nochlin's famous question about the museum art world). It's "why have there been no great women comics artists until recently?"

And the answer, of course, is "antiquated social constructs that are finally starting to go away." Anyone who pays much attention to contemporary art comics knows that Lynda Barry and Alison Bechdel and Megan Kelso are as good as it gets right now, and Hope Larson and Marjane Satrapi and Carla Speed McNeil and a bunch of others I could mention get name-dropped plenty too. Still, because of those old social constructs—and because comics take a very long time to draw, and it takes a long time for most cartoonists to hit their peak of power—there are a lot of men who had a head start.

Look at the best contemporary American cartoonists in five or ten or fifteen years, though, and I bet there'll be a lot more women among them. There's a new generation of young women drawing comics already—although it'll be a few years before most of them can get beyond the "really promising" stage. The generation behind them is devouring manga the way no generation of American girls has grown up on any comics form before, and these young artists have the advantage of Internet culture to give them artistic peers; in a few decades, some of them will be making better comics than we can even imagine now. The gender imbalance among cartoonists is ridiculous, but it's gradually dissipating—at least in art comics and manga.

Mainstream comics' creators, on the other hand, are still overwhelmingly a boys' club; they'll need a bit more time. It doesn't help that women lead characters in superhero comics are outnumbered by men something like ten to one. There's also the familiar complaint of what those women tend to look like—the stereotype of the top-heavy bombshell being the only body type superhero artists know how to draw is frighteningly close to true. Of course, virtually every major male character in mainstream comics has rippling muscles beneath skintight clothes too, unless he's a villain, in which case he's also got the option of being really ugly or lanky or doughy—a Doctor Octopus or Kingpin or Lex Luthor. As I've noted earlier, the way characters in mainstream comics are drawn is supposed to trigger a visceral, somatic response, and that can include sexual attraction or repulsion. But any reason people don't like something is a valid reason.

Beneath the gender dynamics of the comics themselves, there's something a little insidious about the way people's initial contact with comics has historically happened. (Again, this is changing now, but this is the way the story *has* gone in the past.) Kids relate to superhero comics by identifying with their characters—understanding, on some level, that the struggles of the colorful characters on the page are metaphors for their own isolation and longing for power, identity, and acceptance. That identification happens in private, in kids' own little fortresses of solitude. The superhero is somebody who's different from everybody else; the superhero story has rituals and formulas that grow comforting through repetition. Spend enough time reading and thinking about them and comics themselves can become a fortress, a way of isolating oneself from the rest of the world.

One thing's for sure about people who are devoted to a subculture based on ongoing fantasies and frustrated by their perception of a lack of connection with the rest of the world: they make really good customers. Over the last couple of decades, the American comics mainstream has made a few stabs at drawing in new customers from outside its core constituency of a few hundred thousand diehards—aiming the occasional title at young kids who might want to pick up something exciting at a newsstand or drugstore, reaching out to adults who'd rather read projects like *Criminal* or *Y: The Last Man* as squarebound paperbacks once or twice a year than pick up floppies once a month, launching projects like the Minx line of graphic novels aimed at teenage girls. Mostly, though, the industry has circled the wagons, dedicating itself to serving its biggest fans, at the expense of letting new readers into its fellowship.

Before the shift started happening sometime in the '80s, the assumption was that every comic book was somebody's first; that usually meant a certain amount of repetitive exposition, but every issue was potentially an on-ramp. Now, many new issues of long-running series—and sometimes even new series' debuts—are so inbred and rooted in continuity with other comics that it's nearly impossible for a new reader to make sense of them. That has painted mainstream comics into a corner: once publishers figure out what that core audience wants, they devote their resources to making and marketing the same thing again and again, with gradually diminishing returns, all the while assuring whoever's left in the audience that the product is made just for them.

The problem is not only that you need a graduate degree in continuity to understand what's happening when you pick up a typical mainstream comic right now, although I'll discuss that more in the next chapter. It's that some of the codes and traditions associated with mainstream comics—not simply in their stories or the way they represent their characters but in their format and presentation and scope and economic apparatus—are stupid and useless, and they're tolerated and *perpetuated* because that's the way comics work. To question them is to question the edifice of comics itself; to object to them is to mark yourself as outside the circle of understanding and to risk the fury of the faithful.

I've been on the receiving end of that fury myself, although not under my own name. It started one day in 2003, when I was chatting with my friend Heidi MacDonald, who was then coediting The Pulse, a popular comics-news Web site. We were complaining to each other that there didn't seem to be a lot of smart, harsh comics criticism on the Web, and that a lot of the way readers talked about mainstream comics was to judge them on how well they played to the visual and storytelling conventions their readers expected, instead of on their worth as art or entertainment as such.

Then we remembered Sidney Mellon, a critic who'd had a column in a long-dead weekly comics-news magazine in the '80s. Sidney was the fanboy to end all fanboys; he talked and thought in warmed-over clichés from Marvel's in-house promo pages, he used lots of words he clearly didn't quite understand, and he couldn't fathom why anyone would read Donald Duck or Maus when they could feast their eyes on real literature like Uncanny X-Men. Like a lot of amateur critics, he couldn't disguise his presumption that he could write his favorite comics better anyway, and he was forever nattering on about the "graphic fantasy trilogy" he wanted to write, Thunderskull.

Sidney Mellon, it turned out, was a put-on by a couple of comic book writers—the columns were written by Gerard Jones, and the pimply, bespectacled kid in the columnist photo was a young Mark Waid—but it took people a little while to figure that out. (There was eventually an issue of Sidney Mellon's Thunderskull published; the only thing I remember about it was a caption that read "Erstwhile. . . . ") Who, Heidi and I wondered, would be the Sidney Mellon of today? We realized that somebody who didn't read comics at all would have the same sort of "how can they say that?" effect.

Together, we devised a nonexistent reviewer of our own: Jess Lemon, an undergraduate of indeterminate gender who had no particular interest in comics but had been asked to review one every week as part of an internship at The Pulse (arranged by a comics-loving older brother). The idea was that Jess had no idea what he/she was talking about, but everything he/she wrote would be the brutal truth.

I ended up writing all the Jess Lemon columns myself, with a bit of invaluable guidance from Heidi. The debut column pointed out that the first issue of a new *Outsiders* series was categorically incomprehensible to anyone who wasn't thoroughly steeped in bad superhero comics and was pretty stupid anyway; the initial responses were cautiously amused that The Pulse would ask a non–comics reader to write reviews. Then Jess was accidentally "outed" as a girl, and Internet commenters' misogynist knives came out: Who does this dumb little girl think she is? and so on.

It took a while for most people to catch on that Jess was a jest. (At that summer's Comic-Con International, somebody stood up at a panel Heidi was on and demanded to know whether or not Jess was a real person.) In the meantime, I invented a bit of backstory for her: her difficult relationship with her brother Andy and her real goal for the summer, which was reading all of Dickens at the rate of a novel every week—I tried to drop a few Dickens references into every column.

Here's my favorite column I wrote as "Jess":

Since I've been writing these reviews, I've been getting into the habit of asking my brother Andy to show me what comics he brings home from the store every week. He likes it when I do that. This week, though, I noticed him palming one comic book under another one as he was flipping through his stack for me, and I called him on it. He acted all surprised as he pulled out VAMPIRELLA/WITCHBLADE, whose cover shows two women who look like the ones on the posters he used to hang over his bed, wearing very skimpy outfits in the middle of a snowstorm. (You can tell it's cold—one of them is, uh, having a reaction.) "Oh, yeah . . . this one," he said, totally not fooling me. "You know, this has some really strong women characters in it." Oh really!, I said, and snatched it out of his hand. I think what I heard then was him clicking his front teeth together.

My friend Stacy has a rule: she won't go to a movie or read a book unless she knows that it's got a) two women who b) talk to each other about c) something besides a man. I will give VAMPIRELLA/WITCHBLADE credit for this much: it is Stacy-safe, since it involves two women talking to each other about killing monsters. But when people say they like stories with strong women characters, they don't necessarily mean strong in the sense that they can lift things, they mean they want *interesting* women characters. Like Dora Spenlow in *David Copperfield*: she's not strong, really, in any sense of the word, but she's an actual character— you get the sense that she has a life when she's not on the page, and the kind of person she is is part of what drives the story. This comic has a couple of women who seem to be *very* physically strong, but . . . well, let me try to explain what happens in it. I would put a spoiler warning here, but there aren't actually any surprises to spoil.

Sara Pezzini, a New York police detective whose car nonetheless doesn't have a front license plate, starts an incident report by announcing that she's never going to file it. (Why? Because if she didn't narrate an unfileable report, there would be no narration to try to make the story make sense.) In snow so deep it makes her stop driving in the middle of the Brooklyn Bridge, which has mysteriously not been cleared and even more mysteriously has no other drivers on it, she's gotten out of her car (to hold up some flares) when two other women run (yes, run) past her. The first one knocks both flares out of her hands and steals her gun without her noticing. The second one is Vampirella, who is running at top speed in foot-deep snow while wearing spike-heeled boots and some kind of one-piece boob-sling/thonglet contraption that would embarrass Lil' Kim, and who throws the first one off the bridge. Curiously, Vampirella's "running" position looks sort of like a tree pose in yoga, but she does seem to be kicking up a lot of snow. Perhaps whoever wrote this comic has experience sprinting in deep snow with spike heels on—write what you know, they say.

Now, of course, Detective Pezzini calls for backup. No, wait, she doesn't. Instead, she pulls out the gigantic magic claw-weapon on her hand. No, wait, she doesn't do that either. She does, however, explain that she forgot to do both of those things (in the report she doesn't intend to file), and gets back in her car, which is mysteriously able to move again and even more mysteriously grows a front plate on the next page, and drives to the Brooklyn side of the bridge, where the high-speed *Stuff*-foldout deep-snow spike-heel footrace is continuing. Before getting out of her car to pursue them in the falling snow, Detective Pezzini apparently takes *off* her jacket, the better to show off her boob-hugging turtleneck-T-with-printed-on-badge (of the kind that's so popular with NYC cops these days).

When Detective Pezzini catches up with the two women, the one who stole the gun shoots Vampirella and escapes; instead of pursuing the shooter, Detective Pezzini collapses like she's been shot too, even though she hasn't. When she gets up, Vampirella's wound is healing, and the little gold eagle logo has disappeared from the crotch of her thong/sling outfit. Vampirella takes off after the shooter, in a contorted pose that allows her to show off both buttcheeks and both boobs simultaneously. They chase the shooter to a broken-down building of some kind, where Detective Pezzini announces that "we need to resolve this, and I have the tool for the job," whereupon the gigantic magic claw-weapon shows up on her hand and shoots out a cloud of glowing green stuff.

Then a bunch of mind-controlled zombies and a huge wolf-creature attack them—none of them have visible cleavage, so the artist seems to have lost some interest by this part. Vampirella tells Detective Pezzini to "find your gun," throws her a silver bullet (the story makes a point of mentioning that it's not clear where Vampirella's been hiding it, which still doesn't make it okay), and gets her to shoot the wolf-creature with it, whereupon everything's okay again. In a one-page coda, Detective Pezzini is home and dry, watching Vampirella leaping between snow-covered rooftops in her spike-heeled boots and typing that knowing that Vampirella is out there makes her feel "a little less alone."

This leaves a number of questions unanswered. For instance: why is Detective Pezzini dressed as a cop (with curly strawberry-blond hair) on the inside of the comic and as a swimsuit-issue model (with straight brunette hair) on the cover? What exactly is Vampirella doing here, and why? How is anything different at the end of this story than it was at the beginning? Is there anything at all that it's possible to care about, anywhere in this comic?

That last one's got an answer, actually. I wanted to go to my brother and say: look, you sometimes like to look at drawings of really stacked women wearing buttfloss and boob-slings and high heels and contorting themselves into impossible positions, you know it and I know it, and it's *okay*. Really, it's okay. That's what you like, and that's what the people who made this comic know people like you like. But there's something sort of not-okay about thinking that it's *more* acceptable if it happens with a story to justify it, especially if the story's as stupid and lame as this one. The monsters aren't scary at all, they're just symbols of stuff that used to be scary when we were little. And maybe the women aren't actually sexy to anyone either—they're drawn so badly that it's hard to imagine it—but just symbols of pictures, or ideas, that the people who this comic is made for used to think were sexy. Or maybe they still do. In any case, I didn't say anything to Andy about it. I just put it back in his bag, and he didn't ask me about it either.

Credit where credit's overdue: Stacy's rule is lifted from a great old "Dykes to Watch Out For" strip by Alison Bechdel. I wrote thirteen columns as Jess, and poor Heidi had to deal with everybody thinking *she* was writing them; nobody guessed it was me. By the end, though, the joke had pretty much run its course—I couldn't keep Jess knowing nothing about comics forever, and I wanted to end it while it was still funny (to me, anyway). In the final Jess Lemon column, she vanished mysteriously, in the middle of reading *The Mystery of Edwin Drood*. I hope somebody thought that was amusing.

Why I Love My Culture

So why do we put up with comics' codes and cults and endless failings, their cycles of empty hype, their dirty halls of dirty boxes pawed through by lonely seedy people? Because comic books are *awesome*, and their culture is as much a blessing as a curse.

Comics culture couldn't have attracted as many people as it's attracted, with all its off-putting annoyances and idiocies, if it didn't also offer some genuine delights. The flip side of the Comic Store Guy's sneer of "you mean you don't know?" is that it's a culture that really does privilege deep knowledge of its history and present; the culture, as it turns out, doesn't take itself very seriously at all and is very happy to open its doors to anyone willing to take comics themselves seriously. The comics community encourages unmitigated enthusiasm and unmuted pleasure, especially because those are mocked by other subcultures that don't permit them.

For a medium usually experienced by individual readers in their individual homes, reading comics is linked to a pretty nifty social apparatus. It's a springboard for debate and a grounding for friendship. It has pleasant little rituals: the weekly trip to the store, the occasional larger trip to a convention, the post-reading discussion (in person or over the Internet), alphabetizing back issues for storage. To the extent that it allows people to live in a fantasy world, it allows them to live in an extraordinarily rich fantasy world. The apparatus of continuity that's accumulated around comic books gives readers access to the rewards of taking enormous bodies of entertainment very seriously and combing them for flashes of deeper meaning, whether that meaning was intended or not—even, sometimes, a kind of transcendence that's only present by accident.

My favorite manifestation of comics reader culture, I think, is something called "The Lesser Book of the Vishanti." It was written in 1977 by a woman named cat yronwode, who had a lot of time on her hands at that point (she went on to be the editor in chief of Eclipse Comics in the '80s and has since published part of her manuscript on her Web site). Yronwode was an admirer—no, let's say a *fan*—of *Dr. Strange*, a series about a "master of the mystic arts" that had been running since the mid-'60s. She decided to put together a comprehensive and coherent guide to Dr. Strange's system of magic, retro-engineering it from whatever parts of it had been published in the comics—this despite the fact that the spells the character cast and mystic artifacts he used had obviously been made up on the spot, probably on tight deadlines, by the various people who'd written Dr. Strange stories for close to fifteen years. Reportedly, *Dr. Strange*'s writers eventually came to rely on "The Lesser Book of the Vishanti" as a reference tool.

One other benefit of immersion in comics culture is that it lets readers enjoy even bad comics. "Bad" is another one of those loaded terms, so it's worth kicking it around a little to see what it gives up. Bad comics are the ones with something interfering severely with their ability to give pleasure as a coherent piece of work—inept or slapped-together writing, clumsy or generic art, two-dimensional or one-dimensional characters, a sense of having been hacked out to meet a deadline as a piece of product.

But some bad comics, especially bad old mainstream comics, can be wonderful in their way. What's good about them isn't their badness or their trashiness: it begins with their desperate desire to entertain. (Why *old* comics, in particular? Because they had to leap off the newsstands into customers' hands, which means they had to promise a good time on their covers as loudly as possible and deliver it on the inside.) Newsstand-era comics, whether or not their craft has held up over time and whether or not they seem insultingly dumb now, were almost always insanely *fun*—a lot of them are bulging at the edges with style. They're not necessarily campy, in the sense of making a deliberately failed attempt at seriousness; usually, they don't bother trying to be serious in the first place, or if they do, they hide their seriousness beneath a thick coating of nuttiness. They're willing to risk overambition or ludicrousness in the hopes of scaling the heights of readerly delight; the only sin they won't brook is boringness.

And something else comes to light when you've read a lot of mediocre comics: an understanding of how they're part of a process that results in good ones, an appreciation for the history of the form that doesn't fall prey to longing for it to be the way it once was. Read enough comics and you achieve the broader insights of seeing artists and their shared techniques develop, styles rise and fall, inane concepts reconsidered in ways that make them meaningful. Even bad comics' antsy aspiration to be thought of as something other than the trash they feared they were has its charm when you recognize the little steps they took toward being meaningful. There's pleasure in noting their little successes—and in mocking their dorky failures.

That pleasure, like most of comics' pleasures, is a shared one. The secret language of comics is the argot that comes from the experience of searching for gems together in a huge pile of rubble and being able to slough off the rubble's grime with a laugh. A few years ago, a challenge went around the Internet's comic blogs: "100 Things I Love About Comics." The examples some people listed were the kind of flashes of inspiration that happened when cartoonists' desire to make something really entertaining worked out. Others had to do with the rituals and incantations that belong to comics' context; still others were favorite minor characters or unsung creators.

A lot of the things on my own enormous list of the things I love about comics are covered elsewhere in this book. Here, though, are some of the ones that aren't. In no particular order:

- The sound effects in Howard Chaykin's early-'80s science fiction satire *American Flagg!*—crowding the borders of every panel in a convincing evocation of sensory overload, not to mention that some of them were pretty hilarious on their own, like the guns that went PAPAPAPAPAPA-OOOOOO-MOW! MOW! MOW!

- Paul Gambi, the "crime tailor"—a very minor '60s-era DC character whose job was making supervillains' costumes (those fur collars!)

- The short period in the Norse mythology/superhero series *Thor* when Stan Lee was convinced it would be more dramatic to end every word balloon without punctuation, and was correct

- "Son of the Sun," the first *Uncle Scrooge* story by Don Rosa, drawn on spec as an audition and an homage to the decades-earlier Scrooge stories by Carl Barks—Rosa, who ended up as a full-time Scrooge artist, spends the length of the story trying so hard to be funny and impressive and true to the Barks tradition that his panel borders practically shake, but it totally works

- The low-key desperation that seeps like a ceiling leak into Mark Gruenwald's *DP7* stories, the one bright spot in the otherwise legendarily awful "New Universe" line that Marvel launched in the mid-'80s: a group of "paranormals" on the run discover that they have nothing in common but mutual protection and nowhere to go that's safe

- Dishman, John MacLeod's minicomics superhero, whose entirely useless power is to clean and put away dirty dishes by waving his hand at them (he got it from radioactive Fiestaware) and who feels compelled to try to fight crime with it anyway

- Fred Hembeck's free-associative satire on comics culture, *Abbott and Costello Meet the Bride of Hembeck*

- The half-dozen Batman stories written in the '80s by Alan Brennert, a television writer—this was back in the days before television writers often went slumming in the lower-paying world of comics—who had a real eye for the central tragedy of the character

- Vanessa Davis's untitled story about a young goose breaking an old goose's neck—a sketchbook doodle that pretty obviously kept suggesting or rather *demanding* more until it turned into a story

- "68 Pages—No Ads from Cover to Cover!": the proud declaration on the cover of DC's "Dollar Comics" circa 1980

- *Howard the Duck* #16, for which writer Steve Gerber, realizing that the story scheduled for that issue wasn't going to be finished in time, banged out a long, amusingly meandering, free-associative prose essay about the state of comics and the "dreaded deadline doom"

- Stephen Grant's desperate heroine Whisper, perpetually endangered by people who think she's a ninja, pleading "I don't even know what a ninja is!"

- Tarquin, a sleazy little scholar in Andrew and Roger Langridge's *Art D'Ecco*, attempting to get the perplexed woman he's interviewing to admit that her work is really about "Mysticism and the Sublime in Aotearoa"

- Aliens in the science fiction series *Nexus* routinely greeting each other with "What it is" (which subsequently became the title of the series' letter column)

- The names that would appear month after month in letter columns, back when there *were* letter columns, especially a fellow named T. M. Maple (the initials stood for The Mad)

- *The Journal of M.O.D.O.K. Studies*, a mock-academic journal of which some fan has published at least three issues, all about a ludicrous old Captain America villain (the initials stand for Mental Organism Designed Only for Killing)

- The obsession Mike W. Barr, who wrote various mystery and Batman-related comics in the '80s, had with Ellery Queen— specifically with Queen's idea of providing all the clues needed to solve a mystery and then telling the reader so

- Boom Tubes, the deus-ex-machina means of transportation in Jack Kirby's early-'70s "Fourth World" comics

- Richard McGuire's indelible short comic "Here," a nearly abstract story about the passage of time (its few characters are almost

totally off-panel) whose influence has echoed through art comics
for decades

- Murphy Anderson's inks on Curt Swan's pencils in '60s and '70s
  comics—their feathery details softened the stiff edges of Swan's
  drawing and brought out the genial power in the way Swan drew
  Superman and his supporting cast

- Eddie Campbell's sweet-and-bitter *After the Snooter*, in which
  Campbell's long-running, quasi-autobiographical *Alec* series becomes fully autobiographical (he stops changing his name on the
  page, basically)

- The '60s-era "Atomic Knights" stories in *Strange Adventures*, a
  postapocalyptic scenario in which a team wearing ancient plate-
  mail, which turns out to be radiation-proof, sets about rebuilding
  the world after a 1984 atomic war

- The running gag in René Goscinny and Albert Uderzo's beloved
  European series *Asterix* about people stuffing parsley in their ears

- "Glx sptzl glaah"—the transliterated baby talk spoken by the pre-
  verbal kids in Sheldon Mayer's charming *Sugar & Spike* series

- The incantatory power of the little text boxes that used to appear
  at the beginning of Marvel comics, explaining each series' premise—I can still recall a chunk of the one from *X-Men*, with its
  swaggering rhythm: "Cyclops. Storm. Nightcrawler. Wolverine.
  Colossus. Children of the atom, students of Charles Xavier, *mutants*—feared and hated by the world they have sworn to protect!"

- The tour-de-force opening scene of the first issue of William
  Messner-Loebs's *Journey*: a nineteenth-century backwoodsman
  being chased by a bear through the Michigan wilderness for four-
  teen riveting pages

- The cover of the next-to-last issue of *Planetary*, on which the title
  of the comic itself didn't even appear—just a jigsaw-puzzle-style

image of one of the characters, about to put the final piece in place

- Scott McCloud's *DESTROY!!*, an oversized 1985 one-shot (later reprinted in 3-D) in which he tried to get all the grand Kirbyesque superhero violence out of his system in the course of one story, in which two long-underwear types smash Manhattan in the course of a fight. Final line, spoken by the kindly police commissioner amid-the rubble of the World Trade Center (!!): "Well, at least no one was hurt!"

- The duotone effect used to print Max Allan Collins and Terry Beatty's early-'80s detective comic *Ms. Tree*, which somehow gave it the effect of an old pulp magazine

- The conclusion of "Strontium Dog," a long-running serial in the weekly British comic *2000 A.D.*, in which the bounty-hunter hero is staked down in the desert for a few weeks, struggles against his bonds, can't escape, and eventually expires—not the ending anyone saw coming

- Marc Hempel's first *Gregory* book, a set of short stories about a hopelessly insane, nonverbal, institutionalized little boy whose only friend in his padded cell is a rat who keeps getting killed; it is played for laughs and is actually kind of adorable

- Todd McFarlane's much-imitated cover for the first issue of the *Spider-Man* series launched specifically as a showcase for McFarlane's artwork: the character perched among a cascading array of webs

- Ron Regé Jr.'s "Ouch!" ads for Tylenol, for which he toned down exactly none of his cracked, distorted, clear-line style

- Larry Marder's *Tales of the Beanworld*, a sui generis series about talking beans inspired by Native American mythology and Marcel Duchamp's "Large Glass"

Larry Marder's *Tales of the Beanworld,* a Duchamp-inspired
series about a cartoon ecosystem. ©2007 Larry Marder.

- The cubist-inspired cartooning technique Mary Fleener used for
  her autobiographical comics in *Slutburger*

- "Hypertime," the actually-it's-*all*-true plot device along the lines
  of Jorge Luis Borges's "The Garden of Forking Paths," invented to
  explain all inconsistencies within DC Comics

- The tradition of the opening "splash page" in old comics, sort of
  the equivalent of the "emblematic shot" in early cinema—an
  oversized panel on the first page of a genre-comics story that was a
  literal or symbolic representation of a conflict or dramatic moment that would happen later in the story. The sort of story it was
  to be having been determined, the narrative proper could begin
  with a quiet moment, since the reader knew that something exciting would be happening later; the only question was how the
  story would get there

- Marvel's '60s twist on the splash page: beginning in medias res
  with an action scene that would go on for at least a few pages and
  catching up with whatever background had to be covered via subsequent exposition or flashbacks

- Mike Grell's twist on the Marvel-style splash in his '70s and early '80s fantasy comic *The Warlord*: making the first page of the story a multi-panel narrative lead-in and then having a single, enormous image blanket the second and third page of the story

- The conclusion of the final issue of *Legion of Super-Heroes* before its mid-'90s relaunch, in which the old continuity ends with a brave farewell from the original three members of the group before blankness eats the last remaining bit of their timeline—and then the final four pages of the comic are totally blank

- R. Sikoryak's hilariously on-the-mark adaptations of classic literature into the forms of specific comics: *The Scarlet Letter* as a "Little Lulu" story ("Hester's Little Pearl"), Kafka's "The Metamorphosis" as a series of "Peanuts" daily strips ("Good Ol' Gregor Brown"), and maybe most impressively the entirety of Dante's *Inferno* condensed into a page's worth of "Bazooka Joe" strips

- The *Batman Chronicles* story, written by Devin Grayson, which made the sexual power-play undercurrents of Batman and Catwoman's relationship all but explicit

- Kalo, the forgotten *New Yorker* cartoonist in Seth's *It's a Good Life, If You Don't Weaken*, many of whose readers thought Kalo must have actually existed

- Not so much the superhero Hostess pastry ads that ran in the '70s, but the joke of throwing pastries at villains to distract them that has persisted in comics ever after

- Along the same lines, the "Hero-Halo" of the *Doom Patrol* character Flex Mentallo—a riff on a Charles Atlas ad that had appeared in so many '60s comics that readers could be counted on to catch the allusion

- Jules Feiffer's *Tantrum*, a two-hundred-page comics story about a middle-aged man who decides to become two years old, drawn around the same time as his old employer Will Eisner's *A Contract with God*, but obviously much, much faster

- Colleen Coover's minicomic *Star of the East*, a heartbreaking little improvisation based on three words given to her by her partner, Paul Tobin

- The "Judge Dredd" stories published in *2000* A.D. in the '80s in which Dredd, the quasi-fascist policeman who protects a gigantic future city, takes time off from fighting crime to quash the city's nascent pro-democracy movement—writers John Wagner and Alan Grant were very aware that there was a repugnant subtext to their hero, and cheerfully exposed it

Every one of those gives me joy to see and to recall, as well as to share with other people who've experienced them, or to pass along to other people who want to see them too. That's what I love most about comics as a culture: it's united not just by liking the same sorts of things but by communicating about them. The medium is built on a tradition of entertainment and reflective pleasure and out-and-out fun, and the enjoyment of it is redoubled by people who care about it talking about it—and arguing about it—with each other.

CHAPTER 4

Superheroes and Superreaders

Why Superheroes? Why??

There is no way of getting around it: if you are going to look honestly at American comics, you are going to encounter superheroes. The spandex wall is the public face of the medium, and its monolithic presence is what leads to the conflation of the superhero genre and the comics medium by people who don't know any better. ("Comic book" as a pejorative basically means "characteristic of superhero comics.") For artists and readers who are interested in comics as a form of artistic expression, there's something horribly off balance about that. It's as if virtually all mainstream Hollywood movies were Westerns, or all prose novels that didn't come from tiny experimental conclaves were Regency romances.

Before the art-comics movement came along, mainstream comics were virtually always genre-based. Still, there used to be a wide variety of genres on newsstands: Western comics, war comics, horror comics, sports comics, romance comics, funny-animal comics, crime comics, teenage-humor comics (which still persist in the form of the Archie line, like a tiny vestigial organ). With the rise of collector culture—readers who liked to piece together individual pamphlets into larger histories—superheroes slowly took over, and the others drifted out of existence. (It didn't hurt that the mainstream companies' editorial staffs, by the late '70s, were almost entirely composed of people who'd come up through superhero fan culture.) New mainstream comics about anything other than superheroes aren't entirely obsolete, but they're definitely anomalies; if there are three war comics running at the same time, it's like some kind of harmonic convergence.

Virtually every major American comics artist has worked with superheroes' iconography at some point or other, even if only parodically, as a way of setting their work apart from the genre. Even superheroes' absence means something. In 2005, the popular comics writer Warren Ellis set up a Web site called The Engine for discussing comics; its ironclad rule is that there is to be no discussion of superhero comics, period—including the ones Ellis still writes. A few years ago, the terrible comics publisher CrossGen was founded on the principle that what people really wanted to read was *genre* stories and announced that they would publish all sorts of genre comics *besides* superheroes. They were very proud of their array of genres and of the big names from the superhero comics world they had hired to come and work for them. The company folded quickly and ignominiously. (Their comics were terrible for other reasons, too, but the anecdote still holds.)

Of course, picking up a superhero comic book right now, if you're not already immersed in that world, is likely to make you feel simultaneously talked down to and baffled by the endless references to stuff you're already supposed to know. But immersion in that world isn't just what they require; it's what they're selling. Contemporary superhero comics *aren't* really meant to be read as freestanding works, even on those rare occasions when their plots are self-contained. They're not even necessarily meant to be individual creative statements, although some of them are.

Instead, superhero comics' readers understand each thirty-two-page pamphlet as a small element of one of two gigantic narratives, in which most major characters have thematic and metaphorical significance. The two big stories have names—corporate names: Marvel and DC. (Or "the Marvel Universe" and "the DC Universe." DC, by the way, stands for *Detective Comics*, a series launched in 1937 and still running today, so DC Comics technically means Detective Comics Comics.) Each company's superhero comics are collective histories of a fictional place that now has so much backstory attached to it that no one person knows it all. That depth, that collective psychology—the historical forces summoned up within the fiction by individual writers and artists who at first thought they were just telling stories to hold the kids over for another month—is the reward for absorbing the weird, yellowing contents of superhero comics' long white boxes.

The older parts of the big stories are also more accessible to readers now than they've ever been before. In the '70s, if you'd missed some crucial episode in the past, your only hope of seeing it was to scour the back-issue bins or to wait until it was reprinted as filler in an oversized special issue or in the occasional paperback book like *Origins of Marvel Comics*. With the shift in the comics economy to a book-driven model, any major new storyline in monthly comics is quickly collected into a book that stays in print as long as there's demand for it, and in the past few years, both major companies have started reprinting the '60s and '70s stories that are the cornerstones of their meta-narratives in cheap, fat, black-and-white volumes.

All of that, in turn, is why DC and Marvel have an unbreakable duopoly on the costumed-hero concept. (They also share a trademark on the word "superhero," which perpetuates that duopoly.) Virtually all superhero comics of the past twenty years or so are either:

1. stories that take place in the main Marvel or DC universes; or

2. about slight variations on the characters from those comics, published by those two companies (like Marvel's "Ultimate" line, which jettisoned forty years of convoluted continuity to relaunch some popular characters from scratch in a new shared setting); or

3. commentaries on older comics of one company or the other or both (like Erik Larsen's *Savage Dragon*, an homage to the storytelling traditions of mid-'70s Marvel comics, or Brian Michael

Bendis and Michael Avon Oeming's *Powers*, a police-procedural satire of the conventions of superhero comics); or

4. showcases for big-name cartoonists to demonstrate their chops on terms more their own than what either of the Big Two would permit (Todd McFarlane's *Spawn*, Jim Lee's *WildC.A.T.S.*, Alan Moore's *Top 10*); or

5. failures, commercially and artistically.

Some of the Big Two's hegemony, of course, has to do with their economic clout within the comics industry: success perpetuates success, and it can also freeze out small players. But their dominance is also related to what's interesting about the costumed-hero thing in the first place, which is what particular characters and their histories *mean*, and how that meaning has piled up, page by page, over decades. Within each of the two big stories of superhero comics, the interaction of familiar characters over time is a ritualized enactment of the ideas their readers and creators have about culture and morality or, in some cases, a testing ground for them. Style and "events" sell mainstream comics in the short term, and we'll talk about those later on. But the first aspect of them that readers attach themselves to, and often what they stay attached to, is characters.

Superhero comics are, by their nature, larger than life, and what's useful and interesting about their characters is that they provide bold metaphors for discussing ideas or reifying abstractions into narrative fiction. They're the closest thing that exists right now to the "novel of ideas." That's what's kept this particular weird little genre so closely connected to its much broader medium: a form that intrinsically lends itself to grand metaphors and subjective interpretations of the visual world goes well with characters who have particular allegorical values. Superhero cartoonists can present narratives whose images and incidents are unlike our own sensory experience of the world (and totally cool-looking) but can still be understood as a metaphorical representation of our world. That's something that's very easy to do in comics and very hard to do in any other medium. It's not the only thing that comics do well, or what comics do best—but it's something that can be pulled off *easily* only in comics.

Curiously, though, even some great characters' creators sometimes don't understand their symbolic resonance. Take Spider-Man, for instance. Pressed for an explanation of why he's been so popular for so long, a lot of cartoonists—including Stan Lee, who cocreated him with Steve Ditko—suggest that it might be that he's sort of cool-looking, or that he's got "real problems" (a well-meaning but overbearing aunt, a bruised public image, perpetual broke-ness), or that there's something strangely abject about his powers and persona. Readers—at least adolescent readers who feel perpetually misunderstood—can *relate* to him, the argument goes.

But what all good Spider-Man stories have in common, beginning with the eleven-page story that introduced him in the final issue of a science fiction/horror anthology called *Amazing Fantasy* (previously *Amazing Adult Fantasy*, "the magazine that respects your intelligence!"), is their exploration of the relationship between power and the obligation to use it correctly. Lee even spells it out in the endlessly quoted final line of that first story, "with great power there must also come—great responsibility!" If you've somehow managed to avoid encountering that origin story, its plot is that Peter Parker, a teenager from a poor family who has just gotten superhuman abilities, has an opportunity to stop a fleeing burglar but figures that it isn't his problem; the burglar goes on to kill his beloved uncle. The central theme of *Spider-Man* from then on is the friction between what Peter wants to do and what he believes he's required to do, given what he's *able* to do.

Ask longtime readers what their favorite Spider-Man stories are and they'll always name the same ones: "Spider-Man No More," "The Night Gwen Stacy Died," "The Death of Jean DeWolff"—the stories that explore that theme best. In the famous sequence in *Amazing Spider-Man* #33 that I'll discuss in the chapter on Ditko, he's trapped under a gigantic piece of machinery and convinces himself, painfully,

Writer Stan Lee and artist Steve Ditko make the theme of *Spider-Man* clear from the get-go, in his first appearance, *Amazing Fantasy* #15.
©2007 Marvel Characters, Inc. Used with permission.

to lift it up, free himself, and rescue his aunt: there's the power/responsibility theme right there. The best-loved Spider-Man artists (Ditko, John Romita, John Romita Jr., Todd McFarlane) have their own followings, but even more run-of-the-mill artists have drawn some Spider-Man stories that have succeeded on the strength of their thematic resonance.

One that I particularly love is 1987's *Spider-Man Vs. Wolverine* one-shot, by Jim Owsley, Mark Bright, and Al Williamson. It looks like just another exploitative piece of product (make two popular characters fight on the cover; watch it sell), but the point of its fight scenes and spy clichés is putting Spider-Man in a situation that's a moral quandary for him and wouldn't be for anyone else: an international intrigue that everyone tells him he should stay out of because he's out of his league. He can't—because of the power-and-responsibility thing—and his doing what his ethical code obligates him to do at every turn ends up making matters far worse. It's not a particularly graceful or subtle comic book, and it wouldn't have anything like the same impact for somebody who hadn't already read a hundred other stories about Spider-Man, but it's an unforgettable *superhero story* whose force comes from the core idea of its protagonist's history.

Virtually every major superhero franchise, actually, can be looked at in terms of a particular metaphor that underscores all of its best stories. The metaphorical subtext of a character usually doesn't jump out at readers immediately—it often takes a while to take shape—and it's not the most important thing about any *individual* superhero comic. (That would be the pleasure of the text itself: the plot, the art, the action, the crazily broad concepts that make them fun page by page.) But that subtext deepens the experience of the surface text, and over time it makes characters meaningful parts of the master "universe" narratives.

Some more examples: The X-Men, who have spent most of the last twenty-five years at the top of superhero-comics sales charts, are mutants—accidents of modernity who are unlike ordinary people and despised for it even as they slowly amass cultural capital. One faction of mutants wants to assimilate into mainstream society; another wants to break off from it altogether. The subtext is pretty obvious, and X-Men stories tend to be, on some level, allegories about difference and identity politics. (They're often specifically about sexual identity: mutations tend to show up in adolescence. Some people get just zits and pubes; some people get unstoppable red force beams coming out of their eyes.) For a while, when Grant Morrison was writing *New X-Men* in the late '90s, he tried to reroute the series' dominant metaphor into evolutionary leaps and what it might mean to be "post-human." And then, after he left, the X-Men titles went right back to being about identity politics.

Green Lantern has a "power ring" that can essentially do anything he wants it to, if he concentrates hard enough; his good stories aren't about a guy in a green costume flying and making giant green pliers but about will made manifest in the world. The series also posits that the rings can be used only by fearless people and that they need to be "charged" regularly in a ceremony that also requires reciting an oath; well, of course, if you're going to be exerting your will in the world, you need to check in with the principles behind what you're doing on a regular basis. For most of the '70s, Green Lantern was teamed up with Green Arrow, whose mastery of archery was part of a Robin Hood metaphor: he was an outspoken social-justice advocate who counterbalanced the might-makes-right aspect of Green Lantern's persona.

The Flash's power is that he can run at something like the speed of light, which makes for a cool streak-of-light visual effect but doesn't intrinsically lend itself to much of a metaphor. The most fondly remembered Flash stories, though, were the ones from the '50s and '60s, and what made them work was that they were actually about the hard sciences—the character was a police scientist, the stories were scattered with scientific "Flash Facts," and their resolutions always involved some application of science (or, sometimes, pseudoscience). His enemies committed crimes involving scientific principles: chemical elements, the light spectrum, heat, cold, weather, mirrors. And he occasionally fought a time-traveling magician, Abra Kadabra, whose "magic," it was painstakingly explained, was actually advanced sixty-fourth-century science.

The Fantastic Four—a woman, her brother, her husband, and her husband's friend—provide a way for cartoonists to play with the idea of difficult extended-family structures, with a little bit of earth/air/fire/water symbolism thrown in. (That would be, in order, the Thing, the Invisible Woman, the Human Torch, and Mr. Fantastic.) *Legion of Super-Heroes* has been relaunched, reformatted, and rebooted at least half a dozen times, and the creators of its most recent incarnation, Mark Waid and Barry Kitson, came up with a smart angle for it: it's about the distance between youthful idealism and adult realpolitik. The Hulk, a milquetoast scientist who turns into a huge, stupid monster when he gets angry, is a terrific metaphor for the dehumanizing effects of rage. Wolverine (who first appeared in a Hulk story), on the other hand, is about the struggle to *contain* rage. Little boys ask who's stronger, the Hulk or the Thing; what matters about that fight isn't that one is green and one is orange but that the question can also be understood as "which is the greater power, blinding anger or earthy groundedness?"

Oddly enough, the "what does this character metaphorically stand for?" schema is toughest to apply to the three most famous superheroes, Superman, Batman, and Wonder Woman. Here's a stab at it: Superman and Batman are both about human perfectibility. Superman is effectively the perfect person: capable of doing anything, humble and compassionate, so in love with being up-to-the-minute that he's a reporter. The catch is that he's not actually human, except to the extent that he's made himself human, and his one real weakness—Kryptonite, the remnants of his home planet—is the thing that reminds him that he's not a real Earthling.

Batman, conversely, has pushed himself to the edge of being greater-than-human—and what he's defined as the peak of human-

A cover, drawn by Jim Aparo, from the long-running Superman/Batman team-up series *World's Finest Comics*. "World's Finest" #253, ©1978 DC Comics. All rights reserved. Used with permission.

ity is dangerousness and a lack of weakness. His relentless drive, though, has made him (for all practical purposes) psychotic: he's a benign psycho but barely functional as a person. His enemies mostly get sent to an insane asylum rather than a prison—they're like him but malign rather than benign, as virtually everyone who's written Batman comics over the last few decades has hammered in. And his drive is the kind that parents often pass on to their children; hence his parental relationship with Robin, whose symbolic value is as a son trying to learn from his father's experience and wisdom without making his father's mistakes. (The peculiar parallel between Superman and Batman is why stories featuring both of them work so well—the series with the charmingly old-fashioned title *World's Finest Comics* teamed them up almost every issue for more than thirty years.)

And Wonder Woman? As conceived by William Moulton Marston, aka Charles Moulton, who created the character, she was very specifically an excuse for stories about sexual domination and submission. They appear in drag as children's fables, of course, but that's what they're about, and if you doubt me, count the number of times characters are tied up, chained, or bound in a "magic lasso" in any Golden Age Wonder Woman story. After a certain point, that didn't wash, of course; in the early '70s, a few writers tried to make *Wonder Woman* a series about the feminist movement, and more recently writer Greg Rucka has also worked the human-perfectibility angle, making Wonder Woman an ambassador from Paradise Island who explicitly tries to teach the world to become more like her.

The same principle goes for their enemies. Superman's nemesis Lex Luthor is a Nietzschean "superman," who believes the world should bend to his desires and never stops reminding Superman that he's an alien. And even before Alan Moore and Brian Bolland's *The Killing Joke* set up the Joker as a man whose Job-like suffering destroyed his mind and made him want to become a cruelly laughing force of random suffering inflicted on others, it was obvious that that was what he was, and that his fights with Batman were two kinds of madness pitted against each other: one the madness of assuming you can turn the chaos of urban life into order, one the madness of human frailty and violence without meaning.

Conversely, very few superhero characters who don't have some kind of strong underlying theme can support interesting stories. Hawkman has been around for decades because he's got a great look—a man with a hawk helmet and enormous wings. But hunt for a canonical good Hawkman story, and you'll come up blank. The series has been relaunched and cancelled over and over in the course of the last quarter century, playing on the early Hawkman stories' science fiction background or the archaic weaponry that Joe Kubert used to draw the characters with or the theme of reincarnation, but nobody's ever figured out how to make it really work. *Thor* has survived for a long time on the strength of its connections to Norse mythology, but there's not much interesting about the character Thor himself, and the franchise itself has run out of steam—Ragnarok can happen only so many times. And virtually every other superhero who's failed to catch on, over and over, from Blue Beetle to Dazzler to the Martian Manhunter, fails because there's nothing about *their* stories that keeps them from being generic superhero punch-ups.

It can take a long time for a new character to get integrated into the master-narrative matrix, too; combined with the fact that superhero-comics readers are, out of necessity, nostalgics, that means it's very difficult to introduce significant *new* characters with any hope of catching on. The premise behind the Sentry, a Marvel character introduced in 2000, is a clever riff on that dilemma: his creators suggested that the Sentry had been around for almost forty years but that everyone had forgotten all the classic Sentry comics from the past because they'd had their memories psychically erased. (The Sentry also came with a preformed subtext: he's also his own archenemy the Void and spends most of his time crippled by his internal struggle—a neatly wrapped little metaphor for severe depression.)

One other useful thing about the superhero genre is actually the opposite of the black-and-white good-guys-and-bad-guys pattern for which "comic book morality" is still shorthand: it's an ideal framework for discussing the complexities of morality and ethics. It used to be that the good guys did right because they were good people, and the bad guys did wrong because they were greedy or insane or just plain evil. One side's groups were the Justice League of America and the Defenders and the Seven Soldiers of Victory; the other's were the Crime Syndicate and the Secret Society of Super-Villains and the Monster Society of Evil.

That's now the condescending, cynical political spin on international relations that the American government pumps out on a regular basis, and superhero-comics writers have made their analysis of "good" and "evil" much more interesting. The trend didn't really start until the mid-'90s, after *Watchmen*'s intimation that maybe the mass-murdering villain could be in the right and the earnest heroes in the wrong had had a chance to sink in. (Dan Jurgens anticipated it in a very mild way with his 1986 series *Booster Gold*, whose hero, a money-hungry time traveler, invariably does the right thing for the wrong reasons.) But ethical action has become Topic A in twenty-first-century superhero comics; a lot of the best and most significant ones address the question of means and ends and where they intersect with violence and history and the notion of what constitutes moral action.

Thunderbolts, a Marvel series launched in 1997, was the first to address those ideas head-on: the Thunderbolts, as conceived by initial writer Kurt Busiek, were a group of villains posing as heroes and acting in the public interest to gain the world's trust, with the intention of betraying it later on. Ed Brubaker and Sean Phillips's 2003 series *Sleeper* is about a hero who's gone undercover to join a team of villains and has become so seriously morally compromised that he no longer knows if he's acting in any interest other than his own. (Brubaker pushed the metaphor as far as it could go—the main supporting character in *Sleeper* is Miss Misery, who gets her powers from vices and acts of cruelty.) Mark Millar's writing for *The Authority* and *The Ultimates* all but explicitly draws parallels between superheroes imposing their will on unwilling noncombatants for what they see as the good of "their side" and contemporary U.S. foreign policy. And then there's the awful but very popular Brad Meltzer–written *Identity Crisis* miniseries, of which more shortly.

The Secret Society of Superreaders, or How Long Underwear Characters Grew Up

Superheroes are the public and private shame of American comics. They're a Peter Pan façade that refuses to grow up, the idiot cousin that the whole family resents for being the one who supports them and brags about it. They're omnipresent; they're eternally the same; they're the part that acts like it's the whole.

Most of all, they're something that people tend to discover as children, and it's deeply embarrassing to enjoy the same things as an adult that you enjoyed as a child, even if you're not enjoying them for exactly the same reasons. It's suspect enough to be nostalgic for the comics of your youth, to the point of buying deluxe $50 hardcover collections of stories that were created for disposable 12-cent newsprint periodicals. To want to own the original comics is, in a way, to be swept off one's bearings by nostalgia. To keep buying stories about characters you adored as a child, out of something like team loyalty, or in the hope that they'll give you the same kind of thrill you got from their comics as a ten-year-old, is desperate and (if they don't give you the response you want) kind of pathetic. To *actually get* the same kind of thrill you got as a ten-year-old means that something—probably something important—hasn't changed since you were a child.

It also suggests that you're sublimating "adult" impulses into something that's not exactly maturely sexual. Every formal convention of superheroes can be read as something on the continuum between amusingly pervy and genuinely sick: the skintight outfit, the mask, the double life, the incident in which one's true identity was formed, the way the first interaction with everyone of one's kind is a physical tussle, the kid sidekick. Oh, God, the kid sidekick. That alone has come in for enough "deconstructions" that . . . well, we get it already.

And when there's shame, there's an opportunity to capitalize on people who want to overcome it. For most of its existence, the American comic book industry has been trying to convince its readers that they should be not ashamed but proud. Let's go back for a moment to that first Spider-Man story, in *Amazing Fantasy* #15. Stan Lee's first caption on page one begins, "Like costumed heroes? Confidentially, we in the comic mag business refer to them as 'long underwear characters'! And, as you know, they're a dime a dozen!" Like costumed heroes? *Sucker!* But you know what? You're reading something better now! Within a few months, Lee had changed his tune a little—or, rather, developed his public persona: a smiling huckster forever talking up his goods' similarity to Classic Literature, which meant Shakespeare and not a lot else.

Ever since then, superhero comics have been steadily and earnestly pressing toward adulthood, toward the idea of being seen as *mature*. A few early-'70s issues of *Amazing Spider-Man* and *Green Lantern/Green Arrow* concerned drugs, which was a big deal at the time, since that meant they weren't entirely suitable for small children. In the early '80s, the industry batted around the idea of a ratings system like the one American movies use and ended up with the prevailing euphemism to print on covers: "mature readers." (Mature readers, you see, are the ones who can handle strong language and naked ladies.)

The initial praise outside the comics world for *The Dark Knight Returns* and *Watchmen* didn't mention that they were well-wrought as much as that they were "grown-up." In 1987, Spider-Man married Mary Jane Watson, and a few years later Superman married Lois Lane. Not coincidentally, the core constituency of superhero comics has been steadily getting older, and the comics have been playing to their audience's concerns, as a way of trying to be more "mature"—Captain America hasn't yet attempted to calculate his Medicare prescription-drug benefits, but it's only a matter of time.

The fact is that open-ended *franchises*, like all the big-name superheroes, are fundamentally unable to grow up in some sense. Their stewards are charged with maintaining the marketable things about them, which means that significant, lasting change is almost impossible to get past the marketing department, or past sentimentally attached readers. If the new way doesn't work out—and it almost never does—it's time for the "cosmic reset button," as fans call it: a contrivance that restores things to their original state. Superman will always be Clark Kent, will always be the last survivor of Krypton, will always have Lois Lane and Jimmy Olsen and Perry White around. The X-Men will always be associated with a "school for gifted youngsters" run by Professor Xavier, who will always be a bald psychic in a wheelchair, even if he's healed for a little while. Spider-Man will always take care of his fragile Aunt May; when she died of age and infirmity some years ago, it threw off the balance of the franchise, so it was declared that the Aunt May who had died had actually been an artificially aged actress, and the real Aunt May was just fine, and so on.

Children are only too happy to deal with limitless stories whose resolutions leave things exactly as they were at the beginning; there's no need for Scooby-Doo's friends ever to age or change. The adults that superhero comics' readers have grown into, though, demand stories that go somewhere. So the producers of superhero stories are forced to present the *illusion* of real and lasting change. Over the last few decades, the two big narratives have been in near-constant turbulence, roiled by one big "event comic" after another—stories that cross over with scores of ongoing series and may change the fundamental premises of some of them for as much as a few months. Superhero readers can rattle off a list of them: *Infinite Crisis, Crisis on Infinite Earths, Secret Wars, Secret Wars II, Secret War, Armageddon 2001*, The Age of Apocalypse, *Zero Hour*, The Onslaught Saga, *Millennium, DC One Million, House of M*, Decimation, The Death of Superman. The events keep appearing, because they keep selling: in the summer of 2006, *Civil War*, the flagship title of an immense crossover in the course of which Spider-Man unmasked, became the best-selling pamphlet-form comic in years.

There's another, slightly more dubious adult objection to the conventions of superhero comics: they're "unrealistic." (Of course they're unrealistic! That's the *entire point!*) So real-world settings and consequences started creeping into them in the '60s, when Marvel made the radical move of replacing superheroes' fictional hometowns—Metropolis, Star City, Gotham City—with a recognizable New York. In the '70s, Howard the Duck set up camp in a grotty Cleveland and tried to run for president. "Put on a costume and fight crime in the streets . . . You'd have to be crazy," the ad for *The Badger* read in 1983. Below the caption was a picture of the mentally ill hero, suited up and glaring.

The natural next step for "realistic" superheroes is that they would try to change human society from the ground up. There's a potentially interesting story there; the problem is that there's scarcely a story to write after it, and it would cause the kind of permanent change that's fatal to ongoing franchises. So when it's been brought up, it's generally been outside the two master narratives. Alan Moore's '80s series *Miracleman* ended with Miracleman and his family announcing that because they

Howard the Duck runs for president in 1976. ©2007 Marvel Characters, Inc. Used with permission.

were more powerful than anyone else, they were abolishing money and governments and declaring a utopia. (Neil Gaiman, who wrote the subsequent *Miracleman* stories, got cut off halfway through the story he wanted to tell by publisher Eclipse Comics going out of business, but the parts that were published concerned the slow failure of the Moore/Miracleman political and social system.) More recently, *Squadron Supreme*, *Stormwatch* and its sequel *The Authority*, and *The Ultimates* have all imagined superheroes instigating profound changes in the world, and their writers have all pretty much written themselves into corners—the scope of *The Authority*, in particular, was shocking at first, but it's now gotten so huge that there's basically nowhere left to take it anymore.

Still, there's a way in which the superhero genre *has* legitimately grown up over the past seventy years. It's the same way anybody grows up: by accumulating complexity and depth from experience. Superhero-comics readership has matured, too, just because a lot of those readers can be counted on to have read hundreds or thousands of superhero stories. Often-reprinted comics have become a canon of their own within the genre. (When Joss Whedon and John Cassaday show Kitty Pryde standing up and declaring "now it's my turn" at the end of 2006's *Astonishing X-Men* #15, they can pretty much count on their readers recognizing it as an allusion to Wolverine striking the same pose at the end of 1980's *Uncanny X-Men* #132.) But the cumulative mass of not-especially-distinguished superhero comics is at least as important: there are certain images and archetypes and kinds of incidents that have been internalized by readers and creators—traditions and conventions of the superhero idiom that are so familiar that tweaking them can pass for creativity.

That has led to the rise of superhero metacomics, whose point is commentary on the conventions of superhero stories or on familiar characters who are represented in a sort of thinly disguised roman à clef way. Metacomics may pay lip service to being universally comprehensible, but they're really aimed at what I call "superreaders": readers familiar enough with enormous numbers of old comics that they'll understand what's really being discussed in the story.

The first metacomics came about as a bit of whimsy, around 1970: DC's Justice League of America met the Champions of Angor (a group of characters meant to be understood as Marvel's team the Avengers) in the same month as the Avengers met the Squadron Supreme (who were the Justice League in all but name). The tongue-in-cheek conceit of *Defenders*, which began in 1972, was that the Defenders were a "non-team," whose stories rebelled (a little bit) against the tropes of superhero-team comics. 1986's *Watchmen* was the first comic to seriously mess with the conventions of superheroes: the cape (of an offstage character that gets caught in a bank's revolving door, whereupon he's shot dead by robbers), the loner-hero (Rorschach, an obsessive, psychotic loser), their practice of never really changing the world (as we learn near the beginning of the story, the heroes won the Vietnam War, and consequently Richard Nixon is in his fifth term).

After that, the floodgates for entire series of metacomics were open: *Damage Control, Astro City, Powers, The Boys, Top Ten, Nextwave*. The Five Swell Guys in *Promethea* are effectively the Fantastic Four, and so are the Four in *Planetary*, a series in which thinly disguised analogues of characters from comics and pulp fiction are introduced in nearly every issue. Rob Liefeld's character Supreme is Superman in all but name; Mr. Majestic from Jim Lee's *WildC.A.T.S.* is Superman too. So is Apollo from *The Authority*, whose lover is the Midnighter, a Batman analogue. The Elite, who fought Superman in *Action Comics* a few years ago, are in turn stand-ins for the Authority, and their leader

UH -- UCHUM --
MY NAME'S JESSICA
JONES AND I -- UH --
I NEED TO SPEAK
TO CAPTAIN
AMERICA.

I'M SORRY, BUT
THE AVENGERS ARE AWAY
ON A MISSION -- HELPING TO
KEEP THE WORLD A SAFER
PLACE FOR YOU AND YOUR
FAMILY TO LIVE.

BUT WE
THANK YOU FOR
STOPPING BY.

PLEASE STEP
BACK FROM THE
GATE.

Jessica Jones of *Alias*, out of her league among the superhero world's power players. Written by Brian Michael Bendis, drawn by Michael Gaydos. ©2007 Marvel Characters, Inc. Used with permission.

Manchester Black is a stand-in for Apollo, who is of course a stand-in for Superman himself. And yes, if your head is spinning right now, that's fine, because there's no way to even make sense of this sort of stuff unless you don't just read the occasional superhero comic but are fanatical about them.

More and more superhero series are readable really only as metacomics, because they're mostly about where their plots and characters are positioned in the matrices of the big superhero narratives. The best one was probably Brian Michael Bendis and Michael Gaydos's sly, raw-edged *Alias*, whose protagonist, Jessica Jones, is a former super-heroine who couldn't cut it in the big leagues; she's retired her costume, become a private investigator specializing in cases involving the cape-and-cowl community, and started drinking too much, and her sex life consists mostly of uneasy liaisons with other third-tier Marvel characters. The reader is expected to understand the social protocols of Jessica's life—which characters are her peers and which ones are out of her league—and the final storyline of the series constructs a metaphor for rape out of a terrible thing that can happen to a superhero-comic character but not to an actual person.

One of the most popular superhero comics as of this writing is 52, a weekly DC series that's totally locked into the DC metanarrative. The concept is that it happens in "real time" during a year when Superman, Batman, and Wonder Woman are all missing, and that therefore there's some kind of heroism void that other characters rush to fill. (The series' protagonists include Renée Montoya, formerly one of the main characters in a nifty metacomic called *Gotham Central*, a police procedural set in Gotham City, whose cops have to deal with costumed types interfering with their cases.) At a panel discussion before the first issue of *52* appeared, one of the series' writers, Greg Rucka, mentioned that the writing team was trying to make it work a bit like Google Earth: a map of an entire fictional world, with some points in much clearer focus than others. Every issue of *52* is filled with allusions to long-forgotten characters and long-out-of-print stories, as "Easter eggs" for the most fanatical readers, and every element of the plot is directly tied to events in other comics past and future. It's exactly the kind of thing I love—but then again, it's aimed at people like me who breathe the rarefied air of ten thousand yellowing back issues, and I can't even begin to explain its plot to people who aren't superreaders.

Then there are comics in which writing-for-superreaders, misguided "realism" and "adultness," questioning the morality of "heroes," the contemporary demand for the illusion of change, and the commercial draw of "event" stories add up to extraordinary awfulness. I'm speaking, of course, of DC's *Identity Crisis*, the most egregiously terrible comic book of all time. There have been many more inept comics, of course, and more unpleasant comics, but no others that suffer from quite as pungent a combination of deafening hype and resolute refusal to offer any kind of gratification at all to their readers.

Identity Crisis was a big event in mainstream comics by any standards. Written by best-selling prose novelist Brad Meltzer and drawn (glitzily if not distinctively) by Rags Morales and Michael Bair, it topped the comics sales charts for most of its seven-issue run and was reprinted in a fancy hardcover volume. The plot involves a terrible secret from the Justice League of America's past that comes to light in the wake of the shocking murder of Sue Dibny. What's that? You don't know who Sue Dibny is? Why, she's the beloved wife of the Elongated Man! The wise-cracking down-to-earth soul of *Justice League Europe* in the '80s! Um . . .

Well, there's a problem right there. For anyone who's not a super-reader, Sue's death can have no emotional resonance at all. Superreaders, on the other hand, will note that having Sue murdered and mutilated—and earlier raped by a minor supervillain—is at best a gross misuse of everything that was interesting about the character, whose role in earlier stories was always to act as a sort of Nora Charles type, a grounded counterbalance to her protean, daffy husband. On top of that, she's killed immediately after discovering that she's pregnant, an emotional device so cheap that Tearjerker Depot usually just leaves a crate of its ilk out front in the hopes that someone will take it.

For an event story line that was promoted outside the usual comics-shop circles, *Identity Crisis* can't possibly make much sense to readers who aren't already intimately familiar with its dozens of characters and their long-established relationships. Even so, it might still work as an adventure story, if its plot weren't riddled with ludicrous implausibilities. Superhero comics' readers are willing to take it on faith that a man can fly, but this one also asks us to believe that a grotesquely out-of-shape man who's just been shot, fatally, three times in the chest can still throw a razor-edged boomerang hard enough to pierce his shooter through the heart; that a one-eyed man with a sword can stab someone who can move at the speed of light; and that a happy-go-lucky supporting character of forty years' standing can have turned into a psychotic serial killer without anyone noticing anything amiss. Also, the solution to its central mystery is that Sue was killed by *tiny footprints in her brain*, a revelation to which the only reasonable reaction is deep embarrassment for everyone who devised or greenlighted it.

Worst of all, the entire story hinges on the idea that its heroes have secretly acted nastily and venally, and covered it up, again and again, for years, to protect their own interests. (Seeing them starting down the slippery slope of the cover-up and debating its morality for more than a few panels could have been a gripping plot thread; making it a years-old fait accompli feels like a cheat.) It's possible to make a great story out of questioning heroes' morality, or out of bringing out a familiar character's dark side, as long as it seems to be raising the stakes rather than changing the rules. Meltzer's story, though, requires virtually every character to act entirely unlike what we've seen of them for decades' worth of comics and ignores their metaphorical significance, so that it can pull off its lazy, sordid shocks. There's no pleasure in *Identity Crisis*, no sense of the adventure or triumph or fun that its characters were created for—only violence, betrayal, and witless flailing. It's relentlessly, hideously grim and melodramatic, from Superman shedding a tear on the original cover of the first issue to the dribbling pathos of its ending.

Near the end of *Identity Crisis*, Meltzer quotes Arthur Miller: "An era can be said to end when its basic illusions are exhausted." His intention seems to be to plant the final coffin nails (or razor-sharp boomerangs) in the Silver Age of superhero comics, the era when troubled and flawed characters could nonetheless be relied upon to do right in a crisis, when there was always a vein of lightheartedness in their stories, even at their darkest. The stories of that era were intended to delight children, the logic appears to go, so if we extinguish the possibility of delight, we can make sure that the genre is truly mature.

But what *Identity Crisis* is presenting, in effect, as exhausted illusions are the idea of heroism itself—that anyone can have a reliable ethical compass at all—as well as the ideas that consistency of character counts for more than bean-counting "continuity," and that even the most consequential parts of a huge fictional meta-narrative should speak to an audience greater than long-devoted fanatics. Without those principles, the superhero genre is itself exhausted of everything but an endless loop of brightly colored brutality.

Superheroes Need Style Too: Daredevil, Birds of Prey, and Guilty Pleasures

The peculiar thing about all that shame over superhero comics is that there are a lot of really good ones. (I suspect that if they didn't so totally dominate the American comics mainstream, there'd be a lot less free-floating contempt for them.) Like anything else, they can be done well or badly, and they're usually done badly—but there still seem to be at least two or three released every week that keep me coming back for more, and after twenty-five years, I'm not bored yet. Beyond the genuinely first-rate stuff, there's a big, sloppy mountain of superhero comics that are flawed but fascinating, like worthy B-movies—stilted or ludicrous or maybe just not quite all there, but full of life and graced with at least some aspect I love. And then there's a mountain range's worth of worthless ink and pulp, most of which I've read so you don't have to.

One big difference between art comics and superhero comics is what their readers look for in them. What matters most in art comics is the way the cartoonist communicates his or her content—the creator is always an almost-tangible presence. What matters most in superhero comics is *what happens to whom* and *what it looks like*—the actual plot and dialogue, and the content of the images, are what provoke the most immediate reaction from their readers.

That doesn't mean that style doesn't count for a lot in the context of superhero comics; it just means they can get along without a lot of it. I'm being slightly snarky here, because there's no such thing as a totally neutral style. But superhero comics default to a narrow range of style that's meant to make them immediately engaging (because they are, above all else, entertainment, and entertainment is useless if it isn't engaging). It's also meant to make them fit into the context of those grand corporate narratives—the way a character looks in a particular comic book can't be *too* different from the way he or she looks in another one published the same year.

What draws superhero comics' readers to particular individual comic books is partly favorite characters and the promise of major consequences in the big narrative. Putting Wolverine or Batman on the cover of an issue guarantees at least a slight bump in sales (although a lot less than it used to, since the most popular characters have now been pimped half to death); indicating on the cover that an issue is a crucial component of a crossover like *Infinite Crisis* or *Civil War* can pump up sales, too. (A certain amount of that effect is the semi-bogus collectibility factor, of course.)

But one of the biggest sales draws for superhero comics right now is star creators, who are now invariably credited on the cover. And a marquee-name writer or artist, on his or her own, is less effective than a marquee-name team. When superhero buffs talk about their favorite comics of the past, they usually name their favorite pairings of writers and artists, as well as the series those teams worked on: the Chris Claremont/John Byrne *X-Men*, the Steve Englehart/Marshall Rogers *Detective Comics*, the Marv Wolfman/George Pérez *New Teen Titans*, the Tom and Mary Bierbaum/Keith Giffen *Legion of Super-Heroes*, the Mike Baron/Steve Rude *Nexus*, the Denny O'Neil/Neal Adams *Green Lantern/Green Arrow*, and so on.

All of those teams collaborated long enough to build up a substantial body of work with a specific tone and visual aesthetic. Claremont and Byrne's X-Men, for instance, were prone to extended bouts of soap-operatic self-reflection even in the middle of cosmic fight scenes, and the rounded, smooth forms Byrne drew always seemed about to bounce off the page; Englehart and Rogers's *Detective* was marked by an Art Deco–inspired design sense and a loopy, decadent air—even their other collaborations (*Coyote* and *Madame Xanadu*) don't have quite the same vibe. All of them also understood the symbolic and metaphorical value of the characters they were working with, and they let their stories and even

The Joker's Art Deco menace, from *Detective Comics*, written by Steve Englehart and drawn by Marshall Rogers and Terry Austin. From *Batman: Strange Apparitions*, ©DC Comics. Used with permission.

their stylistic choices proceed from it. Without that kind of formal unity of purpose, it's possible to create entertaining or memorable superhero comics, but rarely great ones.

As a sort of case study in what I'm talking about, the most impressively realized aesthetic of any recent superhero series belonged to Brian Michael Bendis and Alex Maleev's 2001–2006 run on *Daredevil*, an ornately zigzagging narrative about moral blindness and double lives, with a hero sinking irreparably into a pit he's dug for himself. Bendis is the most prolific writer in comics right now—he usually writes at least five monthly series at a time—but his collaboration with Bulgarian-born artist Maleev had a distinct, understated, security-camera perspective on the demimonde of crime, law, and the press. They managed to make *Daredevil* their own, a doubly impressive feat, considering that almost everyone who worked on the series for the past twenty years has struggled and failed to get out from under Frank Miller's shadow.

Daredevil was launched by Marvel in 1964 as a superhero comic with a "shocking" twist—the hero is blind! and a lawyer! because, all together now, *justice is blind!* And he dresses up in a spandex devil suit because he lives in the Hell's Kitchen neighborhood of New York! The series spent the next fifteen years limping along as the poor cousin of *Spider-Man* and *Fantastic Four*. When Miller, then an unknown twenty-two-year-old cartoonist, and his artistic collaborator, Klaus Janson, began their work on the series in 1979, it was marginal and generic. They quickly reworked it into something far darker—both visually and metaphorically—and more interesting than it had been; I'll discuss their work on it a bit more in the chapter on Miller and Will Eisner.

After Miller left the series in 1983, though, *Daredevil* became the comic book Frank Miller used to do. Nearly everyone who attempted a *Daredevil* story after them was either trying to send "a valentine to Frank Miller," as Bendis calls it, or to rebel against his legacy. Bendis and Maleev fell into the latter category—their *Daredevil* looks and moves nothing like Miller's. From the beginning of their first issue, Maleev unleashed a drawing style that's sometimes been called "photorealistic," which it isn't, exactly—it's wildly, unmistakably stylized, even when he's clearly working from photographs of cityscapes or models. But it's believable, even seductive, in the same way a grainy surveillance tape is seductive. And their opening story line, "Underboss," caroms back and forth in time like a ricocheting bullet: a model in miniature of the way Bendis's four-year plot loops around and through itself, revisiting key moments from different perspectives.

That splintered, documentary approach is appropriate for Bendis and Maleev's overall story, one of whose major themes is information and evidence and how they inform the relationship between the law and justice. (That relationship is the essence of Daredevil's symbolic value, at least in Bendis's take; this simply wouldn't have made sense as a Spider-Man or Green Lantern story, for instance.) At the center of it is a nasty metacomics twist on superhero comics' sacred tenet of the secret identity. Beneath his mask, Daredevil is a trial lawyer, Matthew Murdock, and nobody else knows it—except for a bunch of other superheroes, and various ex-girlfriends, and his partner at his law firm, and a trusted reporter or two, and a rather large number of people who've seen him with his mask off, and a bunch of murderous ninjas, and—oh, yes—a Hell's Kitchen crimelord known as the Kingpin. And the Kingpin's family knows too, and so do a handful of friends they've blabbed to. Following a mob power struggle, one morning Matthew Murdock wakes up, and his secret is on the front page at every newsstand in Manhattan.

There's no going back. From that moment on, he's in a morally untenable situation, and everything he does makes things worse. The only response he can have is to start lying and make all of his allies lie for him too. He denies everything. He files lawsuits that he knows are fraudulent. He beats the Kingpin half to death, drags his unconscious body into an underworld bar, and declares himself the new boss of Hell's Kitchen. Then the narrative abruptly jumps forward a year, and things really start going downhill.

The second half of the Bendis/Maleev run fills in the gaps of the missing year bit by bit and suggests what happens when a hero chooses to rule in Hell (or its kitchen) rather than serve in Heaven. Murdock

has taken on the responsibility of single-handedly saving his community, and he can't even save himself. He's forced to break ties with his allies; he becomes the pawn of greater legal powers than his own; he's de
facto a Kingpin himself. Bendis hints briefly that Murdock might have
had a nervous breakdown before everything went wrong, then makes it
clear that he's just made one terrible error in judgment after another,
out of pride and shame. By the final Bendis/Maleev story line, "The
Murdock Papers," the hero is trapped and desperate, under attack on all
sides, and he's made it impossible for his friends and allies to do right,
either. His allegiance to the law over the truth has made justice impossible for him.

Maleev isn't much for heroic poses, either. His artwork has the appearance of a newspaper photo that's been blown up and photocopied
until it disintegrates into blotches and grains—the backgrounds in his
outdoor scenes appear to actually be degraded photographs, and his
characters' body language and facial expressions are indicated more by
jagged, scribbly flickers of ink and spackled folds of shadow than by
clear, continuous lines. (Often, a blown-up detail from one panel becomes another.) He also varies his stylistic approach a little for each
story line: in a sequence that deals with the history of the rulers of Hell's
Kitchen, Maleev uses a metacomics visual technique, drawing flashbacks to the early days of Daredevil's career as simpler line art, colored
with slightly off-register patterns of dots against an off-white background, to suggest the look of '50s-era four-color comics on yellowing
newsprint.

Naturally, all sorts of other characters and gimmicks keep things
lively, too: a sexy ex-Soviet spy called the Black Widow; a couple of
cameo appearances by Spider-Man; the illegal drug Mutant Growth
Hormone; a woman known as the Night Nurse whose clinic patches up
injured heroes, no questions asked. It's melodramatic, pulp-fiction stuff,
and what keeps it from getting soggy is Bendis and Maleev's shadowy,
low-key delivery. Bendis's dialogue is crisp and fragmentary, often David
Mamet–inflected; his favorite trick is to give the reader just enough in-

Alex Maleev's post-photorealist technique on display in a sequence from
Daredevil #66 written by Brian Michael Bendis. ©2007 Marvel Characters, Inc.
Used with permission

formation to get a sense of what's happening, letting crucial context slip
out bit by bit much later. His Matthew Murdock thinks and talks like a
lawyer, convinced that he can make the legal fiction that he's not Daredevil true if he keeps repeating it, even as the story's gap between what's
just and what's legal keeps widening. And the violence of Bendis's *Daredevil* isn't grand or bloodless: it's quick, confusing, and horrible, and its
victims are haunted or ruined by it.

The Bendis/Maleev *Daredevil* belongs to the first tier of superhero
comics, the stuff that gets reprinted again and again, and occupies the
prime positions in the two big company narratives (it's already been re-
released as a set of oversized hardcovers). The second tier, of entertain-
ing-but-not-great comics, works a little differently. As good an example as
any of that second tier is the seven recent issues of the DC superhero series *Birds of Prey* reprinted as a book with the title *Sensei & Student.* The
cover of the paperback carries a blurb from *Entertainment Weekly,* "A

well-written guilty pleasure," a backhanded compliment if ever there was one. If it's well written, why is it a *guilty* pleasure? What exactly is fun about it, and where does the guilt come in?

The first few things to be guilty about are obvious from the cover: six hot-looking babes in tight-fitting outfits, a series name with a little trademark sign next to it, and nine last names listed below the subtitle. The book is the work of a factory's worth of artists, along with a single writer, Gail Simone, whose take on the characters she's working with dovetails smoothly with the way other writers have defined them in the past. The basic setup of *Birds of Prey* is a Nero Wolfe kind of scenario, in which Oracle, a wheelchair-bound ex-superheroine and computer genius with ties to Batman, works with a couple of field agents, notably Black Canary, who's been in the hero game for many years and has a lot of psychological baggage. In *Sensei & Student*, Black Canary teams up with two untrustable assassins to try to find the people who murdered her teacher.

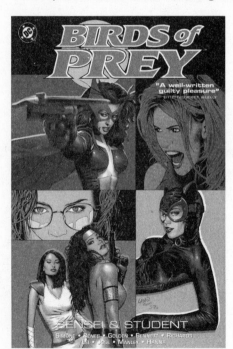

"A well-written guilty pleasure," as its cover blurb puts it. *Birds of Prey: Sensei & Student.* ©DC Comics. All rights reserved. Used with permission.

It's absolutely a pleasure to read, although some of its thrills are a little sleazy—the phrase "kickboxing in wet lingerie" comes to mind—and it's drawn in the smooth but generic style that future historians will call "mainstream comics circa 2005." A lot of its fun, though, comes from how deftly Simone handles superhero conventions (not "subverts" or even "tweaks": she's happy to play them straight), especially this story's connections to the larger, and unbelievably tangled, backstory of the DC universe. Just as an example: Cheshire, the poisoner and international terrorist, is also the mother of a baby whose father is Black Canary's ex-boyfriend Green Arrow's former sidekick, a small-time superhero, ex-junkie, and inveterate fuckup called Arsenal. (Draw a diagram if it helps.) Fortunately, Simone doesn't assume that her readers already know all that, but everything her characters do and say to each other is colored by their histories, and that's what drives the plot.

She also stakes a lot on Black Canary's symbolic value as a vehicle for examining the ways people define themselves by their relationships to others. For many years' worth of comics, Black Canary's role had been Maid Marian to Green Arrow's Robin Hood, or the link between a new generation of heroes and its predecessor (which included her mother, the previous Black Canary) and the new one—her very occasional solo stories didn't really have a conceptual grounding of their own, other than "blonde in fishnets." Simone's smartest move with *Birds of Prey* has been to turn that very lack of definition into a subtext for the character. She keeps things moving on the surface level of the story, too; there's something entertaining happening on almost every page. But nobody's ever going to refer to "the classic Simone/Benes/Golden/Bennett/Richards/Lei/Jose/Manley/Hanna era of *Birds of Prey*," because as much fun as it is, it doesn't really have an aesthetic of its own. That's not a reason to feel guilt for enjoying it—it's just a sign that *Sensei & Student*'s genuine pleasure is also a limited one.

CHAPTER 5

Pictures, Words, and the Space Between Them

What Cartooning Is and How It Works

The most significant fact about comics is so obvious it's easy to overlook: they are *drawn*. That means that what they show are things and people, real or imagined, moving in space and changing over time, as transformed through somebody's eye and hand.

That transformation is incredibly important. Film and photography intrinsically claim to be accurate documents, even when they're not: they always have the pretense that they are showing you something you would have seen exactly the same way if you'd been present at the right time and place. (That's true whether they're depicting a stack of books in a basement or a light-saber battle on the Death Star.) Comics don't work like that. When you look at, say, a Will Eisner drawing of a tenement in the Bronx, you know that what you're seeing represents a tenement in the Bronx, and you believe on some level that it's real, because it's in front of your eyes. But you also understand that you're not seeing an actual building or a building you could have seen unaided by the drawing. What you're looking at is a manifestation of Eisner's style, a personal interpretation of what that sort of building looks like. Isolate

Not a literal document of a Bronx tenement: a Bronx tenement filtered through Will Eisner's eye and hand. 'Contract with God.' ©1978, 1985, 1989, 1995, 1996 by Will Eisner, from *The Contract with God Trilogy: Life on Dropsie Avenue* by Will Eisner. Used by permission of W. W. Norton and Company, Inc.

and enlarge a detail of it so tiny and fragmentary that it looks like an abstract collection of shaky lines rather than like a building, and it'll still be identifiable as an Eisner to someone familiar with his work.

For the most part, historically, the visual part of comics has been *drawing*, rather than any other kind of image-making. As with so many things about the medium, that's an accident of history and economics—pen-and-ink drawings are relatively fast to make and cheap to print clearly, and having one artist draw pencil roughs and another refine them with ink made it possible to crank out lots of pages in a hurry.

In fact, when I talk about "drawing" in this book, I usually mean a specific kind of drawing: cartooning. (Artists from the fine-art world who draw are much faster to make the distinction.) The difference is that drawing in the conventional sense is usually supposed to represent real-world beings and objects; it's concerned with their mass and interaction with light much more than their outlines, and its result almost always suggests a relatively static moment. The idea of classical drawing is to capture, as accurately as possible, something the artist is looking at. Where it simplifies the details and shades of the subject—which it necessarily does, because no drawing can look exactly like its model—it generally simplifies them *retinally*, in a way that suggests what they look like to the eye. The way style comes into it is partly through the artist's misperceptions and accidental misrepresentations and partly through the choices the artist makes in the service of retinal simplification. (For these reasons and others, drawing has historically been the red-headed stepchild of painting, but that's another discussion.)

Cartooning is a whole different game. Its chief tools are distortion and symbolic abstraction; it usually begins and sometimes ends with contour and outline, and it relies on conventions that imply the progression of time. Cartoonists can draw characters who look only vaguely like actual people do, and backgrounds with only the faintest hints of real-world complexity, and get away with it—often, that's the idea. The simplifications of cartooning are symbolic even more than they are retinal: there are universally accepted scribbles that stand in for what mouths and noses and motion and sweat look like. Other kinds of visual shorthand imply other temporal, spatial, and emotional effects. Over the last hundred years or so, cartoonists have developed an immense repertoire of tricks and passed them on to those who've come after them.

Scott McCloud's *Understanding Comics* and *Making Comics* are the standard guides to the unique codes of cartooning, and to visual interfaces in general—he's a born taxonomist and communicator, and he's got a thoroughly worked-out model of how cartooning's abstractions function for the reader. Briefly: he claims that simpler, more symbolically abstract representations of people are easier for readers to identify with than realistic drawings are, and that therefore bold, not terribly detailed cartoons of characters, especially if they're contrasted with more realistic-looking settings, make it possible for readers to imagine themselves in the fantasy world of the comics narrative. I can't quite buy into McCloud's evenly spaced, triangular continuum of realism, geometrical abstraction, and symbolic abstraction—the latter two categories seem closer together than he proposes—and I think there's a much bigger leap from symbolic abstraction of images to written language than the gentle hop he suggests. But our differences may have to do with the way we tend to explain things. McCloud likes to make categories; I like to make generalizations and excuses.

There's another important way in which cartooning is different from drawing, in practice: it usually depicts invented or fictional people and settings, or in some cases real people and settings that are supposed to be looked at as if they were fictional. That's not a universal law—any rule that claims that, say, Joe Sacco's superb reported comics about

Visual subjectivity in the context of reportage, from Joe Sacco's *Palestine*. ©2007 Joe Sacco.

Palestine and Eastern Europe "are supposed to be looked at as if they were fictional" is a very bad rule. Still, even Sacco's work uses "cartoony" distortions and caricatures; his drawing relies on careful observation, but its style indicates that his stories are subjective interpretations of those observations. (The same goes for memoiristic comics by Guy Delisle and Alison Bechdel, most of the artists who work with *American Splendor*'s writer Harvey Pekar, and many others.)

The "cartooning as interpretation" effect is also the reason that when recognizable people from the real world, drawn realistically, show up in narrative comics, there's always something off-puttingly fake about them. If Garry Trudeau didn't substitute simple icons for the politicians who appear in "Doonesbury," or if Dave Sim didn't distort the thinly disguised comedians and cartoonists who pop up in

Cerebus into outrageous caricatures, the cognitive dissonance of seeing images that tried and failed to match up to the reality of actual people's appearances would wreck the stories around them. Real-world celebrities have occasionally turned up in mainstream comics—in the late '70s, Spider-Man encountered *Saturday Night Live*'s Not-Ready-for-Prime-Time Players in an issue of *Marvel Team-Up*, for instance—and it never works. Even the most valiant attempt, an oversized one-off called *Superman Vs. Muhammad Ali*, published in 1978, drawn by American comics' pioneer of anatomical realism Neal Adams, and way more entertaining than it might have been, comes off as earnest, unfiltered kitsch for reasons even beyond its ludicrous premise.

There are a few kinds of art that have appeared in comics besides line drawings, none of them terribly successfully—again, I'm making generalizations about the enormous majority of comics that already exist, not suggesting that the form has impermeable boundaries. Photo-comics, or "fumetti," have been around for decades, but there haven't been any noteworthy ones yet, at least in English. Painted comics have been appearing regularly since the early '80s (when they were made more feasible to publish by advances in comics' printing technologies), but most of them are just posher variations on pen-and-ink cartooning.

That's not necessarily a bad thing—Melinda Gebbie's mixed-media artwork for *Lost Girls* is exquisite and inspired by pen-and-ink technique—but only a few cartoonists, most prominently Bill Sienkiewicz, have taken much advantage of the distortions and abstractions that paint can offer and conventional drawing techniques can't. As I write this in 2006, quasi-realistic painted comics by the likes of Alex Ross (not the music critic) are very popular, but they suffer from a commitment to looking "just like the real thing." Ross's painted upgrades of standard superhero-comics imagery are stiff and glossy, as misguidedly "realistic" as colorized black-and-white movies. His images, meticulously painted from photographs of models, come off like inspirational office posters starring Batman or Wonder Woman. They exude grand seriousness, but they leave too little to the imagination.

Back, now, to pen-and-ink cartooning and the outlines that it makes the artist impose on everything seen within the borders of the panel. (Again, there are exceptions: David Lloyd's artwork for *V for Vendetta*, for instance, avoids outlines as much as possible, and Alex Maleev's work on *Daredevil* alternates outline-based cartooning with a blotchy style that imitates the look of multiple-generation photocopies of photographs.) In the real world, objects don't have lines defining their edges, they just end. Still, the convention of the contour is so familiar that drawing teachers struggle to get their beginning students to draw objects as areas of light and darkness rather than outlines. That might have something to do with how ubiquitous cartooning has become.

The cartoonist's line defines the shape of the comics image, but it's never *just* a border: it's a signature, or rather a marking of territory as the artist's. As with the Eisner example mentioned above, most first-rate cartoonists have an instantly identifiable line. Just a few strokes are enough to call entire bodies of work to mind: the "clear-line" style Hergé developed for the *Tintin* books (in which forceful lines maintain an almost uniform density and are rarely used for shading), the lusty, ragged brushstrokes of Craig Thompson, the "dead," single-thickness mechanical lines of Chris Ware, the tremulous Rapidograph squiggles of Robert Crumb, the oscillating scribble that blurs the edges of the half-revolting human flesh Dave Cooper draws.

The line itself is an interpolation, something the cartoonist adds to his or her idea of the shape of bodies in space. In a cartoon, every object's form is subject to interpretive distortion—even when what's being distorted isn't a real image but a distant cousin of something real. A consistent, aestheticized distortion, combined with the line that establishes that distortion, adds up to a cartoonist's visual style, no matter how intentional or unintentional it is. A person, as drawn by Megan Kelso or Peter Bagge or Ron Regé Jr., doesn't look much like a human being seen by the eye—but also always looks like a Kelso or Bagge or Regé character, and looks enough like a human being that the reader immediately makes the leap.

The distortion of cartooning has only one hard limit. It has to be legi-
ble—the reader has to be able to recognize everything and everyone in
the image very quickly. McCloud calls comics "the invisible art," and
part of that invisibility is the medium's tradition of effortlessness. It can
be a pleasure to stare at a cartooned image for a long time, taking it all
in, but nothing turns a reader off faster than not being able to tell what
she's looking at. (A few cartoonists have experimented with a deliberately difficult, visually ambiguous style, but it generally hasn't gone over
too well.)

Again, every great cartoonist has a specific, intensely personal style,
and so do most decent-to-middling cartoonists. Mediocre cartoonists'
work blurs together; bad cartoonists generally either don't have enough
control to work up a style of their own or fail the legibility test. The best-
remembered, best-selling mainstream comics of the past have been the
ones whose artists were naturally gifted storytellers, encouraged to let
their stylistic quirks show: C. C. Beck's Captain Marvel stories, Jack
Kirby and Steve Ditko's '60s work, Frank Miller's *Daredevil*, John Byrne
and Terry Austin's *Uncanny X-Men*. Even Carl Barks's humbly eccentric *Donald Duck* and *Uncle Scrooge* stories, with their characters drawn
to Disney model sheets, are little wonders of style. He wasn't allowed to
sign them when they were originally published, but his admirers could
easily recognize work by "the good duck artist," as they called him.

It's curious, then, that the American comics mainstream has spent
most of its history trying to force its artists to conform to a "house
style"—the idea being, apparently, that consistency is more commercially viable, or less confusing, than innovation. (That's probably true to
some extent; it's also the case that a cartoonist who can be replaced with
someone else who draws roughly the same way doesn't have much bar-
gaining power.) But even some of the most dedicated company men
have been able to assert a little bit of personal flair, or at least weren't
able to expurgate it—enough that almost anyone who's drawn more
than a couple of dozen comics is remembered fondly by some segment
of comics-reader culture.

(A cartoonist friend once showed me a page of original comics art from her collection—one of the innumerable ads for Hostess Fruit Pies starring various superheroes that ran in American comics in the '70s. She might have seen it as an amusing piece of kitsch advertising, and probably did to some extent; she might have seen it as a little story about characters from *Aquaman* comics, and probably did to some extent. But what she said as she pulled it out was, "Hey, check this out: a Curt Swan page! Wow, Swan really couldn't draw sharks." Swan, who drew *Superman* for decades, was a solid, reliable, workmanlike, unspectacular artist, the sort whose work could almost pass for "generic funnybook." It's a sign of our own submersion in the comics world that my friend and I both immediately thought of the thirty-year-old advertisement as "a Swan original.")

The fact that drawing style is the most immediate aspect of comics means that what you see when you look at a comic book is a particular, personal version of its artist's *vision*—not what the artist's eye sees, but the way the artist's mind interprets sight. That's not unique to comics, of course: it's true of any artist who creates a two-dimensional image meant to represent a three-dimensional scene, real or imagined. Since comics are cartooned instead of conventionally drawn, though, they're more obviously distorted by the artist's vision. And what narrative comics convert into an interpreted two-dimensional image is actually four-dimensional: space *in time*.

Decorating the Blank Walls of the Fourth Dimension

Comics suggest motion, but they're incapable of actually showing motion. They indicate sound, and even spell it out, but they're silent. They imply the passage of time, but their temporal experience is controlled by the reader more than by the artist. They convey continuous stories, but they're made up of a series of discrete moments. They're concerned with conveying an artist's perceptions, but one of their most crucial components is blank space.

To understand what's happening when you read comics, and what makes some of them work better than others, it's useful to think about how the process of reading them actually works. I'll spell it out (with the understanding that this is the *default* way that comics look, and that a cartoonist can violate any of these principles): The viewer looks at a printed page and sees a series of drawn (cartooned) images, surrounded by borders, with empty space between them, each one a representation of a single moment or very short, continuous span of time. Some of those bordered images also include text, surrounded by lines or other visual cues that indicate whether it's to be read as speech spoken (at the time of the moment seen in the image) by one of the characters in the scene, or as speech by another character who's not visible in the panel, or as narration from an omniscient source.

This is all pretty obvious stuff if you've had a little experience reading comics, but the more closely you look at it, the weirder it gets. For the sake of not getting entirely lost in the poppy fields of theory, let's look at how it pans out on a specific page of a comic book story. I've selected it fairly arbitrarily: page 38 of the Canadian cartoonist Seth's 2004 book *Clyde Fans Book One*, which collects the first half of a story he's been serializing since 1997. (On the title page, Seth calls it "a picture novella"—yet another name for the same thing.) The page in question is very simple, with seven panels and a single character, Abraham Matchcard, a retired fan salesman. He walks down to his basement, hangs up his hat, and starts to tell a little joke about salesmanship.

There are two different kinds of information on this page, which collectively make up this segment of *Clyde Fans*' narrative: drawn images and written words. They're vastly different things, they work in different ways, and comics require them to be jammed together constantly. The argument about the relationship between "painting" and "poetry"—the generic classical terms for image-making and word-assembling—has been going on for a long time, and the earliest people to try to figure it out concluded that painting and poetry were basically different forms of the same thing. Simonides of Keos's formulation was *"poema pictura loquens, pictura poema silens"* (roughly: "poetry is a verbal picture, paint-

Seth's *Clyde Fans*, pg. 38. From *Clyde Fans, Book One*, ©2007 G. (Seth) Gallant.

ing is a silent poetry"), which Horace later reduced in his *Ars Poetica* to the more familiar phrase *"ut pictura poesis"* ("as is painting, so is poetry"). That's true mostly in the very broad sense that both are ways of representing perception.

Poetry, though, has the advantage of relatively fixed meaning and the disadvantage that it's limited by the boundaries of vocabulary and language; painting has the advantage of infinite shades of variation and the disadvantage that any kind of perception that's not visual is much harder to communicate with it. If you want to describe a particular shade of yellow, poetry will get you as close as a modifier or two, but no closer, and painting will get it exactly; if you want to describe a particular psychological state, poetry will get you very close indeed, since psychological states tend to be defined by language, and painting will do its best by way of visual association or metaphor; if you want to describe a particular taste, poetry will get you as close as a modifier or two, and painting will shrug its shoulders and give up.

Abraham's first line of dialogue on this page of *Clyde Fans* is: "A young salesman was instructed to go out and make as many calls as he could." It's possible that a series of drawings (rather than a single drawing) could get the basic meaning of that across, although it would take an enormous amount of space and effort and still not capture the way the phrasing suggests that it's the first line of a joke, or the vagueness of the instruction that pays off in the punch line. But words can only loosely describe Abraham's appearance: to say that he's a squat, slope-shouldered, balding older man with a moustache and a purposefully dignified look doesn't capture the specificity and weight of the way Seth draws him, or the sort of body language and facial expressions the artwork implies, or the way he moves through the scene.

Here's where Gotthold Ephraim Lessing's 1766 essay *Laocoön* comes in. Lessing rebutted the *ut pictura poesis* principle; space, he claimed, was the domain of painting, and time was the domain of poetry. Any particular panel of a comic book can encompass as much space as a person can see at once (projected onto a two-dimensional picture plane), although it usually trims most of that space off with its borders to focus on whatever's important to the narrative. Time, on the other hand, has to be shaved very thinly to fit in a comic panel, which is generally understood to be an image of a single moment. Scott McCloud demonstrates in *Understanding Comics* that a single panel can imply the passage of time, but only with the help of symbolic tricks: special kinds of lines that imply speed and motion, showing the same figure or different figures at slightly separated moments in time across the direction that the eye scans the panel, or, most easily, language.

Language, especially dialogue, that's included in a panel of comics gives it a temporal dimension. Look at Abraham Matchcard's first line of dialogue on the *Clyde Fans* page again. It takes four or five seconds to read out loud; that means that the panel represents at least that much time, since we understand that the next panel doesn't "happen" until the dialogue has been spoken. Abraham's line also describes something that happened in the past, projecting the possibility of something ("go out and make as many calls as he could") that would extend over another span of time. Time is the domain of poetry (or language), because language takes time to experience, and because it can describe time, or describe change over time, easily in a way that pictures can't.

The novice comics reader's question is, "Which do you look at first, the words or the pictures?" The answer is that you look at both of them at once. On a first reading, at least, it's possible to take in a comics panel's picture in just about exactly the time it takes to read the associated words. (That's assuming that the picture is clear enough to make out what's going on in it without some puzzlement.) In any case, you don't look at a given panel's image for *less* time than it takes to read all the words in it.

That's why readers tend to hit the brakes when they encounter wordless sequences; a single image without text is read as a pause, and a longer sequence without text demands some scrutiny. Without language acting as a "timer" or contextual cue for understanding the image, every visual change causes the reader to stop and assess what exactly is happening, and how long it's supposed to take. (Skilled cartoonists can manipulate that phenomenon for pacing, to guide the eye slowly or quickly across the page.) Look at the first four panels of the *Clyde Fans* page. The second and fourth have visual time cues—two puffs of smoke rising from Abraham's cigar. That's not what smoke looks like, but we understand that each puff is supposed to indicate a couple of beats' worth of pause. The fourth panel also has a little bit of text in its old sale posters, which slows us down again as we make it out from the visible fragments. How long does that whole sequence last? It takes a little while to read—not as long as the amount of time that we understand elapses as Abraham smokes, hangs up his hat, and walks toward the back of the room, but perhaps longer than it would if there were a single word or two in each panel.

To recap: there's an element of space in any one panel of comics and an element of time in some comics panels; the domain of the word-and-image combination is both space and time (the latter in the continuous form in which we usually experience it). When we add another panel, though, something else happens: a gap in time and then a jerk forward.

"Change over time" is roughly the same thing as narrative—one thing happens, then another thing happens. But showing change over time, and being experienced over time, is also what multiple-image comics do, whether they use language or not. You look at one image, then you look at another, and you note what's changed between them.

What's happened between the panels is the viewer's vantage point moving through time and (usually but not always) through space. (The only case in which movement through space doesn't happen is the technique some cartoonists occasionally use of drawing consecutive panels that are exactly the same size, with exactly the same perspective on a scene.) That movement is *strongly* in one direction—the direction of the panel-to-panel flow—but it's not *exclusively* in one direction. Look once again at the *Clyde Fans* page. Your attention may be mostly focused on a single panel at a time, but you've got the entire page full of pictures in your line of sight at the same time, maybe two pages. (You can also usually see your own hands and the environment in which you're reading; they're visual information too, but they're easier to ignore, since they're three-dimensional, real rather than drawn, and not part of the narrative.) You see seven images of Abraham going about his rounds, all at once; you see the basement from seven angles, all at once.

As a reader, you're ultimately in control of the speed at which the page progresses. You can linger over each panel; you can observe a tier or a page or a two-page spread as a composition and get a sense of the whole thing at once; you can look back at panels you've already read (you can scarcely *not* do that, when you're observing what change has happened between panels) or turn the pages backwards at will. And you can reorient yourself in the story with a glance, because you've got a visual cue for where you are on the page and in the narrative.

Panels aren't the only thing on the page, though. Between them, there's blank space—a "gutter," it's called—whose borders are also the borders outlining the images. (Some comics, both old and contemporary, have only a line between panels, or dissolve into blankness without specific panel borders. The bordered gutter has become the default, though, because it's the clearest indication that there's a distinction between where the panel's image goes and where it doesn't.) That gutter is where the fun happens.

For one thing, readers get to fill in the lapse of time represented by the blankness of the gutter. Another big idea that Lessing's *Laocoön* contributed to the way people talk about art is relevant here: the idea of the "pregnant moment." He argues that a single image in static visual art is most dramatic when it's the moment from which time radiates in both directions, suggesting what's happened before it and what's about to happen after it.

A lot of the most effective individual panels in comics are pregnant moments, which give birth not to the next but to the space before the next. (The single-panel "Dennis the Menace" strips I mentioned back in chapter 1 work the same way, usually with the help of their captions; they're funny because they suggest something happening at a moment they don't show.) Look again at that *Clyde Fans* page. We don't see Abraham setting his hat on the faucet, we see him reaching his hat toward it; two panels later, we don't see him standing in front of us, we see him walking toward us, his back foot lifting off the ground, his face and upper torso about to emerge from shadow. There's a little thrill in filling in the rest. A metaphor for sequential comics' chain of panels that might work as well as pregnancy, in fact, is walking: each step is a fall that's caught by the next.

Scott McCloud refers to the process of imagining the relationship between the image in one panel to the image in the next as "closure," and certainly there's an element of that in how the pregnant moment leads us as readers from panel to panel. Between panels 3 and 4 of *Clyde Fans'* page 38, for instance, the reader imagines Abraham Matchcard hanging his hat up, taking his cigar out of his mouth, and swinging his arm down as he walks toward the back of the furnace room.

What we don't imagine quite as much is our own motion as observers. Between the same two panels, the viewer's perspective on Abraham has changed—the light from upstairs, which was shining on the back of his head, is now illuminating his right side as he walks away—but we don't imagine ourselves rotating clockwise around Abraham and taking a few steps back as he turns to his right, because we don't think of ourselves as being in the scene, even though Abraham is addressing us all but directly. The change of angle just reads as a sort of directed, invisible omniscience.

On the other hand, there's more to the immersive experience of comics than what's visible in their panels and what specific actions happen between them. A lot of the pleasure in reading comics is filling in *all* the blank space beyond each panel, as far as it can go in both space and time, with the drawing on the page as a guide or set of hints.

The *Clyde Fans* page shows only the basement's furnace and pipes in fragments, but we can piece together what the whole room looks like, as well as how it's lit, how Abraham carries himself, how he uses his cigar as a prop when he's talking. The size, shape, and content of each panel is how Seth directs our focus, but we understand through the cumulative effect of all the panels what's beyond the edge of each one. That edge is a frame—a device borrowed from gallery art. When it surrounds a single image on a wall, it suggests that what's inside it is more important than what's outside it; when it surrounds each one of a group of images on a page, its implication is more that the part of the scene that the artist is spelling out for the viewer stops there. These particular frames are not perfectly straight, and they don't have a consistent thickness: they've got the same wobble as Seth's other brushstrokes, so they declare that they were made by the same hand that drew the image within them.

In fact, comics omit far more visual information than they include. They're a series of deliberately chosen visual fragments that don't represent the time between or the space around panels. And because they're cartoons, they omit most of the details of the things they actually do depict in a panel. Instead, they present the rudiments of physical forms—a few details that stand in metonymically for something in reality (or something reality-like in the imagination), even if they aren't an actual detail of that thing. As an example, look at Abraham in panel four of the *Clyde Fans* page. He has six hairs on the back of his head, each one a thick brushstroke. That's not what hair looks like, and of course a more "realistic" look at the back of his head would show more and smaller hairs; from looking at Seth's drawing, though, we make the imaginative leap to understanding what the character's scraggly, far-receded hair looks like.

Leaps of the imagination are an enormous pleasure, and comics are particularly good at sparking them. Their narrative is one kind of guide; their style is another. They're full of enticing blank spaces, in both space and time, for readers to decorate in our minds. But what they look and feel like when we flesh them out isn't the same way we perceive our own environments. Instead, comics are a guide to imagining the visual aspect of a story as it's transformed through the cartoonist's perception.

That's a wonderful kind of escape from the reader's own perception. The comics medium was built on the idea of escapism and the pleasure that goes with it. Genre comics promise an escape into a more intense and exciting version of the world; art comics promise an escape into a kind of vision very different from one's own. Sometimes, both forms deliver it. The job of the cartoonist, in any case, is to make the reader do most of the imaginative work of moving from panel to panel through the narrative, but to make that work as engaging as possible.

One gauge of the goodness of comics is how much they excite the imagination—what the reader perceives beyond and between the borders of their panels. As far as the actual story is concerned, that means the life that a comic's characters and setting have beyond its pages, the same principle that applies to any kind of narrative art. But it can also mean the extent to which a cartoonist can temporarily hijack a reader's visual imagination into something that feels like an environment whose every detail is determined by decisions or accidents of the cartoonist's style, whether it's actually visible on the page or not.

The broader philosophical implication of many comics, to one extent or another, is: *there is another world, which is this world.* The places that cartoonists draw are very different from the ones where readers live; every element of the comics world is created by the artist's hands. The cartoonist's image-world is a metaphorical representation of our own, though, and it can be mapped onto ours. It can even be more meaningful in some ways than an accurate depiction of our image world—the same sort of relationship that prose fiction has to reportage.

In one sense, that's the way comics represent the subjectivity of vision (and experience), as I mentioned back in chapter 1. It's easy enough to follow a comics story despite its visual distortions and temporal gaps, which means experiencing space-through-time in a way that's different from our personal perspective. But the concept of a literal separate reality that is also, in consequential ways, default reality is something that a surprising number of first-rate cartoonists deal with fairly explicitly: David B.'s monstrous, swirling interpretations of his and his brother's cracked understanding of the world in *Epileptic,* the pitched quasi-physical battles in the metaphysical setting of Stan Lee and Steve Ditko's *Dr. Strange,* Grant Morrison and Alan Moore's evocations of Kabbalistic taxonomies, the blurred borders between waking and dreaming in Hope Larson's *Gray Horses* and Chester Brown's *Underwater,* and on and on.

Even the old DC Comics scenario of infinite "parallel Earths" (the planet where most of the stories published in the '60s and '70s happen is "Earth-One," the one where older stories happened is "Earth-Two," the less significant one where the readers live is "Earth-Prime") plays into the same idea. Experiencing a world that's in the same place as "default reality" but significantly different is also a working definition of schizophrenia, of course, as we'll see a few times in this book's remaining chapters.

PART TWO

REVIEWS
AND COMMENTARY

A Small Disclaimer

The essays that follow are not meant to constitute a "best of" or "suggested reading" list. They're just about comics and cartoonists I think are interesting to discuss.

The comics I've picked to write about here aren't any kind of "representative" sampling of what's out there, either. A couple of major biases worth noting: they're all books that are available in English, and they're mostly by Americans, because that's what I've been exposed to most and what readers of this book can find most easily; they're overwhelmingly by men, because most of the interesting long-form comics projects published to date have been by men—although, as I've mentioned, I expect the gender balance of cartoonists to shift dramatically over the next decade or two. I haven't addressed any manga, and I've treated the original "underground comix" movement only in passing. Almost all of the comics I discuss at length are currently in print in book form, except for Jim Starlin's *Warlock*, which has been reprinted several times and really ought to be again (for the record, the best-printed and easiest-to-find version is a six-issue miniseries called *Warlock Special Edition*).

There are, however, some very big names I'm barely mentioning or neglecting outright in the following pages: Jack Kirby, Robert Crumb, and Hergé all jump to mind as artists without whom a *comprehensive* book about comics would be shockingly incomplete. Some of my personal favorites aren't in here, either; I feel compelled to at least mention Jim Woodring's *The Frank Book*, Eric Shanower's *Age of Bronze*, Peter Blegvad's *Leviathan*, and Lynda Barry's *One!Hundred!Demons!*

But I'd rather smash, or at least ignore, the idea of a canon of comics for two reasons. The first is that canons aren't made to last, especially for an emerging medium; they grow and change with what critics, educators, and readers find useful over time, and I'm more interested in starting discussions (and arguments) about comics than settling them with any kind of self-appointed authority. The second is that a lot of the comics I treasure most are somehow dodgy or flawed, and I'd rather explain what brings me joy about them than endorse them unequivocally. So the rest of this book is a tour of some notable spots on an enormous landscape — not all or even most of the peaks, just points from which further investigation can be rewarding.

CHAPTER 6

David B.:
The Battle Against the Real World

Our tour has to start somewhere, and it might as well start with one of the highest peaks: the French cartoonist David B.'s singular book *Epileptic*. It's a memoir like no other, about two brothers and the way their alienation from default reality changed their lives, one sinking into disease and horror, the other rising to command his vision and communicate it through his art. It's also about its own obsessive, mesmerizing visual style and the way its cartoonist developed that style. The story of David B. and his epileptic brother doubles as the story of how an artist's eye and hand develop through life experience and how this artist's ability to communicate his understanding of the world through comics saved him.

As *Epileptic* begins, it looks as if it's going to be concerned with the objective facts of a family history: there's a short scene with thirty-five-year-old David B. encountering his battered, bloated older brother, and then a flashback to 1965, when Pierre-François Beauchard (B.'s original name) was a five-year-old boy in Orléans, fascinated by history and warfare. Almost immediately, though, realism starts to give way to metaphor. We see Pierre-François, or "Fafou," as his family called him, surrounded by gigantic pen nibs, fifty-centime coins, and comic books—his way of representing their importance in his early life, a simple image for a simple moment. A few pages later, B. displays two of his earliest drawings; they're as crude as any child's, but it's possible to see in them the faintest hints of his mature style.

Then Fafou's older brother, Jean-Christophe, starts to have epileptic seizures, and the family effectively comes under his disease's control. Through the rest of the '60s and the early '70s, they move all over Europe, trying to find some kind of effective cure for Jean-Christophe's epilepsy. Doctors fail them; gurus fail them; mystics fail them; macrobiotic diets fail them; exorcists fail them. Nothing brings them relief. Young Pierre-François imagines, though, that the adults he encounters have access to the powers they claim and has images in his mind of what that broader world looks like. He slowly descends into a madness of his own, less malign than his brother's but just as powerful. He becomes obsessed with the idea of another reality and with drawing battles and fantasy monsters.

In a chilling sequence midway through the book, David's family begins to collapse, and the barrier between his visual understanding of fantasy and his reality erodes. His fantasy life becomes an armor he imagines as literal, protecting Pierre-François from the bloody chaos of his brother's illness but also threatening to seal him off from the world altogether. At the same time, he starts to see a sort of second, metaphorical layer to his physical surroundings. The artwork in *Epileptic* tracks his perceptions, becoming increasingly elaborate and design-heavy. His dead grandfather has the head of a long-beaked bird. His brother's epilepsy is a sort of alligator-mouthed serpent with an endless body. The skeletons of soldiers, in their uniforms, are everywhere.

Almost exactly halfway through the book, David (a name he believes he's "prevailed over the disease" by adopting) begins to record his dreams and gradually gains control of his waking visions—and sets about turning them into the stylized imagery we're seeing on the book's pages. To build a "bulwark against sorrow," he begins his career as a cartoonist, drawing the crazed, surreal stories that led to the peak from which he drew *Epileptic*: "Who will seize the reins of power by putting the 50 madmen back in the correct order? . . . Who is this man leading a flayed child by the hand?" As David reckons with his baffling visions, Jean-Christophe's condition continues to deteriorate; he bloats up under heavy medication, surrendering to deranged nostalgia for the indulgences of his childhood. The epileptic brother, too, has visions and believes that he's a prophet, but his prophecies are the rootless babblings of a madman.

What dominates the book, though, isn't Jean-Christophe's interior landscape. It's David's and, in one terrifying sequence near the end, the prophecies David imagines his brother imagining: "mighty oceans" and missiles and Chinese soldiers, portents in a teabag and a magazine, landscapes dominated by Jean-Christophe's fat, sweater-clad form, which becomes a charred corpse and then a skinny, angel-winged spirit accompanied by an arrow-shaped God and dozens of disembodied eyes. In the dream sequences that occupy many of *Epileptic*'s final pages, David imagines his brother's face altered again and again by "an invisible adversary"—but the artist himself is the one changing it.

That's not a lot of plot for a 360-page book, but B.'s point isn't to tell stories from his screwed-up childhood or even to explain the story of his life. (To read it as a family history or a portrait of circa–1970 French subcultures is to fail to look at the pictures.) What he's actually doing is guiding readers who are used to reality as it can be captured by photographs into the profoundly different way he perceives the world, partly by relating the specific experiences that led him there and partly by representing everything not as his eye apprehends it but as his consciousness alters it. To give yourself over to *Epileptic* is to willingly be trotted into the deep shadow of Jean-Christophe's sickness, changed by it, and finally shown a safe route away from it by his brother. The book is also a very clear demonstration of what comics can do, as drawn narratives that require the reader's imagination to play along, that nothing else can. And it's impossible to imagine it being adapted into any other medium: to lose the specific work of B.'s drawing hand would be to lose *Epileptic* itself.

Comics are the art that B. turned to even as a child, attracted to their capacity for symbolism, and he supersaturates the book with layer after layer of metaphor, eventually crowding out literal representation almost entirely. It's a frightening transformation, so B. eases it with the magisterial assurance and grace of his linework, and the crisp, solid-black areas and feathery, woodcut-inspired etched patterns that balance each other's weight. His work is a pleasure to look at as a series of compositions, even if you don't consider their content or let them add up to their devastating sum.

In *Epileptic*, everything is simultaneously its real-world self and its distorted fantasy self, charged with mystical significance. When people and things are seen in their usual physical forms, B. draws them in a gently mannered style, noses and mouths plainly outlined, objects stripped down to simple contours; unreal things and imaginary entities are creatures of almost pure design, surrounded by blackness or by amorphous, seeping things. There's nothing approaching "correct" perspective, even in the scenes in real-world settings. Distances and shapes are determined by psychology, not compasses and rulers.

B.'s visions didn't leap into his head on their own. The part of *Epileptic* that deals with his childhood includes digressions on all the alternate philosophies or practices that the Beauchards encountered and tried on in the course of their quest for a cure, and each one suggests how its visual iconography drifted into B.'s mind and art. In particular, a three-page discussion of Rudolf Steiner and Anthroposophy becomes a breathtaking display of hermetic symbolism replacing literal representation. At one edge of each page is half of a mannequin: the first, for instance, has a sundial head surrounded by stars, the epilepsy-serpent coiled up in its hand, a book in front of a fireplace for a belly, the bones of its arms and legs visible. A few pages later, B. shows us the destruction of Steiner's Goetheanum by the German far right and tells us that Steiner saw it as "the handiwork of Lucifer"; the image of a building in flames, with a pile of bricks behind it, looks like a Blakean vision of hell, and Steiner is fish-scaled, holding a bone, alligator-jawed, a spiral of the epilepsy-snake making up his face.

Most of all, the armies and armor that Jean-Christophe and Pierre-François read countless books about and drew as children become the metaphors for David's understanding of all human struggle, and their meticulous duplication of armor's patterns becomes the template for the visual patterns he finds in everything. (That's true even beyond *Epileptic*. Two of the very few other stories by B. that have been published in English touch on the same themes. "The Armed Garden" concerns a fifteenth-century war between two sects that believed God had revealed the true nature of the world to them; "The Veiled Prophet" is another fable about prophecy, violence, and images that direct reality.) When he imagines himself locked "ever more tightly in my armor," a suit that covers his entire body, he draws himself bent over and contorted like his brother, with the epilepsy-serpent looping around him, curling into and around his head.

The other vision that has become part of *Epileptic*, of course, is his brother's, which by necessity we can only ever see refracted through B.'s own. He avoids showing it as much as he can, although he tries in a few sequences late in the book, in addition to the horrific depiction of his brother's prophecies. In another passage, he imagines his brother's life in Paris: going to the opera, collapsing with seizures, being beaten by the police. Each page is framed by a distorted, stretched version of Jean-Christophe's body (with the stupefied eyes and open, bucktoothed mouth that B. always draws on him), until the last, when the serpent whose zigzag outlines have been showing up in the background throughout the sequence swallows Jean-Christophe and takes over page-border duties from him.

There's also a brief sequence in which Jean-Christophe has a psychotic episode while looking at an abstract painting (the opposite of representational cartooning?), seeing its indefinite shapes as falling bodies: "It's death! It's death!" David convinces him that they're just shapes—but by then the scratchy, round form of the imaginary bodies' heads has shifted from the canvas to Jean-Christophe's own head. This is not entirely a case of "illness as metaphor," as Susan Sontag put it; it's at least as much a case of metaphor as illness. As B. points out, his own condition as an artist is not entirely dissimilar from his brother's: "Those electrical discharges in my brain, like explosions, that's what they are! . . . If I push myself I'm sure I could trigger more serious seizures." The thought is accompanied by a burst of bold, glowing angles around his head, as sharp as a woodcut artist's knife or a scimitar. Every panel of the book is a little world-deforming explosion. The same epileptic spasms of unreality that destroyed Jean-Christophe are what transformed the boy Pierre-François into the artist (the *cartoonist!*) David B. and allowed him to "forge the weapons that will allow me to be more than a sick man's brother."

Epileptic, it should be noted, is the title of the book's American translation (by Kim Thompson), not an English version of the original title, *L'Ascension du Haut Mal*—a phrase that's not nearly as graceful in English (it means, roughly, "the rise of high evil" and alludes to grand mal seizures). *L'Ascension* was originally published as a series of six volumes, by L'Association, a French company that a group of cartoonists including David B. launched in 1990. Back then, the big French publishers generally commissioned forty-eight-page, full-color, hardcover graphic novels at a standard size—the format of *Asterix* and *Tintin*, and still the default format for mass-market comics in France. L'Association promptly set itself apart by publishing mostly black-and-white books, mostly in paperback, with formats and length determined by its artists. Its books often sell only a few thousand copies, but most of the company's clout is cultural: the publishers to which it originally set itself up as an alternative have come to follow its example.

Other L'Association cartoonists' work has started to appear in the United States, too, including Joann Sfar's splendid, warm fantasy about Algerian Jewish culture in the 1930s, *The Rabbi's Cat*, and Lewis Trondheim's howlingly funny "Road Runner" via a Samuel Beckett project, *Mister O*. Most notably, *Persepolis*, a two-volume memoir by B.'s former student Marjane Satrapi, has become a hit even beyond the usual American alt-comics circles. Satrapi's a perceptive writer, and her story—about growing up in Iran during its fundamentalist revolution, then moving away to Europe and back again, and more broadly about how politics affected the way Iranians lived—is more engaging on its surface than B.'s involuted self-reflection.

Still, it's hard for me to see Satrapi's artwork in *Persepolis* without being distracted by its obvious debt to *Epileptic*. Her deliberately flat, two-dimensional images are almost homages to B.'s fiercely squashed perspective and military-tapestry figures, but they're usually just simplified representations of real perception; they don't have B.'s scary mystery or sense of raging, overwhelming floods of imagination. My ambivalence about Satrapi in this context has a lot to do with the fact that her success in English has overshadowed B.'s; when I show people *Epileptic*, they often note that it takes after *Persepolis* a bit. (Vice versa!) In her more recent books *Embroideries* and *Chicken with Plums*, though, Satrapi's drawing style has evolved into something more her own.

As far as visual flair is concerned, though, *Epileptic*'s only rival among the other L'Association books that have appeared in English so far is the single-named Killoffer's horrifying, solipsistic fugue *Six Hundred and Seventy-Six Apparitions of Killoffer*. It begins as a misanthropic diary of the artist's trip to Montreal—something like Dostoyevsky's Underground Man on holiday—and, when the text runs out after a few pages, evolves into something very different. Killoffer imagines himself endlessly duplicated, rampaging across a city with a bunch of Killoffers, all chain-smoking and grungy, letting his hateful id loose on himself and everyone else, until everything in sight becomes an "apparition" of Killoffer, beating and killing and raping the other versions of himself: every line he draws might be a part of himself, or his blood, or something that might turn into him and destroy its maker.

What many of the L'Association artists have in common is an incredibly strong association between self and style: their work, or at least the works that have appeared in English, tends to have at least some kind of autobiographical content and to be drawn in a style that favors distinctiveness over representation. David B. left L'Association a few years ago, but he's still cultivating the territory of *Epileptic*. In the project he's serializing now, *Babel*, B. has returned to his childhood with Jean-Christophe and their dreams, concentrating more on their fascination with military violence and his own conception of "the King of the World." Even his drawings of the war between Biafra and Nigeria, though, are really mostly drawings of his own internal landscape, with its symmetries and serpents and spirals. "The King of the World was the King of Images," B. writes. "Words couldn't describe him. Only drawn lines had the power to trace his features."

CHAPTER 7

Chester Brown: The Outsider

There's a kind of key to Chester Brown's work tucked away at the back of his collection of "short strips," *The Little Man.* "My Mom Was a Schizophrenic," drawn in 1995, is a six-page, fifty-four-panel story that doesn't mention Brown's mother again after its title. Essentially, it's a summary of Thomas Szasz and R. D. Laing's unorthodox ideas about schizophrenia: that, even though it's generally understood as an illness, it's defined by "beliefs and behavior" rather than by physical symptoms, that it's what happens when people "accidentally enter the psychedelic state without drugs," and that it's mostly experienced as painful and unhappy because of its cultural "set and setting."

Most of the rest of Brown's work is, one way or another, about people whose beliefs and behavior are out of step with their cultural context. His characters try desperately to figure out the ground rules for living in their world or at least square up their subjective vision of reality with the way everyone around them seems to understand it. At first, that theme presented itself as absurdity: the early issues of his self-published minicomic *Yummy Fur*, later reprinted in the comic book of the same name, featured surreal, nutty vignettes, a couple of pages long, each of which stopped when Brown ran out of funny ideas. And then a free-associative six-page trifle called "Ed the Happy Clown," concerning a clown with a

Chester Brown explains Szasz and Laing's ideas about schizophrenia, from *The Little Man.* ©2007 Chester Brown.

broken leg, a plague of rats, and a plane dropping pygmies on a city, turned into an enormous serial that went on for most of a decade.

Ed the Happy Clown has turned out to be the story Brown can't get rid of. It initially appeared, in bits and pieces, in most of the first eighteen issues of *Yummy Fur.* The first *Ed* book collected the early installments; *The Definitive Ed Book*, published in 1992, included the first two-thirds of the *Yummy Fur* serial, ditched the final third altogether, and appended a new four-page ending. In 2004, Brown began revising the entire project, with yet another ending in mind, but also began reprinting its earlier form as a series of nine comic books (printed a little bit smaller than standard comics size—out of step again), and ultimately decided to scrap his new revision on the grounds that it wouldn't be an improvement on the previous version. The "correct" ending remains up in the air.

The first few chapters of *Ed* are brief, violent, surreal, disturbingly hilarious gag strips that seem to have nothing to do with each other. An episode of "Adventures in Science" involves a professor studying the giant squid's masturbation techniques ("The project had been a failure. The squid just wasn't showing any interest in itself"); Ed turns up again

in a version of the "Jack and the Beanstalk" story involving Frankenstein, aliens, and a cannibal named Christian; a hospital worker named
Chet Doodley (as in "Chester the artist") discovers that his hand has
fallen off for no particular reason; and, in a two-pager called "The Man
Who Couldn't Stop," we see ten straight panels of a man sitting on a toi-
let. In the final one, he thinks, "Hmn . . . can't seem to stop."

At times, the early parts of *Ed* are like a scatological game of Exquisite
Corpse that Brown is playing with himself; the challenge he ends up presenting himself is the schizophrenic's tic of perceiving patterns where
there are no actual patterns to be found. About thirty pages into *Ed*,
Brown starts trying to tie all of his unrelated jokes together into a master
plot. Ed ends up in a jail cell next to the Man Who Couldn't Stop and
the host of "Adventures in Science"—the jail explodes from the torrents
of excrement pouring out of the dead M.W.C.S.—and Chet dreams
about the Catholic saint Justin (apparently not the same as the best-
known martyr Justin). In the version of Justin's story Chet had heard as a
child, Justin cuts off his own hand to keep himself from stealing; in
Chet's dream, Justin's wife cuts it off when she finds him masturbating.
Chet stumbles over the unconscious, shit-covered Ed, sees a copy of
"Lives of the Saints," goes off to the woods to have sex with his girlfriend
Josie, tells her that the lesson of St. Justin is that "you have to cut off from
yourself the thing that is making you sin," and stabs her to death.

If this seems pretty fucked up—especially if Chet is meant to be a
stand-in for Brown—yes, it is, and it gets more so. In short order, we discover that Josie is actually still alive, but that she and Ed have been kidnapped by the surviving pygmies, and that somehow in the course of the
shit explosion, the head of a Ronald Reagan from another dimension has
appeared on the end of Ed's penis. (He looks nothing like the Reagan we
know, although he's the president of the United States in his home dimension.) And so on. Most of *Ed* after its first few chapters is concerned
with picking up the threads of the early sections and trying to make it look
like they were always meant to go together, in the context of as much
body-horror and violence and mangled theology as Brown can cram into
the story. Eventually, Josie finds out that she survived because she died

"while actively engaged in a grievous sin," and is therefore a vampire. (A pair of vampire hunters, Quincy and Quincy, obviously modeled on Quincy Harker from *Tomb of Dracula*, briefly show up.) Josie gets her revenge: seducing Chet again, then killing him before he has a chance to repent, so that he'll go to Hell. (Maybe he's not so much of a stand-in.)

To say that Brown eventually lost the plot isn't quite fair, because there wasn't really a plot to lose, but after Chet's death, *Ed*'s force diminishes considerably. The "definitive" 1992 edition keeps going a bit further, through an amusing gross-out episode involving a multiple penis transplant, then whisks most of the characters (including Ed) off the board and leaps straight to an ending in which Chet and Josie are wordlessly reunited in Hell. It's not surprising that Brown can't seem to settle on a conclusion, because there can't actually be a definitive form of *Ed*. It's unfinishable, because finishing it would mean some kind of narrative closure, and the premise of *Ed*—as much as there is one—is that everything makes sense as a big picture eventually, but absolutely nothing can be relied on from moment to moment. The story is a scatological doodle built into a monument, brick by brick, but it's the kind of monument that can be abandoned only with its ragged walls reaching up toward a nonexistent roof.

There's another world; the question is whether this one or that one is less horrible. From *Ed the Happy Clown.* ©2007 Chester Brown.

The back pages of *Yummy Fur* while *Ed* was running (and later) were occupied by Brown's very free adaptations of the Gospels of Mark and Matthew. Obviously, Brown's work involves his wrestling with Christianity and sometimes fighting dirty. But he's also fascinated with the scriptural (and apocryphal) Christ as the prime example of someone whose idea of reality was enormously different from the way everyone around him understood it, and who actually communicated his conception

Brown shows us the process of revising the way we get to see his own autobiography, from "Showing 'Helder'" in *The Little Man*.
©2007 Chester Brown.

of this world and the next convincingly enough that other people came to agree with him. Brown's version of Mark follows the original in a fairly straightforward chapter-and-verse way, although he translates some of the dialogue freely to underscore his characterization of a blunt, glowering, gaunt-faced Christ—Mark 7:18's "And he saith unto them, Are ye so without understanding also?" (in the King James translation) comes out as Jesus snapping "How stupid ARE you?"

After *Ed* dribbled to its conclusion, *Yummy Fur* started to feature some of Brown's autobiographical work, later collected in *The Playboy, I Never Liked You*, and *The Little Man*. One story, "Helder," is a straightforward piece of observational memoir, about Brown's experiences with an awful neighbor in his apartment building. It was followed in the next issue by "Showing 'Helder,'" about the process of constructing "Helder" as a comics story: arguing with a friend about the way she's represented in it, consulting a fellow cartoonist about the pacing and dialogue in one scene, trying to make the whole thing work. ("Showing 'Helder,'" unlike most of Brown's comics, is drawn without panel borders; both stories are reprinted in *The Little Man.*) Even his own accounts of his own experiences, Brown suggested, weren't to be trusted as gospel—his life could be raw material for his work, but it might not have happened the way he remembered, and every panel of the way he represents it is selected and framed, figuratively and literally, for artistic effect.

After *Yummy Fur* ended, Brown launched a series called *Underwater*, a very odd and not especially effective piece of fiction about the acquisition of language in babies. The protagonist, a newborn at the beginning of the series, hears everything as gibberish, so we see it as meaningless strings of letters. Eventually, she starts to make sense of a few words and begins to distinguish between dreams and waking life; by then, though, both readers and Brown had grown bored of *Underwater*, and it ended before the story could conclude.

The late *Yummy Fur/Underwater* period is also where Brown's drawing style settled into its present form: a poker-faced, almost ascetic approach, with the tone of an eccentric but very patient explanation. Nearly everything is seen in deadpan middle distance or as a tiny detail against an enormous, empty expanse of blank space, black nothingness or agonizingly fine cross-hatching. His characters are all represented with a few simple lines, although the lines look as if they've been drawn with glacial slowness. The composition of each individual panel is formally graceful, even classical, but its emotional content, if it might have any, is muffled or deadened; any feeling that comes from his artwork has to come from a deliberate appraisal, not from the sorts of bodily responses to drama or sex or danger or disgusting things that he used extensively in *Ed*. He's not trying to create something dull (although *Underwater* sometimes is); he's just rejecting a set of tools for manipulating his readers, declining to argue that anyone else needs to share his vision of the world.

Brown is less concerned with the page as a visual or narrative unit than almost any other comic book artist; occasionally, in *Yummy Fur*, one story would end, and the next would begin on the same page. Eventually, his work started to gravitate toward a strict grid of six square panels on each page. (He draws each panel on a separate piece of paper, so he can adjust the pacing as he pleases without having to redraw entire pages when he adds or subtracts a beat.) And he's another one of the cartoonists, like Crumb and the Hernandezes, who draws his panel borders freehand, so that their wobble becomes another expression of his handiwork.

The next major project Brown attempted after the collapse of *Underwater*—and the only nonautobiographical one he's inarguably completed—was drastically different from anything he'd done before: *Louis Riel*, a "comic-strip biography" of the nineteenth-century French-Canadian rebel and politician. Riel hasn't achieved PBS-level fame in the United States, but his story is legendary in Canada, where Brown lives: He led two uprisings of the part-white, part-Indian Métis over land rights, winning execution for his efforts. The Métis rebellions involved a lot of intricate political maneuvering—hardly the stuff of action-packed comics or even a story that seems to demand a visual interpretation. What seems to have attracted Brown to the subject, though, is the way Riel himself perceived the events of his life, and the conflict between subjective experience and historical nonfiction.

Riel developed a messianic complex, and perhaps schizophrenia, in his later years and declared that God had appointed him to save the Métis people. (His time in exile included stays in an asylum.) That pathology must have struck a nerve with Brown, who found in Riel another protagonist whose perception of the world was at odds with his surroundings. The version of Riel we see in the book is, for the most part, perfectly rational—at least by his own standards. He simply believes that the world is controlled by an active God whose will he knows for certain. Brown seems sympathetic to Riel's cause (the Canadian government that destroyed him is depicted as a bunch of scheming buffoons) but not necessarily to his actions.

The challenge for the artist-historian, then, is to balance Riel's view of the world with its view of him. Brown's solution is to put as much distance as possible between his comic and "you are here"–style history. His tone in *Louis Riel* is disarmingly uninflected and "cartoonish"—his characters have small heads, chunky bodies, oversized noses, and blank, *Little Orphan Annie*–style eyes. The steady rhythm of identically sized

Brown making no bones about taking some liberties with history to turn
it into his art, from *Louis Riel*. ©2007 Chester Brown.

panels makes the most conventionally dramatic scenes in the book (escapes, battles, executions) its most visually understated. If anything, he
errs on the side of drawing history as *less* interesting than it was, and
sometimes he deliberately avoids conventional drama altogether. The
obvious way to illustrate, say, Canadian soldiers' 1870 occupation of the
Red River settlement would be to show the chaos on panel. Instead,
Brown gives us a static, four-panel shot of Riel sitting at a table, reading
a letter about it. The idea is to emphasize that the book is not a representation of the past as it happened; it's Brown's personal interpretation
of the way that he imagines Riel might have experienced it.

The same goes for the book's dialogue. Where it's not pulled from
the historical record, it's deliberately flat and expository ("if only we had
a royal proclamation signed by Queen Victoria") or disconcertingly casual (Riel on returning to his mother's home: "Hi Mom!"). If Brown
doesn't know exactly what was said, he makes it clear that he's making it
up—he doesn't want to seduce readers into presuming he's omniscient
just because he's telling the story.

That doesn't mean his storytelling isn't seductive; even when Brown's
pacing in *Louis Riel* is perverse, it's never dull. For the sake of the story's
flow, he's made substantial elisions and revisions to the facts that are a

Louis Riel in the presence of God—a scene in which "history" becomes purely subjective, twice over. ©2007 Chester Brown.

matter of historical record (and annotates every deliberate inaccuracy in the book's notes). His linework is expressive and spare, almost ecstatically austere: He can suggest a coat or a tree—the light on an object and the weight of it—with a few judicious, scraggly lines. And he's become a master of solid white and black spaces. The courtroom where Riel's sanity is debated is jet-black except for lawyers, witnesses, and their furniture. The battlegrounds that led the rebel to this gloomy chamber are bleak expanses of snow.

In *Louis Riel*'s central incident, a brief, deadpan eight-panel sequence, Riel, on a hilltop near Washington, D.C., finds himself in the presence of God, who declares Riel to be Prophet of the New World. On the book's cover, we see Riel on that same hilltop, staring raptly into the sky. He sees his Lord compelling him to free his people, but all we can see him looking at are empty gray clouds. Brown is suggesting that this is the central problem of relating history: when vision itself becomes so subjective that it makes all the difference, nonfiction's claim of objectivity is dangerous at best.

CHAPTER 8

Steve Ditko: A Is A

Once you've seen Steve Ditko's hands, it's hard to forget them. Not the hands of the famously private cartoonist himself—not many people have seen those. The hands he draws on his characters, though, are unmistakable: expressively gesticulating, fingers pointing in all directions, casting spells or shooting webs or passing judgment. Ditko doesn't have as big a name outside comics' inner circles as his reputation among cartoonists would suggest—there'll never be an awards ceremony named after him—and his deliberately low profile has a lot to do with it. Insisting that his work speaks for itself, he's refused to be photographed or interviewed since the early '60s, and his prickly, loopy individualism has kept fame at bay. Still, he's the ghost haunting the last forty years of American comic books. Over time, his incandescent drawing style darkened, clotted, and shriveled into something much less easy to like, but more like a product of the art-comics world to which he's never suggested he feels any kinship. If his work has a single constant theme, it's I'm Not Like Everybody Else.

Ditko's artwork is often crude and unpretty, on its surface: understated and flat, full of crabbed, ugly characters. It's also impossible to shake. In his '60s prime, he was a master of composition, body language, and storytelling flow, and his best ideas have become part of the visual language of comics, even as his work's concerns have become tediously limited and his drawing has drifted away from narrative and even representation. He'd be assured a place in the pantheon of comics if his only legacy was Spider-Man, whom he cocreated with writer Stan Lee in late 1962. Ditko drew the first thirty-eight issues of *The Amazing Spider-Man*, the canon on which every Spider-Man comic since then is built. He devised the famous blue-and-red costume—a brilliantly weird piece of design, festooned with spiderwebs and featuring a totally covered-up face with two enormous white swooshes for eyes.

More importantly, though, Ditko devised the visual tone of Spider-Man comics: imperfect bodies perpetually moving through the air. Nobody ever looks especially healthy in his *Amazing Spider-Man*. Peter Parker, in or out of his costume, is a scrawny kid with insectoid body language (the specific poses Ditko drew him in were imitated successfully in the *Spider-Man* movies); Dr. Octopus is a sweaty creep with a terrible bowl haircut. Mary Jane Watson's model-perfect face famously didn't appear on-panel until after Ditko had left the series and been replaced by John Romita. When there's sexual tension in Ditko's *Spider-Man*, there always seems to be something repressed and sour about it. (He shared a studio for years with bondage/fetish artist Eric Stanton and has claimed they didn't collaborate, but Ditko expert Blake Bell has a Web site on which he points out some work credited to Stanton that's clearly Ditko—those hands are the giveaway.)

The setting for Ditko's *Spider-Man* is a hyper-real New York City, nothing but skyscrapers and water towers and docks. And its characters are always seen in choreographed motion: diving into upside-down springs, leaping, ducking, moving around each other. Every figure seems to jut into the next panel, even though they never violate the boundaries of the panel borders; you can sense the arcs of everyone's movement from one image to the next. Lee's dialogue and captions are sometimes charmingly corny, sometimes just glib and prolix, but you can tell exactly what's happening without reading a word.

Beyond the first Spider-Man story—a short piece that appeared in the final issue of an all–Lee/Ditko horror anthology series, *Amazing Adult Fantasy* (renamed *Amazing Fantasy* for that issue)—the most

Spider-Man trapped under a huge hunk of metal: a Ditko tour-de-force (with dialogue by Stan Lee) from *Amazing Spider-Man* #33.
©2007 Marvel Characters, Inc. Used with permission.

reprinted Ditko artwork comes from 1966's *Amazing Spider-Man* #33,
by which point he was plotting the series' stories as well as drawing
them. The scene is a series of pages in which Spider-Man lifts and
crawls out from under an enormous piece of machinery in a flooding
room, and it's become comics' equivalent of the Odessa Steps sequence
from Sergei Eisenstein's film *Battleship Potemkin*—a scene so formally
masterful that every subsequent cartoonist has internalized it, even
those whose work has nothing to do with superhero stuff. (*Love and
Rockets*' Jaime Hernandez includes a wickedly funny little homage to it
in his story "Bob Richardson.")

What's great about it is that the entire sequence depends on body
language—Ditko doesn't even get to use facial expressions, since
Spider-Man's mask covers his entire face. It's just one guy and a big
hunk of metal (with water dripping down from above a little more intensely in every panel), but over the course of five pages, Ditko shows us
despair, hope, exhaustion, self-recrimination, anger, resolve, and finally,
desperate victory. It's exhilarating just to look at.

A Ditko psychedelic extravaganza from *Strange Tales* #138
(with dialogue by Stan Lee). ©2007 Marvel Characters, Inc. Used with permission.

At the same time, Ditko was developing a very different visual style
for his other major collaboration with Lee, the stories about a "master of
the mystic arts," Doctor Strange, that appeared in *Strange Tales*. *Spider-
Man*'s characters struggled against the laws of physics in a stylized representation of the real world; the characters around Doctor Strange were
freed from those laws and that world altogether, floating freely in other-
dimensional space filled with curving, scribbly design elements. There
are almost no right angles in Ditko's Doctor Strange stories other than

panel borders. Over and over, though, there are images of weirdly shaped portals through which even weirder planes of existence can be seen, and the implication is that the rectangles on the printed page act as the same sort of portal for the reader.

Doctor Strange supposedly lives in New York City, too, but virtually all we see of it is his curvy, un–New York-like Greenwich Village townhouse. Every few panels, there's a new psychedelic explosion; Strange's nemesis is Dormammu, a "dweller in the realm of darkness" whose head is an indistinct, striated red shape with holes where its eyes and mouth should be, surrounded by billowing yellow flames. If *Spider-Man* was, at its core, a vehicle for exploring the relationship between power and personal responsibility, *Doctor Strange* was, whether or not Lee and Ditko admitted it (they didn't) or even intended it, a vehicle for talking about drug culture.

Still, it was an earlier set of Lee/Ditko collaborations that provided the groundwork for Ditko's later work. In the early '60s, the two of them produced a small mountain of short horror, suspense, and science fiction stories for anthology comics like *Tales to Astonish* and *Amazing Adult Fantasy*. Most of them are corny twist-ending tales with titles like "The Terror of Tim Boo Baa," but Lee knew how to spur Ditko to do his best work, and they're drawn with the single-minded force of nightmares. The artwork is largely close-up shots of distressed characters, with little or no background, which makes the world the protagonists inhabit seem as suffocatingly tiny as the scope of the stories themselves. "Help!" opens with an image of a man clasping his ears as he's surrounded by seven screaming disembodied mouths; "Those Who Change" begins with a gigantic close-up of a huge-eyed reptile's head beginning to emerge from prehistoric ooze. The blunt alienation of these early pieces is still shocking now, and the way Ditko draws the characters' hands alone tells the stories almost as much as Lee's words.

'60s hipsters thought that Ditko's urban realism and trippy visions meant that he was one of them. They couldn't have been much more wrong. Around the time that Ditko fell out with Marvel Comics in

1966, he became fascinated with Ayn Rand and objectivism, and his work started to take on a severe and increasingly strident right-wing tone. He spent the next few years drifting from gig to gig, rarely spending more than a few months on a single project and usually drawing without the passion he'd brought to Spider-Man and Doctor Strange. For a little while, he worked for the cut-rate Connecticut company Charlton Comics, where his most significant creation was the Question: a hero in a suit, hat, and tie, with no face—just a blank pink blot—and ruthless contempt for moral relativism. At a subsequent stint with DC Comics, he created the Hawk and the Dove (a pair of superhero brothers, whose personalities were exactly what you'd guess) and the Creeper (a yellow-skinned, green-haired, red-maned, screeching maniac; great visual, not too interesting otherwise).

Ditko might have continued to crank out cool-looking superhero characters over the next few decades, and sometimes he did: Shade the Changing Man, Starman, Static, Speedball. Most of his mainstream work after 1970, though, was superhero hackwork. Ditko continued to work intermittently for DC and Marvel, but by the mid-'80s, he was phoning it in, hardly bothering with even basic anatomy and perspective, as his lines grew looser and loopier. For a while, he was drawing *ROM, Spaceknight*, a series based on a battery-operated plastic toy.

His passion lay elsewhere. For most of the '70s, '80s, and '90s, he was creating Ayn Rand–inspired comics that are beautifully designed and composed but barely narrative and almost unreadable; they're explicitly didactic and so heavy-handed that it's impossible to imagine them swaying anyone's opinions. He started publishing them in fanzines and moved on to black-and-white comics, published by individuals rather than companies, with titles like *Mr. A.* (another hero in a suit and hat, whose motto is the objectivist tenet "A is A") and *Avenging World*. Ditko's name on the cover was enough to sell a certain number of copies, and he could write and draw whatever he pleased—mostly about objectivism and how there's no middle ground or gray area in morality. A 1974 black-and-white Ditko one-shot called

. .*Wha. .!?* features an "Editorial" on its inside cover (by publisher Bruce Hershenson) that's actually sort of an anti-editorial: "This comic book has been entirely written and drawn by Steve Ditko, without any 'editorial direction' whatsoever."

Perhaps he could have used a little editorial direction. The first piece in . .*Wha. .!?* involves a man with half his face hidden who's got a sort of ventriloquist's dummy that kills with a "silent voice": the letters in phrases like "you must die" and "mercy peace pity" fly out of its mouth in physical form and bludgeon people. That could make for a cool, weird little story, if the characters weren't saddled with dialogue like: "It is definitions that cause man's inhumanity. Measurement is at the root of all human suffering. We hurt with words yet no word is true or false, right or good. For a better world we should only recognize and use kind words . . . devoid of meaning which can only be arbitrary [*sic*] or convention, anyway. 'Judging' is an example of an evil, cruel word. How dare anyone set up a standard to measure any aspect of man! We should all be thought of . . . spoken of equally well, no good from bad, innocent from guilty! Mercy is kindness . . . justice is cruelty!" That's *one* word balloon, by the way.

But consider that date again: 1974, years before there was really such a thing as an art-comics movement. Ditko would always have a reputation as a Marvel-superhero guy (although he never returned to Spider-Man), and he didn't really fit in with the underground-comix crowd. His objectivist comics, though, were visually far wilder and uglier than his mainstream work had ever been, since they proceeded from his ideological concerns and what he felt like drawing rather than the dictates of the marketplace. Also, he owned them. (As a good acolyte of Howard Roark, he'd figured out that self-determination goes well with distinctive style.) At times, they look like compressed versions of the monster stories he'd done with Lee, stuffed with close-ups of faces twisted in rage or horror. They suffer from his failures of imagination—they're virtually all in the idioms of leaden morality plays and tough-guy genre stories—but they seem like a not-entirely-successful stab at inventing art comics.

Even after other artists started publishing style-centered, personal, not necessarily smooth-looking comics, Ditko paid them no mind: 1997's *Strange Avenging Tales* looks for all the world as if it might have been the follow-up to . .*Wha. .!?* Planned as an ongoing series, it lasted only one issue. (It can't have helped that publisher Fantagraphics included a text page that mentioned his "didactically repetitious Randian tracts" and the artist having been "brainwashed by Rand.")

Ditko's most significant venue for most of the '90s was the "Ditko Packages," black-and-white paperback projects published by his booster Robin Snyder. One of them, 1991's *The Ditko Public Service Package*, is a wonderfully eccentric piece of cartooning. It's a bitter, crotchety 112-page rant about the comics industry, drawn with so much gusto you can imagine Ditko's pen ripping into the paper—spatters of pointillist shading, images made of distorted letters, pages upon pages of human faces distorted like stretched Silly Putty, speed lines and exclamations and brains (yes, brains) flying around everywhere. In the middle of it, there's an apropos-of-nothing page composed solely of musical notes in a swaying, looping array—an exercise in the kind of compelling visual composition Ditko could still pull off in his sleep.

His stories, on the other hand, were plain awful. In one, an anthropomorphic page of comics art weeps with happiness at being "a fully integrated visual idea . . . I'm . . . I'm truly beautiful! True art!" What the talking page depicts is a man in a suit and hat slugging a couple of thugs, with a caption and a few word balloons. But then, at the command of a crew of greedy, selfish editors, the page is rewritten and redrawn, and it despairs—when we see it again, it's got more captions and word balloons, plus some sound effects, and the characters are wearing superhero-type costumes. The difference, frankly, seems to be of degree rather than kind. (Call my complaint sour grapes if you like: there's also a story about a "comic critic" who throws a tantrum at comics that aren't good enough for him. Just in case somebody doesn't get the point, Ditko draws a shark beneath him on one page, saying "Yuck! . . . Worse than junk food or pure garbage . . . friend ate one . . . sick for a month.")

Ditko continued to draw hundreds of pages a year through the '90s but hasn't published any new artwork since 2000, by which point his storytelling gifts seemed to have abandoned him, leaving nothing behind but pure nerve-wracking style: arguing faces, abstract doodles, hectoring moralism. 2000's *Steve Ditko's 32-Page Package, v. 5* is a collection of one-page strips called "Tsk! Tsk!" and possibly the whiniest comic ever published. Every page has *some* representational element—a pair of hands, a judge's desk and scales, an abstracted suggestion of a face—but the lines are drowning in a lake of words that all make the same point. As entertainment, or even as an argument, the *32-Page Package* is unbearable. As art, it's kind of fantastic. Ditko's words are design elements as much as his lines, and he's pared his drawing down to ultraminimal, furious gestures that pounce off the page.

In one typical "Tsk! Tsk!" strip, "I'm Indifferent," we see half of a face. On its left, there's a list: "Facts Truth Reason Logic Honesty Integrity Justice Virtues Producers Achievers The Earned The Best." The right side of the face is overwhelmed by wobbling squiggles, and in a shaky hand, Ditko has written to the right of it: "Anti-Facts Lies, Falsehoods The Irrational Contradictions Dishonesties Corruption Injustices Vices Parasites Looters The Unearned The Worst." And at the bottom: "I Refuse to See the Distinction Between Opposite Identities." The dozen or so lines that make up the character's nose and mouth, and even the squiggles, are concentrated essence of Ditko, ugly and tense and crabbed but absolutely clear in their rhetorical import.

By the end of the pamphlet, he gets to the point: Stan Lee keeps getting the credit for creating Spider-Man, and Ditko is indignant about it. He reprints a jovial open letter from Lee saying, in essence, of *course* Steve cocreated Spider-Man, everybody knows that—and then follows it with another strip in which he quotes Lee telling an interviewer, "Spider-Man, he's the most famous character I created," alongside a half-crushed set of scales and a bunch of worried faces behind bars.

Ditko doesn't need to worry about his legacy; his fingerprints are all over other people's work, as well as his own. As we'll see later on, Alan Moore and Dave Gibbons's landmark *Watchmen* is, in some sense, one long tribute to him, and Jim Starlin's *Warlock* pays overt homage to him too. Before Todd McFarlane created his popular horror comic *Spawn*, he made his name with work on *Spider-Man* that was a slicked-up variation on Ditko's style. A few years ago, Peter Bagge wrote and drew a sharp Ditko parody, *The Megalomaniacal Spider-Man*, in which Peter Parker becomes obsessed with objectivism. And Ditko was recently credited for his unwitting contribution to Neil Gaiman and Andy Kubert's tribute to the Marvel of the '60s, *1602*: a scene in which we briefly see another dimension. That image is simply a reprint of a panel from a forty-year-old Ditko Dr. Strange story. After all this time, it's still riveting and alien—a glimpse of a world so different that it could come only from somebody desperately dissatisfied with his own.

CHAPTER 9

Will Eisner and
Frank Miller: The Raconteurs

The Eisnershpritz

There's a certain kind of rain that falls only in comics, a thick, persistent drizzle, much heavier than normal water, that bounces off whatever it hits, dripping from fedoras, running slowly down windowpanes and reflecting the doom in bad men's hearts. It's called an "eisnershpritz," and it's named after the late Will Eisner, one of the preeminent stylists of twentieth-century comics, who never drew a foreboding scene that couldn't be made a little more foreboding with a nice big downpour.

Eisner deserves his veneration in the comics world. He was one of the most gifted, innovative storytellers American comics have produced, and his work has had a lasting impact on the aesthetics and the economics of the medium. The comics industry's annual awards are named after Eisner; until his death in 2005, its honorees had the thrill of being handed an Eisner Award by Eisner himself. (I was one of the awards' judges in 2001 and have never been starstruck as badly as I was meeting him.)

Neil Gaiman begins his 2006 introduction to *Will Eisner's New York* by noting that "when, almost two decades ago, the publisher of a magazine of comics criticism attempted to find someone to write a 'hatchet-job' on a book by Will Eisner, nobody would step up to the plate . . . and the publisher was forced to write the article himself." The implication is that only someone with a heart of coal would be gauche enough to criticize Eisner. Nobody's above criticism, though, and as much as I admire Eisner and treasure his work, it's hard for me to enjoy most of it without some severe reservations.

Eisner's '40s series *The Spirit* was the high-water mark of superhero comics for decades. The lead feature in a weekly comic book inserted into newspapers (in lieu of a Sunday comics section), it starred a hero whose mask was fairly incidental: the rest of the Spirit's costume was a crisp

Eisner brings on the eisnershpritz, from the opening scene of *A Contract With God.*
©1978, 1985, 1989, 1995, 1996 by Will Eisner, from *The Contract With God Trilogy: Life on Dropsie Avenue* by Will Eisner. Used by permission of W.W. Norton and Company, Inc.

blue suit and hat with a red tie. *The Spirit* hit its stride in the half-dozen years after World War II, when Eisner (and his assistant and frequent ghostwriter, a very young Jules Feiffer) started using it as a springboard for an impressive variety of storytelling techniques and kinds of stories.

"*Spirit* sections" had a few hallmarks: exquisitely designed title pages, on which the words "The Spirit" appeared a different way every week (as an ad on the side of a building seen through a roof window, scraps of paper blown in the wind, a headline on a newspaper); beautiful femmes fatales with campy, punning names (Lorelei Rox, Sand Saref, Sparrow Fallon); situations in which the Spirit would get badly beaten up (and, perhaps, cuddled afterwards by the femme of the week). Other than that, anything went. A *Spirit* story could be a straightforward detective adventure, a satirical take on the new trends of postwar culture, a ghost story, a little Ring Lardner–style sketch. Readers never knew exactly what to expect.

The real attraction of *The Spirit* was Eisner's drawing—you might even call it his showmanship. There's something formally dumbfounding on almost every page of prime-period *Spirit*. He knocks out panel borders to let the page's negative space do extra work, aims his picture plane so it cuts through walls and ceilings and the ground, makes panels look like movie frames or file cards or pages from a children's book, and interrupts stories for fake "commercial breaks," all in the interest of keeping the story moving as smoothly and entertainingly as possible. His characters are rumpled and rubbery, emoting like ham actors; Eisner captures every gesture at its most scenery-chewing moment.

The best *Spirit* stories have been reprinted over and over (sometimes in versions Eisner redrew decades after their first appearance), and they're still a delight to read: the brutal showdown with the Spirit's nemesis, the Octopus; the introduction of vamp-among-vamps P'Gell; the bitter little morality tale "Ten Minutes"; the tale of how Gerhard Shnobble discovered too late that he could fly. A few years ago, DC Comics started reprinting all the original *Spirit* stories in handsome-looking hardcovers—the same "Archives" format they use for other old comics they own the rights to—and the cartooning in Eisner's 1946–1950 *Spirit* books is at least twenty years ahead of its time. Parts of them are more like seventy years ahead of their time.

But open up almost any volume, and you're going to run smack into the most embarrassing stumbling block of the series: the Spirit's thick-lipped, bellboy-attired sidekick Ebony White, sometimes accompanied by his pal Bucken Wing. Yes, those were the sorts of caricatures that were common currency at that time; yes, Ebony makes a few stabs at greater dignity in *The Spirit*'s later years (and is also briefly replaced by an Eskimo sidekick named Blubber—not really an improvement—and then by a stereotype-free and personality-free white kid named Sammy). There's no getting away from the awfulness of the stereotype anyway. If readers have to actively historicize every page Ebony appears on to keep from cringing too hard to see the rest of what Eisner's doing, there's a big problem. That's probably why the *Best of the Spirit* volume published in 2005 is more properly the Just-About-Ebony-Free Best-Of.

It's an unimpeachable introduction to Eisner anyway. The 1949 story "Visitor" isn't one of his most famous stories, but it's a seven-page textbook in how a comics story's formal tricks can serve its plot. The first page, unusually for *The Spirit*, doesn't start the story—it's a symbolic "splash" image, a huge picture of the moon with a profile of the Spirit's head superimposed within it, and a mysterious woman standing on some kind of planetoid in front of it. We don't see the woman, Miss Cosmek, again in person until page four; instead, the story proper begins with a police report (on a black column running down the left side of the page) about a mysterious explosion during a bank robbery (shown as ripped gray-tone drawings that look like burned photographs) and the Spirit investigating on-site. One panel shows the scene of the crime surrounded by white space, as if it's a prop on the page's stage, and the next shows us the Spirit and a pair of cops, in shadow, through a hole blown through the wall—but all we see of the "wall" itself is more white space.

The next page is mostly exposition, but you wouldn't suspect that from its abundance of visual spectacle. It begins with a dramatic overhead long-shot of the Spirit walking along a skinny alleyway (echoing the column-on-the-left composition of the previous page) and goes on to encompass three consecutive images of a conversation with a heavily accented Italian landlady ("Mrs. Pizza") that are respectively from a slightly tilted perspective, looking up a winding staircase, and peeking in through a keyhole in a ramshackle apartment, then a broad comedy routine involving Mrs. Pizza's toddlers crawling all over the Spirit while he's trying to use the phone, then some establishing shots of Miss Cosmek's house—on top of a cliff, by a lighthouse, breakers like upside-down Eisenshpritz crashing against a lookout marker, with dozens of gulls flapping overhead. That's all on *one page*, mind you, and there's a staggering amount of plot and playfulness crammed into

A page from the *Spirit* story "Visitor"—one bit of formal inventiveness after another. From "The Visitor," ©1949 by Will Eisner Studios, Inc. All rights reserved. Used with permission.

the remaining four, too, including a charming, silent nine-panel sequence to end the story.

Eisner drifted away from *The Spirit* in its last few years (and the leaden, run-of-the-mill artwork by other members of his studio suggests that his adventurous techniques didn't rub off), but the science fiction theme of "Visitor" showed up again briefly in some odd strips at the end of the weekly strip's run in 1952, in which the previously street-bound Spirit led an expedition to the moon. After its awkward final weeks, in which *The Spirit* shrank to four pages and incorporated some gorgeous artwork by science fiction artist Wally Wood (as well as garbled last-minute fill-ins when Wood couldn't meet his deadlines), Eisner spent most of the next few decades working on instructional comics for the U.S. Armed Forces.

His next great leap came in 1978. *A Contract with God and Other Tenement Stories* was a stand-alone book of four broad, melodramatic comics stories about the residents of an old Jewish tenement in the Bronx. It wasn't serialized, it didn't belong to any particular genre, it didn't look like either mainstream comics or "underground comix," and the cover of the paperback edition (depicting a man walking up tenement steps in a driving Eisenshpritz) was captioned "a graphic novel by Will Eisner." It wasn't the first book-length visual narrative (Eisner mentioned Lynd Ward's novels-in-woodcuts from the '30s as an inspiration), and he wasn't quite the first person to come up with the phrase "graphic novel," but that's the name that stuck.

A Contract with God also introduced Eisner's mature drawing style— a looser, more idiomatic, more fiery version of his *Spirit*-era technique. Freed from a limited page count, he let his images grow as big as they needed to and used panel borders only as occasional graphic elements; as often as not, backgrounds would dissolve into a patch of thin vertical or horizontal slashes, fading from consciousness like the borders of the reader's visual field. His characters' body language became more rubbery and more stagily expressive than ever before. The whole thing looked exquisite, and for the first time, cartoonists had a model for what long-form art comics could be. The problem was that it was a badly flawed model, because the stories themselves are club-footed and mawkish. They flow along frictionlessly—Eisner knew how to suck readers into a narrative—but his ironies are cheap, and his attempts at profundity aren't very deep at all.

Over the next twenty-seven years, Eisner wrote and drew about a dozen more graphic novels, with increasing seriousness of purpose. They're all drawn with ferocious, assured verve and are frustrating to try to read: leaden fables populated by oafish Everymen, chops-licking businessmen, women who are almost inevitably either inscrutable erotic temptresses or hen-pecking harridans, and the occasional autobiographical stand-in. He also drew several books of shorter sketches of his beloved New York street scenes and two of the earliest books to analyze how comics work: his groundbreaking 1985 how-to treatise *Comics and Sequential Art* and its sequel, 1996's *Graphic Storytelling and Visual Narrative.* And he settled into his role as the universally loved elder statesman of comics.

Eisner's importance—and the gift for soulful, essence-capturing drawing that never left him—let him get away with a lot, though. His final graphic novel was the posthumously published *The Plot: The Secret Story of the Protocols of the Elders of Zion,* hailed as an important testament in the way that good artists' posthumous work tends to be whether it deserves it or not. As always, the artwork is splendid: a crew of scraggly characters with grand body language, perfectly idiosyncratic layouts and design, and a range of techniques from woodcut-inspired linework to impressionistic ink-wash. There's even some eisnershpritz. The subject matter is potentially fascinating, too: the most persistent anti-Semitic libel, "The Protocols of the Elders of Zion," a plagiarized, repeatedly discredited batch of murderous lies that's still reprinted all over the world.

Regrettably, *The Plot* is a train wreck of a book. Despite the title, there's no plot to speak of, just a pile of undigested factoids about the *Protocols,* stagily arranged into scenes in which all the dialogue is exposition. In the middle of it, there's an unfinishable seventeen-page scene in which prose passages from the *Protocols* are pasted in side by side with the sections of Maurice Joly's 1864 *Dialogues in Hell Between*

Machiavelli and *Montesquieu* that they paraphrase. (The story of the *Protocols* is more complicated than that, actually, and Umberto Eco's introduction to *The Plot* mentions some sources for them that Eisner doesn't.) Eisner-the-writer, it turned out, stuck Eisner-the-artist with a nearly impossible task: turning a story with virtually no visual elements and no narrative drive into a sequence of images. More than any other cartoonist of his era, Eisner attempted to leap from light entertainment to art. But there wasn't a leap to make, and *The Plot* suggests he didn't realize that what was most valuable about his art was his mastery as an entertainer.

Sinners and Saints

Eisner's most prominent disciple is Frank Miller, the writer and artist of the *Dark Knight* and *Sin City* projects and probably comic books' biggest marquee name right now. There's a book of conversations between them, *Eisner/Miller*, that's modeled on *Hitchcock/Truffaut*, and in 2006, Miller announced that he would be writing and directing a movie of *The Spirit*. The film will give Eisner's work the widest circulation it's had since at least the '40s, which is some kind of karmic payback: when the young Miller made his initial mark with his early-'80s work on *Daredevil* (in collaboration with inker Klaus Janson), the *Spirit*-era Eisner was his biggest and most obvious influence.

What Miller brought to *Daredevil*, previously a third-rate series that had come to sell so poorly it had been demoted to bimonthly publication, was an almost outlandishly bold sensibility. The New York of its setting became an Eisneresque urban landscape of steam and bricks and shadows, updated for the electric '80s; the narrative tone became savage noir, with bracing outbursts of consequential violence; the characters became crisp, grotesque caricatures, talking in clipped and stylized patterns. Miller's drawing proceeded from his striking design sense, and his covers for *Daredevil* practically leaped off the stands and punched readers in the face. Also, there were ninjas—lots of ninjas, including Daredevil's ex-lover, an assassin named Elektra. (The terrible

Miller's impeccably designed cover for
Daredevil #189: the hero facing a hail of
ninja arrows. ©2007 Marvel Characters, Inc. Used
with permission.

Daredevil and *Elektra* movies were both mash notes to Miller's run on the series.)

After *Daredevil*, Miller essentially had carte blanche within the mainstream comics world. The next big project he took on was *Ronin*, an incoherent but spectacular story about a samurai warrior and a future city. It wore its artistic influences on its sleeve: the French cartoonist Moebius and the *Lone Wolf and Cub* comics by the Japanese team of Kazuo Koike and Goseki Kojima. (At the time, almost nobody in America had heard of manga.) It made a splash when it was published in 1983 and 1984, partly because Miller dictated that it had to be printed beautifully on high-grade paper stock, which was unheard of for an American comic at that time.

After that came Miller's greatest hit: *The Dark Knight Returns*, a four-issue miniseries published in 1986, for which he reunited with Janson. It was a Batman story, set a few decades in the future, in which the battered old hero comes out of retirement for one final stab at cleaning up his corrupted city, accompanied by a spunky young girl who's the new Robin.

The Dark Knight Returns tipped over most of the superhero clichés within kicking distance and extrapolated adult psychological complexity from forty-five years' worth of Batman stories in which it had mostly been lacking. Miller treated Batman as a sort of benign psychopath: a man driven by his parents' murder to dress up like a bat and fight crime with his fists, who repeatedly enlisted children into his private war. The standard phrase used to describe *TDKR* and the comics that followed its example was "grim and gritty," which wasn't entirely fair. The book's mood is dark and brutal, and Batman's interior-monologue narration couldn't get any grimmer: "Something explodes in my mid-section—sunlight behind my eyes as the pain rises—a moment of blackness—too soon for that . . . ribs intact—no internal bleeding." (Dave Sim parodied its tone expertly in *Church & State:* "Cardiac arrest. Acute uremic failure. Leakage in the left ventricle. Mustn't. Black. Out.") Still, *TDKR* is larded with comedy, if rather black and sour comedy: any character who isn't either a hero or a bastard is an object of ridicule.

TDKR was a huge hit, and its collected edition has never stopped selling (although it's been redesigned a few times). Curiously, a lot of its initial buzz seemed to be about what it *wasn't*—a typical Batman-and-Joker story, unstylish and lily-livered—rather than what it was. Still, a lot of superhero comics suddenly aspired to be just like it, or as much like it as they could manage. Across the board, fight scenes got more brutal than they'd ever been before; ichor flowed everywhere; heroes and villains quickly acquired dark psychological motivations for their actions; a sense of eschatology crept into superhero stories, as their battles became battles for the soul of modernity. The rough-riding, macho pronouncements of Miller's Batman ("Tonight, *I* am the law. Let's ride") became disconcertingly common. And the "prestige format" of nicely printed, squarebound forty-eight-page stories about future or past or alternate-world versions of familiar characters spent the next fifteen years being flogged to death.

What ought to have made more of an impact on mainstream comics, though, was Miller and Janson's stylistic distinctiveness and sense of design. Miller had finally found a technique of his own that didn't owe much to Eisner or anyone else: hard-angled vectors crashing into each other, thick and thin, jerking everything into crinkly forms, decorated with tiny, eccentric lines that earlier comics printing techniques wouldn't have been able to reproduce. (*TDKR*, like *Ronin*, was given the deluxe-paper treatment, and its individual installments were square-bound: the message was that this was no floppy little ordinary monthly funnybook.)

And Miller's design for *TDKR* brilliantly allowed him to pack it densely with plot and details. Almost every page is based on a sixteen-panel grid, although most pages combine a cluster of those sixteen spaces for a larger panel or substitute television shapes with caption above them for a couple of spaces (TV commentators act as a sort of idiot Greek chorus for the story). Some panels bleed out to the margins of the page beyond the confines of the grid itself—the four-by-four checkerboard is a pulse underlying Miller's storytelling, not an unvarying rhythm. He's absolutely in control of the book's pacing and dynamics, from its quiet, wry moments of character interplay to the triple-fortissimo climax. When he gives us a full-page shot of Batman riding a rearing horse straight toward us with his gang of followers behind him against a roiling night sky, it's corny and over-the-top, but it's as huge a moment as he wants it to be anyway.

Following a handful of late-'80s one-off projects and collaborations with artists including Geof Darrow and Dave Gibbons, Miller spent most of the '90s writing and drawing *Sin City*, a loosely linked series of stories—or "yarns," as he calls them, which sums up the problem with them concisely. They're all about being hard-boiled. Really hard-boiled. Tough. Manly. Not wimpy. And hard-boiled. And dark. The women are dames. Real dames. The men are real men. Some of them need killing. Some of them are just the kind of men to do it. The hero of the first one, having gotten his first dose of the electric chair, declares, "Is that all you got, you pansies?" I mentioned the hard-boiled thing, yes? Also, there are ninjas. One of them is a dame ninja on Rollerblades (which, okay, is kind of cool). And there are very tough men with guns. And dames, real dames, with red dresses and lipstick. And so on. Miller has written and drawn *seven volumes* of this stuff, not to mention codirecting a successful and excruciatingly faithful movie adaptation, with two more to come.

Obviously, film noir is a big, big touchpoint for *Sin City*—and that also goes for the new art style Miller developed for it, which cranks up

Miller's tightly controlled pacing on *Batman: The Dark Knight Returns*—the grid's presence is felt even when he extends over the edges of it. From *Batman: The Dark Knight Returns*, © DC Comics. All rights reserved. Used with permission.

the chiaroscuro effects he's always favored as high as they can go, light and dark exploding against each other and sending shrapnel everywhere. (When it rains in Sin City, we get the Miller version of an eisnershpritz: cruel, freezing splinters of ink and light.) His drawing is violently powerful, solid, passionate. But there's also something off-putting about the whole affair, which is that the same stark black-and-white contrast extends to *everything* in the *Sin City* books. What kept a lot of classic film noir intriguing was the deep, murky gray morality beneath the sharp contrast of its appearance, and *Sin City*'s morality is anything but gray. There's something monotonous and almost infantile about the way the series' characters are all either supermen, patsies, or demons; the bad guys aren't just evil, but snorting, cackling, puppy-crushing evil.

Fortunately, he broke away from the clichés of *Sin City* with his ridiculous 2001 sequel to *The Dark Knight Returns*, variously known as *DK2* or *The Dark Knight Strikes Again*. It's much less controlled than the first *Dark Knight*—actually, it's pretty much off the rails, and its tone rarely dips below a full-throttle attack-yodel. It's longer than the first book, too, although it reads a lot faster; instead of reusing the sixteen-panel grid, Miller just makes everything huge and spectacular (although he throws in a thirty-three-panel page for the hell of it).

TDKR wasn't exactly crying out for a sequel, and the odd thing about *DK2* is that Miller doesn't seem to have anything more to say about Batman. The "Dark Knight" in the title is a sales hook, more than anything else—an excuse for Miller to trigger the fireworks, smash all of DC Comics' toys, and kick over the sandbox. The best-remembered sequence from *DK2* is actually a sex scene between Superman and Wonder Woman, and Miller brings in every crazy Silver Age gimmick he can think of (if you don't happen to know what the Bottle City of Kandor is, a major plot point makes no sense).

If *Sin City* pushed the contrast level of black-and-white cartooning as far as it could go, *DK2* cranks the dial all the way in the opposite direction: its colors (by Miller's longtime partner Lynn Varley) are eye-gougingly bright, garish, and blurry, and Miller's linework is so thick and chunky it seems to have been drawn with a big knife—he never uses the *Sin City* standby of solid black where Varley can stick in a bombastic computer color effect instead. One advantage Miller finds in drawing characters with colorful, immediately recognizable costumes is that he doesn't have to be too precise about their bodies or features, so they get the same wild, gleeful distortions as everything else. It's a blow against the anatomical hyperrealism of mainstream comics, as vernacular and stylized as any art cartoonist's work.

Still, Miller seems unclear on what kind of story he's telling, other than a really loud, not very serious one. There's cheesecake, presented in a way that poses unconvincingly as a critique of cheesecake; there's outright comedy, but his contempt for most of his walk-on characters gets irritating quickly. There's also some very flat characterization. In the first *Dark Knight* book, Miller's heroes had psychologies and at least hints of interior life. In the sequel, they've got speech patterns, but that's it—they're inscrutable gods, clashing in the sky, the one-dimensional power fantasies superheroes are always accused of being.

Most of all, there's politics, posing as disgust with politics of all kinds. Instead of the blatant Ronald Reagan of *TDKR*, the U.S. president in *DK2* is nothing but an electronic construct, manipulated by the wicked Lex Luthor. The leftist hero Green Arrow and the rightist hero The Question are both objects of ridicule, along with witless television ideologues; there's also some satire about America's curtailment of civil liberties, although it feels pasted onto the

A kiss of Wagnerian proportions: Miller's thick-lined, triple-fortissimo cartooning from *The Dark Knight Strikes Again*. From *Batman: The Dark Knight Strikes Again*,

plot. Miller tries to suggest that the story's politics are neither left nor right—a lot of ideologues, left and right, like to claim that they're presenting a "fair and balanced" viewpoint.

But if the story's glorification of violence and its dominion of the strong over the weak are so ludicrously out of proportion that they don't quite count as cryptofascism, Miller can't stop stacking the deck: his combatants are totally right-on or irredeemably evil in a way that allows for no moral quandaries at all, which is at least crypto-reactionary. More recently, he's gotten a little more overt about his politics. Back in 1984, *Batman: Holy Terror* was the first working title for a project that eventually evolved into *The Dark Knight Returns*; Miller recently declared that he would be using it at last, for a story in which Batman takes on Al-Qaeda. (Oh dear.)

Unexpectedly, *DK2* has aged better than *TDKR*. The original *Dark Knight*'s earnest, controlled rancor feels a little tired now; the fun of the sequel is that Miller seems completely unfettered, as if he's got no goal in mind but to make the biggest, gaudiest, most overheated comic ever. By its end, he's almost entirely sacrificed plot to spectacle—you can almost hear the "1812 Overture" in the background. If it's annoying on any level, for its ideology or its fannishness or its gaudiness, that's sort of the point: what it tries to do most is provoke a reaction. The blazing delight Miller obviously took in drawing it makes it easy to get swept along by his craft and boldness and quash one's readerly objections until the book is over—at which point they all pop up again.

CHAPTER 10

Gilbert Hernandez:
Spiraling into the System

Gilbert and Jaime Hernandez have been publishing their work side by side in their comic book *Love & Rockets* for most of the last quarter century. The brothers have almost never collaborated; they each take up about half of the space in each issue of the series (with very occasional contributions by their brother Mario), and the books collecting their work are mostly separated by brother. Their styles are complementary (in a sort of Lennon-and-McCartney way), but they're very different, and they've each got their partisans. (For clarity's sake, I'll refer to them by their first names.) Kevin Huizenga's brochure for the Center for Cartoon Studies lists some of the essential questions cartoonists ask: "What is the relationship between comics and caricature? What is art? What is knowledge? Gilbert or Jaime?"

One way of thinking about the differences between them comes from the four "tribes" of cartoonists Scott McCloud proposes in his book *Making Comics*: "classicists" who put beauty and craft first, "animists" who try to make their characters and plot come alive, "formalists" who are interested in playing with the boundaries of comics itself, and "iconoclasts" whose ideal is self-expression and fidelity to the grubby quirks of reality. Jaime, as we'll see in the next chapter, is basically an animist in classicist drag: his sense of line and composition is exquisite, and he draws extraordinarily pretty people (which is why his work is easier to like than Gilbert's). But what he's really most interested in is his characters and their inner lives, and his work is almost entirely propelled by the interactions of a cast whose stories he's been documenting for decades, with a fairly consistent tone and focus.

Gilbert's comics, on the other hand, look like the work of an iconoclast—he's got a rough, wobbly line and a pervasive interest in grotesquerie, he highlights the wrinkles and flaws in everything he draws, and he's fond of one-off experiments in which he lets his id run wild on paper. He's more willing than his brother to fall on his nose, and he's created some pretty terrible comics (as well as some excellent ones) in the course of expanding his range.

Beneath that iconoclastic surface, though, Gilbert's got a thick layer of animism too: he's also devoted to exploring the lives of a small group of characters and the way their pasts have shaped them—so devoted, in fact, that he's repeatedly tried and failed to break away from telling stories about them. Beneath *that* layer, he's a formalist at the core, whose specialty is investigating just how telegraphic comics can be and how much he can imply with how little. He's a master of the space between panels, and his work constantly toys with readers who think they know how to negotiate their way through that space. And he's even more interested in the bigger picture of the bonds between his characters, and between them and their social context, than he is in their actual personalities: he sketches out his characters, but his passion is for illustrating the systems they belong to.

To make one last comparison to his brother—it's not entirely unfair to compare them, since they've both talked about being inspired by each other's work—Gilbert's the faster cartoonist of the two brothers, by a considerable margin. His projects outside *Love & Rockets* have the inchoate energy of a kid running around trying to burn off a sugar high. For a while in the early 2000s, he was writing and drawing his half of *L&R* as well as two other series—*Luba* and *Luba's Comics and Stories*, both about the supporting cast from his *L&R* stories—and contributing

AS WELL AS GIVING BATHS FOR A LIVING IN THOSE DAYS, CHELO WAS ALSO A MIDWIFE. SHE CAN TELL YOU STORIES.

The first panel of the first Palomar story already suggests the series' themes of personal and family history, and its ever-present sexual tension. ©2007 Gilbert Hernandez.

to the *Measles* anthology of children's comics. He also took a stab at writing the superhero series *Birds of Prey* (for which he turned out to be poorly suited), made a bizarre film called *The Naked Cosmos*, and developed a significantly different drawing style, based on meticulous stippling and compulsively repeated brushstrokes, for a peculiar stand-alone graphic novel called *Sloth*.

Still, the core of his work is his contributions to *Love & Rockets* and its direct spin-offs, and the most famous chunk of it is the stories collected as the five-hundred-page volume *Palomar*, about the inhabitants of a tiny, fictional Central American town. The first few Palomar stories were pretty clearly written under the magical realist influence of Gabriel García Marquez's *One Hundred Years of Solitude* — one character is even named "Soledad." Fairly quickly, though, the focus of the stories shifted to the extended family of a character he's never been able to shake.

Gilbert doesn't follow his characters' lives in real time the way Jaime does, but we've probably seen three decades or so of his character Luba's life history; as time goes by, her hair has grayed, her eyes have developed bags under them, and her back has rounded over from the weight of her sagging breasts. More than once, Gilbert has claimed to be through with Luba or to have one last story to tell about her and her clan, but there's always another one, it seems. Even after he moved his attention out of Palomar proper, he serialized the frantically convoluted graphic novel *Poison River* about Luba's family history, then its sequel *Luba Conquers the World.* That was followed by the short stories collected in *Luba in America* and *Luba: The Book of Ofelia* and most recently (as of this writing) a new series of comics, *New Tales of Old Palomar.*

Luba initially appeared in "BEM," Gilbert's visually striking but incoherent science fiction story in the first couple of issues of *Love & Rockets*, as a half-naked adventurer with flowing hair, electric eyes, and an enormous rack, the last of which was her primary identifying characteristic at first. She was an internally blank fantasy object for only a few months. Ever since then, the stories about her have traced the internal existence and home life and tangled personal history of someone who's painfully familiar with being other people's fantasy object and has something of a weakness for it anyway—which is why she's ended up having so many children with so many different men. (All the kids look a bit like her and a bit like their respective fathers; one of Gilbert's gifts is suggesting the subtleties of facial expressions and features with a few unkempt lines.)

Most of Gilbert's significant characters, from Luba on down, are defined in part by their sexual desires and fetishes, and the clash of sexualities warps or drives a lot of his plots. He may be the most sex-obsessed great cartoonist; his only real competition for that title is Robert Crumb, and Crumb is more concerned with exploring his own desires than illuminating his characters'. In the early '90s, Gilbert drew a hard-core porn miniseries, *Birdland*, for Fantagraphics' cash-cow Eros line; it's as sweethearted, amusing, and character-driven as it's possible for a story with a money shot on almost every page to be, and it ends with a bizarre little fantasia in which all the characters have traded genders, an idea he reprised fifteen years later in *Sloth*. It may also be the only pornographic comic whose characters were interesting enough to be carried over to a PG-rated context: a few of them subsequently became regular cast members of *Love & Rockets*. At the other end of the scale, Gilbert also gets points for his short stories in the children's comic *Measles*, starring an inquisitive little girl named Venus; when we finally meet her parents, they turn out to be characters from *Birdland*, a few years older, fully clothed, and all settled down. Well, where did you *think* kids came from?

But the prime example of Gilbert's fascinations as a storyteller—interconnectedness, erotics, juggling an enormous cast of characters—is *Love & Rockets X*, originally serialized between 1989 and 1992 and slightly revised for its book publication in 1993. (When it appeared in installments in *Love & Rockets* the comic, it had the same title as the series, confusingly enough; the X was added because it was the tenth volume of the Hernandezes' collected works.) Among some readers, *L&RX* has a reputation as "the one where Gilbert finally went off the rails." It's actually the one in which he figured out that he could control the speed at which readers had to absorb his work, and that he could cram in an enormous amount of depth and complexity if he forced his audience to slow way down.

The title of the story is a little conceptual knot: Love and Rockets is a Los Angeles punk band within the story, which shares its name with a real-life English band who named themselves, in turn, after the Hernandez brothers' comic. At first, it looks like the central incident of *Love & Rockets X* is going to be a performance by the L.A. punks at a party at the home of their bass player's high-society mother. But that's just the MacGuffin that the first half of the book is organized around. The performance never happens, and by the time you realize it hasn't happened, the story's already zoomed far past that point, toward where it's really going: a portrait of L.A. in the racially charged moment when it was building up to the riots that would tear it apart a few years later, the city's party culture was beginning to collapse under its own weight, and the United States was preparing to invade Panama.

The jacket copy on the first book edition of *Love & Rockets* X describes it as echoing Robert Altman's *Nashville*, which is partly true—the most obvious resemblances are the ensemble cast (there are more than forty characters with significant speaking roles) and a big musical event as the vantage point on a broader historical moment. *L&RX*, though, isn't just about America in 1989, it's about the smoldering

Three characters who all think *Love & Rockets X* is about them. ©2007 Gilbert Hernandez.

tension under Los Angeles in particular: a social system whose tensions of class and race and sex and language and culture were insupportable and about to erupt into flames.

One of the cleverest formal elements of *L&RX* is that it messes with one of the unstated premises of most comics, and in fact most narratives: they have a protagonist, or a character with whom the reader's sympathy is supposed to rest, or at least are about a group of characters who have something in common. All of this story's characters believe that they're its hero; a lot of them soliloquize or even address the reader in idle moments, as if we're supposed to be paying attention to them in particular and everyone else is just the supporting cast. Sometimes they stare admiringly into mirrors, checking out their makeup or their war wounds. But the reader's eye flutters over and past them, always drawn away by some psychological showdown happening nearby or by the scene changes that happen too quickly for us to identify too closely with anyone.

That's probably fortunate. One side effect of *L&RX*'s focus on the city's culture and its awful inequities is that there are no characters in the book who won't betray readers for identifying too closely with them, and not many others it's entirely possible to loathe. Gilbert is clearly fond of some characters and has it in for some others, but he mostly likes to lead us into thinking of caricatures with familiar traits as stereotypical examples of a particular subculture, and then yank the rug away. The enormous, bitter gangbanger Erf'quake turns out to be a genuinely nice guy when he's not putting on a hard-ass pose for his friends; a violent white supremacist and his girlfriend get a playful little sex scene; the only conventionally beautiful girl in the book, a bulimic half-Jewish, half-Muslim teenager named Kris Niznick with a crush on a Mexican flower seller, spends most of the book looking like some kind of half-tragic heroine — until her final scene, a little monologue in which her selfishness and casual, oblivious racism are painfully evident.

And race, in particular, is never simple in *L&RX* (or in Gilbert's work in general). A dreadlocked teenager named Igor, asked what his ethnicity is, answers, "I'm Mexican and I'm black — *and* I'm Chinese and Indian and Aborigine and Inuit and Jewish and *Martian* — so you gonna buy a hubcap or what?" Steve, a white surfer punk, is as close to a color-blind character as there is in the book, and he's effectively the reader's guide in the opening sequence, which lays out the territory of the story: he zooms on his skateboard from a poor black neighborhood to a posh white neighborhood, then catches a ride with a couple of Valley girls to the garage where Love and Rockets is rehearsing, develops a crush on Riri, the Mexican girl who's cleaning bassist Rex's house, and drops her off at her home. But later we see Steve embarrassed by a stupid prejudice of his own: he remembers beating up another kid (who later became his friend) for being a long-haired metalhead, and not understanding why his victim didn't fight back. Everyone has to define themselves by what they're not, it seems.

Steve drops out of the story for a while, but the soap-opera complications grow like kudzu. Riri is having difficulties with her girlfriend Maricela — Luba's daughter — and they're both illegal immigrants under the threat of deportation; Maricela's making eyes at Kris, the daughter of a gay Vietnam vet/producer of political documentaries named Mike, who's got a thing for Igor, whose friend Sean Ogata is having a clandestine affair with Bambi Dibble, whose boyfriend Carl's little crew of

"Aryan" losers is perpetually fighting over who's really the whitest and is living in terror of being identified by the elderly black woman they beat nearly to death, and on and on.

These are the raw materials of melodrama, somewhere between *La Ronde* and *La Haine*, and there's a certain pleasure in watching the clichés of romance stories and racial-tension stories play themselves out. But Gilbert is as uninterested in validating stereotypes about genre as he is in stereotypes about people. The secret to *L&RX*'s tragedy—as well as its comedy, of which there's plenty—is that it's forty different stories, all happening at cross-purposes; nobody's willing to sacrifice their self-interest to anyone else's plot.

The way Gilbert presents the story deliberately avoids giving any particular character or narrative thread much more weight than any other. As with Chester Brown's *Louis Riel*, the basic unit of the story and its visual compositions is its uniformly sized panels, not the page. (The book of *L&RX* has been published in two different formats—one with six panels on each page, one with nine.) And every scene is cut down to the bone and then to the marrow, with just enough information to build a context for it. That means some of the dialogue is barely diluted exposition, but again, it's always exposition for the version of the story in which the speaker has a starring role.

The first half of *L&RX* gradually escalates in complexity, setting up all the characters and their relationships as they head toward the party where Love and Rockets is going to play, playing up everybody's most grotesque attributes, and going for the comedy of exaggeration whenever it can be shoehorned in. When a conversation goes over a few characters' heads, the dialogue is rendered as abstract symbols; a punk singer, screaming a count-off into a microphone, has an open mouth half the size of his head (with teeth drawn as a jagged abstraction) and a tiny spiral for an eyeball. A car in motion is always a little bit off the ground, with a puff of smoke coming out its back. Almost every scene, though, is darkened and shifted by some mention of the atrocities in the civil war in El Salvador or of American involvement in Central America.

Gilbert Hernandez makes the most of cartooning's capacity for abstraction and visual shorthand, from *Love & Rockets X*. ©2007 Gilbert Hernandez.

The centerpiece and turning point of the story is a long, chaotic party scene in which everyone's in the same place and nobody's in the same mind-set. (Fritz, the lisping psychiatrist from *Birdland*, is wandering around the background of one panel, muttering, "the puny anth . . . one day I shall be mathter of the world. . . .") The combination of drugs, booze, culture clash, and hormones is toxic enough that someone almost gets killed. Once the madness hits its peak, though, the pacing of the story abruptly slows way down, and a sequence of calm, silent panels of the ocean as the sun sets and rises signals a transition to Palomar, where Steve has ended up. Gilbert doesn't have characters that are specifically Salvadorian or Panamanian, but he does have the Palomarians—actual characters, not faraway abstractions, above whose heads the promise and threat of the United States hovers like a boot.

With the Palomar interlude, Gilbert's caricatures become less rambunctious and more sympathetic; nobody's only comedy relief, or only a one-dimensional type anymore. And then the pacing speeds up again, cutting rapidly between a series of dramatic clashes and sexual disasters set up in the first half. (Kris's awkward, tentative assignation with Maricela—"I don't think I know how to do it right . . . checking for lumps, I mean . . . show me"—is interrupted by her freaking out on discovering that Mike's in a swimming pool with Igor. As the star of her own story, she gets to follow her desires, but her father's homosexuality is an unforgivable betrayal.) After a startling act of violence that wraps up one plot thread, L&RX becomes almost as densely packed as it's possible for comics to be: the story's final sixty-six panels are sixty-three separate scenes.

A single panel, for instance: Igor and his girlfriend Wanda standing on a bridge, wordlessly, with rolling clouds behind them—he's looking at her, she's looking up and away, and it's clear from their body language that they're breaking up, or rather that she's breaking up with him. Next panel: Steve in Palomar, holding a suitcase, being addressed by the bedridden Luba (in Spanish, which he doesn't understand), whose newborn baby, Concepcion, is being soothed by her cousin Ofelia. (The dialogue here is pretty much exposition but presented as character comedy: "Now listen, boy," Luba is saying, "I don't know how big California is, but if you see Maricela anywhere near Guadalupe, you report back to me *immediately*.") Next panel: Mike holding a Star-of-David necklace, telling his daughter, "I'll save it for you, Kris," and Kris on her bed, cross-legged, sorting out some papers, muttering "whatever"—in the brackets that indicate she's speaking Arabic. Next panel: Maricela knocking over flowerpots and screaming at her terrified boss (in Spanish), "You want to call immigration, you fuckin—I'll give you a reason—." The boss's "AIEE" word balloon is cut off by the edge of the panel.

And so on. Flash, flash, flash, flash—this goes on for pages. We don't need to be told what happened between where we saw Maricela last (naked in fetal position on her bed, crying over Kris) and the scene in the flower store, or between the flower-store panel and where we see her next (kicking at her jail cell wall); we fill in the earlier part of the argument, the threat to call *la migra*, the arrival of the cops. We don't need to see any more of the conversation between Mike and Kris to see her coldness toward him, or hear anyone explain that she's trying to renounce the Jewish half of her identity as a fuck-you gesture to her dad.

Part of the quick-cut final sequence of *Love & Rockets X*—each snapshot expands into an entire off-panel scene. ©2007 Gilbert Hernandez.

Still, comprehending all of that comes with observation and a bit of thought. In any real-time meaning, the final sequence of *L&RX* would be a string of non sequiturs; absorb it even at the normal speed of comics reading and you'll be lost. But Gilbert's trying to outdo the normal process of closure that readers apply to the space between panels. With every abrupt scene shift, we have to work hard to puzzle out where we are and how the fragment we're seeing clicks into the matrix of the story—not just each character's plot, but the panels before and after each image, and the social and political context of mutual incomprehension that includes them all.

They don't even understand how their stories connect to each other, but Gilbert does, and so do we; he's kind enough to give some of his characters some kind of happy ending, if they're willing to move beyond their parochial worldviews. And then he moves his readers' perspective up and out, too. The last character we see is Steve, in a long shot with his surfboard, walking back toward California; it's followed by an abstracted, dappled wave on the ocean, then a *Powers of Ten*–style series of increasingly distant images of the Earth from space. The system whose workings the story has followed is a small part of a greater one, and a greater one than that.

The grand formalist gestures of the book aren't just a way to tinker with the medium's boundaries of time and suggestion. They have a moral weight, because they expose the animist habit of identifying with particular characters at the expense of others. Gilbert is not suggesting that fascination with individual characters is a trap; there's no better example of comics animism than his career-long love affair with Luba, as unsympathetically as he sometimes depicts her. *Love & Rockets X*, though, is ultimately about his larger concern—the forces that shape people and societies—and the effort it demands from its readers echoes the slow and difficult process of understanding those forces.

Jaime Hernandez: Mad Love

It's easy to like Jaime Hernandez's comics for the wrong reasons. His drawing is eye candy, his dialogue is perky and witty, and basically everyone who went to indie rock shows in the '80s has read his work in small doses: "Oh, right, the Maggie and Hopey stories, I always really liked those; a friend of mine has a cat named Hopey." Those two characters are at the center of almost all of his work; in their archetypal form, Maggie is a curvy, bisexual Mexican-American mechanic, and Hopey's her skinny, punky, attitudinal best friend, roommate, and sometimes lover. From their reputation, you'd think Hernandez's comics were an edgier version of *Laverne & Shirley*.

You'd be wrong. Read as a group instead of one at a time, his stories become something much richer and darker. The first fifteen years' worth of Maggie-and-Hopey stories, drawn between 1981 and 1996, have been collected in a wonderful seven-hundred-page hardcover, *Locas*, and they flow into a fantastically intricate narrative about dozens of friends and relations that spans two decades. Hernandez is a master of showing how bodies and faces, and even body language, change over time with a few of his perfectly assured lines. His characters all have pasts and perceptions and inner lives, even if we don't know about them for years; they grow and change, on-panel or off, sometimes radically. Chepa, the gray-haired, bespectacled mom who turns up late in *Locas*, is just barely recognizable as the ferocious gang member who'd appeared in the background a few times ten years earlier.

Almost all of the stories involving Maggie or Hopey have to do with their friendship in one way or another, but the two of them spend much more time estranged than together. They're actually roommates only briefly; lots of people gossip for the first few hundred pages of *Locas* about whether or not they're a couple, but on the same page where we see for the first time that they *are* lovers, we find out that Hopey's sleeping with her band's guitarist too. Immediately after that, Maggie and Hopey are separated—thanks to a small, off-panel act of betrayal that's only clear from context later on—and barely see each other for the rest of the book.

Hernandez wrote and drew the first quarter or so of *Locas* before he found his voice as a cartoonist. It's still pretty great, but it's very different from the rest. Maggie is unequivocally the star of the early stories, a tough, cute mechanic who goes on crazy adventures involving giant lizards and killer robots; the glamorous science fiction life isn't her world, but she sort of wants to be part of it. Occasional short stories are just about Maggie and the group of friends she sends letters home to, especially Hopey—they're drawn more cartoonishly, with less shading and "realistic" detail, but Hernandez's heart seems to be more in them.

He starts to discover his strengths with 1983's "100 Rooms," which appears in *Locas* in its later revised and expanded version. It's the first time Hernandez really addresses the class issues that are part of the subtext of his later work. Almost none of the characters in the Maggie-and-Hopey stories ever get above the middle-class line, and most of them go through a rough patch at one time or another. There are a few big exceptions: Rand Race, the handsome young daredevil Maggie works with in the earliest stories, is some kind of culture hero, and Maggie's childhood friend Penny Century has married the "multi bulti billionaire" H. R. Costigan—the one hundred rooms are in his mansion. By that point, though, Maggie's already starting to feel awkward around that moneyed world, and her chance at belonging to it is slipping away.

The scene in *Locas* where Jaime Hernandez tells us his characters' real names and shifts to a new style of storytelling. ©2007 Jaime Hernandez.

And then, a quarter of the way into *Locas,* Hernandez reveals the full names of the six women he's been telling us about, and everything abruptly falls into place. (Maggie's full name is Margarita Luisa Chascarrillo, and Hopey, it turns out, is named Esperanza Leticia Glass—a nice allusion to J. D. Salinger's own series of linked short stories.) He adopts the sparser, cleaner drawing style that he's used ever since, and he figures out that the science fiction plots are actually way less interesting than his characters' personal lives and the way they interact. From that point onward, his work is devoted to getting psychological perspective on the *locas'* lives and histories and to giving all of his characters life and depth.

That's where the casual *Love & Rockets* readers' affection came from early on, and maybe why Hernandez's later work is emotionally rougher. It's easy to develop a little crush on the young Maggie and Hopey: they're cute punk girls, and they also seem cool and endearing and even admirable as characters—as people, really. Those first images, the ones that endure in readers' heads, are what those characters are like before they develop much depth, though. It's not as easy to get crushes on them when Hopey gets a little older and can't grow up enough to stop taking her friends for granted, or when Maggie loses

heart and starts wasting her mechanical gifts on repairing copy ma-
chines. Still, those painful moments make people who've been following Hernandez's stories for years, and have built up some kind of
relationship to his characters, start loving them even more.

Hernandez revels in the nonrealistic shorthand conventions of cartooning—sweat drops flying off anxious faces, puffs of smoke, speed
lines, plaid patterns that cheerfully ignore his carefully observed folds of
clothing, little kids with enormous heads and wide-open wailing
mouths and dots for eyes. But he's also fastidious about drawing bodies
that look like real bodies, and he's got an incredible sense of composition and flow—almost every panel of his work is beautiful on its own.
Look at any later page of *Locas* without reading the words, and it's instantly clear what's going on from everyone's body language. And his dialogue is unlike any other cartoonist's, except maybe his brother's:
stylized but convincingly vernacular, often reduced to the crucial fragments of a conversation that suggest the rest.

In the second half of the book, Hernandez discovers his favorite storytelling device—flashbacks, which let him keep the main narrative moving forward while he fleshes out the characters' history. (He usually
jumps into and out of them with no warning; the only clue about when
they're set, in general, is the way characters look and dress, but he's so
sensitive to those details that that's enough.) The longest story in *Locas*
is the 120-page "Wigwam Bam," a sparkling ensemble comedy about
broken friendships and corrosive jealousy, which echoes the book's
sleight of hand in miniature. At first, it reads like a Maggie-and-Hopey
situation comedy, built around the mystery of who put Hopey's picture
on an orange juice carton's missing-persons announcement. It starts
with a howlingly funny scene involving our heroines at the worst New
York City fashionista party ever, which abruptly cuts to a punk rock
flashback: an even worse party in 1980 L.A., with a fat man in sun-
glasses muttering about human sacrifice and a muscle-bound female
wrestler bellowing, "Who wants to fuck?"

Back at the New York party, Hopey and Maggie have a spat over
Hopey's ability to "turn [her] 'ethnic half' off whenever it's goddamn

The NYC party scene from the beginning of "Wigwam Bam." ©2007 Jaime Hernandez.

convenient." After that we see Maggie in flashbacks, we see her friends talking about her, we see her family—but we never see her in real time for the rest of "Wigwam Bam." She's the real missing person here, which most people reading it when it was originally serialized didn't even notice, because Hernandez keeps distracting the reader with bravura displays of cartooning: a string of TV fragments between channel flips, some *Li'l Archie*–inspired kid comedy, and a routine involving a Lucille Ball type with a fetish for twenty-something women who pretend to be little girls. Beneath the giggles and fireworks, though, there's a growing sense of sick despair and loss that bursts open in the story's final section.

"Bob Richardson," which concludes *Locas*, defines his sort of comedy by what kind of conclusion it *isn't*. First, Hernandez gives us the classical comedy ending—a double wedding—but it's a brief, silent sequence, with Maggie visually separated from everyone else. Then we get the sitcom happy ending: Hopey and Maggie are back together, situation normal, the last two-thirds of the book was just a bad dream—which, of course, is promptly exposed as a lie. Finally, there's the real ending, which is more satisfying than either of its alternatives, and funnier: a few words of dialogue and an exquisitely choreographed series of drawings that say more about his characters and their relationship than any words could.

Hernandez's fascination with the way personal history accrues and resonates means that his stories have grown more powerful as his characters have more of a past; he also sometimes likes to leave characters alone for a few years so they can spring something on us when they reappear. After the stories in *Locas* (which ended with the conclusion of the original *Love & Rockets* series), Hernandez spent a few years paying much more attention to his supporting cast than to either Hopey or Maggie, although they made occasional appearances. (Maggie turned up at one point newly divorced; we hadn't even known she'd gotten married.) *Ghost of Hoppers*, serialized in the revived *Love & Rockets* over a four-year period and published as a single volume in 2006, was his first book in a while to focus entirely on Maggie. The "Hoppers" of the title is the neighborhood of Huerta, a mostly Mexican town in California, where she grew up, and the site of a lot of the story's understated action.

As *Ghost* opens, a year or so has passed since the end of 2003's *Dicks and Deedees*, and Maggie is older, sadder, and a little worse for wear; she's managing a rundown apartment complex in the San Fernando Valley and worrying that she's gotten boring. Her greatest years are behind her, and she knows it. Her childhood friend Isabel "Izzy" Ortiz has written a well-received book about their hometown, although she's either seriously mentally ill or, if you ask her, involved in an ongoing struggle with the devil. Maggie and Hopey, who's now a bartender, still talk on the phone and occasionally hook up. And, despite her better judgment, Maggie's getting involved with Vivian Solis, nicknamed "the Frogmouth" for her rasping voice, an ex-stripper who works on a terrible local talk show and can't stay out of really stupid kinds of trouble. Vivian provides a lot of the book's prickly comedy, as when she explains to Maggie that she's kinda-sorta dating the fiancé of a woman who hit her with a bottle (and injured Hopey's eye):

"The fiancé, he said I move real good. He really likes my French way."
"French? Earlier you said you're pura Chicana, girl."
"Fuck that. French is way more exotic than Chicana."

Maggie and the Frogmouth talking in *Ghost of Hoppers*—note how the characters' movement lets Hernandez rotate the viewer's perspective 180 degrees.
©2007 Jaime Hernandez.

"I'm Chicana."

"Oh, right on. Chicana to Chicana all the way, sister."

Maggie is in her late thirties in *Ghost of Hoppers*—one reader's carefully worked-out online chronology suggests that she was born in 1965, which seems reasonable. She's gradually put on a lot of weight since she was a bombshell teenager in the early issues of *Love & Rockets*, she's started to get bags under her eyes and chin, and her posture isn't what it used to be, but Hernandez makes her look gorgeous. He obviously loves to draw her and to be faithful to the way her body looks as it ages.

Maggie has changed a lot psychologically since the end of *Locas*, too; she doesn't feel like she fits in *anywhere* anymore. She spends a lot of the book shuttling between L.A. and Huerta, propelled by a hilariously blatant MacGuffin—a "folk art thing" the Frogmouth stole from a boyfriend's place, which has found its way to Izzy's house in Hoppers. (Izzy thinks that the devil is getting back at her by causing trouble for Maggie, and in fact Maggie keeps seeing shadowy manifestations of the kind Izzy's obsessed with: a huge black dog, a swarm of flies, a salamander with human hands.) What she finds, though, is a whole lot of dead ends; her family has moved to another neighborhood and become a "Mexican Beverly Hillbillies," and Hoppers is so alien to her now that she gets lost in its streets when she tries to drive away. Back at the apartment complex, one of the tenants is an eight-foot-tall superheroine called Alarma (we see her in only about a dozen panels), and Maggie, who was once at least a bit player in that world, has become its furtive spectator.

There's a lot of backstory here; fortunately, Hernandez has a gift for dialogue that implies most of it without coming off as blatant exposition, and *Ghost's* early scenes, especially, are funny enough that they keep things moving while he clarifies who's who. But the story also picks up emotional and thematic momentum from everything he's done before. One of its subplots, for instance, is the question of whether Hopey has ever told Maggie she loves her. (At the end of the first chapter, Maggie hears her say, "I love you, y'know"—on a phone that Izzy later points out was broken at the time.) Maggie can't remember if Hopey's ever actually said the words or not, but she has—once—not that Hernandez ever mentions it in *Ghost of Hoppers*. In a 1986 story included in *Locas*, "The Return of Ray D.," there's a flashback to 1980, when Hopey told Maggie, "That's why I love you so much! You are such a weirdo!". . . a few seconds before the first time she kissed her.

Hernandez knows that, of course. He knows every detail of his dozens of characters' lives, and throwaway comments in his stories may not make sense until three or five or ten years later. Still, the subtleties of his characters' interactions really appear only on re-reading. On the surface, *Ghost of Hoppers* is a straightforward story about a woman taking stock of her life; despite the technique Hernandez has picked up from his brother of jump-cuts within each scene, it reads so smoothly that you have to make a conscious effort to slow down and note what else is happening.

Fortunately, the creamy grace and crisp geometries of Hernandez's artwork make it worthwhile to slow down and stare. His sense of composi-

Maggie walking alone in *Ghost of Hoppers,* through an effortlessly pared-down landscape. ©2007 Jaime Hernandez.

tion is one of the sharpest in comics; almost every panel in *Ghost of Hoppers* is balanced between audaciously bold white and black areas. (A house illuminated by moonlight is blackness interrupted by four tiny white squares for a window, a white parallelogram separated by horizontal lines for the lit side of the roof, and a white squiggle for a tree cut off by the roof's other diagonal.) Where the earliest *Locas* stories looked labored over, with ornate cross-hatching and lighting effects, his most recent pieces seem effortless in the way that, say, "Peanuts" does, as if Hernandez just happens to have put a single perfect line in the perfect place.

In the book's final chapter, Izzy's house has burned down, and Maggie (whose coffee may or may not have been dosed with acid by a trio of penny-ante Satanists) wanders near its ruins, seeing the whole history of the building and its curse: the people who lived there before she was born, herself and Izzy playing in front of it as little girls, a birthday party in her teenage glory days, Izzy making a final deal with her devil. The conventional way to handle this sequence would be to show the ghosts of Maggie's past passing in front of her. What Hernandez does, though, is trickier—the book's title is singular, and Maggie is, as she puts it, "an old graveyard ghost" herself, hovering around the fringes of scenes she experienced and things she never saw, in the building where she once belonged. That's the difference between memory and history, Hernandez suggests. Memory can lose a crucial detail—like, say, the declaration of love that Maggie's aching to hear—or dissolve into immaterial nostalgia, but the past is real, immutable, and growing all the time, and it's haunted by the present.

CHAPTER 12

Craig Thompson and
James Kochalka: Craft Versus Cuteness

Two ideas that have poisoned a cross section of contemporary writing in general have also seeped into comics a little bit. One is the sentimental memoir—the first-person story that explains why the author is in the right and why the author's pain and sadness are more sad and painful than yours. The other is the toxic maxim "write what you know": the idea that, even in fiction, an author's imagination has to be directly limited by his or her personal experience. The rise of autobiographical or semiautobiographical comic books brought those ideas into play in comics and opened up the question of how cartoonists might best represent their own experience.

A few underground cartoonists of the early '70s, especially Justin Green and Robert Crumb, were ahead of the memoiristic curve— Crumb's favorite kind of self-representation was, and mostly still is, to dig up the thoughts and impulses he was least proud of (his sexual obsessions, his internalized racism) and shove them into the light, as a joke on himself. Crumb also drew some of Harvey Pekar's earliest comics stories, beginning in 1976, when Pekar launched his autobiographical comics series *American Splendor*. Especially in those first years, Pekar rarely let us see anything like a significant moment in his

life. Instead, he focused on relentlessly quotidian incidents and conversations: interactions with coworkers, domestic non-events. *American
Splendor* was a refreshing kind of memoir, focusing on the ordinary and
valorizing it over the extraordinary. Pekar liked to emphasize that he was
nobody in particular, just a file clerk in Cleveland. And every few pages,
readers saw a different artist's interpretation of his words, in a way that
broke the illusion that the only person telling the story was the person it
had happened to.

In the '80s and early '90s, a lot of notable small-press cartoonists started
focusing on autobiographical work, especially confessional or unsparing
stories about themselves. Joe Matt was probably the cruelest: in his
Peepshow series, he depicted himself as a porn-obsessed, penny-pinching,
emotionally immature jerk. Julie Doucet's hilarious *Dirty Plotte* was a
portrait of the artist as a slovenly, hormone-crazed, impulse-control-free
ball of trouble; Eddie Campbell's stories about "Alec McGarry" were self-
evidently the artist amusedly viewing himself with as much detachment
as he could muster. (His 2006 graphic novel, *The Fate of the Artist*, is
mostly about taking that artistic detachment from himself so far that it becomes alienation from himself.) The most striking comic about its artist
to come out of the '90s, though, was Dan Clowes's *Ghost World*, later
adapted into a movie of the same name: Clowes himself puts in a cameo
appearance, but the story's protagonist is a disaffected teenager named
Enid Coleslaw—an anagram of Daniel Clowes.

James Kochalka and Craig Thompson both arrived in comics in the
mid-'90s, around the time the autobiographical wave was cresting. The
most important comics both of them have done are about themselves,
and they've also both published books about cute cartoon characters who
are fairly clearly themselves in disguise. The two of them run in the same
circles, and they've actually collaborated on a minicomic, but their work
is, on its surface, almost entirely dissimilar. Kochalka has a curious grudge
against the idea of "craft" and prefers to reduce characters and objects to
their most primal forms; Thompson's work is mostly gesture-capturing
semi-realism that interprets his subjects as he perceives them. They're
both ridiculously graceful at what they do, but they're both sometimes

tripped up by an insidious kind of sentimentality—a sense of self-justification that becomes an inability to think outside "what they know."

Kochalka's enormously prolific: in the past decade he's published over a dozen books, and for more than seven years he's been drawing a daily four-panel autobiographical comic strip, "American Elf." He's also something of a comics theorist; his essays on the medium and his aesthetic-statement comics are collected in a book called *The Cute Manifesto*, whose most provocative statements are his attacks on "craft" (sample essay titles: "Craft Is the Enemy"; "Craft Is Not a Friend") and his suggestion that cuteness is the highest form of beauty and the greatest goal of art. Obviously, both of those are deliberate raspberries in the face of the two major strains of fine-art tradition: one of those strains maintains that craft (or technical virtuosity) is the essence of the artist's work, and the other, although it doesn't have much use for "craft" in the old sense, distrusts cuteness—or anything that activates the reptile-brain sense of pleasure without complexity—as kitsch or worse.

The beginning of Kochalka's "The Cute Manifesto." ©2007 James Kochalka.

You can draw a diagram of the sort of oppositions Kochalka has in mind:

Craft plus cuteness: "Wallace & Gromit," Norman Rockwell
Cuteness without craft: James Kochalka, Jeff Koons
Craft without cuteness: Chuck Close, Alex Ross
Neither craft nor cuteness: Robert Ryman, Mike Diana

Quick examination reveals that Kochalka's schema, as tempting as its rejection of two different kind of orthodoxies may be, is just about totally incoherent. The first problem is that his idea of "craft" is free-floating—"trying to draw well," he suggests, is an attempt at something "illusory," since there's no such thing as objectively good drawing. That's pure sophistry: there's no drawing that everyone *recognizes* as objectively good, but cartoonists need to be able to draw things the way *they themselves* want them to appear. (To put it another way: they need to be able to draw images that produce whatever reaction they're hoping to produce in people who look at them.) That goal—matching (or at least correlating) the marks the hand makes to the image in the head—requires experience, skill, a personal and specialized tool kit. Kochalka argues that self-expression is one of the most important things in life, and I don't disagree with him. But self-expression for the rest of the world's consumption means you need the ability to express yourself in a way that's interesting to people who don't know you, and nobody is born with that any more than with the ability to climb a mountain or diagnose a disease.

Kochalka's fondness for cuteness, on the other hand, is based on the principle that everybody likes cute things—that they give pleasure by definition. He doesn't really even pay lip service to the reason that contemporary aesthetics often find cuteness suspect: the sensations it provokes bypass the intellect and go straight to the reptile brain, making it uniquely easy to use as a sugar-coating for poisoned or malicious content. Cuteness is an effect that's very easy to evoke, and we've gotten so used to it selling something that to *not* question what it's covering up is to be a sucker for it.

What it's usually selling in Kochalka's comics is James Kochalka as a brand. Virtually every project of his is drawn in the same simple, "childlike" style, with thick lines and bold outlines, and even beyond "American Elf," a lot of his work is directly or indirectly autobiographical or self-valorizing. ("Magic Boy," the protagonist of a handful of his books, is Kochalka in all but name; outside comics, he leads a band called James Kochalka Superstar.) He's not always the hero of his autobiographical work—he's been known to show himself acting like a jerk—but as fond as he is of lots of people who aren't James Kochalka, his work doesn't particularly try to suggest what's going on in their heads. The really annoying aspect of his comics isn't cuteness but sentimentality: his constant evocation of the very simplest emotional states (uncomplicated sadness, uncomplicated prettiness, uncomplicated love) under the pretense that they are somehow more real than states that aren't quite as easy to evoke.

Kochalka makes some very broad claims for his medium in "The Horrible Truth About Comics." ©2007 James Kochalka.

As much as I resist Kochalka's work on ideological grounds, though, I can't bring myself to dislike a lot of it, because so much of it really does offer the sense of delight he promises. One of my all-time favorite T-shirts is one that Kochalka drew as a benefit for the Comic Book Legal Defense Fund, with his cute, filthy-minded cartoon frog character, Fancy Froglin, explaining his outfit: "I am wearing little pants to hide my genitals. It is the law!" His comic for kids, *Peanutbutter and Jeremy*, is as adorable as he wants it to be; his *Monkey Vs. Robot* project is built on a smart metaphor for the distance between intuition and thought (unsurprisingly, he tends to come down on the intuition side). And that thick-lined technique of his is marvelously expressive: his insistence on simplicity means he makes every mark do the work of many. Perhaps we could call that ability "craft"?

Whatever craft is, Craig Thompson's got miles of it. He's written and drawn three books and a few shorter projects, but his best-known work by far is 2003's *Blankets*, which won the Eisner, Harvey, and Ignatz best graphic novel awards in the same year—a 582-page brick of a book, described on its cover as "an illustrated novel." (That's yet another attempt to come up with a better synonym for "comic book.") It's anything but a novel, though: it's a memoir—a deeply sentimental memoir—of the crucial period of Thompson's youth in which he discovered his art, fell in love for the first time, and broke away from the evangelical Christianity in which he'd been raised. The blankets of the title are the ones made of snow that cover Michigan and Wisconsin, where the story takes place, in the winter, as well as cloth blankets: the one that Thompson and his brother shared when they slept in the same bed as children, and the quilt that his first girlfriend (called Raina in the book) sewed for him and gave him on a high school vacation when he slept (fairly chastely) in her bed.

Early in the book, Thompson shows us a scene from his childhood when he asked a Sunday school teacher if he could praise God with his drawings, and she replied that he didn't need to draw God's creation, since He'd already drawn it. The prayerful visual grace of *Blankets* seems like an attempt to prove her wrong; as a showcase for Thompson's masterful, fluid drawing, it's a glorious piece of work. But it's also enormously frustrating to read, because as much as Thompson can make the world fresh through his interpretation, he barely gives anyone else in the book credit for being a whole person. As a teenager, Thompson thought of Raina as his muse—a mysterious, perfect, alluring creature who inspired him to create art, then pulled away from him when his ardor grew stifling. (You have to give him credit for excruciating honesty, though—he shows himself masturbating over Raina's *handwriting*.) At the dramatic climax of *Blankets*, Thompson calls her to tell her he's severing his ties with her, then burns everything she's given him except the blanket.

The book's flashbacks to Thompson's childhood have a gently mocking, self-conscious tone—in one infamous scene, he recounts an argument with his brother that became a literal pissing match. (Great detail: a cutaway to a literal cutaway view of the urinary system from an anatomy book, with a sound effect reading "GUSH" below it.) Where

Raina is concerned, though, *Blankets* is almost as starry-eyed and self-important as Thompson apparently was at the time. He never gives her anything like interiority or suggests that she might have had any significance other than being a perfect, stainless Celia for his work.

That lack of empathy extends to almost all the other characters in the book, who tend to be either saintly or despicable—the latter category includes a long list of hard-line Christians who terrorized Thompson in his youth and adolescence. A fat, buffoonish older man warns him not to go to art school, telling him the story of how his brother's experiences with life drawing led him to pornography addiction and then homosexuality. Raina's mother is saddled with dialogue like, "Now that your father doesn't live here, he's finally helping out with responsibilities—and for our family, it's crucial. But for our marriage . . . it's too late." Cue the strings.

None of this is as irritating on a first reading as it becomes with later reflection, though, because Thompson is so gifted at sweeping the reader along with him. His drawing has an incredible sense of flow, not just from page to page or from panel to panel but within and around every panel. The reader's eyes zoom around each image in a swooping motion, propelled by his vigorous, curving lines. On one page, Craig and Raina are making snow angels; her hands and word balloon and the "FWOMP" sound effect of her falling into the snow pry open gaps in one panel border, and the tops of the trees open the top of the next panel. There can't be a much sappier image of young love than making snow angels, but he actually captures the sensation of falling into the softness of snow and seeing the borders of your vision open up to the sky.

Even the quietest sequences in *Blankets* can be visual tours de force, like a passage in which Craig's lying awake next to Raina, listening to her breathing and heartbeat, "the gentle murmur of spirits in the room" and falling snow. Each of the sounds is represented by its own gorgeous, distinctive design, and as Thompson introduces each one, he integrates it into the page's images, until the progression culminates in an outrageously beautiful drawing of the two characters asleep in each other's arms, surrounded by a lush, organic hurricane of all four

Craig and Raina fall into the snow in *Blankets*. ©2007 Craig Thompson.

sets of abstractions—with a small inset drawing of Raina's unplugged alarm clock in a much plainer style.

Thompson had earlier drawn another book, *Goodbye, Chunky Rice*, which covers a lot of the same thematic territory as *Blankets*, except that Thompson's stand-in is a little cartoon turtle who's realizing he has to

The visual patterns of sound in *Blankets*. ©2007 Craig Thompson.

move on to the next phase of his life. But his best book, as far as I'm concerned, is a much more informal one than either *Blankets* or *Chunky Rice*: *Carnet de Voyage*, a 224-page travel diary banged out in a little over two months while he was on tour in Europe and Morocco in the spring of 2004. "This is not 'the Next Book,'" begins his introduction, which he

Craig Thompson's observational, casual drawing in
Carnet de Voyage. ©2007 Craig Thompson.

calls a "disclaimer"—that would be the long-promised *Habibi*, which as
of this writing still seems to be a few years off.

Freed from the responsibility of making a Great Work like *Blankets*,
he's able to just draw: Marrakesh markets, Gnawa dancers, Swiss moun-
tainsides, a diagram of how raclette is made, a woman he has a fling
with in Barcelona. It's enticingly casual—there's a short jam with
French cartoonist Lewis Trondheim, a quick drawing of Thompson by

American cartoonist Michael Allred, and a few other cameos by artists Thompson passed his "carnet" to at one point or another. All the architecture is minutely observed and rendered loosely in his fast, rough strokes; it all looks mythical, fantastical, more impressive than any more-literal image could be.

Carnet is also a more honest kind of memoir than *Blankets*, in some ways: it's Thompson's environment as he sees it in real time, rather than retrospectively transformed into drama. In *Blankets*, he casts himself as a confused young hero, achieving his solipsistic victory by casting off the people and ideology that threaten to bring him down; in *Carnet*, he's just an observer (whose observations include his own reactions), and an exceptionally skillful one—his visions aren't fogged by after-the-fact self-regard or by the need to spin his experiences into a "novelistic" arc of character growth. Midway through the book, he shows us his meeting with the French cartoonist Blutch, one of his biggest influences, who says of his own drawing that "there is nothing real, but everything is exact . . . just the juice of reality." The same goes for Thompson's work at its best.

CHAPTER 13

Hope Larson:
The Cartography of Joy

By the time the Canadian cartoonist Hope Larson published her first graphic novel, *Salamander Dream*, in 2005, she had already been the toast of the independent comics underground for a while. Her early, handmade minicomics staked out her conceptual territory: the world of dreams, where things are always becoming each other. *Salamander Dream*, though, was the comics debut of the year. It's a simple fable for children about imaginary friends, nature, and growing up, and its curving, mutable lines perpetually seem to be evoking three or four different images and ideas at once. There's a passage near its end that kids will read as two of its characters at play in the microscopic world of cellular biology; they won't notice its erotic undercurrents, but their parents will.

Like *Salamander Dream*, Larson's second mass-produced book, 2006's *Gray Horses*, is a very slight story whose depth comes from its exquisite visual design and imaginative resonance. Its protagonist is Noémie, an exchange student from Dijon, France, who's come to Onion City (a thinly disguised Chicago) to study art. She talks to herself, and thinks, in French, but every French sentence also appears in an English translation. Noémie has left a boyfriend behind, but she's mostly interested in exploring her confusing new environment and taking as much delight in it as she can. She makes friends with a fellow student named Anna, carries on a nervous at-a-distance flirtation with a photographer, and gets flashes of homesickness. And, at night, she dreams about a little girl named Marcy, who rides a horse to the mountains to conceal a special photograph.

That's not much of a plot, but Larson isn't really interested in straightforward narrative; she's interested in investigating systems and in coming up with novel ways to map them. (The book's endpapers, title page, and acknowledgments page all involve fragments of maps, which is no accident.) Even the

Making lemonade on a summer afternoon in *Gray Horses*. ©2007 Hope Larson.

smallest processes are fair game for close consideration here. Instead of simply drawing a horse grazing in a field, Larson devotes a page to cartoony, cameo-shaped images of the horse leaning into the grass, taking a bite, chewing it a few times, swallowing, and leaning back down. One lovely, relaxed scene diagrams, bit by bit, the mechanics of a lazy summer afternoon: a fan blowing, a half-eaten plate of cookies, someone stirring a pot of lemonade syrup, a girl lying on her friend's bed and doodling in a book. Mostly, though, what Larson's charting in *Gray Horses* is the overlapping categories of perception, documentation, and imagination, and what art has to do with all three of them.

More than any other North American cartoonist of the moment, Larson focuses on her characters' sensory impressions and not just visual imagery—she loves sound effects (and integrates them into the lines and composition of her drawings) and even tries to give hints of scent and taste and texture. Anna introduces herself by noting that she lives in a bakery across the street from Noémie's apartment; her word balloon extends into an arrow, pointing to a little spot illustration of a building shaped like a loaf of bread, with smoke coming from its chimney (we understand from this that Noémie has a scent association with the bakery) and a young Anna standing in front of it. That image, in turn, has an arrow emerging from it that points to another word balloon: "I'm Anna." As the two girls shake hands, there's a "rumble" sound effect— written in cursive, with the beginning of its "r" curved around into another arrow that indicates where the elevated train is coming from. And when the train arrives in the next panel, it appears as a stylized curve over Noémie's head, crossing the stem of her word balloon.

This sort of thing goes on throughout the book. Noémie's story is cute and charming if you zip through it, but it's much more fun to linger over every set of panels and let them provoke sense-memories. One big theme of *Gray Horses*, as with *Salamander Dream*, is the flow of the world's images and sensations between the real and imaginary realms: wrinkles in a blanket become a dream image of grass in a field, the moon half-concealed behind a cloud becomes a skipping stone in a hand. A breeze carrying the scent of flowers is represented as an array of wavy lines, a couple of which form the word "shhh" and a couple more of which go into Noémie's nose. When she dreams of a horse carrying a sick girl, coughing, through a fire, we see her hair as licks of flame and smoke; as she wakes up, the dream space evaporating behind her head is the negative image of the flames, and she's hearing somebody coughing in the next room.

The horse of Noémie's dreams is the book's central visual motif: it's echoed by the image of the horse on her room's wallpaper, a horse in a cave drawing from France, an invisible-ink blot of lemon juice on paper that Anna "develops" with a lighter, and shadows of leaves on Noémie's face in a Polaroid picture. Fragments of the horse's shape are implied everywhere. This, Larson suggests, is how the imagination works: the artist's mind perceives patterns and then extends them.

So it's curious that photographs and their fixed specificity are also so important in *Gray Horses*. Photography is the medium that draws Noémie both to her dream's subject and to her nameless suitor, who takes pictures of her from a distance and leaves a few with her when she falls asleep in a park. ("Trust me, you don't want to date a photo kid," Anna tells her. "They have issues.") The way Larson uses photos for most of the story, they're safeguards for memory in a way that drawings aren't but maps are; they preserve the physi-

Reality and dream sensations conflated on a page from *Gray Horses*. ©2007 Hope Larson.

cal world as it really is. The sick girl, Marcy, is on a mission to conceal a photograph of her siblings; her parents have burned the rest of her germy possessions (shades of *The Velveteen Rabbit*!), but that one piece of documentation means everything to her: "I don't want them to burn it! I don't care if I die!" And when Noémie falls asleep in her new apartment, she's got a photo of her back-home boyfriend propped up by her bedside; as she exhales, her breath takes on the form of that picture.

The only aspect of Noémie's artistic education we really see is the slides shown in her art history classes, which click past like the shutter of a camera. (By the end of the book, Noémie has become an avid photographer: "I want to remember everything here," she says.) In one scene, Noémie, falling asleep in her new apartment, hears a bell ringing outside her window and wonders what it could be; the inset picture that

Is it a photo, or a drawing? ©2007 Hope Larson.

explains the sound isn't just a drawing of a man pushing an ice cream cart—it's a drawing of a Polaroid of a man pushing an ice cream cart, and the cart has a tiny word balloon with a single musical note coming out of it. You wouldn't see a word balloon on a real Polaroid, of course, but the point is that the photographed image is what's really happening.

Inescapably, though, the "Polaroid" is actually a hand-drawn, personal representation of a Polaroid. Given that *Gray Horses* is a book about the expression of creativity through mutable images, there's a lot more photography than drawing going on in it. But Larson's drawing could scarcely be less photorealistic: her brush lines are bold and elegantly wavy, and she uses as few of them as she can get away with to imply everything from facial expressions to foliage. (When the book's bold style makes something in her drawings look ambiguous, she's got the endearing habit of slipping in explanatory labels with arrows: "bread crocodile," "watermelon-shaped cookies," "leak in ceiling.") Besides black and white, every page of the book uses a flat peach tone whose wobbly spread defines the borders of the panels Larson never outlines: the suggestion is that each drawing is a personal field of view, not a window into an objective reality.

The argument that photography documents and preserves the world and that drawing transforms it into something not quite true that belongs to the artist is slippery, though. Even within *Gray Horses*, Larson doesn't quite make it outright and contradicts it by the end of the story. Marcy's photograph, an artifact of Noémie's dream world, slips into the reality of Onion City; Noémie finds a way to return it to the realm of the imaginary and frees herself from her own history by sending a photographic relic of the past she's leaving behind into the world of dream horses, too. That doesn't make a lot of literal sense, but it's not supposed to. Dream logic is the only way to make a map of the processes of joy, and Larson is already becoming a master cartographer of the psyche.

CHAPTER 14

Carla Speed McNeil:
Shape-Changing Demons,
Birth-Yurts, and Robot Secretaries

In the middle of Carla Speed McNeil's eighth collection of her *Finder* series, *Five Crazy Women*, a five-page interlude called "Brief Wake" is a little wonder of economy and narrative force. There's not much to its plot: Chane, the mother of a newborn whose relationship with the baby's father is taboo in her tribe, comes to a "sin-eater" called Jaeger to get him to symbolically remove the stain from its conception. Jaeger takes a little blood from the baby, smears some over his own eyes, drinks the rest, tells them to go in peace, then heads down to the river to be ritually cleansed.

But there's more to it than that, because one of McNeil's central fascinations is the clash of cultures. Chane and Jaeger's encounter happens in the courtyard of an apartment building within a dome-covered city, in a neighborhood where it's always night. They belong to the same tribe—they've got the same sort of eyebrows and a similar facial structure—but she's half-assimilated into urban life, with a short hipster haircut and a friend who's glowering at her for seeking out a sin-eater for a bloody ritual instead of just going to a priest. The first time we see

Chane approaches Jaeger to take away her baby's sin in *Five Crazy Women*'s "Brief Wake." ©2007 Carla Speed McNeil.

Jaeger through her eyes, he's a monster coupling with demonesses; a panel later, he's a shirtless guy half-asleep in a corner. The guests at the party include a centaur and a few other "genetic constructs" (a couple of whom are discussing Alison Bechdel's *Fun Home*). The "shallow bowl" Jaeger uses to collect the blood is an ashtray. And Chane presents her baby to him in a plastic infant car seat—the kind you'd buy at a department store.

McNeil describes *Finder* as "aboriginal science fiction," although "anthropological science fiction" is probably closer. It's about cultures both pretechnological and postcybernetic, with all their totems and taboos, and the sparks that fly when they come into contact with each other. The science fiction part of the premise, though, allows her to bring in basically every idea and image she likes from history, technology, and pop culture, real and imaginary—talking dinosaurs, robot secretaries, tribal rituals, speed dating, Devo songs, and plenty of stuff from Sir James Frazer's *The Golden Bough*. The nameless world she's built as the series' setting is constructed out of cut-up and drastically rearranged scraps of our own, with all of its elements in new relationships. The core of the *Finder* stories is the anthropology of that world and the way it defines the microcosmic experiences of her characters—and, by extension, the way the culture of McNeil's readers defines their lives.

Since 1996, McNeil has been writing, drawing, and publishing *Finder* and its graphic novel collections (eight to date) through her company, Lightspeed Press. The protagonist of *Finder* tends to change from volume to volume, although Jaeger the sin-eater makes at least a walk-on appearance in every book so far and takes center stage in five of them. Jaeger is a half-breed transient who's a "finder"—a member of a secret society of tracker-scouts. Being a sin-eater means that he's a ritual scapegoat for members of his tribe, who believe that he doesn't have a soul. Jaeger can recover quickly from almost any injury but grows sick and weak unless he gets hurt regularly. As an outsider everywhere he goes, he's always some kind of cultural go-between; most of *Five Crazy Women* is about the way that his alienated restlessness, and his ability to absorb the worst other people have to offer, extends to his relationships with his lovers. In the words of its first chapter's title: "Beware of Dog." (Another character McNeil keeps returning to is Vary Krishna, a young dancer attending an exclusive academy for aspiring temple prostitutes; the shorter stories about her are collected in a volume called *Mystery Date*.)

McNeil has worked out her world's socioeconomic systems and subcultural quirks so comprehensively that she can take them for granted as background information for her stories—the sort of tossed-off concepts that gave the original *Star Wars* and *Dune* their depth. The collected volumes include endnotes to explain some of their less obvious details. In *The Rescuers*, for instance, we see a posh neighborhood infested by a kind of kudzu that grows jabbering video screens everywhere; McNeil's annotation describes how it evolved from a "self-regulating streetlight," but you don't need to know that to boggle at its presence.

The *Finder* world's population is concentrated in multi-layered, domed cities, full of elaborate but messy technology. Most of their residents belong to clans, each of which has customs of its own and a certain level of genetic uniformity—members of some clans look almost exactly alike. Wealthier urbanites have data-port jacks surgically implanted in their heads for transferring information. (Many also know how to read, but it's considered an old-fashioned skill.) Nomadic tribes, known as "Ascians" (as generic a term as "Native American"), generally live outside the cities but sometimes set up camp inside them; Jaeger identifies as an Ascian. There are some genetically engineered people with animal heads and features, too, and humans also interact with the world's semi-humanoid species (like the lion-like Nyima, whose females are bipeds and whose males, except for their king, are quadrupeds) and with intelligent but totally non-humanoid creatures. And there's a bit of magic around, but it's generally pretty low-level, more useful for temporary possession by spirits or divination than for doing much of substance.

That's a lot to swallow at once, and there's a lot more. The advantage of *Finder*'s high-concept overload is that McNeil never runs out of remarkable stuff to draw—she always gives the sense that she knows *exactly* what her settings look like, and she's got so delicate a touch for faces and their expressions that she can draw dozens of characters who look almost identical but are still distinct. The disadvantage is that the constant stage-setting can impede the plot's flow. The first couple of volumes, in particular, are so overwhelmed with clever ideas that they're sometimes hard to follow. (Fortunately, the books are self-contained and don't have to be read in order.) McNeil didn't entirely hit her stride until the fourth *Finder* volume, *Talisman*, and it's not a coincidence that it's her most tightly focused story: it's about a girl who falls in love with a book, loses it, and becomes a writer in her attempt to find it again.

Well, imagine that—a storyteller inspired by other people's stories. McNeil's not shy about borrowing ideas, passages, and images she's fond of, and she's careful to identify her sources in her annotations; within the first few pages of *Talisman* alone, she quotes Michael Ende's *The Neverending Story*, Oscar Wilde's "The Selfish Giant," Stephen King's *Rose Madder*, Octavia Butler's *The Parable of the Sower*, and the movie *Night of the Hunter*. It's also the first volume to delve into her other favorite subject, creativity and the difficult pleasures of the artistic process. (The scenes in *Mystery Date* in which Vary is dancing aren't just lovely to look at; they've got a genuine respect for dance as a discipline—Vary is perpetually training, limbering up, testing out body movements.)

She followed *Talisman* with its much longer conceptual flip side, *Dream Sequence*, which addresses the dark side of imagination and creation; it's about a scrawny, wireless-antenna-haired guy named Magri White whose dilemma is that he's a place rather than a person. His brain is a lucrative virtual-reality environment, "Elsewhere," but a monster from his subconscious is attacking its visitors. The story pits simulation and reification against each other—it's a blunt metaphor for the agonies of creating (or re-creating) culture, but it also suggests how immersion in a fiction can blur the lines between creator and consumer.

McNeil mostly drew *Dream Sequence* in a swirling, elaborately crosshatched style, to mimic its chaotic stream-of-consciousness narrative. Her next long narrative, *The Rescuers*, is thematically concerned with inflexible boundaries, and its layouts are brutally geometrical. Even so, every few pages McNeil pulls off some kind of visual tour de force: a ritual in which Ascian girls, drawn with flowing chiaroscuro, try to call on a benevolent spirit to possess them; a dark forest scene whose setting is nearly obliterated by charcoal smudges; and especially the story's conclusion, where the narrative literally implodes with a sequence in which panels following most of the plot threads get tinier and tinier until they're crushed into illegibility. (You can work out what's actually

Or, rather, a drawing of a drawing of a painting of a photograph.
From *Dream Sequence*. ©2007 Carla Speed McNeil.

happened, but it's McNeil's way of drawing attention to the parts of her story that are more important.)

Constructed around a set of events loosely inspired by the kidnapping of Charles Lindbergh's baby, *The Rescuers* is named in tribute to the Margery Sharp book, or maybe the Disney movie, or both. It's a mystery story in which culture clash negates the possibility of the crime ever being solved, an upstairs-downstairs story in which the upper and lower classes in the same household have such different mind-sets that they can barely understand each other, a story about stolen children in which nobody gets rescued.

The setup is that the year-old son of a baron of one of the city of Anvard's lower-ranking clans has been kidnapped. As it turns out, kidnapping rich people is so common in Anvard that it's considered borderline legal, if troublesome, and the baron's wife sends out a televised message to the kidnapper, trying to micromanage the baby's care: "He must not be fed chicken, turkey, quetzal, or other bipeds, or risk developing allergies. . . . If he cries without his stuffed squid, I'm sure we can work something out." Jaeger, though, discovers that the situation is worse

Totemic taboos in *The Rescuers.* ©2007 Carla Speed McNeil.

than it seems—and that even though he knows who the kidnapper is, local law makes him powerless to do anything about it. Meanwhile, the baron's estate is being managed by a crew of nomadic Ascians, one of whom, a young woman named Lohena, has just given birth to twins—a serious taboo in her tribe—and is trying to figure out how to keep one of them from being put to death before her period of seclusion in the birth-yurt ends.

The pieces are in place for something like a happy ending, but things don't really work that way in McNeil's cosmology. Instead, the grinding inability of the story's two central cultures to communicate means that things work out disastrously for everyone. "*What* kind of people *are* these??" one Ascian woman snaps about the nouveau riche clan she's serving. "That woman in there, she tried to feed the children *animal milk*!" The baron and his guests, meanwhile, can't stop condescending to the impoverished, half-starved Ascians: "Oh! How *do* these native girls stay so slim?" (In an earlier volume, *King of the Cats*, a group of Ascians are offered sanctuary by Munkytown, a domed city that's a giant amusement park—as long as they agree to pitch their tents and perform in "Noble Savage Land.") And the ideological core of *The Rescuers* is an ongoing argument between Jaeger and a kitchen maid named Lydia about whether or not you can "pick and choose *parts* of a culture to *tack on* to your life."

Why is that important? Because one major function of culture is determining who can be exiled or killed when resources can't support everyone. The idea of the painful division between the drowned and the saved recurs throughout *The Rescuers*—at the beginning of the story, a teenage Ascian boy has just shot a couple of male lizard-bird creatures that invade game birds' nests, and an older woman tells him that he's wasted his bullets: "If there are too many of anything, it's the *girls* you have to kill." The drowned ones aren't the same all over, though. There's no deeper chasm between cultures than their ideas of who deserves to be spared and which unfortunates' only hope is to be rescued from a wicker basket by someone from another tribe. McNeil's take on that conflict is framed as a science fiction detective story, but its tone is as primal as folklore.

CHAPTER 15

Alan Moore:
The House of the Magus

Prospero's Comic Books

Alan Moore declared a few years ago that he was just about done with comics—that he was breaking his wand, like Prospero, and heading off to putter about elsewhere. It was an unusual thing to announce, since not many artists of any kind make a point of letting it be known that they're quitting their best-known medium. In any case, Moore has indicated that he's not entirely opposed to the possibility of writing another comic book at some point. But every time I hold a new Moore book in my hands now, I silently count the number of his comics I still have some hope of seeing for the first time: another *League of Extraordinary Gentlemen* volume or two? That not-yet-titled graphic novel Avatar Press reportedly commissioned? Perhaps the never-published third issue of *Big Numbers*? Am I missing any last scraps?

Moore is one of the few comics creators whose work I actively collect—as prolific and inconsistent as he's been over the last quarter century or so, I still buy anything with his name on it. Even his most minor or slapdash pieces almost always inform the way I understand his major work. And the major work still sends out shockwaves, years after it's been completed. It's not at all correct to say that the last twenty-five years of the history of comics are the history of Alan Moore's career, but it's fair to say that it sometimes seems that way.

Even while he's still nominally in the game, Moore has indisputably made it into the Hall of Fame: he's one of the pillars of English-language comics, alongside Jack Kirby and Will Eisner and Harvey Kurtzman and not many others. He's also the grand exception in that hall, since the other pillars are artists—and, more often than not, writer/artists. Moore is a writer almost exclusively, although his famously hyper-detailed scripts always play to the strengths of the artists he works with. His published artwork mostly consists of a few comic strips from the late '70s and early '80s that he (wisely) drew under pseudonyms including "Curt Vile" and "Jill de Ray" (homonyms for composer Kurt Weill and child-murderer Gilles de Rais).

That makes him the chief monkey wrench in comics auteur theory. The main reason that almost nobody's willing to say that a single cartoonist is *categorically* superior to a writer/artist team is that such a rule would run smack into Moore's bibliography. In fact, a handful of cartoonists who almost always write the stories they draw have made exceptions for Moore—Jaime Hernandez, Mark Beyer, and most memorably Eddie Campbell, who's still probably best known as the guy who collaborated with Moore on *From Hell*.

Campbell's quasi-autobiographical graphic novel *After the Snooter* includes a couple of chapters in which Moore appears as "the magus." ("The Magus Is House-Proud" concerns the house Moore bought with his share of the proceeds from the *From Hell* movie.) The nickname mostly comes from Moore's fascination with magic and the occult, with which he's deeply involved these days; he plays the part, with his flowing hair and beard and rings on every finger, and he's cowriting a book to explain his system of magic, although he's already explained a lot about it in his series *Promethea*. (More on that later.) But it also may have something to do with the particular strengths of his writing, chief among which is the archetypal wizard's trick: transmuting base metal into gold.

In his own recollection of the night, *I Keep Coming Back*, he's in the Ten Bells afterwards, a crucial site in *From Hell*. "I don't mean to do it. It just happens. Write about a place and you're cemented to it." Geographical locations become significant in his work.

In another pub, in his home town, he's painted on the ceiling in the company of 19th century poet John Clare. His grand subject narrows till it becomes this town; its presence, its history.

NOT PAINTED ON ANY CEILING EXCEPT IN HIS OWN HEAD

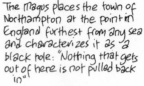

The magus places the town of Northampton at the point in England furthest from any sea and characterizes it as "a black hole": "Nothing that gets out of here is not pulled back in."

Alan Moore as "the magus" in Eddie Campbell's *After the Snooter*.
©2007 Eddie Campbell.

Virtually every comic Moore has written is inspired by some kind of pop-culture source of the past that he can elaborate and improve on. He's far from the only cartoonist who's fascinated by the miraculously bizarre comics he stumbled onto as a kid or the mass entertainments of earlier generations in general. Moore's specialty, though, is tapping into and magnifying their power with care and enormous craft, and at his best, he makes his source materials seem like sloppy knockoffs of his comics. The totally original major creations in his bibliography can be counted on the fingers of one hand: *V for Vendetta* (essentially a polemic in support of anarchism, which would be hard to pull off with established pop-culture characters), the less-than-thrilling graphic novel *A Small Killing*, the never-finished *Ballad of Halo Jones*, the never-finished *Big Numbers*. Almost everything else is Moore playing in somebody else's sandbox. The protagonists of *Watchmen* are thinly disguised versions of characters from '60s Charlton Comics series; *From Hell* elaborates on the premises of Stephen Knight's *Jack the Ripper: The Final Solution*; *D.R. and Quinch* is just the characters from National Lampoon's "O.C. and Stiggs" stories in alien drag; Moore's run on *Supreme* is a homage to the Superman stories of the '50s and '60s; *The*

League of Extraordinary Gentlemen and *Lost Girls* both star characters scooped up from the public domain.

What seems to draw Moore to preestablished characters and premises is that they always come with associations attached to them, and he's got a particular knack for probing those associations for their soft spots, then squeezing firmly. Moore's debut in American comics, cover-dated January 1984, was as base as base metal gets: a fourth-rate monster comic on the verge of cancellation, *The Saga of the Swamp Thing*, coasting on a not-too-successful movie and a handful of good comics by the character's creators Len Wein and Berni Wrightson in the early '70s. Within two issues, Moore had turned the series' premise inside out and made it his own.

For the next four years, he used *Swamp Thing* as a platform to show off his chops, in collaboration with a half-dozen artists, most notably Steve Bissette and John Totleben. One character's dialogue, isolated and placed end to end, formed a series of Elizabethan sonnets. A two-issue sequence was partly printed in an alien language that Moore devised, complete with its own grammar, and left to readers to translate from visual and contextual cues. In a six-month span, Moore's *Swamp Thing* included a delicious tribute to Walt Kelly's comic strip "Pogo"; a fill-in quickie that ultimately provided a lot of the groundwork for Neil Gaiman's *Sandman*; mainstream comics' first issue-length psychedelic sex scene; a grandly failed experiment called "The Nukeface Papers"; and the first appearance of John Constantine (who'd go on to star in his own series and movie).

This was spectacularly clever stuff, for the most part—Moore is clever even when he's not much else. But he'd also identified what was interesting and useful about Swamp Thing as a character. Wein and Wrightson's original stories about the character had been an excuse to investigate the broader idea of what monsters are and mean. They'd had Swamp Thing travel across the United States, encountering monster archetypes (a Frankenstein-like "patchwork man," a werewolf, a witch). Moore's year-long "American Gothic" storyline had the same structure, but this time each horror-archetype monster was explicitly connected with one of the monsters of the American national psyche: the werewolf story was also about repressed feminism (think lunar cycles), the zombie story concerned Americans' gun fetish, and so on.

Moore understands the potency of cheap, popular entertainment and its formulas, which is why he's so interested in already-famous characters. He's a connoisseur of pop wonders and cool trash and successful hackery of every era, because there's a kind of magic about them: they answer readers' needs to understand their own culture and experience. *The League of Extraordinary Gentlemen*, Moore and Kevin O'Neill's series about a team of secret agents comprised of heroes from Victorian pulp literature like Captain Nemo and the Invisible Man, plays up the terrors of Victorian culture that were expressed over and over in its cheapest literature: the dangerous allure of the British Empire's exotic fringes, uprisings by "Mohammadans" and "Chinamen," science gone amok, sexual libertinism. The wretched movie version of *League* missed one of Moore's great jokes: in the film version, Dracula's old victim Mina Harker is terrifying because she's a vampire; in the comics, she never lets on whether she's a vampire or not—she's terrifying because she's an independent woman with no time for Victorian social codes.

It's curious, then, that Moore has such a troubled relationship with having his own work be a significant part of mass culture. His response to being screwed creatively or financially by the entertainment industry has usually been to flip it off and walk away—in the last few years, he's repudiated the movies based on his work (and refused royalties from them) and even asked to have his name removed from some of his books. When he created the all-Moore-all-the-time "America's Best Comics" line in 1999, the idea was that he'd be writing four or five comics every month and that they'd be super-pop fun. (First sign of tongue in cheek: something called "America's Best" written by a very English gentleman.) By the time the line trickled to a halt in 2005 and 2006, he'd obviously lost interest in all its titles except the hermetic *Promethea*, and issues were crawling out months apart. A final *ABC* A-Z miniseries was launched, with stories by other writers about the line's characters, but without Moore's name attached, *ABC* turned out to

The "fascist cabaret" scene from Moore and artist David Lloyd's *V for Vendetta*. From *V for Vendetta*, © DC Comics. All rights reserved. Used with permission.

have no pop-cultural force at all: sales were so abysmal that A-Z was cancelled midway through.

So how does Moore reconstitute the semi-artless entertainment he loves into something more resonant? For one thing, he respects it as entertainment, and he's a natural entertainer himself: a magus leading a tour of his mansion's mysterious, colorful rooms. Open one of his stories to any page, and something interesting will be happening; open it to the first page, and it reaches out and drags you in by the collar. If nothing dazzling is happening in the plot, he'll come up with something clever to keep the story moving. (Years after reading it, I can still quote from memory the song the chanteuse in V *for Vendetta*'s fascist cabaret sings: "So if some blonde and blue-eyed boy would care to teach me strength through joy/And make sure all my liberal tendencies are cured/If it should be decreed by fate that you invade my neighboring state/Then you will find my frontiers open, rest assured.") And, as with most clever bastards, he can be whoopingly funny when he's in the mood. My favorite joke of his appeared in *The Bojeffries Saga*, his variation on the Addams Family/Munsters concept: a milquetoast vampire shuffles into a health food store and asks (in semi-gothic lettering) for some "soy blood." Oh, yes, says the proprietor, soy blood, I understand it's very good in vegan black puddings.

Moore also genuinely respects comics' visual component. It's more than respect, actually: he obviously *loves* cartooning, he lets the pictures he dictates tell at least as much of his stories as his words do, and the scripts he writes for the artists he collaborates with are mash notes to their particular capabilities. With *Watchmen*, he took advantage of Dave Gibbons's precise, diagrammatic understanding of three-dimensional space and willingness to draw, as Moore put it, "whatever absurd amount of detail you should ask for, however ludicrous and impractical"; with *Big Numbers*, it was Bill Sienkiewicz's protean stylistic variety; with Alan Davis and John Totleben's respective stints on *Marvelman/Miracleman*, it was Davis's sensuous line and rippling, idealized figures and Totleben's obsessively dense, grueling, slow-moving sense of texture.

Moore's weapon of choice, though, is formal, closed-ended structures—stories planned from the beginning to have a discrete number of segments of identical length, with certain things happening in each segment. He likes to plan ahead, and he's very fond of symmetrical forms. It's not surprising that the magical system he explains in *Promethea* is so thoroughly symmetrical or that he so often uses mirror imagery in his stories. Sometimes the predetermined thematic unity of his work can be almost stifling—there's a looseness, a willingness to improvise, that's missing from most of it. (As a friend of mine puts it, Moore can't just impress you; he has to tell you how much he's going to impress you first.) Fortunately, he loves to mess with the associations readers attach to his stories' genres and structures as much as the ones we attach to the characters he uses. *V for Vendetta* is set up as a three-act mystery: Who is V? The mystery formula dictates that by the end, he'll be dramatically unmasked. By the end of the actual book, we haven't found out who he is; instead, we've found out why it doesn't matter who he is.

The danger in admiring an artist as much as I admire Moore is blind idolatry: imagining that his work is by definition good or that his contribution is enough to salvage any project. That's not really a risk with

Moore, who's very often been happy to measure out a tiny portion of his cleverness and phone something in for a quick paycheck. (*Spawn/WildC.A.T.S.! Voodoo! Fire from Heaven! Violator/Badrock!* Oy!) Also, he's got a few tics that are innocuous at first and gradually more unbearable the more you read of his work: using "upon" for "on"; employing two adjectives joined by "and" where just one, or two with a comma, would do; and, most of all, the rhythm he uses to imply high seriousness.

Whenever he or one of his characters has something meaningful to say, the language Moore uses shifts into an iambic gallop: da-*dum*, da-*dum*, da-*dum*. It's there in V's big speeches, in William Gull's monologue about the architecture of London in *From Hell*, in all the dramatic scenes of *Lost Girls*, and particularly in Moore's prose novel *Voice of the Fire*, beginning with its first sentence, spoken by a man in the year 4000 B.C. with a very limited vocabulary: "A-hind of hill, ways off to sun-set-down, is sky come like as fire, and walk I up in way of this, all hard of breath, where is grass colding on I's feet and wetting they." The final chapter of *Voice of the Fire* is in Moore's own voice, or a more aestheticized version of it: "The mutter of our furnace past grows louder at our backs, with cadence more distinct."

Cadence doesn't get much more distinct than Moore's—he's got writerly style to the point where you need to look at only a few panels to tell he's written something. It's a style that's hard to parody or imitate, and other comics writers haven't borrowed from it nearly as much as they've lifted his throwaway ideas. "Twilight of the Superheroes," an unpublished proposal for a never-executed project that made it into samizdat circulation about twenty years ago, became hugely influential anyway; "Mogo Doesn't Socialize," a short twist-ending story done as a backup filler piece for *Green Lantern*, has become a significant piece of DC Comics canon. He doesn't always give his all, but sometimes, even for his most minor pieces, he comes up with some brilliant ideas.

That's actually what's kept me buying every trivial piece of Moore's work I can find since I first noticed his name on the five-page joke twist-ending stories he wrote for the British weekly comic *2000 A.D.*, almost twenty-five years ago. His major work bellows "major work" at deafening volumes, but a lot of his ephemera is terrific ephemera. If his little stories didn't have the Magus's name attached to them, they'd be the sort of miraculously bizarre comics one might remember fondly having stumbled upon as a kid.

Watchmen: *What Makes the World Tick*

I first read Moore and Dave Gibbons's *Watchmen* when it was serialized as a twelve-issue miniseries in 1986 and 1987. I was a teenager working at a comic book store in Michigan, and it was obvious from the front cover of the first issue alone — its logo running up the side of the comic instead of along the top, its image a cryptic extreme close-up with no character anywhere in sight — that *Watchmen* was something revolutionary. Every time a new issue was released on a Friday, that Saturday turned into an impromptu all-day salon in the store to discuss it.

We needed to talk about it; we were so dazzled by its newness that it was hard to wrap our brains around it. I remember, about halfway through the series, my boss commenting that it was odd that we were so far into the story and we hadn't yet seen the Watchmen use that name as a team. Of course, there's no team of characters called "The Watchmen" (and no definite article in the book's title). The title is a reference to *what* it's about in a broader sense, not *who* it's about, and it comes from a quote from Juvenal that appears in the story as graffiti on city walls: "Who watches the watchmen?"

The plot of *Watchmen* is clever enough that it deserves not to be spoiled for those who haven't read it, although it's far from the most important aspect of the book. The premise is that it's 1985, the world is on the verge of nuclear war, the superheroes who had changed the course of history-as-we-know-it were forced to retire more than a decade ago, their lives are falling apart, somebody has started assassinating them, and the most screwed-up one of the lot — a borderline-psychotic loner who goes by the name Rorschach, after the perpetually shifting, symmetrical inkblot design on his mask — decides to find out what's going on.

Those superheroes are the watchmen, not the Watchmen. The story does, on the other hand, involve a team of characters from the '40s called the Minutemen—with its whiff of history and patriotic rectitude, that's the sort of name a superhero group of that era actually could have had. Both the minute and the watch are part of the book's theme of time, its measurement, its effects, and its terminus. One major character, the son of a watchmaker, has come unmoored in time, and he's free of temporal causality and the morality that goes along with it. (As readers, we're able and even encouraged to move backwards, against the flow of the narrative, too.) The most prominent visual motif of the book, an arrow or line point-

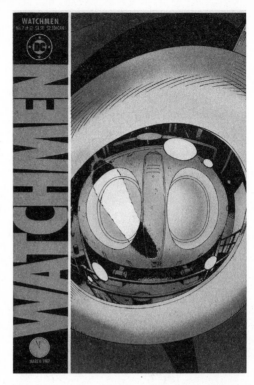

The "doomsday clock" in disguise on the cover of *Watchmen* #7, by Moore and artist Dave Gibbons. "Watchmen" #7, ©1987 DC Comics. All rights reserved. Used with permission.

ing just left of the top of a circular shape, alludes to a clock poised at a few minutes to midnight—specifically, to the "doomsday clock" of the *Bulletin of the Atomic Scientists.* We see it repeated as a splatter of paint on a window, as a smudge wiped away from dust on a pair of goggles, as a line on a radar screen.

Watchmen's structure centers on large and small symmetries. Chapters that advance the plot (odd-numbered in its first half, even-numbered in its second half) alternate with biographical chapters about individual characters (vice versa). Within the story, there are symmetries and reflections everywhere, most spectacularly in the fifth chapter, which is visually symmetrical back to front: the chapter's first page is laid out as the mirror image of its last, and so on, with every major element of every panel's composition reflected on the other side of the story. The thematic anchors of the ninth chapter are the two moments in which one character sees her reflection—first in a snow globe, later in a bottle of perfume called Nostalgia—and understands who she really is, in a moment straight out of Jacques Lacan's theory about the "mirror stage" and the "imaginary order."

The formal rigor of *Watchmen* means that some of its gestures come off as airless and overdetermined: *every* scene shift in the book, for instance, is marked by some kind of verbal or visual connection between the end of one scene with the beginning of the next, and some of those segues are a little on the ridiculous side. ("We see every connection," announces a newsagent. "Every damned link." Cut to another character adjusting his cuff links.) On a first reading, Moore and Gibbons's imposing style covers up hiccups in the plot that become more apparent once you get away from it long enough to think about it. There are hints that one character might have been the product of Nazi eugenic experiments, but they're never followed up on. Another character just happens to have made a duplicate copy of his diary—a ridiculous contrivance without which the ending wouldn't work. An ongoing routine involving something called the Institute for Extraspatial Studies is clearly supposed to go somewhere and doesn't.

For the most part, though, the book is constructed with watchlike intricacy; almost every one of the tiny details Gibbons has somehow crammed into its panels signifies *something* of import to the story. In the first chapter, Rorschach grabs a handful of sugar cubes out of an old associate's kitchen, and for the rest of the book, you can trace where he's been by where the cubes' wrappers have been scattered. The perfume and candy ads that appear on billboards in backgrounds always feature a particular corporate logo and suggest the way that company's owner exploits the zeitgeist for personal gain. The editorial cartoons in the story's right-wing newspaper, *The New Frontiersman*, have a style very much like the style in the comic book one character is reading (well, they're both drawn by Gibbons)—in fact, the comic book, it's mentioned in passing, was drawn in the '50s by an artist named Walt Feinberg, and we see the *New Frontiersman*'s editor inquiring after "that idiot Feinberg," and a cartoon signed with the initial F.

Even the storytelling techniques and page format Gibbons uses for *Watchmen* practically tick. His line art is understated, even muted, with no sense of motion and very little cartoony distortion; each panel shows a discrete, infinitely thin slice of time. The entire book is constructed on an even nine-panel grid or, occasionally, combinations of those panel areas. A few scenes alternate one kind of image with another for a sort of "tick-tock" effect, like the scenes in chapter 5 in which a neon sign blinks on and off outside a bedroom, alternately lighting everything in red and casting it in darkness. The occasional double- or triple-wide panel doesn't have just more visual information than a panel that takes up a ninth of the page; it has a proportionately greater emotional impact. There isn't actually a full-page image anywhere in the first eleven chapters; the twelfth and final chapter opens with six consecutive full pages, which feel like six consecutive unexpected gongs of a clock.

The careful choreography within a nine-panel grid—and the use of full-page images for shock impact—is obviously inspired by the look of a lot of Steve Ditko's comics in the '60s, and Ditko's shade hovers over the whole book. As I mentioned earlier, *Watchmen* was originally proposed as a story about a group of characters published by Charlton Comics: Nite-Owl was Blue Beetle, the Comedian was the Peacemaker, and so forth. (There's a little allusion to that in the text piece after chapter 6, where it's mentioned that one character grew up in the "Lillian Charlton Home.") For a few years in the late '60s, Ditko drew some of Charlton's comics, most notably a half-dozen unforgettable stories about a character called The Question, who was the inspiration for Rorschach's appearance and attitude. The Question was the first real mouthpiece for Ditko's interrogation of superhero morality—he believed that there were no gray areas between black and white and that the guilty should be brutally punished, no questions asked (see chapter 8).

Rorschach strikes a Ditko-hero pose in *Watchmen* (written by Moore, drawn by Dave Gibbons). From *Watchmen*, © DC Comics. All rights reserved. Used with permission.

That absolute, inflexible moral certainty is closer to the standard for superhero comics than Ditko imagined, though, and it's what dooms Rorschach. *Watchmen* systematically undermines the entire premise of adventure stories: not only that evil can be vanquished and that doing good can save the world but that "good" and "evil" are easy to apply. It upends the principles of heroic victory and heroic self-sacrifice, and at the end it looks like the saving of the world may not have been a good idea anyway. And its big love scene is scaldingly bitter: "Was it good for you?" one of the lovers asks, helplessly. "Did the costumes make it good?"

But *Watchmen* is still a pleasure to read, because it's also a first-rate adventure story of exactly the kind it has a grudge against. There's suspense and mystery: Who killed the Comedian? What's with the mysterious island? How will atomic war be averted? There's an aerial rescue, a prison break scene, a showdown at a secret hideout, and exquisitely fleshed-out characters. Moore supposedly intended Rorschach to be a contemptible figure, a mass of half-rotted tough-guy heroic clichés that add up to a pathetic human being, but damned if those clichés don't still have power in them—there's a dignity about him that makes readers love and pity him.

It is a truth universally acknowledged that a graphic novel in possession of a good plot must be in want of a movie adaptation. *Watchmen*, bless its twisted heart, is totally unfilmable—not that people haven't been trying to figure out how to turn it into a movie for twenty years, but it's so heavily invested in *being a comic book* that to take it away from its native medium would be to rip all its bones out.

The most obvious sense in which *Watchmen* is tethered to comics is the fact that it's specifically about comics' form and content and readers' preconceptions of what happens in a comic book story. Beneath that surface, though, it relies on being a comic book for its crucial sense of time and chronology. The amount of time the reader has to spend working through the story isn't the same as the amount of time the events in the story encompass—it's longer—and the direction in which the reader experiences the story isn't linear but keeps skipping backwards to revisit the past, as the narrative does.

Perhaps somebody at some point has read *Watchmen* straight through, but one of the joys of reading it is flipping back to see how images and scenes have been set up. The title page of each chapter—originally the cover of the pamphlet version—is a good example of Moore and Gibbons's passionate formalism: it's always an image with some symbolic relevance to that chapter's story, but it's also a close-up on a detail from that chapter's first panel. (When I interviewed him a while ago, Gibbons said he thought the proper cover for the book collection was the one it currently has: an extreme close-up on the smiley-face button with an arrow-shaped spatter of blood that appears in progressively greater context on the first chapter's cover and in every panel on the first page. Formally speaking, that makes sense. I still prefer the cover that was on the paperback edition for its first fifteen years: a freshly shattered window, with glass shards and the button hovering in the air. It's a beautiful twist on superhero comics' conventions of showing fights, motion, and scenes from the story—instead, we see a frozen, motionless image of the instant after the fight has ended, which is also the instant before the story proper begins.)

Watchmen is full of look-at-me-I'm-a-comic-book devices. Its progressions of images are choreographed in ways that would be impossible to pull off in any other medium (in chapter 9, for instance, there's a variation on the filmic zoom-out that begins with a close-up on two characters and gradually pulls back far enough to see the outline of the planet they're standing on from space). The book's panels are full of enough salient details that it's not just possible but necessary to linger over them. We see one character's narrative voice represented by his handwriting, which would look like a freaky postmodern gimmick in a prose book but functions as a natural visual cue here.

There's also a sort of "polyphonic" trick that Moore and Gibbons return to a few times over the course of the story, in which language or dialogue from one scene is attached to images from another, usually giving the words some kind of second meaning. They use it a lot, in particular, in the scenes involving *Tales from the Black Freighter*—the comic-within-a-comic that's being read by a kid on the street corner whose occupants act as a sort of Greek chorus within *Watchmen*. (If you read all of *Watchmen*, you actually see all of one issue of *Black Freighter* and bits of two others.)

A running gag in *Watchmen* concerns how nobody was interested in superhero comic books once actual costumed superheroes started appearing in the '40s; instead, the genre that caught on was pirate comics. The joke, of course, is that stories about superheroes are as formally limited as stories about high-seas piracy, and it's an accident of history that they ever caught on. (In one panel, we see a comic book store called Treasure Island, advertising *X-Ships* in its window.) In the real world, a company called Hillman published four issues of *Pirates Comics* in 1950, EC Comics published seven issues of *Piracy* in 1954 and 1955, and that was that.

Tales from the Black Freighter wasn't a real series—although Joe Orlando, who'd been an EC artist in the '50s and was a vice president at *Watchmen*'s publisher DC Comics in the '80s, drew a *Black Freighter* page that appears within *Watchmen*. The pirate comic is named after a line from Bertolt Brecht and Kurt Weill's *The Threepenny Opera*, in its Marc Blitzstein translation: the refrain of "Pirate Jenny," in which a put-upon maid imagines "the ship, the black freighter" pulling into port and its crew killing everyone else in town, then disappearing out to sea with her. (Brecht's German lyrics never mention a "black freighter," just a ship with eight sails and fifty cannons.)

The *Black Freighter* story we see the kid reading is jolting and compelling on its own—one Internet wag has suggested that the only way to make a decent *Watchmen* movie would be to adapt the *Black Freighter* sequence and jettison the rest. It's also pretty clearly a grotesque, colorful allegory for what's going on in the broader *Watchmen* story, and by its final chapter, the language and images in each of its panels are being connected to the world within *Watchmen* but outside *Black Freighter*. The open question, though, is exactly how that allegory works—who the man sailing a raft kept afloat by the gas-inflated corpses of his crewmates is supposed to be; whose attempt at heroically coming to the rescue causes the disaster he'd meant to prevent. (The likely answer changes as the story progresses and never quite becomes definite.)

In the page of *Black Freighter* that Orlando drew, the hideous pirate captain stares straight out at the readers—both one and two levels of fiction up from him—and announces: "I walk a lurching timber world, a reeking salt-caked hell/And yet, perhaps, no worse a world than yours." Just as *Black Freighter* is a metaphorical representation of the world of *Watchmen*, that world is a metaphorical representation of our own, a simplified and caricatured mirror image. As above, so below (or, if you prefer, "as left, so right"). Our New York is theirs, without the pretty plug-in electric cars; the American invasion of Afghanistan in 2001 chillingly recalled the one in *Watchmen*; most of all, the "destroy it to save it" calculus of *Watchmen* is the same one its readers face in the atomic era.

A scene from *Watchmen* (written by Moore, drawn by Dave Gibbons), weaving in and out of a scene from *Tales from the Black Freighter*. From *Watchmen*, © DC Comics. All

A clock a few minutes before midnight isn't symmetrical; a clock at midnight is. The overarching metaphor of *Watchmen*—the idea that all the clever stuff with superheroes serves—is nuclear eschatology: a blinding and unstoppable disaster that's perpetually descending, a clock perched at a few minutes to midnight. Graffiti artists spray Hiroshima-couple silhouettes on walls. People keep sickening and dying from radiation poisoning. Dr. Manhattan is the child of the Manhattan Project—a force that was once politically expedient and has become unpredictable and hugely dangerous. Death, in *Watchmen*, hits exactly like the atom bomb and has exactly the same effect.

One more memory I have of reading *Watchmen* when it came out: putting down the final issue, picking up the next comic book in my stack that week, and thinking, "No, I can't read this now; after *Watchmen*, it's obsolete." (I was young.) All superhero comics from then on, it seemed, were going to be either pre- or post-*Watchmen*. Within a year or so, the entire comics mainstream was following its example, sometimes in interesting ways (cartoonists got much more interested in design, and word balloons and captions mostly disappeared from covers), sometimes in irritating ways (the "grim and gritty" mood of *Watchmen* and *The Dark Knight Returns* became the default tone of superhero comics). Thought balloons—a device native to comics if ever there was one—also became rather less common, partly because *Watchmen* eschewed them.

Watchmen was one of a handful of stories Moore published in the late '80s (along with the conclusions of *V for Vendetta* and his tenure on *Miracleman*) that imagine the end of culture as we know it, replaced in every case with something more utopian, if problematic. Shortly thereafter, a lot of mainstream comics began to involve enormous, city-destroying or world-ending calamities, although their creators imagined them as disasters rather than revolutions leading to something glorious. Moore had the advantage of closed-ended narratives, in any case: once you've set up a utopia, it's hard to tell stories about it.

Those weren't the last apocalypse/utopia stories Moore would write, although he took a break from that theme for a while. The final one, though, is hinted at in a background gag in *Watchmen*, a pair of brothers who run the Gordian Knot Lock Company (motto: "They'll never undo this sucker!") and the Promethean Cab Company (motto: "Bringing light to the world"). If the conclusion of *Watchmen* is about the Gordian knot—the kind of disorder that responds to only a violent solution—then *Promethea* is about enlightenment in the sense of revealing the secret order in everything.

Promethea: *Micro and Macro*

When *Promethea* began its thirty-two-issue comic book run in 1999, it looked like it was going to be Moore's riff on Wonder Woman: a story about a superheroine with mythological connections, one of the flagship titles of Moore's whimsical America's Best Comics project. By the time it ended, it had turned into something very different: a rather wonderful excuse for Moore to explain his version of hermetic Kabbalistic philosophy. Moore has occasionally told interviewers about his close relationship with the second-century snake-deity Glycon, about which he's both dead serious and very funny. "The *idea* of the god *is* the god," he's said. That's the thesis behind *Promethea*, which he's described as "a magical rant seemingly disguised as a superheroine comic."

Promethea's artists, J. H. Williams III and Mick Gray, developed a lavish, eccentric visual style for the series, in which almost every two-page spread is unified by decorative design elements and—once again—symmetries. Williams is something of a chameleon—his covers to the individual *Promethea* comics alluded to Alphonse Mucha, Peter Max, Winsor McCay, and whoever else seemed appropriate.

In the first of *Promethea*'s five book collections, though, Williams and Gray's art is mostly a graceful variation on the standard superhero comics mode, and so is the story. College student Sophie Bangs lives in an alternate-world, modern-day New York City that's full of flying cars, futuristic technology, and "science-heroes." As the series begins, she discovers that she's the latest incarnation of Promethea, a mythical heroine born in fifth-century Egypt whose physical presence can be invoked by acts of imagination and creativity. (Sophie becomes Promethea by writing poems about her.)

Through Book 1 and the first half of Book 2, *Promethea* is Moore at his most playful, having fun with his setup and setting. Sophie's foil is her snarky best friend Stacia, whose favorite pop-culture icon is a lovely, daffy running gag: something called Weeping Gorilla, who appears on omnipresent billboards sobbing into his fur and thinking bummed-out thoughts ("We probably expect too much from George Lucas . . . "). The high-tech sensory overload of *Promethea*'s New York is packed with delicious details that Moore never bothers to explain—it's only natural that the city's mayor has multiple personalities, even before he's possessed by demons. (Newscast chatter: "Speaking yesterday, the Mayor said 'I am Legion. All shall kiss my smoldering hoof.'") And the chaos in the street scenes frames the series' contrast between the material and spiritual worlds nicely.

Midway through Book 2, though, things start getting weird. Sophie meets a grubby, creepy old magician, Jack Faust, who says he'll teach her about magic in exchange for sex with Promethea—and she takes him up on his offer. An entire chapter (an issue of the original comic) is devoted to a Tantric sex scene, complete with extensive discussion of the magical significance of clothing and sexuality. At the beginning, it's impossibly squalid—the idea of the gorgeous heroine in bed with a pot-bellied, warty letch is meant to make the reader squirm hard. ("Who re-maindered the book of love?" thinks Weeping Gorilla on the sign outside Faust's filthy apartment.) But the chapter's tone gradually turns grand and psychedelic (if not exactly erotic), then oddly tender, and it lays the foundation for the rest of *Promethea*: the idea that there's magi-cal symbolism in everything, no matter how debased.

The second book concludes with a flabbergasting visual and verbal juggling act: a chapter called "Metaphore," in which the twin snakes on the caduceus Promethea carries explain the history of humanity to her, in rhyming couplets, by way of the sequence of major-arcana Tarot cards. The snakes are named Mike and Mack, as in "micro" and "macro"; they can't keep straight which one is which. (Again: "as above, so below.") Their Tarot isn't *quite* the traditional version, though. Every card from the common Rider-Waite-Smith deck is redrawn as a cute lit-tle cartoon, and "Judgement," for instance, is replaced by Aleister Crow-ley's suggestion, "The Aeon," its angel replaced on the card by Harpo Marx (symbolizing Harpocrates, the Greek god of silence) honking rather than blowing his horn ("ankh ankh"—oh yes, he's wearing clothes decorated with ankhs, rather than the angel's cross).

Every page of "Metaphore" also includes a set of Scrabble tiles spelling out a relevant anagram of "Promethea" ("Ape Mother," "Me Atop Her," etc.—each page's tiles are "scored" with a corresponding let-ter of the Hebrew alphabet rather than a number), plus backgrounds de-picting icons of human culture from that stage of history, plus a painted image of Crowley (aging over the course of the chapter from a fetus to a corpse, and telling a joke that's a metaphor for how magic works), plus a tiny little devil or angel (on the left- and right-hand pages, respectively), plus decorative "go-go checks" that allude to '60s comic books.

Apparently emboldened by the fact that Williams and Grey's hands hadn't yet fallen off or strangled him, Moore threw the plot out the

248

Moore and artists J. H. Williams III and Mick Gray expand the Crowleyan Tarot card "The Aeon" into a page of *Promethea*'s "Metaphore." From *Promethea Book 2*, © DC Comics. All rights reserved. Used with permission.

window for most of Books 3 and 4 and devoted them to an extended explanation of the Kabbala's Tree of Life, the map connecting the *sephirot* or spheres representing God's attributes (or states of mind) in the Jewish mystical tradition. The links Moore suggests between the Kabbala and the Tarot are that the twenty-two major arcana correspond to the twenty-two paths between *sephirot* on the Tree of Life, and that, more importantly, both systems are useful as allegorical representations of the range of human experience. The conceit of *Promethea*'s middle act is that Sophie and her spirit guide, the previous incarnation of Promethea, spend a chapter apiece traveling through metaphorical representations of each of the ten Kabbalistic *sephirot* (plus an extra "invisible sphere" Moore sneaks in between the third and fourth).

There's a lot of ungainly expository dialogue in those two books ("This is the fourth sphere, right? 'Chesed,' there on the arch above the Jupiter symbol. I think it means mercy"). Their ratio of profundity to claptrap varies with the reader's openness to semi-digested Crowley, and occasionally Moore threatens to sprain an eyelid from winking so hard. (Sophie meets Hermes, who tells her that gods, as "abstract essences," can be perceived only through linguistic constructs like "picture-stories." Picture-stories? she asks. "Oh, *you* know. *Hieroglyphics. Vase* paintings. Whatever did you *think* I meant?") Some readers complained at the time that they felt that Moore was lecturing at them, and that's absolutely true. But complaining about *Promethea*'s transformation from a graphic novel to a graphic textbook is missing the point: the idea of it isn't to tell a story so much as to present a gigantic mass of arcane philosophy as entertainingly and memorably as possible.

In fact, the Kabbala volumes of *Promethea* are thrilling, partly because they're total eye candy. Williams and Gray draw each chapter in a style of its own, with a color palette dominated by the part of the spectrum associated with that chapter's sphere. Chesed's panel backgrounds are painted with blotchy, Van Gogh–inspired brushstrokes, suffused with blue; Binah, the realm of the whore Babalon, is drenched in blacks and dark, tinted grays, with outlines that crinkle like woodcut prints. The colors of the highest sphere, Kether, are traditionally white and gold, and its chapter is illustrated almost entirely in shimmering, pointillist golden yellow. When the story gets back to Earth a few pages later, it's hard to readjust, although Williams keeps up the delirious compositional tricks from the Kabbala section.

That leaves Book 5, set a few years later, in which some leftover bits of good-guys-versus-bad-guys plot from the early stages of the series get mopped up, and yet another eschaton-turned-utopia arrives: Sophie becomes Promethea one last time in order to end the world. "End," not "destroy." "The world is our systems, our politics, our economies . . . our ideas of the world!" an earlier Promethea explains to her; the apocalypse she brings on is, as Promethea's name suggests, more like bringing light to those ideas. In the penultimate issue, and a tie-in published later in Moore and Chris Sprouse's *Tom Strong*, we see life continuing much more happily after the world ends.

As entertaining as it is, most of Book 5 is an exercise in clearing the decks for the final chapter, and by then it's clear that Moore has arranged the series into thirty-two chapters for a reason. The final one is thirty-two pages long, each page corresponding to one of the Tarot's twenty-two major arcana or one of the ten spheres of the Kabbala. (They can be read in the order printed in the book, or they can be assembled into two four-page-by-four-page arrays—which form gigantic images of Promethea—and read in that order instead.)

This time, it really is a lecture, consisting of a nude Promethea fluttering around candy-colored background abstractions and limning Moore's cosmology, which centers on snakes, psychedelic mushrooms, sensory overload, the human imagination, and language and art as consciousness-altering tools—especially in comic book form. There is no pretense of narrative, just a circular monologue ("As readers, you are physical beings engaging in a DNA snake-dance with me, a fiction, your immaterial, lunar imagination"), abetted by captions that invoke mythology, literature, science, and a little too much pseudoscience ("The butterfly's random fluttering from one point to another also accurately models how thought follows a fractal path from concept to concept").

Without the rest of the *Promethea* series, it would make no sense at all, and even in the context of the story that's led up to it, it's rough going. As a philosophy of life, it's questionable at best; it's a huge pill, and it would be unswallowable without the smooth sugarcoating of Williams's artwork. As an aesthetic philosophy, though, it's astonishingly fertile, recasting the mind as the "radiant heavenly city" Moore promises, populated by the gods that live in the human imagination, and laid out according to the road maps he's presented in the guise of a grand adventure story. He may be the only human who lives there right now, but at least he's inviting the rest of us.

Lost Girls: *I Am Curiouser and Curiouser*

"Tell me a story," a young girl asks at the beginning of Moore and Melinda Gebbie's dizzying graphic novel *Lost Girls*. We can't see her; all we can see, for the entire first chapter, is a mirror with an ornate carved frame and whatever happens to be reflected in it. On the first page, that's a wealthy woman's bedroom in Pretoria, South Africa, in 1913. "Oh, I don't know any stories," the older woman says. "Your little white breasts, they're so lovely. They'll never be as beautiful once you're grown. Will you touch them for me?" All we can see of the woman is her leg, stretched out as she masturbates.

To put it bluntly, the scene is totally creepy; naturally, it's also more complicated than it looks. As it turns out, the woman is Lady Alice Fairchild, a drug-befogged upper-class Englishwoman in her sixties, and she's just talking to herself. The girl is her reflection in the mirror— or, rather, the lost self Alice imagines on the other side of the mirror. Alice has extensive experience with imagination and mirrors; you've probably already encountered her younger self, the protagonist of *Alice's Adventures in Wonderland* and *Through the Looking-Glass*.

The themes of *Lost Girls* are all right there on the first page: storytelling as a way of making sense of the transformations that sex brings about, children's sexuality and its adult exploiters, and an almost modernist formalism—the idea that working within interesting and rigorously defined structures, no matter how outré they are, will yield worthwhile results. (We get the very strong impression that this is what Lady Fairchild *always* does to get off.)

Moore and Gebbie began working on *Lost Girls* in 1990, and the first six chapters were serialized in the early '90s; the rest wasn't published until 2006, by which point the project itself had practically reached the age of consent. The finished version is an exquisite physical object: an expensive, slipcased set of three oversized hardcover volumes, reproducing Gebbie's mixed-media artwork in luminous color. The point of the project, Moore told interviewers, was to make dignified pornography rather than "erotica"—to produce something that was beautiful and well wrought and also overtly, unblushingly about what happens behind bedroom doors.

Another way of putting it is that *Lost Girls* is a really advanced version of the "slash fiction" that fans write imagining sexual liaisons between their favorite fictional characters—a sort of "I Am Curiouser and Curiouser." In short order, Alice finds herself at a hotel on the Austrian border, the Himmelgarten, where she becomes entangled, figuratively and literally, with beleaguered English hausfrau Wendy Potter, née Darling, and Midwestern farmgirl Dorothy "Dottie" Gale, late of, respectively, *Peter Pan* and *The Wonderful Wizard of Oz*. The three of them have stories of their own, though: they've built grand metaphors—pornographic-utopian worldviews, really—around their adolescent sexual experiences. Naturally, those worldviews look very much like Wonderland and Neverland and Oz, right down to the styles of those books' original illustrations, except that everybody's doing everybody else—boys with girls, boys with boys, girls with girls, and a few other permutations. (Toto is virtually the only character from the source books who escapes with his innocence intact.)

It's a brilliant move: Moore and Gebbie have found a consistent, elaborate metaphor of sexual discovery in three books whose authors didn't put it there, or at least probably didn't deliberately put it there. Alice, for instance, tells the story of how her adult identity, and her fetish,

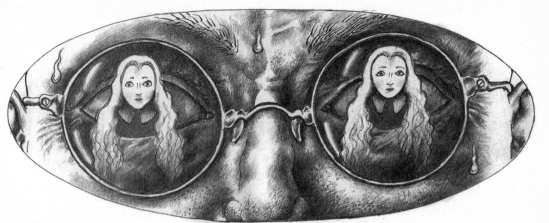

"He was my father's oldest friend, the white hair ringed about his bald, pink crown. He seemed forever anxious; eager to be somewhere else. We called him 'Bunny,' though his actual name escapes me now. In hushed tones, so as not to wake my sister, he complained about the sun and asked if I would come inside to keep him company, awaiting my Papa's return. It seemed ungracious to decline."

Alice, reflected in the spectacles of her molester, the "White Rabbit," from Moore and artist Melinda Gebbie's *Lost Girls*. ©2007 Alan Moore and Melinda Gebbie.

began to form: as a girl, being molested by an older friend of her family—he had white hair and a pocket watch and spectacles and he was known as "Bunny" (of course he's the White Rabbit)—she saw her reflection in a looking-glass. That child, she imagined in that charged, hazy moment, was not just her older self but her true love, forever young and innocent. And the implication of the scene is that she's attracted to actual younger women—maybe children, maybe not—because they remind her of that reflection.

It's an accident of timing that *Lost Girls* is Moore's final major comics work to see print, but it's got one significant difference from his other books. He's very often contextualized his comics as part of some kind of tradition of popular culture (comics or pulp literature), and he's obviously riffing off popular books by Lewis Carroll and J. M. Barrie and L. Frank Baum. But *Lost Girls* doesn't position itself as pop (the way even *Promethea* nominally does), with the disposable, garish trappings of comic books that Moore usually gravitates toward. It's presented as luxurious, exclusive, difficult fine art, and what it's claiming as its kin, at least in the way it encodes attitudes about sex, is fine art: Art Nouveau, Stravinsky's "Le Sacre du Printemps," and the Decadent writers and artists of the turn of the twentieth century.

In fact, *Lost Girls* devises, from a few scraps and hints, the idea of a legacy of pornographic fine art from the prewar era. In every room of the Himmelgarten, instead of a Bible there's a white book of erotic tales and illustrations by famous Decadent fin de siècle types like Oscar Wilde and Aubrey Beardsley (all, of course, pastiched by Moore and Gebbie). Gebbie's artwork is partly inspired by that era's artists even outside the pastiches—her shapes and tones owe more to the ways early-twentieth-century painters, especially Matisse, abstracted the human body than to the way most cartoonists do. Virtually every page is designed and decorated in ways that hint at Art Nouveau; few comics artists care so much about wallpaper. Gebbie sometimes succumbs to the frou-frou soft-focus eroticism of a David Hamilton photograph or an old *Emmanuelle* movie, but most of the time she avoids the clichés of both coy pastel "erotica" and clinical, sodium-lit hardcore, and her sense of color and shade is unparalleled in comics.

So *Lost Girls* is shocking, it's lovely, it's ambitious, it's grandly clever—but is it any good? Yes: it's very, very good, if flawed. Parts of it are some of the most extraordinary stuff Moore has ever written; parts of it made me want to tear my own eyes out. (Some of them are the same parts.) Moore loads every line with thematic weight until it groans, his

Wendy, led astray in an Art Nouveau–inspired sequence from *Lost Girls*.
©2007 Alan Moore and Melinda Gebbie.

idea of what an American farmgirl talks like is ridiculous, and the time-line is a mess: a few weeks' worth of events are spread out over a year, just so the narrative can encompass the riot at the premiere of "Le Sacre du Printemps," the assassination of Archduke Ferdinand, and the out-break of the Great War. Still, even some of his stylistic tics work to his advantage here, like the elevated rhetoric he resorts to whenever he's got a point to make ("an unseen hand undid my blouse, then moved in-side and I sank gratefully into a fauve delirium; the drugging cherry warmth of her"); its galloping iambic meter and lofty, elaborate diction are appropriate for once in the context of the book's heady atmosphere.

There's a lot of that high rhetoric here, because Moore's got an epis-temological axe to grind. He wants to make very sure we get the differ-ence between representation and reality, since he knows perfectly well that, as protectively fond as he is of Dorothy, Wendy, and Alice, a lot of people are going to be extraordinarily unhappy about his setting them up with strap-ons and opium pipes. In one later scene, the Himmelgar-ten's unctuous manager, Monsieur Rougeur, explains that the fictions in the hotel's White Book "are uncontaminated by effect and conse-quence. Why, they are almost *innocent*. I, of course, am *real*, and since Helena, who I just fucked, is only thirteen, I am very *guilty*. Ah well, it cannot be helped." He's in the background of a sequence of panels as he delivers his monologue; the foreground is a series of close-up pene-tration shots, and the top half of the page is a scene of pedophilic incest, lovingly rendered in the style of the Marquis Franz von Bayros, with text pastiching Pierre Louÿs.

All of this is terribly uncomfortable to read; it's meant to be, obvi-ously, because the argument is no fun if it's too easy. *Lost Girls* flirts openly with the idea of adults having sex with children, in everything from the premise of the book to its key sequences to Rougeur's coy admission-of-guilt-as-protestation-of-innocence. If there's a single sexual taboo that still pushes *everyone*'s buttons, it's pedophilia. But one of the strongest effects art can have is a sort of inductive shock—carrying you along some place you don't want to go—and as Moore and Gebbie un-derscore at every turn, no matter what their characters claim, what *Lost*

Wendy's indignation about to be overcome, from *Lost Girls*.
©2007 Alan Moore and Melinda Gebbie.

Girls is showing isn't real. It's imaginary scenarios involving imaginary characters famous for their imaginations. The children's books about them haven't been violated; they're safe on the nursery bookshelf.

For that matter, if Moore and Gebbie have no time for prudes — Wendy's husband, Harold Potter (whose name appeared in *Lost Girls'* early chapters long before J. K. Rowling finished her first book), a stuffy, frigid sort, is humiliated in a handful of rather-too-nasty, farcical scenes — they've really got it in for adult molesters of children. Without giving anything away, a pivotal moment of each girl's story comes when the great and terrible authority figures who've taken advantage of their nascent sexuality are revealed as the tiny men behind the curtain they are.

Lost Girls has a particular erotic obsession of its own, though: the book's frenzy of structure and substructural rigor takes formalism to the point of de Sade–like fetishism. (At least it's formally appropriate.) Each volume is named after a line from one of the source books and contains ten chapters, two of them devoted specifically to Wendy, two to Dorothy, two to Alice, and two including excerpts from the White

Book. Each chapter has its own title and title page; each chapter in the second and third volumes in which one of the women tells her story includes one wordless full-page image directly inspired by a scene from that girl's original book.

More or less every other page in volume 1 has some kind of sexual content; that's ramped up to every page in volume 2, and practically every panel in volume 3 is flat-out hardcore. But by that final volume, the former child stars are fucking against the apocalypse. The war ("that which is most great, which is most terrible") is about to break out, the soldiers are off to the front, and there's nothing left for the hotel's remaining residents to do but lock the doors and screw themselves insensible until they have to run away.

The third volume is the roughest in more than explicitness: the characters enter the sort of pornotopian frenzy they've always imagined and discover that coming back out of the sexual Wonderland is difficult and painful. The final sex scene is curiously feeble—and it's followed not with any kind of afterglow, but with a sorrowful awakening into the world outside the boudoir, as the flames rise across Europe. Whatever awful realities come out of sex, Moore suggests, are a thousand times less awful than the violence that its energy can be perverted into.

The curious—or curiousest—thing about *Lost Girls* is that while it's enormously powerful and gorgeously executed, it's not actually all that sexy, or likely to inspire many fantasies on its own. The kind of release it offers is a fetishist's release: the sense that a ritual has been completed precisely. If it fails as smut, though, it's a victory as art, which is not a bad condolence prize. Like any number of boundary-pushing, button-pushing works before it, it may well require some kind of scandal, or at least a high-placed moralist's denunciation, to find the audience it deserves. It's spoiling for a fight, and it's worth fighting for.

CHAPTER 16

Grant Morrison: The Invisible King

I'm going to spoil the climax of one of Grant Morrison's best comics now, but that's okay—for reasons you'll understand soon, it's better if you know going in how it ends. In the final chapter of his seven-volume graphic novel series, *The Invisibles*, a skinny bald man, the anarchist hero and "ontological terrorist" King Mob, doses his demonic nemesis, the King-of-All-Tears, with a drug that makes its users perceive language as reality. Then he fires a toy gun at him; out of it comes a flag with "POP" written on it. ("A bullet in the right place is no substitute for the real thing," King Mob says.) The King-of-All-Tears naturally pops, and "the supercontext absorbs the King effortlessly, welcoming his quaint ferocity, converting it to narrative."

Most of the hallmarks of Morrison's work are present in that deeply weird scene: reality-bending metafictional freakouts dressed up in action-adventure drag; metaphors that make visible the process by which language creates an image that in turn becomes narrative; a touch of feel-good self-improvement rhetoric; faith in the power of pop and popularity to do magic; and skinny bald men who are stand-ins for Morrison himself, heroically conquering sadness and making the world evolve.

Morrison's writing is the most interesting thing happening in mainstream comics right now, in part because a lot of the best cartoonists of the movement have no interest in superhero franchises' tropes and traps. Pop culture and shared myths, though, are the very center of Morrison's art; he's referred to his cosmology as "pop magick." The point of his comics isn't to subvert or invert the traditions and clichés of the mainstream; it's to revel in them and amplify their power through art, with the ultimate goal of making his readers' world evolve.

This is not quite the same as Alan Moore's project, which is more about aesthetics than potential praxis, but it's not entirely dissimilar, either. Morrison is one of a handful of British comics writers-not-artists who emerged in the mid- to late '80s under the shadow of Moore and took a while to dig themselves out. Morrison's arguably still grappling with Moore's legacy, as we'll see.

Unlike the rest of the British invasion, though, Morrison's got an obvious and abiding love for superhero comics. The first American series Morrison wrote, beginning in the late '80s, were *Animal Man* and *Doom Patrol*—the former a very minor '60s character, the latter a bottom-of-the-class title evidently given to him because he couldn't screw up its sales any further. Morrison instantly figured out what was interesting about *Doom Patrol*: its characters were all nominally "superheroes" because they had something terribly wrong with their bodies. (Robotman, for instance, was a former race-car driver whose body had been destroyed and whose brain had been transferred to a robot shell.) He gave the series a bizarre sense of humor—their former enemies the Brotherhood of Evil became the Brotherhood of Dada; one recurring character was Danny the Street, a sentient, mobile, transvestite *street* (named after British female impersonator Danny La Rue). *Animal Man*, meanwhile, was where Morrison started playing the metafictional games that he's indulged in ever since. Over the course of two years, Animal Man gradually realized that the world he lived in was two-dimensional, made of printer's ink on newsprint stock, and controlled by a single perverse intelligence—a writer named Grant Morrison, whom he confronted in the final issue Morrison wrote.

Subsequently, Morrison has worked on much higher-profile superhero series: *JLA*, *New X-Men*, and his current work-in-progress on *Batman* and

All-Star Superman. Aside from his long-running partnership with a Scottish artist who goes by the pseudonym Frank Quitely (a spoonerism for "quite frankly"), though, most of Morrison's comics are easier to think of as his work drawn by somebody else than as real collaborations. His two most important projects, *The Invisibles* and *Seven Soldiers of Victory*, are both drawn by hordes of artists; they're both, in fact, written in a way that makes being drawn by hordes of artists a strength rather than a drawback.

Morrison has called *The Invisibles*, originally serialized between 1994 and 2000, the central work of his career. It resists description and especially resists plot summary. At a speech at Disinfo.con in 2000, Morrison described it as "my attempt to explain what had happened to me after I'd been abducted by aliens in Kathmandu in 1994," which is as good a starting point as any. (He also noted that he'd gone to Kathmandu in 1994 specifically in order to be abducted by aliens, which should give you some idea of what his sense of humor is like.)

King Mob, near the end of the story, describes a narrative of his own creation, also called *The Invisibles*: "It's a thriller, it's a romance, it's a tragedy, it's a porno, it's neo-modernist kitchen sink science fiction that you *catch*, like a cold." The series is essentially a cracked treatise on the nature of reality, cast in the form of a fast-paced action-adventure story. It is, in a lot of ways, my favorite comic book ever, and I have never been able to recommend it to anyone else with a clear conscience, partly because it's such a ridiculous mess in so many ways and partly because it struck me so much as being *exactly* the kind of story *I like to read*—so much so that it's hard for me to imagine other people being as passionate about it as I am. (This is apparently a common syndrome among its admirers. A few years ago, I made myself a T-shirt with an image from *The Invisibles*; shortly thereafter, I ran into somebody else wearing a homemade *Invisibles* T-shirt and instantly struck up a friendship.)

Before I go on, I should note that even though Morrison is the guy who holds *The Invisibles'* copyright, I don't mean to ascribe it to him alone: he wrote the whole enormous thing but drew only one page of it. The rest was drawn by the aforementioned hordes—eighteen artists in the final four issues alone—and the distinction between text making and picture making in the conjunction of words with images is particularly significant in this story.

A lot of *The Invisibles* is explicitly concerned with the way that time and space can be represented on a printed page, and the idea that if time is the province of language and space is the province of visual art, then the relationship of the two is the province of the comics medium. It also addresses the question of visibility and invisibility (key words: seeing, representation, presence, existence), beginning with the paradox of the series' title (always represented as negative space) and its medium (which is all about visibility). And it's got magical rituals, monsters from another dimension, schizophrenic time-traveling cyborg bombshells, the end of the world, and pacifists with really big guns.

Words can represent things that aren't visible, which images can't, at least without cheating. The fifteenth-century artist Leon Battista Alberti rejected the idea of invisibility in image making altogether: "No one will deny that things which are not visible do not concern the painter," he wrote in his treatise *On Painting*, "for he strives to represent only the things that are seen." *The Invisibles*, though, is riddled with literal and metaphorical transparencies—things that are real but unseen—which it's obligated to represent as part of its story. That's a problem that cuts to the core of the comics medium, and in order to deal with it, Morrison calls into question some of the most basic assumptions observers make about images, narrative, and comics.

The first thing we need to figure out when we look at any kind of visible, representational artwork is what our own perspective on what we're looking at is supposed to be—it's usually so obvious we don't even think about it. When we read any kind of narrative, we ask something analogous about our perspective at the outset. There are three kinds of perspective for a conventional story's reader: we want to know the *intended observer* of the story (who's it meant for? do we need any foreknowledge to understand it?); who's *telling* us the story, and that teller's position relative to the story itself; and (usually) the *protagonist* of the story—the character with whom one's sympathies are supposed to rest.

In *The Invisibles*, the identities associated with all of those perspectives are deliberately ambiguous—or, rather, multiple. For starters, the intended observer is required to break the rule of who the story is meant for, because the prerequisite for reading *The Invisibles* is *already having read it.* The very first line of its first page is "And so we return and begin again," and throughout the seven volumes of the collected *Invisibles*, the reader is called on to remember and anticipate the story in the process of reading it.

Naturally, you can read and enjoy it the first time too—if you couldn't, it would never have survived six years of serialization. (It barely survived that long anyway; early on, Morrison included an essay in one issue, asking readers to masturbate while concentrating on a magical sigil he'd devised to raise the series' sales and save it from cancellation. Sales went up.) Still, large chunks of the story make a lot more sense after the reader has gone through the whole thing. "If you don't get it the first time," King Mob says of the narrative game called *The Invisibles* that he's created (in inhalant-can form, decorated with the cover image from the first issue of the comic book!), "you have to keep running it. It's different every time."

So who's telling the story? It's never specified, and at first we can make the standard assumption that the narrator is invisible and (pretty much) omniscient. If we're willing to observe the fiction from its outside—and getting outside of one's context is one of Morrison's favorite themes—that narrator is effectively just Grant Morrison. Even so, an "omniscient" caption more than five hundred pages into the story asks, out of nowhere, "Which leaves . . . only one question. Who is telling this, and to whom?"

Morrison has a kind of avatar within the story: King Mob, aka Gideon Starorzewski, who writes horror novels under the name Kirk Morrison and is drawn to look a lot like his author. (When King Mob was tortured nearly to death partway through the series, Morrison has noted, he himself promptly had near-fatal medical problems; he took that as his cue to make King Mob fabulously successful and give him a supercool girlfriend, at which point things started going very well for the author, too.) The *Invisibles* game, we learn, is meant to be experienced from multiple perspectives. "It's ragged at the edges," King Mob says, "but you can play any of 300 characters, some more involving than others."

More metatextual knots: *The Invisibles* is also the title of a book that another character, a seventeen-year-old girl named Kay, composes—or rather, revises—in the year 2005, before she travels back in time to become the character Ragged Robin from her story. (For an extra dose of head-spinning-ness, it's gently implied that Kay is also Kay Challis, aka Crazy Jane, a superheroine with multiple-personality disorder who'd appeared in *Doom Patrol* some years earlier.)

"If I write hard enough and honestly enough, I think I can make it real," Kay says. But she may not actually be as honest as she wants to be: "I don't want Jolly Roger to get shot," Robin's caption reads in the scene where the foul-mouthed freedom fighter Jolly Roger is indeed shot. "I don't know if she really did or not but I like her and in my version she doesn't get shot." And her friend Kerry tells her that "even if the guy who wrote *The Invisibles* is for real, he'll be an old man, Kay." Later, the book's authorship becomes even more dubious: "It was called 'The Invisibles,'" Robin tells King Mob in 1998. "I fell in love with the picture of the author. Then it turned out there *was* no author. Or maybe the author was me." There's also *another* book called *The Invisibles* within the story, but it was published in 1960 and seems to have been an exposé of anarchists of the 1920s.

We never see the contents of any of those three versions of *The Invisibles*. We do, however, see the thug-turned-hero Dane McGowan relating the entire story to his dying friend Gaz in 2012, on the day the Mayan calendar runs out and the world ends. Dane also speaks the final dialogue in the last volume and addresses the reader directly on its last few pages. He might have a fairly good claim on being the narrator, except that there's an even stronger claim made immediately before the conclusion. A caption asks: "And this voice talking? Listen to this voice closely. Who is speaking? Whose voice is this speaking in your head and reminding you that freedom is free?"

It's the reader's, of course. It's also an allusive echo. Earlier, Dane's teacher Elfayed quotes his own teacher quoting Rumi: "So what do I have to do to get you to admit who is speaking? Admit it and change everything! This is your own voice echoing off the walls of God." "I've said my bit and it's *your* go now," Dane tells us on the final page—and then, as mentioned above, we "return and begin again." The implication is that the narrator is actually the (intended) reader, who, after all, has already read the story and keeps being prompted to try to remember it.

The identity of *The Invisibles'* protagonist is also up for debate. On a first reading, the series is pretty clearly the story of Dane, the aimless youth who is initiated into a secret society at the beginning and saves the world at the end. But, as we already know, the first reading of this story isn't the correct reading. The heroic archetype is what we assume from experience we're supposed to follow in a narrative, especially in a comic book. Near the end of *The Invisibles*, though, Morrison debunks the idea of the heroic character arc: both "sides" in the conflict, it turns out, are necessary agents of change. "I stopped needing to save the world," says Dane's retired ex-teammate Boy. "Saving is what misers do."

On subsequent readings, it's more interesting to identify another character as the protagonist, especially if you take into account King Mob's comment about "playing any of 300 characters." Perhaps there aren't *that* many whose experiences can be followed as the main arc of the story, but there are more than a handful. (Midway through, there's a nicely executed quasi-Situationist gag in which three of the main characters critique their own unfitness to serve as protagonists.) Morrison has called Audrey Murray (the widow of a security guard killed by King Mob in the first issue) *The Invisibles'* "central character"; that's a bit of a stretch, given that she appears in person on all of ten pages out of roughly 1,300, but it can certainly be read as the story of the extraordinary circumstances surrounding her experience and how she reacts to them.

Once the observer of a narrative has settled on a perspective, the next question is what, exactly, is represented in it. The answer, in *The Invisi-*

bles, goes back to the first question, because what's represented in its panels fragments the reader's vantage point.

Let's go back to Leon Battista Alberti for a moment. One of the central problems he addressed in *On Painting* was a very basic one: how to represent a three-dimensional (3-D) construct on a two-dimensional (2-D) image plane—how to paint a real-life scene, in other words. His solution was essentially to imagine the visible surfaces of the objects in the painting projected onto the canvas's plane and paint where the canvas intersects those projections. *The Invisibles* takes this process another step. Morrison presents the idea that the story's images are not only a series of planar representations of observed three-dimensional space but a series of 2-D representations that are *collectively* supposed to represent greater-than–3-D space-time in a way that can't ordinarily be perceived by a 3-D observer looking at 3-D space.

Some *Invisibles* panels, in fact, are intended to present a view of a segment of space-time *from the outside*, since it can't be represented "accurately" from a particular moment within it. Morrison suggests that an "outside view" of a human being would appear as a gigantic, continuous worm-like structure, including all of that person's physical positions through time—a "time maggot" or "knotted life cast"—which can then be mapped onto the two-dimensional picture plane. "This is your *complete* body, not its section," Dane is informed as he sees the "cast" of his own life; what we understand as a representation of a body in a picture, then, is really only the surface of a temporal cross section of the body. That sounds grotesque, but consider that a milder version of the same idea is a standard part of comics' visual vocabulary: the same body seen in a few positions in the same panel, to suggest the section of its "life cast" that extends over a short span of time.

If the intersection of a "time maggot" with three-dimensional space looks like a person, it follows that other higher-dimensional constructs will be similarly deformed as they are observed in 3-D space, *Flatland*-style: "Just as the interpenetration of a spherical form into a two-dimensional plane is seen as a circle of varying diameters," one higher-dimensional *Invisibles* entity explains, "so too does the interpenetration of /( )/ [*sic*] into your three-dimensional continuum appear as a lens form capable of altering its shape." The lens form in question is probably Barbelith, of which more below.

In short, higher-dimensional forms are distorted twice over by their most literal representations in the picture plane; while we're used to seeing 3-D forms as 2-D images and can compensate for them in our imagination, we're only permitted to see a cross section of a cross section of higher forms. So Morrison is forced to invent other ways of representing space-time constructs projected onto the picture plane from their outside, and he mostly does it by way of a metaphor of fragmentation.

The most sustained leap outside of subjective space-time in *The Invisibles* is the "All Tomorrow's Parties" episode in the sixth volume, *Kissing Mister Quimper*, in which Ragged Robin travels through time and then into the "supercontext" outside it. We see parts of the trip through Robin's eyes (including the visor of the "timesuit" she's wearing) as she moves outside of space; three-dimensional objects first appear artificially flattened and iconic, and her temporal linearity is no longer aligned with everyone else's as she experiences "time and space like an X-ray." After her vision is splintered (literally—her visor is broken), she's able to control her position with respect to space and time, reappearing in 1998 to deliver a message, and then moving into the supercontext or, as she puts it, "allnow."

That's all pretty opaque, but the important bit is the splintering or making-multiple of vision. What Morrison tells us, every chance he gets, is that a higher-dimensional construct (like the complete version of the world in which we readers live) can be correctly perceived only from a multiple perspective. Vision must be *decentered* to see and understand complex constructs; standard stereoptic vision won't do. (Less-than-standard vision is even more hopeless. The two major characters who are killed in the course of *The Invisibles* are both one-eyed.) But the complete human body is "billion-eyed"; if we can experience our own bodies in that form holistically rather than as a cross section, we enter the omniscient supercontext.

One kind of multiple vision in *The Invisibles* is, perhaps, too literal: having a lot of eyes. Near the beginning of the first volume, we encounter a group of demonic servants of something called the Outer Church. They have what they describe as mastery of the fourth dimension, and we know from the start that there's something weird with their eyes, even though we can't see them behind their black glasses. It turns out that their project is replacing human eyes with insectoid, many-image-seeing eyes. "Let me show you the new eyes they have given me," says the sinister school headmaster Mr. Gelt, who's affiliated himself with them; when he's killed, his consciousness is relocated into a beetle.

Robin leaps into the supercontext, written by Grant Morrison and drawn by Chris Weston and Ray Kryssing. From *The Invisibles: Kissing Mr. Quimper,* ©Grant Morrison. All rights reserved. Used with permission of DC Comics.

More interesting than extra eyes are the extra I's that turn up all over the series. Having an unstable definition of the self, in Morrison's cosmology, makes perception of the invisible more possible, since it means the vantage point doesn't have to be fixed. (He's played with that idea for most of his career: his version of Superman's pal Jimmy Olsen in *All-Star Superman*, for instance, is more perceptive than anyone else because his identity is so fluid.)

The Invisibles' most enlightened characters all have multiple identities or personalities. The Harlequinade, an *Invisibles* group who also have the power to control time, share their identity through multiple bodies—it's hinted that they are in fact everyone in the world—and make no secret of what their multiplicity allows them to do: they introduce themselves with the dialogue "This is"/"Pierrot. And this"/"Columbine. I can see"/"invisible things." And the next stage of human evolution, according to the final chapter of the series, is thoroughly unstable personalities, "MeMes," perpetually cycling: "multiple personality disorders as a lifestyle option."

The antithesis of the multiple self is the "I"/"You" sphere represented a few times in the course of the series: a three-dimensional construct that represents rigidly defined identity as overtly as a symbol can. It's literally a sphere made up of the word "I," white on black, and the word "You," black on white, repeated endlessly—admitting of no color, no shade, and no variance in vantage point, not unlike the sort of image Steve Ditko draws to indicate his ethical scale. This sort of Manichaean outlook on selfhood, Morrison wants us to know, is a Very Bad Thing—the sphere initially appears surrounded by messages reading "loser," "I don't love you," and "doctors say it's cancer."

Fortunately, Morrison makes it easier for our own vision of *The Invisibles*, as readers, to be multiple, too. Return and begin again with what we asked earlier: Who's telling this story? Who's making it possible to see? *The Invisibles* is comics, not prose: the creator of its images is, to a significant extent, the person telling the story. But various sections of the series are drawn by roughly twenty artists, and there's no single "true" or "correct" representation of any character. The climactic story line is drawn "jam"-style, with everyone taking a few pages, including the one Morrison himself drew. Morrison nonetheless has a prior claim as the image maker, since he's the one who directed the images via his own use of language.

This is not exactly an unusual condition for comics, but that's sort of the point: comics are sequences of images that are neither continuous (like the "complete body") nor simultaneous. They include the spatial representations and temporal abstractions of images, directed by the temporal representations and spatial abstractions of language. They are,

The dualistic, black-and-white "I"/"You" sphere appears in *The Invisibles: Bloody Hell in America*, written by Morrison and drawn by Phil Jimenez and John Stokes. From *The Invisibles: Bloody Hell in America*, © Grant Morrison. All rights reserved. Used with permission of DC Comics.

King Mob makes his big metafictional move. From *The Invisibles: Counting to None,* written by Morrison and drawn by Phil Jimenez and Keith Aiken. From *The Invisibles: Counting to None,* © Grant Morrison. All rights reserved. Used with permission of DC Comics.

in short, an ideal medium for dividing the reader's consciousness into multiple subjectivities, in the way that *The Invisibles* demands.

Comics are also two-dimensional images, and they give the reader an opportunity to experience transcendence of a construct in the same way that some of the characters in the story do. "From here-is-everything how flat the world seems," the transsexual shaman Lord Fanny notes. In the course of moving outside space, Ragged Robin understands herself as both observer and observed—the fragmentary images she sees of herself are flat but curved and flimsy, like pieces of paper or the individual image-planes of comic book panels. The paper effect also appears when King Mob, explaining that "time and space start to get weird here on the perimeter" of the physical universe, peels back the corner of the panel in which he's speaking. By means of our memory and narration of the story, or "playing" it as a character, we can experience *The Invisibles* simultaneously from two dimensions (on the page) and three (outside it).

Visibility, then, has a certain transitive property. But what does it mean to be *in*visible? Well, literally, invisibility is the combination of being present and not being seen. The key to the question of invisibility in *The Invisibles*, and its most perplexing recurring symbol, is a bit of Morrisonian hand-waving called Barbelith—the lens form mentioned earlier. Barbelith is effectively a "wild card" of meaning: the source of enlightenment, a "cosmic stoplight," a placenta for the evolution of humanity, a physical satellite, a surveillance device; it is always circular or lens-shaped, variously pink or green or red. It reveals and erases memories. As a symbol, it's not only present but persistent, echoed by the spots on Ragged Robin's makeup, King Mob's T-shirt, the Invisibles' badges (characters who identify themselves as Invisibles often wear a blank badge, in the shape of the pins teenagers wear with the images of their favorite band), and a dozen other recurring images, not least the symbol that ends the series, as we'll see.

Barbelith is physically located behind the moon and can therefore never be seen by the unenlightened people limited (by visibility) to linear space-time. But someone whose perspective became multiplied—no longer stuck to the track of moment-and-place—would be able to see it, since that person would see the moon of one moment and the Barbelith of another. And, in fact, the moments when characters in *The Invisibles* find their perspective smashed into pieces (usually by enormous emotional stress or confusion about their own perceptions—the sort of thing that leads to enlightenment in Zen koans) are precisely the moments when they encounter it. Barbelith always manifests itself as enormous, rather than smaller-than-the-moon-from-earth-size; given the proper observer, it's not bound by the rules of perspective.

We, however, are bound by those rules as we read *The Invisibles*, and we have the complicating factor of Morrison's language further affecting our perception. To recapitulate a little: the first thing a representational artwork's observer needs to figure out is the proper perspective to apprehend the artwork; the second is what is represented in the work. Observers who are looking at a comic book, which presents information in two forms at once, have a third basic issue they need to resolve: the relationship between the words and the pictures. To work that out for *The Invisibles*, we first have to examine Morrison's slightly peculiar view of what words and pictures are and can do.

To begin with, Morrison suggests, linguistic representation is innately and entirely different from visual representation. The observer can experience words as polyvalent; they are arbitrary signs for a thing and (when written) not perceived as projections of the thing onto the plane on which they're viewed. Images, conversely, are experienced as correlated representations of visible things themselves.

A recurring theme in *The Invisibles* is imagining the unlikely conditions for exceptions to this particular distinction. King Mob's torturers inject him with a drug called Key 17, which "makes him unable to tell the difference between the word *describing* an object and the object itself." It causes him to see five slips of paper with the word "Finger" written on them as his own severed fingers; one of his torturers is subsequently injected with the drug herself, sees a coffee mug inscribed "World's Greatest Dad," and believes that her father is standing before her. (The "pop" routine mentioned earlier is another version of the same gambit.) Without the drug, attempts to present words alone as the realities they describe are "neuro-linguistic techniques . . . visible . . . as emergent structures": transparent frauds. (Lord Fanny knows "the secret common language of shamans—that language whose words do not describe things but *are* things." But that's not a natural language, and its thing-words don't have words to describe them.)

On the other hand, within *The Invisibles*, even natural language is capable of *generating* reality—causing things rather than being them—and is circumscribed only by the limits on its symbol system. The reactionary aristocrat Sir Miles claims that the alphabet "and all the names it generates were designed to set limits upon humanity's ability to express abstract thought. What you see depends entirely upon the words you have to *describe* what you see." This is emphasized by the business that runs through most of the final volume, in which several of the protagonists have access to the power of an expanded, sixty-four-letter alphabet. It's prima facie ridiculous if taken literally (would speakers of, say, Japanese have an entirely different perception of abstraction than speakers of English?). Nonetheless, the implication is that language determines perception—more or less what linguists call the Sapir-Whorf hypothesis.

Morrison also suggests that language alone is insufficient to the task of describing a higher-dimensional construct from the outside, because language use *causes* reality rather than *representing* its surfaces and is open to distortion. A complicated plot thread involves a crucial line of dialogue that gets disastrously misdelivered and misapprehended: "Edith said to call on Buddha," meant to deliver a message to a time traveler trying to get home with the aid of "the Buddha of compassion," ends up being heard and repeated by a one-year-old as "Edith says to call him Boody," which is how he names his teddy bear.

Even so, the essential power in *The Invisibles* is language use, because it's capable of expressing the invisible. Morrison uses a handful of historical figures as characters, and in one scene, Mary Shelley tells Lord Byron that "poets have a right to vanity and pride; they steal the power of creation from the gods. They remake the world with words and in the image of their dreams. The rest of us must then live in it." Later, King Mob claims that writing literally makes the world, if gradually: "Robin read a story called 'The Invisibles' and wrote herself a part in it until she realized it was all real."

One further, peculiar question remains to the observer of a work of art: Is it "fine art"? Morrison all but preempts the question; he specifically declines the condition of fine art for *The Invisibles*—or, rather, he rejects fine art, along with its associated social baggage, in favor of what he loosely calls "pop." (Of course, it's also reasonable to argue that it's not possible to abdicate fine art–hood.)

Exactly one familiar piece of fine art appears in *The Invisibles*: Picasso's *Guernica*. We see the former anarchist Beryl Wyndham standing in front of it, weeping, in the early 1960s. It turns out, though, that she's perceiving it with the kind of "interest" that, as Immanuel Kant noted in the *Critique of Aesthetic Judgement*, is fatal to a pure judgment of taste (to put it another way, you can't make an entirely fair and dispassionate assessment of an artwork if you've got a horse in the race). As we're later shown, she's seeing it not as Picasso's work but as a literal depiction of the 1937 bombing of Guernica, in which her lover died.

There are also a few more case studies of fine art tucked within *The Invisibles*. The easiest association with fine art is its presentation: nonsequential images on perfectly straight, flat surfaces, displayed as in a

Beryl Wyndham looking at "Guernica." Written by Morrison, drawn by Phil Jimenez and John Stokes. From *The Invisibles: Counting to None*, © Grant Morrison. All rights reserved. Used with permission of DC Comics.

gallery. When two *Invisibles* characters ride a train through a government facility, they see an extensive series of those sorts of images. They're all nicely composed pictures of horrible things: birds chained to a tree, a mushroom cloud, identical drones in an office. That doesn't keep them from being fine art, Kant notes: "Where fine art evidences its superiority is in the beautiful descriptions it gives of things that in nature would be ugly or displeasing. The Furies, diseases, devastations of war, and the like, can (as evils) be very beautifully described, nay even represented in pictures."

Kant also writes, though, that there's one thing that disqualifies pictures as fine art: being disgusting. We see one other "artwork" in *The Invisibles*, signified by its ornate frame: a mirror that's a gateway to the

What she's seeing as she looks at "Guernica." Written by Morrison, drawn by Warren Pleece and Philip Bond. From *The Invisibles: The Invisible Kingdom,* © Grant Morrison. All rights reserved. Used with permission of DC Comics.

Outer Church; out of which a grotesque, oozy, Lovecraftian monster shambles to feast on human flesh, attended by a well-dressed butler. Mirrors are a peculiar case within Morrison's cosmology, since they map higher-dimensional constructs onto lower-dimensional surfaces (in the world as we perceive it, that's three-onto-two). The "magic mirror" that turns up all over *The Invisibles* is always seen as liquid and three-dimensional, rather than flat, and reflects four-dimensional constructs: everything can be seen in it, and it's perceived as "living information." Flat mirrors, though, reflect only some visible aspects of the world and block others; there can always be something disgusting, like the monster, hiding behind their illusion or reflected in them. They are doubly impostors to the throne of fine art, and their imposture is enabled by sharing the accoutrements of art.

While he's toying with the historical framework of art theory, Morrison also gets in a few tweaks at the idea of the "pregnant moment" that comics have adopted from visual art, literalizing it twice in the course of *The Invisibles.* The minor character Edith Manning becomes the commander of time—she bends it, lives to the age of ninety-nine, and dies only when she wills herself to—but she miscarries her only pregnancy

Ragged Robin, free from linear time and literalizing the "pregnant moment," from *The Invisibles: The Invisible Kingdom.* Written by Morrison, drawn by Frank Quitely and John Stokes. From *The Invisibles: The Invisible Kingdom,* © Grant Morrison. All rights reserved. Used with permission of DC Comics.

in the presence of time distortions. The other chief representative of time is Ragged Robin, the time traveler. In 2005, at age seventeen, she imagines having a baby in the future, in a panel whose border is shaped like *The Invisibles'* logo. Robin is apparently pregnant when she begins her second time-machine trip, and when she reappears, depicted as a billion-bodied "time maggot," her time-garbled dialogue begins "baby in a dream on sex." Evidently, she's pregnant with time itself.

If Morrison is eager to distance *The Invisibles* from fine art, though, he tries even harder to position it as pop. It's fashion-obsessed, flippantly allusive, garishly colored, tied to its historical moment, even disposable—the background of one page is crumpled, stained paper, reinforcing its medium's ephemerality. King Mob's email address is RexPop@virgin.net. That's a pun on "rex populi" ("the king of the mob") but also on "king of pop." The POP that pops his nemesis, actually, is the apotheosis of populist "pop."

That scene's language-to-image-to-narrative triple play is followed by an even more vehement example of the same idea. Dane's concluding speech on the final page of *The Invisibles* ends with a four-panel sequence in which words dispense with and replace drawings. He says, in increasingly huge type, "See! Now! Our sentence is up." The second panel has only the words "our sentence is up," with no punctuation; the third is gigantic fragments of the letters U and P and a period; the fourth is as blank and unruled as the Invisibles' badge. But look again at that

The final scene of *The Invisibles*, as Morrison's words displace and then replace images and then disappear. From *The Invisibles: The Invisible Kingdom*, © Grant Morrison. All rights reserved. Used with permission of DC Comics.

period, even bigger and bolder than the one that ends the "Ithaca" episode of *Ulysses*. It's another form of the enlightening, single-color Barbelith shape. This time, though, the sign we see is generated directly by the written representation of language, instead of by its interpretation—the word becomes the visible representation of its invisible power.

The "up" at the end of *The Invisibles* is also, in a way, a call for its medium to grow up. For most people, growing up means giving up the things of childhood—superheroes, say. Morrison, though, has shown no interest at all in ditching the interests of his youth, especially superheroes. Instead, he suggests, growing up means understanding them more fully or using their pop mojo more wisely. (When I talked to him a few years ago, he mentioned that one of his *JLA* storylines had essentially been his way of discussing his depression "and saying: 'Superman—help me! Batman—help me!'") His superhero comics are usually wildly entertaining, because their point is to get his

ideas across to the widest audience he can manage. That's "pop magick": you're much more likely to change the world if lots of people are
paying attention.

Until recently, Morrison's own work mostly fell into one of two distinct categories: rip-roaring action-adventure stories whose conceptual
gestures are largely peripheral (*New X-Men*, his run on *JLA*, the splendid miniseries *We3*) and metafictional/mystical head-spinners for which
the crazy adventure stuff is mostly window-dressing (*The Invisibles*, of
course, but also a handful of shorter projects like *The Filth* and the utterly bizarre *Seaguy*).

The "synthesis" stage of that particular dialectic is *Seven Soldiers of
Victory*, a huge superhero project released as thirty comics in 2005 and
2006 (and collected into four books). The story involves stuff like pirates
called No-Beard and All-Beard riding the secret subway lines under a
New York City filled with every grand architectural project ever proposed but not executed in our world's New York, Frankenstein fighting
monstrous insect-riding slavers on Mars with a steam-powered flintlock,
and the solution to the mystery of the vanished Roanoke colony (they're
still Puritans, but now they're Puritan witches who live with their famil-
iars in luminous-fungus-lit underground caverns and worship the god
Croatoan). It's smart and complicated, and sometimes rushed and baffling, but mostly it's *awesome*, and where *The Invisibles* occasionally
kicks back to indulge its metaphysical side, *Seven Soldiers* starts ham-
mering the FUN!!! button on its first page and never really stops.

Still, it's loaded to the gills with subtext. It doubles as a Kabbalistic
parable that also discusses the relationship between two-dimensional
and three-dimensional existence and features symbolic correspon-
dences with the chakras and elements and planets—nearly every character, object, and incident in it has some kind of distinct allegorical
value. The symbolism, as clear as it is, is almost never made explicit, but
if you're looking for it, it's there on every page. It's mostly in the service
of two linked themes: an explanation of how humanity might evolve to
a higher state (Morrison's old favorite) and how superhero comics
themselves might evolve past their old paradigms into something useful

and meaningful to the present. There have been plenty of revisionist takes on the superhero in the last twenty years or so, but *Seven Soldiers* is the only one so far that suggests what the concept might *become*, instead of pointing it toward some kind of conceptual terminus and flooring the gas pedal.

Seven Soldiers consists of two "bookend" stories and seven four-part story arcs (each originally published as its own miniseries) about bottom-of-the-barrel characters who'd been kicking around DC Comics for thirty years or more: *Shining Knight, Zatanna, The Manhattan Guardian, Klarion the Witch Boy, Mister Miracle, Frankenstein,* and *The Bulleteer.* (The name "Seven Soldiers of Victory" was first used in the '40s, for a third-tier superhero team linked by the slimmest of threads to this one.) Each character's miniseries was drawn by a different artist or team—in the case of *Mister Miracle,* three different artists— and constructed with a different narrative style. The gimmick of the project was that the seven major characters never meet each other— they're not even in each other's frame of reference—but their stories are tightly woven together and collectively form one bigger story that happens over the course of seven days.

In fact, that gimmick is a bit cleverer than it looks. As a rather brilliant, anonymous article at the Web site Barbelith.com (named, yes, after the *Invisibles* thing) points out, one way of reading *Seven Soldiers* is as a specific interpretation of how psychological evolution works, modeled on the "spiral dynamics" theory. Spiral dynamics is a headache to explain, not least because it's got lots of contentious partisans, but the short version is that people and societies pass through various color-coded "levels of psychological existence," becoming progressively more enlightened as a survival mechanism. The Barbelith article argues that each of the seven characters "becomes a 'hero' by rejecting a level which some other character is busily, heroically, attaining"—which is why they never meet—and suggests some specific transitions. Klarion, for instance, goes from blue (ritualized fear of a higher power—in this case, being a part of a hyper-religious, action-circumscribed Puritan society) to orange (working with unexpected opportunities and resources).

It's a curious idea and not exactly far-fetched. Morrison never mentions spiral dynamics in the course of the series, but a lot of story beats support the Barbelith theorist. The implication of *Seven Soldiers* is that you become a superhero by evolving beyond your cultural context—by becoming enlightened and acting on that enlightenment. It's not necessarily something that happens when you get powers and put on a suit. The first "bookend" is narrated by the granddaughter of a minor Golden Age hero, The Whip. She feeds her appetite for thrills by continuing the Whip franchise (wondering if that makes her something other than a "crazy fetish person") and joins a team of other people who also desperately want to be superheroes—many of them souped-up, more badass versions of characters from the past. Before long, they've all been slaughtered for their trouble.

You can read that as a version of the recent history of superhero comics, trapped by nostalgia into repeating sixty-year-old ideas in nastier incarnations. (The big menace of the project is eventually revealed to be an evolved form of something much older that's surviving by strip-mining its own past.) In fact, none of the main characters in the *Seven Soldiers* miniseries *intend* to be "superheroes," as such—the only one with much experience in that category, the magician Zatanna, remarks ruefully that she was "a really *bad* superhero." Also, the only one of the seven who potentially counts as a white American man is Klarion, and even that's a big stretch. Morrison's got nothing against the idea of honoring the genre's past, and *Seven Soldiers* is deeply immersed in continuity, full of little allusions to obscure old comics. But they're *transparent* allusions, designed not to be noticed at all by readers who wouldn't catch them, and when previously published stories contradict what Morrison's got in mind, he cheerfully ignores them.

Instead of presenting each character's story in order, the book collections of 7S alternate chapters of each one (which is how the individual comics were published); the first, following the opening bookend story, is *Shining Knight*, a fish-out-of-water serial drawn with lush grandeur by Simone Bianchi. Sir Justin, the last survivor of the final battle of Camelot, and his flying horse, Vanguard, abruptly find themselves in present-day L.A., stalked by Guilt, a "Mood 7 Mind Destroyer." That's a smart way to work an allegorical reification into a science fiction setting. Sir Justin's Camelot, more than ten thousand years in the past, belonged to the era of the "bicameral mind," and he would of course believe that an emotion like guilt could be an actual entity, speaking to him and tormenting him.

Guilt, in a more abstract form, is also the enemy in *Zatanna*, which concerns a magician who's lost control of her will and the apprentice who helps her find her bearings again. "You want guilt?" she asks on the first page of her story. "I'll give you guilt. My name's Zatanna Zatara. I'm a spellaholic." Zatanna is Morrison's favorite kind of magician: she casts her spells with words, by pronouncing them backward. Her story, drawn by Ryan Sook and Mick Gray with a soft, bold, almost creamy line, also revisits another pet Morrison theme, moving from two dimensions to three. In a séance in its first installment, she encounters an entity that says what she's perceiving as a hexagon is really a cube, or a die (one of several important dice in the course of *Seven Soldiers*). Over the course of the next few pages, she and her companions encounter a series of square planes positioned at right angles in three-dimensional space. Some present themselves as walls, some as floors, some as picture planes (seen from an angle) that distort our views of the characters.

Later, Zatanna moves into a flatter world than her own and briefly tries to escape by reaching out her hand to entities she senses outside her time-stream and dimensional existence. Those entities are, naturally, *Seven Soldiers'* readers, who can move freely back and forth within her linear time sequence; her "reaching out" takes the form of pressing her hand up against the surface of the page. The point, though, is that she's attempting to *transcend* her figuratively two-dimensional (and fictional) existence and pass into our reality. For this, she's rewarded by the "seven unknown men" who live in the dimension above hers (all of whom are tall, skinny, bald, and rather Morrison-like; one of them even wears a DC Comics logo as a tie pin).

Bulleteer, drawn by Yanick Paquette and Michael Bair, is about a different kind of evolution—up and away from the immature sexuality of

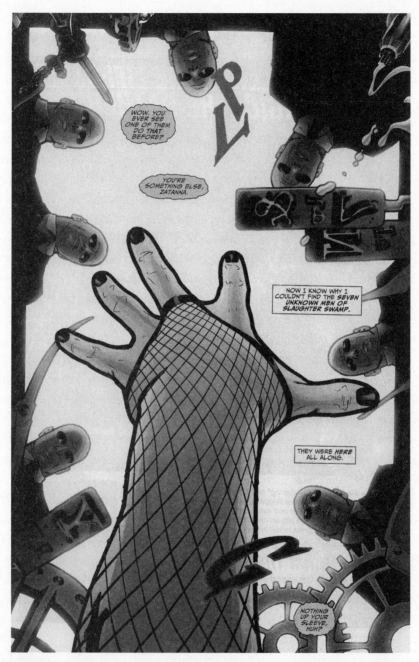

Zatanna reaches out to the Seven Unknown Men constructing the page on which she appears, from *Seven Soldiers: Zatanna*, written by Morrison and drawn by Ryan Sook and Mick Gray. From *Seven Soldiers of Victory, Vol. 3*, © DC Comics. All rights reserved. Used with permission.

superhero comics. Alix Harrower, its protagonist, has gotten impermeable metal skin, thanks to the experiment-gone-wrong that killed her husband, a superhero fetishist who wanted to give the two of them powers. Everyone else assumes that means she has to be a superhero, which is the last thing she wants; she's a good person but has absolutely no interest in beat-'em-up clichés. (Alix always appears in hypersexualized cheesecake poses; every other woman in *Bulleteer* looks more or less normal, except for her rival, a cynical old lady trapped in a body that has the permanent look, too familiar to comics, of a sexy-but-innocent teenager.) In one episode, she finds herself at a convention where fans can meet minor heroes—a harsh but dead-on parody of small comics conventions. The most heroic impulses in *Bulleteer*, actually, come from a supporting character who also appears in *Shining Knight*: Helen "Sky-High" Helligan, whose "power" is her ability to solve problems by getting enough perspective on them to understand them fully. Near the end of the story, Alix's part of the "victory" comes about unintentionally, as a by-product of her compassion and resistance to aggression.

At the other end of the scale is *Frankenstein*, drawn by Doug Mahnke, which is about, well, Frankenstein. (The monster, not the man: he explains that he named himself after his creator.) His solution to every problem is brute force; he has no need for the niceties of plot mechanics. How does he get to Mars and back? He's Frankenstein. How does he travel a billion years into the future? The caption that explains it: "All in a day's work . . . for FRANKENSTEIN!" It's the most deliberately "immature" of the *Seven Soldiers* series, operating entirely on kid logic, with the conflicts between obvious good and obvious evil resolved by good beating up evil. In the context of a project about growing up, *Frankenstein* would be easy to present as somehow not all there or underrealized—but a society without children is in as much trouble as one with nothing but children, and a healthy society in the spiral-dynamics system includes all the levels of psychological existence, not just the highest. At a panel discussion in the summer of 2006, asked what his dream project would be, Morrison replied that he wished he could just keep writing *Frankenstein* forever.

The other three *Seven Soldiers* miniseries are inspired by characters created by Jack Kirby. Maybe that's Morrison's homage to the most fertile imagination in the history of American comics; maybe it's a suggestion that part of what superhero comics have to evolve past is the style that's defined them. (The final episode of the project includes a flashback to 40,000 B.C., when "Earth's first superhero" came into being; that segment is drawn by J. H. Williams III in a precise imitation of Kirby's mature style.) In the '40s and '70s, Kirby drew a generic hero-with-shield called the Guardian, usually associated with a kid gang called the Newsboy Legion. Morrison's brightest move in the 7S version of *The Manhattan Guardian* (with art by Cameron Stewart) is to draw a connection between the character and the news. The new Guardian is the in-house superhero of a daily newspaper ("we don't just report crime—we fight it!").

The original *Klarion the Witch Boy* was a mid-'70s Kirby creation and unusually mediocre in everything except its character design. Morrison's version (drawn by Frazer Irving) discards everything except a few characters' names and appearance; this time, Klarion is one of the aforementioned subterranean inbred Puritans, itching to see the world of "blue rafters" above the caves that are all he knows. Again, that could be a metaphor for mainstream comics, trapped in the underground of a subculture for so long that they've turned pale blue and desperately fear change; Klarion is a hero because he embraces change and wants to break through to the sunlit world above.

The most perplexing *Seven Soldiers* miniseries is also the most explicitly Kirby-inspired: *Mister Miracle*, a lateral look at Kirby's "Fourth World" mythology. The "Fourth World" was originally three linked series Kirby wrote and drew in the early '70s, *New Gods*, *The Forever People*, and the original *Mister Miracle*, as well as his related tenure writing and drawing *Superman's Pal, Jimmy Olsen*. All four titles had some magnificent images and resonant ideas undermined by clumsy writing and idiotic wordplay. They centered on the struggle between two planets, New Genesis (good!) and Apokolips (evil!), and their respective rulers,

Izaya and Darkseid. The latter was after something called the "Anti-Life Equation" that would allow him to destroy free will. Not subtle.

For the last thirty years, there's been revival after unsuccessful revival of the "Fourth World" concepts: other cartoonists couldn't summon up anything like the raging power of Kirby's artwork, and Kirby's own attempt at a conclusion to the story in the mid-'80s was just a mess. Morrison's take on *Mister Miracle* deliberately avoids challenging Kirby on his own turf. Instead of Kirby's familiar Mister Miracle character, Scott Free (ouch), he casts a bald, black American earthling who'd briefly appeared in the original Kirby series, Shilo Norman. The concept of *Mister Miracle*, in all its incarnations, is that the character is a "super-escape artist." As readers of Michael Chabon's *The Amazing Adventures of Kavalier and Clay* know, that particular profession makes a nice metaphor for the kind of escapism superhero comics offer, and the miniseries is largely about how one kind of life can be an escape from another. It is also drawn by three different teams of artists, which actually works just fine, because the protagonist's perspective keeps changing too.

The first three issues of the 7S: *Mister Miracle* are a sidelong take on the "Fourth World." After Shilo Norman escapes from a black hole in which he encounters Kirby's bald god Metron (Morrison has talked about meeting Metron himself in a magical ritual), he experiences a sort of crisis of conscience, in which everything seems freighted with cosmic meaning. "Higher worlds of Manichaean purity locked in a grim, eternal struggle with our earth as their battleground?" his shrink, Dr. Dezard, asks him. "Ideas like that might make you a little crazy if you were to take them seriously." Dezard, however, is a stand-in for Kirby's torturer Desaad—in fact, everything Shilo encounters in his terrestrial life is a "humanized" version of a Fourth World character or concept.

The fourth and final part of 7S: *MM* is a concentrated blast of allusion and signification, starting with its front cover (the chapter-head image in the book collection). The covers of the 7S miniseries' fourth issues are images of the main character leaving or escaping. What we see here, though,

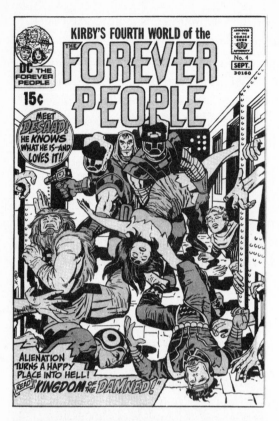

Desaad is introduced in *Forever People*, one of
Jack Kirby's over-the-top early-'70s "Fourth
World" comics. *"Forever People"* #4, ©1971 DC Comics.
All rights reserved. Used with permission.

is Mister Miracle's tombstone:
"HERE LIES MISTER MIR-
ACLE—SUPER ESCAPE
ARTIST—FREE AT LAST."
Mister Miracle's mask is
draped across the front of it.
("Free at last": the escape
artist has escaped from the
"Life Trap," as Morrison calls
it a few times; there's the civil
rights allusion for this African-
American character; and, perhaps, at last the second-
stringer Shilo Norman has at-
tained the status of Scott
Free.) But the image, if you
look more carefully at it, has
something very strange about
it. It's an image of the grave,
seen from an angle, but the
perspective is all wrong. In
fact, it's not an angle shot, but
an *angle shot of* an angle shot:
a two-dimensional view of a
two-dimensional image that
has been rotated through a third dimension. (That effect also appears earlier in *Mister Miracle*, notably on the final page of Morrison's first issue, as
well as in *Zatanna*.) The back door of his grave leads into the world outside and above the comic book's pages; his final escape, at the end of *Seven
Soldiers*' last episode, is through not just the grave itself but the cover of his
own comic book.

The first time we see the tombstone, though, it's followed by a series
of rapid-fire flashbacks to scenes that happened or might have happened or didn't happen in Shilo's life: a crippled, castrated Fisher-King

Shilo ODs on pills; he dies of old age; he practices escaping as a child; he sees his older brother shot to death; he becomes the warden of a super-prison called the Slab and confronts a pair of "God Exterminators"; he dies as an infant; he throws himself in front of the bullets that killed his brother. Finally, he emerges from the black hole for real, which isn't quite the "it was all a dream" cop-out it seems to be at first. Shilo has lived through everything we've seen and escaped to a higher level of consciousness in the process; this has been his initiation ritual, and now his true life can begin.

In other words, *7S: MM* is the hoariest of superhero-comic traditions: an origin story. But what it's the origin of is a certain kind of advanced consciousness—like the other *Seven Soldiers* story arcs, it's a narrative of enlightenment. What Morrison's implying, though, isn't just that superhero stories are exaggerated metaphors for aspects of human experience, but that human experience is in fact the same thing as their titanic conflicts, described in different terms but just as grand. An old man in a wheelchair is also the god Metron; soul-extinguishing despair is also the Anti-Life Equation; a struggle between two people is also the wars of New Genesis and Apokolips.

The cover of *Seven Soldiers: Mister Miracle* #4, drawn by Freddie E. Williams II: a two-dimensional image of a rotated two-dimensional image, hence its odd perspective. "Seven Soldiers: Mister Miracle" #4, ©2006 DC Comics. All rights reserved. Used with permission.

If superhero comics don't speak to the realities of their readers, that's not a problem with the genre but a demand to improve its execution. *Seven Soldiers* is an attempt to simultaneously outline and exemplify that formal leap; its reach sometimes exceeds its grasp. Its premise, though, is that when two-dimensional characters and their stories take on enough complexity and depth, they effectively become real, bursting through the fourth wall or the surface of the page, slipping into their readers' world and charging it with the energy of the fantastic. Morrison desperately wants to inscribe that idea into reality, and this astonishingly ambitious story glimmers with the faint, startling light of magic.

CHAPTER 17

Dave Sim: Aardvark Politick

In March 2004, the Canadian cartoonist Dave Sim published the final twenty-page installment of *Cerebus*, the six-thousand-plus-page comic book epic he'd been writing and drawing since 1977. (Virtually all of it is collected in sixteen volumes published by Sim's company, Aardvark-Vanaheim.) It is an absolute masterpiece—one of the most ambitious and fully realized narratives of the past century. And its flaws are plentiful, wide, and maddening, and penetrate straight to its core.

For one thing, if you want to start at the beginning, you'll have to wade through a few hundred pages of Sim's juvenilia. When he started *Cerebus* at the age of twenty-one, he had no idea that it was going to be more than a short-lived parody of *Conan the Barbarian*—not even Robert E. Howard's original stories, but the early-'70s Marvel comics drawn by Barry Windsor-Smith, whose style is ineptly imitated by the early Sim. He didn't work out the project's scope—three hundred issues, one every month for its final twenty-four years, concerning several centuries' worth of politics and religion in a fictional continent rather like medieval Europe—until a nervous breakdown a couple of years into it.

There's a lot of *Cerebus* that's deliberately derivative, too. Dozens of characters are modeled on real-world celebrities, cartoon characters, and comics artists, and a handful of Sim's jokes will be lost on anyone

A tense moment with "Ham and Mary Ernestway," from *Form and Void*.
©2007 Dave Sim and Gerhard.

without an intimate knowledge of the comics scene of the '80s and '90s. Most of the *Melmoth* volume of *Cerebus* deals with the death of Oscar Wilde; the core of *Going Home* is a series of parodies, pastiches, and paraphrases of F. Scott Fitzgerald (as "F. Stop Kennedy"); *Form and Void* includes a long section adapted from Mary Hemingway's (excuse me, "Mary Ernestway's"—her husband is "Ham Ernestway") African diaries, mostly to set up the argument that Mary actually murdered Ernest, because women are by nature soul-sucking voids.

Oh right. About two-thirds of the way into *Cerebus*, something in its tone abruptly cracks, and the misogynist pus that bubbles up never fully abates after that. (Sim has insisted that he's not a misogynist, just "not a feminist," but he's become rather a single-issue candidate about it; he also claims, for instance, that using *s*'s rather than *s*' for the possessive form of names that end in S is a Marxist-feminist plot. If all you have is a hammer, everything looks like a nail.) It becomes rather tough going if you like your art to be compatible with your politics, unless you're one of the eighty-five people on the planet whose sexual politics are as far right as Sim's.

Make it all the way to the home stretch, and you'll hit the wall, where all but a few readers give up (and Sim's assistant and background artist of twenty years, the single-named Gerhard, nearly quit): the "Cerebexegesis," as it's informally known, a 140-page sequence in the penultimate book, *Latter Days*, whose typeset passages (in tiny type) are a very close reading of the first thirty-eight chapters of Genesis. Very close indeed. The gist of it is that God and YHWH are separate entities, and that the latter (whose name should be pronounced "Yoohwhoo") is the diabolical, female piece of God's spirit who lives inside the Earth, tries to usurp God's rightful place (because isn't that just *like* a woman), and is more or less the Demiurge.

This is, as it turns out, what Sim himself believes, although weirdly enough it's intended to function as a parody of far-fetched exegesis in the context of the story. As he points out, if it turns out to be the truth, he's "the only sane person who perceives reality accurately and everyone else alive today and everyone who has lived in the last six thousand years or so is and was immersed in full-blown schizophrenia." It's accompanied by a cute, intricately realized visual riff on the history of European art movies, Freud and Jung, Woody Allen's career, and Jules Feiffer's and Robert Crumb's drawing styles, but the text itself is unbearable. By the end, the *character who's reading it in the story* gives up and starts listlessly flipping through it.

That's followed by an even more unreadable forty-page explanation of the universe, in pseudo-archaic biblical language and a Gothic font, plus footnotes, for example, "'The light,' then, becomes a *simultaneous* 'living metaphor' of both an electron *and* electron motion; that is, a *simultaneous* 'living metaphor' of both the spirit of God moving upon the face of the waters *and* the wave created by that movement of the spirit of God. The bringing forth of 'the light,' therefore, made merged, simultaneous existence a reality (and the lunatic template which women thus apply to everyone and everything)." Sim reportedly prides himself on incorporating prose into comics, but it's probably much easier to appreciate *Cerebus* if you simply skip over all the typeset parts.

On top of all that, the protagonist of *Cerebus* increasingly resists any kind of sympathy: he's a murderer, a despot, a fool, a fuckup who has plenty of chances to do great things and blows it every time thanks to his pathetic vanity and romantic delusions. When he dies at the end, he is, as a sort of oracle predicts much earlier in the story, alone, unloved, and unmourned. Also, he's an anthropomorphic, hermaphroditic aardvark.

That's the apology—it's hard to discuss *Cerebus* without apologizing, one way or another; the good stuff is coming. Before I get any further, I should note that Sim's personal reputation tends to overshadow his actual work. I'm not interested in addressing any more of the particulars of his biography here, and, having spent all of an hour in the same room as the guy about twenty years ago, I'm not in a position to assess his psychological state. But his I-dunno-maybe-everyone-*else*-is-schizophrenic routine is significant; he's also described himself as a sort of professional schizophrenic, who lives in his invented world at least as much as consensus reality and tends to conflate the two. That's where his art comes from and where it leads.

Cerebus is a novel of (very big) ideas, and one of the biggest is the nature of reality and its relationship both to subjectivity and to the stories that communicate versions of reality. "The definition of schizophrenia—the inability to perceive the difference between reality and fantasy—is, to me, self-evidently ludicrous because it presupposes that there is a universally agreed upon perception of what reality is," Sim has written, and several thousand years ago someone asked something similar. *Cerebus* doesn't refer directly to the Bible until about 90 percent of the way through the series, with one major exception: at the climax of its opening third, there's a version of the trial of Christ, with Cerebus in the Pontius Pilate role. He asks the prisoner before him the same question Pilate asked Christ: "What *is* truth?"

Sim provides plenty of answers, which of course aren't very satisfying—a bitter running joke is that every time any of his characters explain the way things are, either they're lying to serve their own interests or they're simply deluded, even if what they're saying makes perfect sense at the time. Some characters poach their subjective truths word for word from real-world writers; one volume ends with a passage from John F. Kennedy's inaugural address being written on a cell wall by an imprisoned, idiotic "Anarcho-Romantic" aesthete who believes that what he thinks is Cerebus's philosophy (it's not) is the great hope of the common people—or, as most of the characters in power call them, "the peasants and livestock." The scene is set up as a swelling-strings mo-

A quasi-heroic moment from the end of *High Society*, whose context makes it bitterly scornful. ©2007 Dave Sim.

ment, and you can take what he's writing ("we shall pay any price, bear any burden, meet any hardship, support any friend, oppose any foe, in order to assure the survival and the success of liberty") at face value if you like—it just means you're being willfully blind to its context.

Cerebus demands a sort of schizophrenia from its readers, as well: it makes you succumb to its conflation of objectivity and subjectivity and blatant deceptions, and see patterns of meaning in coincidences and unrelated events. There are a handful of extended dream sequences, which seem at first like Cerebus's unconscious mind reprocessing his experiences and on rereading are revealed as prophetic visions. Images and words appear as echoes years before or after their actual occurrence; the reader's world keeps intruding into the fantasy world on the page. Close a volume of *Cerebus*, and veiled allusions to it seem to be everywhere. (The furious, resentful Bishop Powers, so insistent on dogma that he can't see what's in front of him, now seems to prefigure the later Sim himself.)

People who've heard of Sim but haven't actually read *Cerebus* tend to think of him as some kind of cackling Henry Darger figure, endlessly filling up crude volumes of his awful fantasies. They couldn't be much more wrong. He's a shockingly gifted cartoonist, one of the most

Sim and Gerhard turn a very long talking-heads scene in *Church & State*, vol. 2, into a visual spectacle. ©2007 Dave Sim and Gerhard.

innovative storytellers in the history of his medium, and he routinely pulls off technical feats that no other cartoonist would dare. (*Church & State* includes an eighty-page sequence that's little more than two characters in a small room having a political argument and ends with a hundred-page monologue; both are utterly compelling as visual narrative, which spares the reader from the numbing *Fountainhead* effect of the Cerebexegesis.) He draws even grotesque caricatures with absolute certainty of each character's body, not just their expressions and physical shapes but the way they move through space and interact with each other. And Gerhard's micro-detailed background architecture has the same kind of certainty of every beam and stone.

The formal symmetries and echoes within *Cerebus* are spectacular, especially given that every chapter has gone unrevised since its initial publication. The series can be divided into three units, each roughly two thousand pages long and each culminating in a failed ascension into Heaven. Alternately, it can be split into a "male half" and a "female half" (everything we believe is true in the first half is inverted in the second) or on a sort of angle into a "Cerebus half" and an "Astoria half" (which I'll explain shortly). Almost from the beginning, it's loaded with resonances and symbol systems and setups—the final few scenes abruptly detonate thematic explosions whose groundwork had been laid decades in advance.

It's also a novel of characters and character actors—some are one-dimensional types who are there for the sake of the plot or comedy, some have a profound internal life and evolve over time, and Sim loves to screw with readers' perceptions of which ones are which. Jaka, a dancer Cerebus meets early in the series, is set up as his one true love—the thing that can save him, the other half with whom he can eventually be reunited. But after we've had a few thousand pages to work from that assumption, Sim points out, brutally, that we (and Cerebus) know *nothing* about her beyond the surface—that we've simply imagined her as the story's romantic heroine for all the wrong reasons. Then he redeems the idea of their love as redemptive, and then dashes it again, and again. Near the end, the aged, lecherous Cerebus compromises what little is left to him so he can seduce a young woman who doesn't realize that she looks exactly like the long-dead Jaka. It's a devastating scene, and a few readers, unable to bear the idea that the story had perverted their expectations so badly, somehow convinced themselves that it depicted a happy reunion with the real Jaka, magically young again.

What makes the series' twisted mechanics move is that Sim is a hell of an entertainer when he feels like it—the early books, especially, are often knock-down hilarious, and there are flashes of wicked comedy right up to the end. He's especially brilliant as a mimic. When he "casts" a real person (or a character from someone else's comics) in his story, he gets them down immaculately—their speech patterns, their body language, the kind of role they'd be perfect for. Lord Julius, the bureaucrat who maintains a stranglehold on the continent's economics by his control of interest rates (and, after money is abolished, by his monopoly on distilleries), is none other than Groucho Marx. A pair of hammer-wielding, handlebar-moustached, not-too-bright brothers share the voice of Yosemite Sam. Two dissolute princes slumming it in the lower city are late-'60s versions of Mick Jagger and Keith Richards. ("Keef! You 'aven' bin strite since fou'een-ow-*noine*!") The efficient, nannyish, overenunciating functionary who's forever putting everyone else in their places as cruelly as possible is a mercilessly caricatured

Mosher, Losher, and Kosher capture the Three Stooges' body language, from *Latter Days*. ©2007 Dave Sim and Gerhard.

Margaret Thatcher. And the bumbling "Three Wise Fellows" who install Cerebus as the figurehead of a new religion go by Mosher, Losher, and Kosher: they're the Three Stooges.

The Stooges' faith is the caboose on the series' train of philosophical and religious sects, which each define reality their own way. At the beginning, there are the Tarimites, who believe that the god Tarim created everything out of the void; their church is split into feuding Eastern and Western divisions. (Cerebus becomes the Eastern church's pope and immediately announces that unless everyone hands over all their gold, pronto, Tarim will destroy the world by fire. Of course, being an infallible pope means that he gets to dictate the truth: a very dangerous thing.)

The Tarimites' opposite number are the Terimites, who believe that the goddess Terim created everything out of herself. Their affiliates, the Cirinists, believe that the only appropriate requirement for citizenship is giving birth; they lead an iron-fisted agrarian revolution that eventually takes over most of the continent. The Kevillists, a Cirinist splinter group, are basically anarcho-libertarian feminists. Then there are the Pigts, who believe that Cerebus is the Messiah who will lead them to glory, and the Illusionists, who are the reason the series includes at least six *different* characters named Suenteus Po, and more. There are also Jews and Muslims in the world of *Cerebus* by its end, but no Christians—although one major character is crucified, off-panel.

All of this ideological conflict was in the series' background long before it became the focus of the story—where *Cerebus* begins is very different from where it ends up, and its tone changes dramatically from volume to volume. The first book, simply called *Cerebus*, begins with our hero as an itinerant, long-snouted barbarian from up north. In those days, Sim apparently thought an aardvark Conan was a funny idea, and he didn't realize he'd be stuck with it for the rest of his career. Cerebus has some Conanesque adventures, most of them involving parodies of familiar characters, notably Elrod (Michael Moorcock's character Elric with a Foghorn Leghorn accent), the Cockroach (Batman as a babbling lunatic), and Lord Silverspoon (Prince Valiant as a whiny rich kid). By the book's end, Sim is finding his feet as a writer and artist, and Cerebus starts to get mixed up in politics.

High Society is the second and funniest book and by consensus the best place for readers new to Sim to start. It's the one in which Cerebus shows up in the elegant but nearly bankrupt city-state of Iest, gets dragooned into its political intrigues, and eventually becomes its prime minister. In the two-volume *Church & State*, Sim floors the gas pedal, and the arrival of Gerhard's backgrounds radically improves the art. The deposed Cerebus is reinstated as prime minister, then appointed pope, then ascends to the moon on a tower of stone skulls. Instead of Tarim, he meets "the Judge" (drawn to resemble Lou Jacobi in the film of Jules Feiffer's *Little Murders*), who explains the history of his world and his universe to him—its macrocosmic pattern is that the female light is smashed by the male void—and dismisses Cerebus's life as a waste.

The Judge's speech can be read as the dramatic climax of the series or, if you prefer, the first of its three climaxes. When Cerebus returns to Earth for the drawing-room tragedy *Jaka's Story*, Iest has been taken over by the Cirinists' totalitarian, fascist matriarchy, and he takes refuge with Jaka, now a dancer in a pub, and her husband, Rick; meanwhile, their friend Oscar, that is, Oscar Wilde, is writing a book about Jaka's aristocratic origins that's mostly "true" in a Wildean aesthetic sense. Cerebus doesn't even appear in most of the second half of *Jaka's Story*; he returns for the crawlingly paced *Melmoth*, in which he sits traumatized in a café where, upstairs, "Sebastien Melmoth"—Wilde again, but not the same character—is dying.

A frenetic story arc called "Mothers and Daughters" takes up four volumes of the book collections, *Flight*, *Women*, *Reads*, and *Minds*. Cerebus launches an insurrection against Cirinist rule, which is immediately crushed. In its aftermath, he encounters Cirin (the founder of Cirinism—sort of), Suenteus Po (the leader of the Illusionists), and Astoria (the woman who first elevated Cerebus to power and the architect of Kevillism). Cerebus and Cirin begin to fight to the death but are rocketed separately into space, while pages of the story alternate with an exceedingly tiresome roman à clef about the comics industry, which becomes a screed about how men are actually the capital-L Light and women, who, incidentally, can read minds, are the capital-V Void, and if you're guessing that this is where *Cerebus* starts to go seriously awry, gold star.

The other point of "Mothers and Daughters," though, is that it's where Sim ramps up the metafictional games he's hinted at earlier in the series: directly addressing the reader through semiautobiographical proxies and as himself, toying with the levels on which he controls his audience's reality and perceptions. (*Women* also features a delicious parody of Neil Gaiman's *Sandman* comics.) When Sim returns to the plot in *Minds*, Cerebus, stranded in outer space, encounters his creator—"Dave"—who explains his nature and his failures to him, then sends him back home when he promises to change his life.

That's the second climax, at the two-thirds mark; Sim implies that the end of "Mothers and Daughters" is the end of *Cerebus* proper and that everything that comes after it is a sort of epilogue. For the final third, the pacing mostly slackens, and there's an increasing atmosphere of futility and stasis. Cerebus spends all of *Guys* in or by a pub, where he drinks himself insensible for years on end while the world outside its windows is utterly transformed. Eventually, all his friends grow old and leave, and he becomes the bartender. Then Rick, Jaka's old husband, walks in—this is about ten years since we've last seen him. In *Rick's Story*, he's writing a book about his religious conversion, and Cerebus is at the center of his belief system. Shortly after he leaves, Jaka arrives; together again at last, she and Cerebus decide to move up north to his hometown, Sand Hills Creek.

Their trip constitutes the thinly plotted, involuted, visually gorgeous two-volume *Going Home* storyline—the second volume's called *Form and Void*—most of which documents the on-and-off friction between them, interspersed with weird literary pastiches. When they finally get to Sand Hills Creek, everything that's wrong with their relationship detonates horribly.

Latter Days and *The Last Day* are an epilogue-to-the-epilogue. Thirty years or so pass; Cerebus, longing only to die, is abducted by adherents of the religion that Rick has founded around him. With an army behind him, he conquers the continent and establishes his own fascist utopia, then retires. Finally, he encounters Konigsberg, the Not-So-Good Samaritan (Woody Allen), to whom he explains the aforementioned unique interpretation of Genesis. (That's right: explaining Judaism *to* Woody Allen.) Another hundred years later, Cerebus is wrinkled, sick, senile, and dying, and his empire is in tatters; he's written a final testament for his son to use to carry on his dynasty, but his hopes are categorically shattered. He dies, and we find out what happens to him after his death, in a short, blackly brilliant sequence that casts a new light on everything we've seen before it.

That's a lot of plot (and I'm leaving out much more), but it happens in jolts—more than a few times, revolutions change everything while Cerebus is dozing or not paying attention. Sim loves to play with readers' perceptions of time and significance. A twenty-page sequence dissects three seconds' worth of events; a few years pass between panels without remark (the only immediate cue that time has passed is that one character suddenly has gray streaks in his beard). In *Latter Days*, Sim casually mentions that a major character has been dead for a while—and, a few pages later, lets it slip that actually the entire supporting cast of the series is dead.

But the weird, bumpy way Sim presents his world's history, as a series of not-entirely-trustworthy, not-entirely-compatible narratives that focus on immediate details and miss the big picture, is absolutely in line with his rejection of consensus reality. He explicitly opens up *Cerebus* to interpretation: if he makes it clear that he's not emphasizing a lot of the important parts, it's an open question which the important parts *are*.

For instance, *Cerebus* can be read as a story about power and what it means to exert one's will over somebody else, which makes the crypto-anarchist Astoria—arguably the series' most interesting character—its central figure opposite Cerebus, who desires power only for its own sake. The section from Astoria's first appearance to her last occupies almost exactly half the series, and things go straight to hell the moment she departs, rejecting the idea of power altogether and going off to cultivate her garden à la Candide. Like pretty much all the politicians in *Cerebus*, she thinks of herself as a reformer. She's an advocate of democracy because she believes it can lead to women's suffrage, and her split from Cirinist maternalism proceeds from her commitment to absolute self-determination—which turns her into a master manipulator and a control freak. (Even in chains in her enemies' dungeon, she's running the show.) When the crunch comes, of course, the movement she believes she's pointed toward self-determination expects her to lead them.

But no vision of reality can be wholly trusted in *Cerebus*; nothing is unambiguous. The only major character that Sim suggests is actually righteous is Rick, who's a gullible dweeb at first, sweet-hearted but not too bright. In his later years, he's delusional to the point of derangement, interpreting everything in his environment—a bar, a chair, a woman who flirts with him—as a religious portent. The "holy book" he writes is the work of a hopeless, obsessive schizophrenic. He is also, as it happens, the true prophet of God. In order for the final sections of the series to make sense, you have to believe both of those things at once—which goes beyond willing suspension of disbelief and into a deeply uncomfortable realm. That way lies madness. That's the idea.

There remains the great hurdle for readers that the final third of *Cerebus* is just a hard, nasty slog. Besides the excruciating prose interludes and misogynist blather (latter-day Sim writes as if he's expecting to be nailed on hate-literature charges—"total-dick-literature" is more like it), the character interaction that makes the first two-thirds fun is gradually extinguished. Most of the final volume is decrepit old Cerebus locked in a tastefully appointed room, muttering to himself. It's exhausting. You could, perhaps, skip the "epilogue" of the last six books or decide that the series should really be called *Astoria* and bail out when she leaves. But then you'd miss the payoff. And, inconveniently, as *Cerebus* gets sludgier and meaner, Sim gets better as a cartoonist—more expressive, more daring with design, more committed to integrating even his lettering into a *gesamtkunstwerk* of word and image and idea. Think of it as the *Birth of a Nation* of comics.

Maybe Rick is crazy; maybe he really is a holy man; maybe one doesn't necessarily contradict the other. From *Rick's Story*. ©2007 Dave Sim and Gerhard.

This brings us back to the "aesthetics versus politics" problem. It's comforting to see first-rate art that's compatible with one's own political views, but to see first-rate art that's violently opposed to one's own political views is necessary. If your sympathies are even vaguely secular or liberal, then the second half of *Cerebus* is an attack on *you*. It demands a response in the reader's mind, and if you can see past "what a *total dick*," you're likely to come out of it with your own thoughts about gender, power, and the nature of creation (with both a large and a small C) clarified.

Anyone can come up with a grand twenty-seven-year plan for a mammoth work of art, but Sim, along with very few others in human history, actually went through with it. He made the commitment to his story and spent more than a quarter of a century grinding away at it, and he *finished* it, exactly when he said he would. A serious, ambitious, completed large-scale work, no matter how deeply flawed it is, beats a perfectly envisioned but unrealized project every time. At the very least, *Cerebus* is worth reading for the same reason a grand, half-ruined cathedral of a religion not your own is worth spending time in: It's a cathdral. Take what you can from it.

CHAPTER 18

The Dark Mirrors of
Jim Starlin's *Warlock*

The *Warlock* serial that Jim Starlin wrote and drew between 1974 and 1977 is a crazily dense, heady, philosophy-minded space opera that includes some of the oddest and most dazzling mainstream comic books of their era. Starlin's voice—and it's very much Starlin's, since these are some of the first auteurist comics that Marvel published—is spectacularly inventive; his love of design and his roaring, motormouthed prose style gave his story a tone unlike anything else. And there's a pointed subtext about the aesthetic and corporate context of mid-'70s comics just beneath its frenetic surface.

When Starlin started working on the "Warlock" feature in *Strange Tales* #178, he was a promising but still uneven young artist who'd gotten some notoriety for his run on *Captain Marvel*, part of which he'd also written. *Strange Tales* was the kind of title where a loose cannon couldn't do much harm: a bi-monthly series whose recent issues had been devoted to the fourth-tier characters Brother Voodoo and the Golem, now turned over to Warlock, another fourth-tier character, whose series a couple of years earlier had folded after eight issues.

At the time, Marvel historically hadn't been big on auteurs; the guy writing the dialogue and the guy drawing the pictures had almost always been different people. (The one major exception had been Jim Steranko, who'd written and drawn some Nick Fury stories a few years earlier, but Steranko's stories were generally excuses for him to draw cool-looking psychedelic images without much in the way of a plot attached.)

Starlin immediately made it clear that *Warlock* was totally creatively controlled by him, drawn according to his personal aesthetic rather than a "house style"—he even colored a few of the earliest installments himself. (His third issue's credits riff on how unusual the non-division of labor was: it's written by "Sam Jiltirn," inked by "J. L. Minirats," colored by "Ms. Natjiril," etc.) The roughly three-hundred-page serial jumped around between a few series and didn't always live up to the promise of its earliest chapters. Over the last thirty years, though, it's held up exceptionally well; even if the writing is occasionally ungainly, it's always striking to look at and sometimes spectacular.

The story begins with an undigested lump of exposition: a recapitulation of the small pile of comics in which blond, golden-skinned, quasi-divine Adam Warlock had previously appeared. Created by Stan Lee and Jack Kirby in *Fantastic Four* #66 back in 1967, the character had originally been known simply as "Him," which led to a certain amount of pronoun trouble. He'd drifted through a handful of other series, including eight issues of his own title, mostly as a sort of science-fictionalized crypto-Christ figure in a confused *Island of Dr. Moreau* scenario. (Somewhere along the line, he'd picked up the plot device that Starlin focused on most: a vampiric, soul-sucking gem that he wears like a bindi in the middle of his forehead.) Starlin draws the whole opening sequence in the styles of the stories' original artists, with one ingenious twist: the whole thing's narrated by a chatty amphibian-headed creature sitting on a pink chair with eyes and tentacles of its own.

That's the first sign of an idea that Starlin keeps returning to: science fiction as the realm of allegory. For his purposes here, creating stories about distinctly nonhuman creatures is useful as a distancing effect to make them understood as symbolic rather than realistic. When we finally get past the recap, though, we see a beautiful young human woman in a spacesuit being chased by three grotesque alien assassins.

She's one of only two human-color-skinned human types of any significance in the first half of Starlin's *Warlock*; otherwise, virtually every character we meet is physically alien, an arrangement that recalls nothing so much as the cantina scene from *Star Wars*. (Note that *Strange Tales* #178 was cover-dated February 1975, and *Star Wars* opened in May 1977.)

In any case, the monsters chasing the girl turn out to be Grand Inquisitors from something called the Universal Church of Truth, which has "found her soul unsalvageable." Warlock tells her that he'll protect her; the Inquisitors kill her anyway and disappear. He briefly reanimates her, and she explains that the Church is run by a five-thousand-year-old being called the Magus. ("The basic teachings of the Magus are, to say the least . . . admirable! If all lived by his teachings, the universe would be a place of peace! Unfortunately, those teachings only apply within the Church!") Then the Magus himself appears. He looks exactly like Warlock except for purplish-silver skin and a gigantic purple Afro, and explains to him, in a bad-acid-trip visual sequence, that the two of them are in fact "one and the same being!"

Even at the beginning, Starlin is relying heavily on the visual devices that will characterize the whole serial: repetition, symmetry, and inward motion. He'll repeat a little vertical sliver of a panel three or four times, tracking a change in its image (the sequence in which a crackling field of energy extends above the dead woman's head over four panels while the Magus introduces himself is tiny but incredibly effective); he'll compose images whose composition is symmetrical from left to right (often focusing on Warlock's face, with the soul gem reinforcing its symmetry); he'll zoom in to an extremely tight close-up of a face over a few panels. All of those tricks underscore the story's themes: change that isn't progress, dichotomous oppositions, looking into the mind instead of out into perceived reality.

For the next half-dozen issues (in the middle of which Starlin's serial moved over from *Strange Tales* to a relaunched *Warlock* series), we get a brain-twisting time-paradox story concerning the conflict between Adam

Jim Starlin repeats an image with variations as the Magus introduces himself in *Strange Tales* #178. ©2007 Marvel Characters, Inc. Used with permission.

Warlock and the Magus. It turns out that the Magus is in fact Warlock's future self, who was sent to the distant past by an ethics-scrambling being called the In-Betweener and subsequently became a galaxy-conquering tyrant, setting himself up as a god. Trying to find out more, Warlock encounters the Magus's second-in-command, a sunken-eyed Theda Bara type called the Matriarch, who's the other recognizably human character of the story's first half. He succumbs to madness (in a crucial episode called "1000 Clowns," which we'll get to shortly) and ends up joining forces with one of Starlin's pet favorite characters, another demigod called Thanos, who, as his name suggests, is in love with (the personified) Death and wants to prove his love by killing everything.

But the Magus already knows everything Warlock will do and say, because he's lived through it from the other side—he mocks Warlock by playing a sort of actor's mirror game with him as he summons the In-Betweener. The only way to keep himself from becoming a tyrant, Warlock realizes, is "cosmic suicide." He travels forward in time a year or two, meets his mortally wounded future self ("My life has been a failure!" says the dying Warlock. "I welcome its end!"), and steals his own soul. Thanos, "the champion of death," is the victor; time is reset, with another church replacing the Magus's in the past and present; and Starlin abruptly finds himself treading water.

With the main engine of its plot gone, the '70s incarnation of *Warlock* lasted only another four issues. They're not bad, but they're not anywhere near the heights of the Magus sequence. The first is a strained comedy-relief piece starring Warlock's sidekick, a hedonistic troll called Pip who was Starlin's excuse to sneak stuff past the Comics Code (at one point he exclaims, "For the sake of the Great Coprolite!"). It's followed by the two-part "Star Thief" story involving an Earthman in a vegetative state who develops psychic abilities, makes the stars disappear, and manifests a gigantic shark in outer space. The idea that derangement or loss of the senses is the only way for humans to transcend corporeal existence and enter the abstract, conceptual realm that Starlin's been exploring is promising, but, again, the story involves a gigantic shark in outer space, and there's no getting around that. The final issue, a messy attempt to wrap up a bunch of subplots, is so disorganized that it's titled "Just a Series of Events."

Still, Starlin had an actual conclusion to Warlock's story in mind: a conclusive-looking fakeout that ran in 1977's *Avengers Annual* and a sequel that appeared a month or two later in *Marvel Two-in-One Annual*. Both stories nominally star a whole lot of other characters—Spider-Man and the Thing, in particular, play major symbolic (and minor plot) roles in the second—but they're really the wrap-up to Warlock's story. (They also feature the only clear influences from *Star Wars* in the whole thing: a rather Lucas-looking spaceship, a reference to a "tractor beam," and a very Obi-Wan–like line of dialogue: "I felt the psychic screams of unbelieving millions—dying suddenly . . . unexpectedly.")

As Thanos plots the "stellar genocide" for which eliminating the Magus cleared the way, Adam Warlock's life falls into ruin. At last, his past self comes to claim his soul as he dies; we see the same dialogue between the two Warlocks again, and it's even scarier the second time. But his spirit returns for a few moments and transforms Thanos into stone, "the petrified form of his own corruption," before returning to the paradise inside his soul gem.

Despite its inappropriately happy ending, the tone of the whole sequence is unnervingly fatalistic. It was shocking in 1975, and it's still odd now, to see an adventure comic about a hero's utter, abject failure; not too many lead characters in mainstream comics think things like "now I realize that my body is nothing more than a useless shell for my ego." From the beginning of Starlin's story line, Warlock is fated to betray himself, his friends, and everyone else; the Magus, we discover, may be formally a villain, but he's on the side of life, and Warlock is de facto on the side of death. Nearly every time he acts heroically, he makes himself an accessory to genocide. Removing himself from the conflict—by killing his externalized future self—barely helps. The fact that Warlock's death redeems nobody is the final step in Starlin's repudiation of the character's earlier Christian allegory: in this story, organized religion is cruel and murderous, our hero steals souls instead of saving them, and the world becomes lost to him. (In the one striking moment of the "Star Thief" sequence, Warlock returns to Earth to find that his body has expanded while he was out in space—the planet is now the size of his thumbnail, and he's invisible and intangible to it.)

Mostly, though, Starlin used *Warlock* as a vehicle for playing with various kinds of dichotomies and dialectics. There are a lot of neatly two-sided conflicts going on in the series—life versus death, order versus chaos, free will versus predestination, and so on—and the characters are only too happy to discuss their respective ideologies, even in the middle of a fight. The Magus, on seeing Warlock steal a bunch of his soldiers' souls, says, "You've just proven yourself worthy of becoming that which I am! You spout sanctimonious trivia about honor and goodness . . . but to gain your own ends you've just slaughtered a room full of men! You've at last revealed me to be, not a perverted version of your soul, but rather, a true image! A true image that's about to see that you no longer interfere with what has been and will be!" Thanos replies, as he zaps the Magus with some kind of hand-beam-thingy, "Fortunately, a true image, like truth itself, is a subjective concept, one to be accepted or rejected depending on the viewer's prejudices, so . . . MAGUS, I REJECT YOUR TRUTH!" (These are ungainly clumps of text for sure, but you have to hand it to Starlin: it's not like you'd mistake them for anyone else's ungainly clumps.)

Warlock was also one of the first American metacomics—at least part of its subtext concerned the comics industry and the art of cartooning. The crucial "1000 Clowns" episode has the most blatant jokes about the business: Warlock encounters a pair of evil clowns named Len Teans (an anagram of Stan Lee, with an extra N) and Jan Hatroomi (Marvel art director John Romita, with an extra A), who want to adapt him to "house style" by sticking a clown nose and greasepaint on his face. (It's fairly safe to assume that Starlin was unhappy about the company-line consistency demanded of Marvel artists in those days.) The routine involving clowns building a tower of garbage that repeatedly collapses because of the diamonds someone keeps sneaking into it is not exactly subtle, either, and Starlin himself puts in a cameo appearance as a hapless technician attempting to program Warlock.

Other behind-the-scenes references in "1000 Clowns," though, actually tie into a more interesting thematic dialogue in *Warlock*: the struggle between the legacies of Steve Ditko and Jack Kirby, the two most important artists of Marvel's '60s peak. The look of Kirby's comics, filtered through John Romita, had become the look of comics-the-Marvel-way (power, solidity, grandeur), and his early-'70s DC comics were unabashedly the work of a big-name auteur. Ditko's side of the Marvel style (frailty, surreality, outsiderdom), meanwhile, had started to fade from view; by 1975, he'd been drawing ghost comics for Charlton and working on his own experimental projects for a few years.

Starlin's pretty clearly chosen his side: he dedicates "1000 Clowns" to Ditko, "who gave us all a different reality." The reality in question is the way that Ditko had drawn the Dr. Strange stories in the same comic, *Strange Tales*, a decade earlier, and the first page of Starlin's story shows Warlock in the middle of an unmistakable pastiche of Ditko space—

Dr. Strange's weightless realm of abstract geometries and free-floating bubbles and spires.

Warlock himself, of course, is a Kirby creation. But Starlin starts introducing Ditko-style gestures from the beginning—that outer-space chase scene looks like something out of one of Ditko's space-war comics (especially the alligator-patterned spacesuit one character is wearing), and a planet in the background has the crisscrossing curved lines that are a Ditko hallmark. When he zooms in on the soul gem, it's full of stars and planets, looking like nothing so much as Ditko's conception of Eternity from *Strange Tales*.

Both Kirby and Ditko had

Jim Starlin draws Warlock hovering in Ditko-space in *Strange Tales* #181. ©2007 Marvel Characters, Inc. Used with permission.

gotten deeply into the idea of ideological opposites in the early '70s—Kirby with the yes-we-get-it-already conflict between New Genesis and Apokolips in his "Fourth World" comics, Ditko with his bluntly Ayn Randian self-published comics. (The symmetrical, black-versus-white costume of Starlin's In-Betweener could have come straight out of Ditko's *Mr. A*—a neat reversal, considering that the In-Betweener is supposed to represent neither/nor morality, between "good and evil . . . logic and emotion . . . god and man.") And Starlin's pet character Thanos has more than a passing resemblance to Kirby's "anti-life" champion Darkseid.

Kirby, though, always drew a pumped-up version of reality—even his freakiest settings have gravity and perspective and solidity. Ditko, at least in his Dr. Strange stories, drew "a different reality": a nonphysical realm, whose perception comes from magic or madness or drugs. (*Warlock* is a very druggy series, although given that it was a Comics Code–approved title in the '70s, the closest Starlin could come to mentioning it was casual comments from Pip the Troll like, "Say, I wonder what's inside this hookah?") That different reality isn't just what we see in the clowns' world: it's Warlock's mental landscape after he embraces insanity, and later the territory for his fight with the In-Betweener. Physical conflicts, on the other hand, are Kirby's domain. A fight scene in *Warlock* #11 is a blatant Kirby tribute, appropriating his explosive gestures, aggressive foreshortening, and four-panel layout, and the free-for-alls of the final episodes are generally Kirby paraphrases too.

The Kirby/Ditko dichotomy helps to explain the somewhat tacked-on final installment, the *Marvel Two-In-One Annual*. In theory, it's a team-up between the Thing and Spider-Man, which is peculiar, since both of them seem to have been shoehorned into an Avengers story. But it makes sense to include them for the aforementioned symbolic reasons: they're the archetypal characters from Kirby's and Ditko's respective '60s stints at Marvel. Just to rub it in, the story interpolates a discussion between "Lord Chaos" and "Master Order"—the former is drawn as a '70s Ditko distorted head-abstraction; the latter recalls Kirby's '70s creation OMAC without the Mohawk. (Shortly afterward, Starlin would go on to draw a few OMAC stories of his own.)

All of that, though, is an undercurrent to the main thrust of the story. More than anything else, Starlin's *Warlock* is the product of an artist exploring his science fiction interests (he'd evidently been reading a lot of Michael Moorcock) and artistic voice, full speed ahead. The beats of his drawings and his words play off each other constantly; everyone rattles on in that weirdly crabbed prose style, but even the crammed word balloons become design elements on the page, and he gets away with bizarre metaphysical hand waving by making it look cool and thrillingly paced.

See, for instance, the four-page sequence leading up to the first time we see Warlock's suicidal conversation with his other self. The first page (a fight between Thanos and the Magus) includes four big Kirbyesque panels, with each tier punctuated in its middle by a slivered close-up: one side of the Magus's face, the other side of Thanos's. Then we get a sequence in which Thanos's assistant runs away (first a zoom in on her face, then two static shots of an airlock as she escapes through it—the inward movement/repetition trick again), and we see Warlock in his Ditkoesque inner world, looking at "the crossroads of [his] fate"—literally drawn as five blue paths extending into hot pink space, one of them discoloring into black. That's followed by alternating horizontal panels of Warlock purifying and destroying that possible path—an image it's safe to say no writer who wasn't going to draw it himself would ever have thought of—and the ongoing Thanos/Magus fight scene.

After that, we get an extraordinary seventeen-panel page: two panels in which we see the Magus starting to fade out of existence (and our point of view rocks ninety degrees to the side), and then three tiers each containing five increasingly narrow panels (the second tier a bit taller, the ones flanking it equivalent sizes). Each tier is topped with a three-line caption; looking down each tier, we see a zoom in on the symmetrically placed In-Betweener, a static shot on one "life path" as Warlock races along it and dives into the brilliance at its end, the symmetrically placed Magus racing toward us as he disappears, a zoom in on the symmetrically placed Thanos as he rears back his head and laughs to reveal a death's head inside his mouth, and a static shot of an abstract Ditkoesque fleur-de-lis among the stars erupting into a burst of lines and vanishing. It works both as fine-tuned design and as a careening piece of storytelling.

Starlin doesn't seem to have been able to realize some of his grand plans for these characters. In the final issue of *Warlock*, a prophet tells Adam Warlock that over the next year, his life will come to ruin; he'll see the deaths of his friends Gamora and Pip and cause the death of the High Evolutionary (a character from his pre-Starlin series). That's the last we hear of the High Evolutionary, though; the next time Starlin picks up the story (that *Avengers* annual), it jumps ahead to Warlock discovering the dying Gamora, and by the end of the issue both Pip and

314

Starlin lets his design carry the plot in a climactic scene from *Warlock* #11. ©2007
Marvel Characters, Inc. Used with permission.

The second appearance of Adam Warlock's death scene, drawn by Starlin and Joe Rubinstein in *Marvel Two-In-One Annual* #2.

Adam Warlock himself are dead. But that climactic scene—Warlock accepting the death that's come for him, the death we as readers had already seen and were sure he could somehow avoid—is still shattering.

Since the early '90s, Jim Starlin has returned to Warlock a few times, with diminishing returns—bringing the character back at all was a perversion of the dramatic conclusiveness of his death. What there is of Starlin's original story, though, is worth tracking down, as a high point of mainstream comics' generally iffy period in the mid-'70s and as a pointer toward the gradual move away from "Marvel style" that followed its lead, but mostly as an eccentric, engaging entertainment in its own right. The Magus sequence appeared during the fertile moment between the Harlan Ellison–edited anthology *Dangerous Visions* and *Star*

Wars, when SF had an active and exciting avant-garde wing. *Warlock* wasn't just a tribute to that scene; it was part of it, extending experimental SF's formal tricks and druggy madness into comics. If some of its ideas have become clichés over the past thirty years, that's mostly because they were so potent the first time.

CHAPTER 19

Tomb of Dracula:
The Cheap, Strong Stuff

There are two kinds of horror stories. One is matinée horror, in which some kind of monster or grotesquerie rages across a landscape of innocence until it's finally destroyed and the natural order of things is restored. Its threat is neatly defined—it's Frankenstein, a vampire, a werewolf, a plague of zombies, a serial killer in a mask; there are always specific rules for how it can be beaten. The pleasure of reading the story is the pleasure of seeing justice done and the formula cleanly executed.

The other kind of horror story is the kind in which no good ending is possible and humans exist only to be crushed and devoured. The tone of these stories is feverish, and the threat they describe can't quite be mapped out or terminated. Their gist is that "life is painful and disappointing," as Michel Houellebecq put it by way of introducing the form's icon, H. P. Lovecraft. Horror stories of this kind aren't rousing and heartening; they don't give pleasure so much as a sense of vertiginous awe in the face of a doom too huge to escape, a clutch at the pit of the gut that doesn't easily vanish.

Tomb of Dracula, a series that ran from 1972 to 1979, was originally meant to be an example of the first kind of horror, quickly aspired to become the second kind, and sometimes got there. Written by Marv Wolfman and drawn by the penciler/inker team of Gene Colan and Tom Palmer for almost its entire run, it developed a consistent, unique mood and style, ripping away the moral center of matinée horror and replacing it with a frantic desperation echoed in the tempestuous, helter-skelter flow of Colan and Palmer's artwork.

The origin of the series, fittingly enough, had to do with the lifting of a taboo. The initial formulation of the Comics Code, from 1954, decreed that "scenes dealing with, or instruments associated with walking dead, torture, vampires and vampirism, ghouls, cannibalism, and werewolfism are prohibited." When the Code was revised in 1971, it softened a bit: the walking dead and torture were still out, and blood and gore were frowned upon, but "vampires, ghouls and werewolves shall be permitted to be used when handled in the classic tradition such as Frankenstein, Dracula, and other high calibre literary works written by Edgar Allan Poe, Saki, Conan Doyle and other respected authors whose works are read in schools around the world."

Marvel Comics pounced at the opportunity; within months, they'd launched *The Monster of Frankenstein*, *Werewolf by Night*, and *Tomb of Dracula*. There was room in the newsstand-comics mainstream, back in the '70s, for genre comics that didn't have much to do with superheroes; because they weren't the top-of-the-line titles, they often got assigned to inventive young writers and artists who weren't interested in "house style." (Other notable examples: *The Hands of Shang-Chi, Master of Kung Fu*, on which writer Doug Moench and artist Paul Gulacy realized that as long as they threw a couple of pages of Bruce Lee martial-arts ultraviolence into every issue, they could get away with whatever else they felt like; Michael Fleisher's nihilistic scripts for the grim, long-running Western *Jonah Hex*, including a story about the end of Hex's career in which the dead gunfighter's body was stuffed, mounted, and displayed in a touring Wild West show; Don McGregor and P. Craig Russell's "Killraven" serial in *Amazing Adventures*, which began as a riff on *The War of the Worlds* and eventually became a framework for Russell's Wagnerian science fiction spectacle.)

Wolfman, who wrote the last sixty-one issues of *Tomb of Dracula*, was part of that new generation. Gene Colan, who penciled all seventy issues, wasn't: he was forty-five years old when he got the gig, a veteran superhero artist who'd been drawing *Iron Man* and *Daredevil* for years. The first year of the series is a mess, with four different writers and five different inkers, but by issue #12, the Wolfman/Colan/Palmer team fell into place and stayed there.

Their run, as well as a handful of other Dracula-related stories published around the same time, has been reprinted in the first three volumes of Marvel's *Essential Tomb of Dracula*—fat, heavy books printed in black and white on newsprint. It's actually overwhelming to read more than one or two issues' worth at once: for most of its run, it seems to barely know where it's going from page to page. The plot of *Tomb*, though, isn't nearly so much the point as its tone, which deepens from harmless capes-and-fangs fun to suffocating despair.

At first, Wolfman occasionally made the error of telling stories focused directly on Dracula and his actions, which had the unfortunate side effect of making it look as if the reader was supposed to sympathize with the Count. If Frankenstein's monster is a tragic figure, and a werewolf (like *Werewolf by Night*'s Jack Russell) is a metaphor for someone struggling with base urges, a vampire is pure malevolence: not even a sympathetic rogue but a destroyer and sexual intruder. It's hard to get suspense out of putting a deliberately repugnant character in danger. Occasionally, Wolfman tried to force readers to cheer for Dracula, which didn't work terribly well. *Tomb of Dracula* #27, "Night-Fire!" (virtually every issue's title ended in an exclamation point), begins with a scene that's unintentionally funny on several levels: Dracula trapped in a chamber into which holy water is pouring.

Before long, though, Wolfman wisely made *Tomb of Dracula* mostly an ensemble comic, about a group of people who had in common only their dealings with vampires, and to move the spotlight away from the title character as much as possible, despite the requirement of giving customers the blood-sucking action they were ostensibly paying for. (There's at least one issue in which Dracula doesn't appear at all.)

The chief protagonists are a loose collective of vampire hunters, and we mostly see Dracula through their perceptions of him. Frank Drake, a nondescript blond descendant of Dracula, and Rachel Van Helsing, a nondescript blonde descendant of Bram Stoker's Dr. Abraham Van Helsing, were both part of the series before Wolfman showed up. Wolfman's first issue introduced Quincy Harker, the son of Stoker's Jonathan and Mina Harker: an ancient, wheelchair-bound inventor who's been fighting vampires his entire life, he always wears dark glasses and turtlenecks, since decades of vampire attacks have left him with a ripped-up neck and sun sensitivity. Later, the cast grew with the addition of Hannibal King, a vampiric private eye out for revenge on the rival of Dracula's who gave King his fangs, and Blade, a fearless vampire killer and blatant rip-off of Shaft, right down to his girlfriend referring to herself as his "woman." (Other members of the crew weren't as entertaining—the shlubby comedy-relief hack writer Harold H. Harold and his Drac-admiring lust object Aurora Rabinowitz haven't aged well.)

One of the series' signature devices, though, was its shorter-lived supporting characters—much shorter-lived. Wolfman's favorite trick was to introduce a new character with a short biographical sketch or a page or two of low-key conversation, then have Dracula slaughter him or (more often) her a few panels later. Whenever you see a caption in *Tomb* like "Janet Golin and Stu Summers attend school at Harvard. Stu is studying law, while Janet works to become a doctor," you know that Janet and Stu have about a page left to live. That's one of the genre requirements of horror: the evil entity has to maintain its rep for evil by killing off the characters who share the audience's aspirations.

The problem Wolfman (and the writers before him) faced is that another genre requirement of matinée horror—like Bram Stoker's *Dracula*, say, or any vampire movie—is that the plot drives fairly rapidly toward its conclusion, which is the destruction of the evil entity. The structure of a vampire story is a direct progression to its payoff, in which the vamp is vanquished and all the survivors go back to their lives. *Tomb*, though, was a series, meant to go on as long as it kept selling. Every so often, Dracula would get a stake through his heart, and then

Wolfman would have to come up with some reason for the stake to be pulled out again.

It was the pulling out of the stake, though, that transformed *Tomb* to a deeper kind of moral horror—about the willing corruption of the good, rather than just the death of the innocent. In #32 (an even more wretched title than usual: "And Some Call Him . . . Madness!"), Quincy Harker confronts Dracula with a room full of trick mirrors that appear to be surrounding him with crosses, a trap door that opens to drop garlic on him, and so on—the sort of death traps mad villains spring on old-fashioned heroes. In the cliffhanger scene at the end of the issue, Drac has been shot full of arrows and about to expire at the hands of Harker, who's got a justified grudge against the five-hundred-year-old vampire who killed his wife and, earlier in the series, forced him to stake his own daughter, Edith, through the heart.

And then the story becomes genuinely chilling. The dying Dracula tells Harker to call Rachel Van Helsing, who's been kidnapped by a group of vampires who say they'll kill her if Harker lets their boss die. Rachel begs for death anyway—"I'm not important in all this! *Kill him! Kill him!"*—and of course she can't have it; Harker revives Dracula to spare her life. On his way out of Harker's house, Dracula snatches the urn containing Edith Harker's ashes, and Quincy tells him to put it down. "Very well, Harker," he replies. "I'll put it down. *But not before I scatter away the ashes of your stinking offspring, you stupid, insignificant fool!*" He smashes the urn and exits laughing. Harker: "NO!" Apropos-of-nothing caption: "GAMES!"

That's one problem with reading *Tomb of Dracula* now with the expectation that its writing will work in the "literary" way we expect of art comics—Wolfman's prose is purple at best and hilariously overwrought at worst. It's also full of spelling and grammatical errors. One extended story line involves a character named Shiela Whittier; by the time anybody pointed out that's not how the first name is usually spelled, it was probably too late. Or, as Wolfman might have put it: far, far too late!!

Still, *Tomb* is bluntly effective, and it's hard to imagine a subtler version of Wolfman's writing working nearly as well: this is the cheap,

Harker's showdown with Dracula from *Tomb of Dracula* #32, written by Marv
Wolfman and drawn by Gene Colan and Tom Palmer. ©2007 Marvel Characters, Inc.
Used with permission.

strong stuff. *Tomb* makes no bones about being a genre comic—not a twist on vampire horror, not a "subversive" reinvention of vampire horror, but a straight-up, lustily and faithfully executed vampire story whose one unusual aspect is that it opts for the Lovecraftian tradition of trembling hopelessness instead of the monster-movie tradition of vanquished evil. Its text works in the service of its mood: a deliberate, consistent look and feel that's entirely in line with the traditions (call them "clichés" if you like) of its genre. The series is nominally set in the Marvel universe—the superheroes Dr. Strange and the Silver Surfer both put in brief appearances over the course of the series—but its place within the shared Marvel setting's matrix is mostly irrelevant. The *moral* universe of *Tomb of Dracula* is one in which humans are largely helpless prey, hopelessly compromised and adrift in a sea of their own blood, and there's no one to defend them against their vampiric harvesters except God—maybe.

In that sort of environment, as the great pulp writers knew, clichés are useful, because they're moral anchors: affirmations of preformed ideas. The issue where *Tomb* hits its stride, and one of its most entertaining, is also one of its most cliché-ridden, #25 (the last in the first volume of reprints), "Night of the Blood Stalker!" When a beautiful woman walks into a P.I.'s office, desperately seeking help, the caption reads, "I'm a leg-man, understand? And when I take in a pair of dark, slender stems, resting in the doorway of this hovel I laughingly call an office, I take my sweet time before checking out the rest of what's staring at me." And so on. The story marches precisely through the tropes of hard-boiled detective stories until Dracula shows up and blows the whole thing sideways.

All the human characters in *Tomb* are familiar types. They have their roles cut out for them from the start and stay that way until they're turned into vampires and get staked, or jump out a window to avoid getting bitten, or quietly drift off stage. Only Dracula is a free agent, a force unhampered by a moral code. He isn't *only* the cliché with a cape who vants to suck your blood: he is pure vileness, a being so evil that he corrupts everything in his perimeter, making it impossible to do good. (In one sequence, the vampire hunters revive him from another staking so that he can save the world from something even nastier; by way of thanks, he announces that he's about to go kill an innocent person, just to make them complicit in murder.) He deals death to those who don't want or deserve it, denies death to those who crave it, forces parents to destroy their children, and laughs. Justice and the grave are never more than a temporary inconvenience to him. He takes everyone's will away.

Tomb as a seventy-issue unit doesn't exactly read like a single, overarching story—it mostly seems improvised from chapter to chapter, and as with most improvisations, it's got a lot of flab and flailing. By halfway through the series, though, Wolfman and Colan have worked out a distinctive mood: total panic, both in the story's plot and in its images. Dracula believes himself to be noble and believes that he deserves to take whatever he desires, but he is ultimately so unknowable that he's capable of acting honorably just to be contrary. His hunters perpetually fail in the clutch, doubt themselves and their motives, act in bad faith. Death is dealt out meaninglessly and is itself meaningless. Clichés are all there is to hold on to.

What makes *Tomb of Dracula* work as comics, though, is that Colan and Palmer's artwork has the same adrenaline-addled effect. Panels nudge into each other's space, their borders keep drifting away from right angles and being obscured by fog and steam, space is warped or glossed over, and swirling lines are everywhere. In #42 ("A Final Battle Waged!"), one scene happens among blinding beams of light; all we can make out are fragments of Dracula's face and cape, and a box with a brain in it seen from an impossible perspective. The rest is all rushing streaks of ink, mist, and light eradicating the skewed-angled panel borders.

By the final third of the series, everything Colan and Palmer draw begins to sublime into shadow and steam. They develop a swirling, almost abstract line for action scenes, making physical presences dissolve into bursts of motion. There's no reliable sense of gravity, no perspective that isn't warped as if by heat, no setting that's drawn in more than a sketchy, contingent way. Even Dracula's facial features keep shifting. Everything

An almost totally abstract fight scene from *Tomb of Dracula* #42,
by Wolfman, Colan, and Palmer. ©2007 Marvel Characters, Inc. Used with permission.

solid may turn into air, and every mist may be a vampire about to rip somebody's throat out.

There's a cartoonist's rule of thumb that every page should have at least one pair of feet visible—it means that the reader can get some sense of scale and proportionality, in order to see how everything fits together. That's exactly what Colan doesn't want to offer the reader in *Tomb*. His layouts, crammed with close-ups and strangely angled perspectives, violate that rule constantly (much more than his artwork for non-horror comics), so you never know exactly where you are or how big or small anything is. Toward the end of the series, when you do see a foot, it's as likely as not to be the shoe sole of a character leaping away from the reader's vantage point, and the irregular borders of Colan's panels seem like crude attempts to contain images that want to streak across the page.

The final, extended story line in *Tomb* is the most visually impressive of the series and one of the weakest in terms of plot. It's an attempt by Wolfman to produce a grand, coherent story arc about Dracula's struggle with God; sadly, grandness and coherence weren't *Tomb*'s strong points. Dracula ends up married to a quasi-Satanic cultist named Domini, who gives birth to their child, Janus. The kid is somehow or other aged to adulthood immediately and turns out to be an angel who inhabits the painting of Christ that's the only religious relic left in the abandoned church where Dracula has taken up residence. By the penultimate issue, Drac defends a few children against marauding vampires by gripping a crucifix even though it burns his hands. But there's no sense of moral order to the way the religious symbols are used—the upshot of the story is almost "I would have done it, too, if it hadn't been for that meddling God."

Tomb of Dracula abruptly ended with #70 ("Lords of the Undead!")—a double-sized issue, condensed from a longer, already completed sequence in which Dracula got killed yet again. The series' conclusion, in which Dracula and Quincy Harker meet for a final battle in pouring rain and both perish in an explosion, doesn't feel at all final. In fact, two months later Dracula was revived for a new *Tomb of*

Colan and Palmer's artwork for this scene from *Tomb of Dracula* #68 deliberately avoids offering a physical anchor for the reader. ©2007 Marvel Characters, Inc. Used with permission.

Dracula series in an oversized magazine format that didn't have to be approved by the Comics Code (and was therefore much more open to blood, boobs, and cussing); Wolfman, Colan, and Palmer produced a couple of stories for it, but by then they'd clearly lost interest.

Over the quarter century since *Tomb* ended, Wolfman and Colan have continued to collaborate occasionally on related comics: a few more Dracula specials and miniseries at Marvel, a horror series called *Night Force at DC* with another Van Helsing relative in its cast, a project for the smaller publisher Dark Horse called *The Curse of Dracula* (with an entirely different version of the Count), even a parody of *Tomb* for a Simpsons Treehouse of Horror comic. If there's a series right now that's captured the sustained moral rootlessness of *Tomb of Dracula*, it's probably Robert Kirkman's open-ended zombie dystopia *The Walking Dead*. *Tomb*, though, was the product of a moment when comics about monsters seemed freshly permissible, and cartoonists had just started to think about what was really monstrous about them. Wolfman and Colan knew that what's scary about Dracula isn't the blood he spills; it's the thought that he can spill it at any time and that there might be no good reason he shouldn't be able to.

CHAPTER 20

Kevin Huizenga:
Visions from the
Enchanted Gas Station

In "Lost and Found," one of the central stories of Kevin Huizenga's exceptional debut book *Curses*, his character Glenn Ganges flips through the mail, imagining the missing-child and last-seen-with images on "Have you seen me?" postcards as panels in "an accidental graphic novel whose story is mostly hidden, though sprawling landscapes are implied and tragic scenes are hinted at." In Huizenga's comics, everything has an intrinsically interesting story of its own—even junk-mail ads and suburban sprawl and annoying bird noises, things that most people do their best not to perceive at all, become crucial parts of a grand and gradual narrative.

Huizenga's been a cult hero in the art-comics world since the late '90s, initially for his self-published *Supermonster* minicomics and more recently for a series called *Or Else* and a separate *Ganges* project. (He also wrote and drew the Center for Cartoon Studies' promotional booklet, a splendidly bizarre little comic book in its own right.) The nine stories in *Curses* mostly appeared separately in various anthologies over the past few years; all but one of them feature Glenn Ganges, Huizenga's default protagonist, a quiet, literate sort living in the Midwest, usually with a woman named Wendy who's his girlfriend in some stories, his wife in others.

Glenn's not really an autobiographical stand-in, although his perceptiveness and loopy imagination are obviously a lot like his creator's. Sometimes he seems more like Carl Barks's version of Donald Duck: an infinitely durable Everyman in a long-sleeved T-shirt whose life circumstances are whatever they have to be for any given story. Still, one major aim of Huizenga's comics is to explain the complicated systems that shape people's lives and emotions—at least as far as it's possible to understand them. The individual stories here vary enormously in tone and technique and aren't directly connected by plot threads, but they can be read as the components of a single, elliptical narrative about children longed for, found, and lost again, and how people in the world of the living can understand the torments of hell.

Huizenga cares a lot about titles—he's published a minicomic, *Untitled*, which consists of the various titles and logo designs he considered for *Or Else*. (He's also very interested in creative processes; other Huizenga minicomics detail the way he designed a character who appears on three pages of *Curses*, and excerpt the doodles and notes he makes during sermons in church.) The word "curses" is the sort of thing a villain might say in the kinds of simple cartoons that inform Huizenga's drawing style (Hergé's *Tintin*, E. C. Segar's "Popeye"), but living under a curse is also the closest a person can come in the world to damnation: a punishment that needs supernatural intervention before it can end.

The title of *Curses* also refers, more directly, to its best story, "28th St.," a tour de force of cartooning adapted very loosely from Italo Calvino's own adaptation of an Italian folktale, "The Feathered Ogre." The setup is that Glenn and Wendy are trying to have a baby, and it's not working ("You have the most halfass sperms I have ever seen," a doctor informs Glenn). Eventually, he discovers that he's under a curse, and the only way to lift it is to pluck a feather from an ogre who lives under 28th Street—a hellish stretch of stoplights and strip malls in Grand

Rapids, Michigan, where Huizenga once lived.

Like most of *Curses*, "28th St." is drawn in a spare, whimsical, almost old-fashioned cartooning style, built around symbolic abstractions. Glenn has dots for eyes and a line for a mouth; all the cars in the story are the simplest possible "sedan" or "SUV" glyph; a character's surprise is shown by his feet flying through the

An Hergé-style doctor gives Glenn the bad news in "28th St." ©2007 Kevin Huizenga.

air with a puff of speed lines coming out of them. The future baby that Glenn imagines is drawn to look a bit like Swee'Pea from "Popeye."

What Huizenga's really up to, though, is so conceptually tricky that a "realistic" style would make it impossible to render; his artwork's surface simplicity makes the reader fill in the blanks of the transformations Huizenga suggests with a handful of nonchalantly confident lines. On the first page of "28th St.," a tangle of roads with houses alongside them prefigures the next panel's tree branches with birds perched on them. The rest of the story is one long, gliding fluctuation between suffocating reality and hallucinatory fantasy. Glenn, trying to find the feathered ogre, meets a gas station attendant who informs him that he's come to the right place: "This is an enchanted gas station. We have enchanted gasoline. . . . How it works is you got to squirt some in your eyes. Then you have visions." Over the next few pages, the deadened landscape of Home Depots and Jo-Ann Fabrics mutates into abstracted shapes and animal forms; then a rainstorm washes all the scene's new geometries and clots of language away until 28th Street regains its old form. Glenn is directed toward the ogre by one of the "lost boys," the Sudanese refugees in Michigan mentioned in "Lost and Found," who's cursed with insomnia. At the end, the defeated ogre becomes a flock of cursing birds.

The rainstorm that washes away the enchantment of Huizenga's landscape in "28th St." ©2007 Kevin Huizenga.

But it's the *next* story in the book that's actually called "The Curse"—its premise is that Glenn, Wendy, and their newborn daughter can't sleep because they're being tormented by the screeching of starlings. That becomes a springboard for Huizenga to go off on a fascinating tangent about how the birds were introduced into North America and the refer-

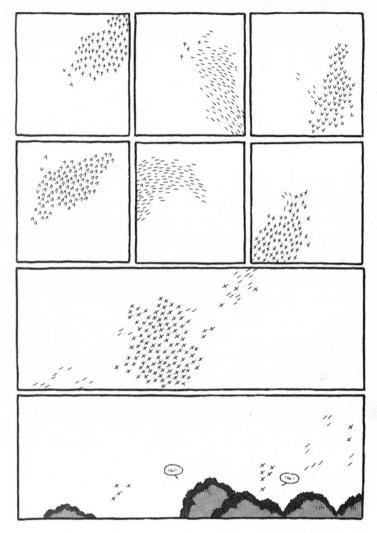

Huizenga's exquisite abstraction of a flock of starlings in "The Curse." ©2007 Kevin Huizenga.

ence to them in Shakespeare's *Henry IV*. One page of the story is nothing but starlings flying in formation, and it evokes their motion with the faintest suggestion: Huizenga draws them as a flurry of dashes, crosses, and Vs. The image on the book's front cover is a flock of single-pen-stroke birds, high above the streetlamps and pylons of a suburban highway.

The rest of *Curses* flows out of or into those stories' concerns. Their "lost boys" and lost children and desperately longed-for babies are echoed by "Case 0003128–24," the one Ganges-less story here, a heart-breaking piece of found text from adoption papers accompanied by Huizenga's pastiche of classical Asian landscape drawing—no people, no straight lines or human-made structures, just floating organic shapes. The insomnia of the Sudanese immigrant and the starling-besieged family reappears in "Not Sleeping Together," evidently set before Glenn and Wendy lived together: a meditation on Indian summer nights whose "holy, warm and humid air mass" makes it impossible for even the dead to rest in their graves. Visions and sleeplessness under-score "Green Tea (Glenn Ganges Remix)," an adaptation of a Victorian ghost story by Joseph Sheridan Le Fanu about a man driven to insanity and suicide by images of a demonic monkey dragging him into "the enormous machinery of hell." In Huizenga's version, Glenn describes a supernatural vision he had in college, then relates Le Fanu's narrative as something he'd come across in a pile of old papers.

The underworld/torment motif is fleshed out in "Jeepers Jacobs," the bulk of which concerns a conservative theologian at his desk writing a tract about the doctrine of hell being "eternal conscious torment." That's a lot more interesting than it sounds, partly because Huizenga depicts Jacobs's ideology and thought process as sympathetically as he can, and also because he uses the natural dryness of its premise (golf! theology! driving!) as leverage for the dramatic impact of the only full-page image in *Curses*: a drawing of the smoke billowing up from the fires of hell, filling the page all the way out to its borders.

Most of the book's themes come together in its final, perfect five-page story. In thirty-two images and fewer than two hundred words, "Jeezoh" plays with the way religious ideas evolve into more informal folk mythology, and it calls into question how much of what's come before it has "really happened" to Glenn and Wendy and how much our desires as readers (or as people living in the world) lead us to try to put together contradictory images into "an accidental graphic novel." It's emotion-ally crushing; what's surprising about it is that it's also cathartic and even funny, a suggestion of a kind of redemption improvised out of desperation.

Curses is full of peculiar, oblique approaches to storytelling — Huizenga favors depth of reflection over narrative drive — but calling the Ganges stories experimental cartooning doesn't do justice to how effortlessly droll and charming they can be. In one brief piece, "The Hot New Thing," Glenn and Wendy hear about *something* from their friends ("We were talking about the HNT at work! It sounds incredible! Let's go check it out this weekend!"), then go stand in line for it, as Huizenga occasionally cuts away to newsmagazine covers ("The Hot New Thing: Is It Safe?"; "HNT2: A Behind the Scenes Look"). Finally, we see Glenn and Wendy going to bed after experiencing the Thing: it blew his mind, she didn't think it was all that special, and he lies awake after she's fallen asleep, silently fuming a little.

That's probably the best joke in the story: the dead-on evocation of the disappointment of a loved one seeing only mediocrity where you've seen profound brilliance. The deeper comedy of the scene, though, is that Huizenga is both Wendy and Glenn, crediting and debunking the hype at the same time. He cares about the sensations and meanings of grindingly mundane things as much as he cares about the mystical glories his Ganges stories always seem to evoke around their edges. When Huizenga distills the sacred and the everyday into the symbolic clarity of his linework, they come out looking like the same thing viewed from different angles.

CHAPTER 21

Charles Burns and
Art Spiegelman: Draw Yourself Raw

"Everything's either concave or -vex," the Danish poet Piet Hein once wrote, "so whatever you dream will be something with sex." In Charles Burns's decade-in-the-making graphic novel *Black Hole*, the natural concavity and -vexity of everything leap out at you: nearly every image is a sexual metaphor, with the distorted clarity and mutability of a nightmare. And sex in *Black Hole* also means body-horror, sickening transformations, and loss. The first page's abstraction—a thin, wobbling slit of light on a black background—opens up to become wider and fleshier, then reveals itself as a blatantly vaginal gash in a frog on a dissecting pan (surrounded by pools and pearls of liquid). That's only the beginning of the book's array of weenie roasts and clumsy tongues and trees leaning away from each other like spread legs.

Burns originally serialized *Black Hole* as a twelve-issue comic book series, beginning in 1995; a *New York Times Magazine* article offhandedly compared the way its enthusiasts followed it to the way *Ulysses* had been anticipated. That's not a particularly useful analogy, not least because Burns's narrative gifts are much more visual than verbal. The only thing the two books really have in common is a formally audacious structure, with a chronology complicated enough that it takes a few readings to work out—*Black Hole* is riddled with flashbacks, flash-forwards, and multiple perspectives. What made each issue of the comic worth the long wait was its sustained tone. Chip Kidd (who designed *Black Hole*'s jacket), speaking on a panel in 2005, pointed out that Burns had managed to keep his drawing style perfectly consistent for the ten years it took to finish. The mood of the story moves in a slow, graceful arc from its initial plunge into repulsion to its final glints of hope; every panel suggests that Burns knew what it would look like from the moment he began the book.

The setting of *Black Hole* is the suburbs around Seattle, circa 1974. Its characters are all high school students: they hang out with their cliques; they're cruel or kind to each other in a high school way; they get high on whatever's available; they're dragged along by sexual urges they barely understand. And there's a disease going around, "the bug." Once you get it, your body changes, and everyone notices. You might just get little tadpole-shaped growths on your chest or bulbous things on your face, or your hair might all fall out, or you might grow a tail, or worse. You are never the same again, and you don't belong at home anymore. "The bug" is, of course, sexually transmitted.

It's not a metaphor for AIDS—too early—or for herpes, or even for pregnancy (although a sobbing girl tells her philandering boyfriend that "maybe now that I'm starting to SHOW you're getting grossed out and want to move on"; what she's showing is webbing between her fingers). The disease these scared, horny teenagers are passing on to each other is, basically, sex itself.

In a delicious touch, the endpapers of the book are close-ups on a page from a high school yearbook. On the inside front cover, we see a selection of mid-'70s teenagers smiling for the camera (with terrible hair, little moustaches, annoying teeth); on the inside back cover, the same characters and facial expressions are reprised, but this time everyone's faces have mutated. (Evidently, everybody got it on in high school in those days.) Look back at the first pictures, though, and you can see the hints of what each of them will become. Burns specializes in drawing people and things that look like they're just beginning to curdle.

...AND I COULD FEEL MYSELF FALLING FORWARD, TUMBLING DOWN INTO NOTHINGNESS.

Keith's horrific vision of his future near the beginning of Charles Burns's *Black Hole.* ©2007 Charles Burns.

Black Hole begins with sideburned teenager Keith Pearson dissecting the aforementioned frog in his high school biology class, with "sweet and perfect" Chris Rhodes as his lab partner. He suddenly collapses and sees a vision of the future: the gash in the frog, a gash in a foot, a huge tear opening up on Chris's back, a hand over a woman's crotch, and then a whirlpool of tiny, iconic images from what follows.

At a party, Chris heads off for a graveyard tryst with a tall, handsome boy named Rob Facincanni; as they're having sex, she notices that there's a tiny mouth on his neck, making groaning noises. But she doesn't realize that she's got the bug until a week later, when she goes swimming with a bunch of her classmates, who notice the skin splitting open along her spine. Before long, she realizes that she's repeatedly shedding her skin, like a snake. Rob apologizes to her, and she kisses his neck-mouth: "It was warm and salty. It was like the ocean . . . a clean, sharp taste . . . and further inside, a tiny tongue. I could feel it trembling, fluttering up against mine." (Burns's work has a lot of virtues, but subtlety is not always one of them.) Soon she runs away from home to live in a tent in the woods, near the bonfire where all the infected kids go, and one day Keith, getting high with his friends, sees Chris's abandoned skin hanging on a tree.

Keith, it turns out, has been flirting with the bug himself. He's been hanging out at a local drug dealer's pad, and an artist named Eliza who lives in the spare room there has her eye on him—she's got a tail, and he's a little turned on by that. Eventually, she has her way with him, and while she's deflowering him, a piece of her tail breaks off in his hand. Meanwhile, something terrible is closing in on the alienated kids; there

A deeply creepy sex scene from *Black Hole*. ©2007 Charles Burns.

are weird, chopped-up dolls appearing all over the forest, people are disappearing from their bonfire clique and never returning, and somebody
swears he saw a severed arm deep in the woods. And there's an image
that keeps popping up of something awful in the forest: a young man
lashed to a tree, a gag around his mouth, his hands tied in front of his
crotch. It might be Keith; it might be someone else; it might not be
there at all.

What makes all these Cronenbergian grotesqueries work is that Burns
doesn't play them for gross-out value—everything looks subdued and formal, and the story's tenor very rarely departs from what you'd see in a
monster-free coming-of-age story. In one scene, a group of rough-living
kids have trashed the house their acquaintance is taking care of for the
summer; in another, a girl stands in the dark, outside a party thrown by a
friend she's fallen out with, realizing she'll never see her again. These
characters are mutated creatures, but their mutations stand in for the
physical and emotional changes of adolescence. The horrors of *Black
Hole* are the horrors of high school, just made more vivid.

Burns's style will be instantly recognizable to people who read more
than a few magazines. His sweating, beady-eyed characters have appeared in a bunch of Altoids ads, and he's drawn the covers of most issues of *The Believer*. His ink brushwork is so clean and assured it almost
seems like plastic frozen into place (even when he draws smoke or
falling detritus, nothing in these images ever seems to be *moving*), and
the panel and page compositions in *Black Hole* are classically pure.

The story strikes a few sour notes near the end with a violent wrap-up
of one of its subplots, but the last chapter is magnificent: two visions of
what can happen after the turbulence of a sexual awakening. In the first,
a pair of Burns's bug-mutated characters run away together, talking
about how they're going to start a new, idyllic life in a new place. It's the
kind of idle fantasy that tends to get cut down by fate, and even earlier
in *Black Hole* it would have been. This time, though, it's accompanied
by a dream sequence that reprises the structure of one of the book's first
scenes, transformed from a vision of hellish squalor into an apparition
of serenity and stark beauty; the implication is that maybe things *will*

work out, that their grotesque fumblings have become something meaningful.

It's followed by an overwhelming final scene, in which we see what Chris has shed her skin—metaphorically, as well as literally—to become. What sex has made of her isn't a monster but a whole being. She can never have her childhood back, as much as she's longing for it; she has to work out a new way to relate to the rest of the world. But on the last few pages, we see another recapitulation of an earlier dream, an image that Chris once thought would be "my end . . . a sparkling ceiling . . . some cheap, glittery shit," under which she was naked, stumbling over ground littered with mangled corpses and bones, broken glass and snakes, things concave and -vex decayed into garbage. As she actually experiences it, it's the beginning of her new life: a million stars in the sky above the icy water, beyond a soft beach where she's buried the symbol of the change she'll remember forever.

Black Hole didn't come out of nowhere; artists like Burns need to develop in a community of peers. In the early '80s, when he started drawing comics, there was no context anywhere in publishing for a cartooning sensibility like his. Fortunately, he ended up drawing for Art Spiegelman and Françoise Mouly's magazine *RAW*, which valued one-of-a-kind cartooning sensibilities highly. *RAW* didn't try to demonstrate that comics could be art; it just assumed that was a given. Effectively, it was an art magazine whose contributors were all mighty interested in comics.

A quarter of a century later, *RAW* looks unnervingly ahead of its time—not just in its overall aesthetic but in the contributors Spiegelman and Mouly nurtured by including them in issue after issue, even when they were still working out their style. (Burns wouldn't have been able to create *Black Hole* much earlier than he did; his early work has a far shallower creepy/campy vibe.) Mark Beyer went on to create the hilariously grim, design-intensive comic strip "Amy and Jordan"; Ben Katchor's recent projects include the deadpan quasi-historical graphic novel *The Jew of New York*; Gary Panter has turned his scribbly drawings and blank-signifier "Jimbo" character into a series of books including the brilliant, berserk *Jimbo in Purgatory* and *Jimbo's Inferno*; R. Sikoryak is still doing his ingenious adaptations of literary classics into totally in-apposite cartoon pastiches.

As I mentioned earlier, a lot of the *RAW* cartoonists have also be-come influential illustrators, and many of them are still working with Mouly now that she's at *The New Yorker*. But it's also interesting that so many of them have settled into doing strongly narrative-based work, too. *RAW* often seemed to be more about pushing the boundaries of visual experimentation in comics than actually telling stories, with one very big exception: Art Spiegelman's *Maus*, his story of how his fa-ther survived the Holocaust, serialized in *RAW* beginning with its sec-ond issue.

For those of us who've been passionate about comics for ages, it's hard not to resent *Maus* a little for being a lot of other people's sole idea of what art comics are like. It's the equivalent of what Bob Marley is to reggae, the one fine example that too often stands in for the whole and becomes an inappropriate model and reference point. Oh, you like comics for grown-ups? I read *Maus*! Personal or political history in comics form? It's like *Maus*! A story about the Holocaust? In the tradi-tion of *Maus*! A graphic novel with any kind of serious intent? Right up there with *Maus*! (That's not Spiegelman's fault, of course, but the tallest poppy is the first to get cut down.) A couple of other recent comics Holocaust memoirs, Miriam Katin's *We Are On Our Own* and Martin Lemelman's *Mendel's Daughter*, are both by cartoonists who seem to have not looked very far past Spiegelman for a model—and not to have noticed the depths and subtleties of his book.

Part of what rankles, of course, is the general perception that *Maus* was a one-of-a-kind work with no historical precedent (and that therefore if you love *Maus*, you can still safely ignore the rest of the medium), when in fact Spiegelman is more deeply attached to the whole history of comics than any other cartoonist this side of Chris Ware. *Maus* doesn't directly allude to old comics the way some of Spiegelman's later work does, but they're a phantom presence all over it, from the four-tier page layout with occasional tilted panels that recalls World War II–era comic books to the way the book's domestic scenes echo the deadpan staging of "family" comic strips like Frank King's "Gasoline Alley." And if *Maus*'s visual style isn't much like the rest of *RAW*, that's because the only thing *RAW* cartoonists all had in common was their devotion to making work that didn't look like anyone else's.

Young punks also find it frustrating that *Maus* is one of those books that seem almost immune to criticism—it's about the Holocaust, it won the Pulitzer Prize, it's the gold standard of art comics. You can't disparage it without looking like a fool, a contrarian, or worse. But its craft actually *is* impeccable; twenty years after its first volume sent out shock waves, it still looks like a masterpiece.

The central device of *Maus*, which gives it a lot of its riveting force, is Spiegelman's trick of drawing Jews with mouse heads and tails and Nazis with cat heads. (Poles are pigs, the French are frogs, and anyone trying to be anything else wears the appropriate mask.) That's as simple as metaphors get, but it's also shockingly powerful, and the more you think about it, the deeper it becomes—real cats don't just eat mice the way they do in cartoons; they torture them first. The book's characters aren't drawn as "realistic" animals, though; they're *cartoon* animals, the mice's faces stripped down to a simple outline, a pair of dots for eyes, and maybe if they're lucky some eyebrows. Spiegelman does amazingly complicated things with the barest possible tools for representing facial expressions, sometimes with the help of a bit of body language.

Again, there's a comics tradition he's working in here: the forms of the mice and cats and pigs are inspired by "funny animal" comics, the peculiar strain descended from animal fables that has as much to do with animated cartoons as it does with early comic strips. But the story is about horrible reality instead of whimsical fantasy, and the actual linework of *Maus* is deliberately unlike the smooth, clean lines of most funny animal comics. Instead, it's rough and utilitarian, mostly drawn with a ragged felt-tip pen, making do with the slightest possible resources, just as Vladek does within the story. The panel-to-panel and page-to-page flow is miraculously smooth—Spiegelman's artwork gives the impression of crudeness, rather than actual difficulty in reading. It's thoroughly cooked; it just looks raw.

The metaphor *Maus* is built on gets even trickier in the second half of the book. (It was originally *Maus II: And Here My Troubles Began*; they're now paired as *The Complete Maus*.) It opens with a sequence in which the Spiegelman-mouse is sketching Mouly as various kinds of animals, all with her signature striped shirt and scarf, trying to decide what animal to draw her as, since she's French. Mouly shows up in the second panel as another mouse, so we know the answer to his question before we know the question.

A bit later, Spiegelman draws himself at his drawing table as a human wearing a mouse mask (a human who's specifically acting as a Jew?), surrounded by flies; his table is perched on top of a mountain of emaciated corpses with mouse heads, and surrounded by reporters and businessmen, all humans with masks tied on, trying to leech off the success of the first *Maus* volume. When Spiegelman goes to visit his shrink, he notes in a caption: "His place is overrun with stray dogs and cats. Can I mention this, or does it completely louse up my metaphor?" Not at all—as his readers, we know what's real and what's symbolic— and in any case, earlier in the story he's drawn Nazi officers with attack dogs at the gates of Auschwitz.

It's only fair that the fame of *Maus* should be reflected in its story. Almost all of Spiegelman's comics work is autobiographical, one way or another, and *Maus* itself is as much about his relationship with his parents and the brother he never knew, and the particular way he's chosen to turn his father's history into small-a art, as it is about Vladek's actual experiences in the Holocaust. The first chapter of the book ends with Art promising not to reveal the story his father has just told him about his love life before he married Art's late mother, Anja; of course, that's precisely what Art's done in the preceding pages. That's a bright neon sign indicating that the reader should bear in mind that although we may be reading Vladek's words about Vladek's experiences, Art is the one telling us this story. And at the end of the first volume, Art is walking away from his father's house, cursing him as a murderer for having destroyed Anja's diaries.

The improbable achievement of *Maus* is how perfectly pitched its formal elements are. Consider some of the things Spiegelman might have done differently. Imagine it, for instance, as a direct adaptation of the way Vladek Spiegelman described his experiences under the Nazis, without any of the material about Art's relationship with his father and his ambivalence about the way he's relating the story, or Vladek's crotchety, English-mangling diction. It would lose the depth of the generational struggle, the echo of the Jewish injunction about telling one's children about the exodus from Egypt, the acknowledgment of how difficult it is to comprehend the enormity of the Holocaust, the heartbreaking flavor of Vladek's voice.

Imagine if Spiegelman used the same language throughout the book but dropped the mice-and-cats metaphor and simply drew all of the characters as people. It would be just another true story of the Holocaust, moving and maybe thought-provoking but a little bit tedious to look at, and it wouldn't have *Maus*'s shock of understanding the situation from a different angle through the metaphor. Imagine if the style he used for the body of the book was the same as the scratchy Lynd Ward woodcut-inspired style that appears in the "Prisoner on the Hell Planet" section (it would be much tougher to read), or if he'd chosen instead to use the broader, sleeker style that's usually used for animal comics or the style he used for commercial art projects like the "Garbage Pail Kids" trading cards (it would have seemed to be trivializing the horror of his father's story). All of those approaches might have been more intuitively obvious than the one Spiegelman took, and any of them probably would have wrecked it. But he got it right.

Spiegelman completed *Maus* in 1991, after working on it for over a decade, and he's been riding the momentum from it ever since—it's the sort of act that's nearly impossible to follow up, so he's mostly avoided doing narrative comics in the last fifteen years. He's published non-comics projects like his children's book, *Open Me . . . I'm a Dog*, coedited a series of comics anthologies for kids (*Little Lit*, a sort of junior *RAW*) with Mouly, and drawn some of *The New Yorker*'s most provocative covers. His first "major" post-*Maus* project, *In the Shadow of No Towers*, is a god-awful mess. Its ten tabloid-sized pages pastiche the iconography and style of early-twentieth-century comic strips as a response to the fall of the World Trade Center, but Spiegelman's drawing is overworked and overcomputerized, and there's no sense of drive or closure to it—it just kind of ends after a while. Still, it somehow became a book, printed on cardstock and padded out with a handful of the original comic strips to which it's an homage; the magnificent Sunday pages the likes of Winsor McCay and George McManus knocked out every week make Spiegelman look like a bit of a slacker for spending a year and a half on ten pages.

The project Spiegelman's been serializing in *Virginia Quarterly Review* for the past few years, a memoir called "Portrait of the Artist as a Young %@?*!"—note the title's allusion to the fake euphemisms of old comics—is as technically accomplished as anything he's ever drawn, but so far it mostly consists of scattered anecdotes from his past. He's also reportedly assembling something called *Meta-Maus*, which will document how he put together the book that was already, in some ways, a documentation of its own creative process. Both *Portrait* and *Meta* are ancillary material, of course; we're not going to get another work on the scale of *Maus* out of him. Very few works by anyone are on that scale.

CHAPTER 22

Why Does Chris Ware Hate Fun?

Chris Ware's work has an emotional range of one note, and he sings it at the top of his lungs, with gusto if not exactly pride. He's the most acclaimed American cartoonist to have emerged in the last twenty years; as reflexively self-deprecating as he is, he's a technical and formal wizard. Ware's a scholar of the history of comics, and almost without exception his own are executed in the idioms of antique light entertainment: top-hat-and-tails design, big-headed kids, wacky flexible animals, cutout dioramas.

But his work also systematically dismembers the idea of light entertainment. Ware forces his readers to watch his characters sicken and die slowly, torment (and be humiliated in turn by) their broken families, and lead lives of failure and loneliness. Commercial amusements, he suggests, make suckers of everyone who consumes them, including himself. So it's strange how thoroughly his ideology of art and cartooning is contradicted by the comic strip artists whose work he's dedicated part of his career to preserving, and how suspicious he is of the ideas of pleasure represented by the things that give *him* pleasure.

Ware's first graphic novel, 2000's *Jimmy Corrigan, the Smartest Kid on Earth*, is a brilliant and exhausting book: a history of a family's pathetic fantasies and painful realities, rendered in a style whose maniacally precise, composed frostiness (every line either perfectly straight or

347

perfectly curved) counterbalances the story's emotional brutality. It had been serialized in his *Acme Novelty Library* series, which swept comics awards ceremonies through most of the '90s; the collected *Jimmy Corrigan* won the Guardian First Book Award in 2001, and Ware went on to be featured in the 2002 Whitney Biennial and draw the *New York Times Magazine*'s first weekly comic strip, a section of his ongoing "Building Stories" project.

"Building Stories" is one of two major works in progress that have been occupying Ware's time since *Jimmy Corrigan* ended, along with "Rusty Brown." While he works on them (and he's indicated that they'll both take years more to finish), he's published three other books, none of them long narratives—they're more like art books, both in the sense that they're exquisite objects and in the sense that they're basically overviews of what the artist has been up to.

The oversized *Quimby the Mouse* collects some of Ware's work from the early '90s, although its back cover is a version of the staggering mural he designed a few years ago for 826 Valencia, Dave Eggers's storefront community center in San Francisco. (The 826 mural is a history of communication and the drives for food, sex, and shelter, in the form of one of Ware's trademark "diagrammatic" comic strips, composed of several hundred panels connected by lines that show how a complicated system evolves over time.) The short pieces inside *Quimby* occasionally echo other cartoonists' work—there's a note-perfect parody of old *New Yorker* cartoons—but they're mostly Ware working out his own voice, especially in a wincingly funny sequence, "Quimbies the Mouse," in which one of a pair of conjoined twins remains young while the other is dying of old age.

Ware's most recent book, which bears the unwieldy title *The Acme Novelty Library Final Report to Shareholders and Saturday Afternoon Rainy Day Fun Book* and is credited to "F. C. Ware" rather than the more prosaic "Chris," isn't quite his long-awaited second graphic novel either. Instead, as Ware explains in an "Apology and Souvenir Comic 'Strip'" on the inside of the paper band wrapped around the *Final Report*'s cover, it's mostly one-page "gag strips" he's drawn as a diversion from his longer stories. "When I drew these strips," he writes, "I was still so deeply dubious of my ability to do 'emotionally resonant' comics that I had to occasionally return to a 'joke' format just so I was able to find the confidence to keep going in a more 'serious' direction."

The apology's a little disingenuous, given the gobsmacking level of craft on display here. Start with the cover: a gilt-embossed design that features "the world's smallest comic strip," 110 tiny panels about love, death, and heartbreak, printed not on the front or back cover, or even the spine, but the *edge* of the hard cover itself. Turn the first few pages, past a series of vicious parodies of old comic books' ads for *Grit* and Charles Atlas, and you'll hit a spectacular two-page map of the heavens and the traditional constellations, à la Ware. View it in the dark, and it becomes an entirely different celestial map—the constellations this time are Ware's characters, printed in glow-in-the-dark ink. That's followed by a brief history of visual art (presented as a series of tiny newspaper-style comic strips), then another grand two-page scheme described as "Our Blueprint of the Universe, as Seen through its Four Physical Types, Principles, and the Opposing Forces of Nature."

It's the sort of marvel that would single-handedly establish another artist's career, and Ware's only started showing off. The centerpiece of *Final Report* is a long, wordless story about the pudgy, masked, omnipotent character that Ware sometimes calls "God" or "Superman" in his comics. (He's not named here, and the story isn't mentioned in the otherwise detailed table of contents.) It occupies twelve pages in the middle of the book and fragments of other pages. Near the story's end, the character is in a prison cell, scraping little drawings onto the cinder blocks with a nail. Then Ware pulls back, so we can see hundreds of stick figures on the wall. If you're willing to stare at the panel hard and long enough to risk eye damage, you'll see that he's drawn a microscopic stick-figure version of *the entire story up to that point*. We are not worthy.

The recurring one-page comic strips that fill most of the rest of the book are more or less in the manner of old full-tabloid-page Sunday color newspaper comics. Most of them have a simple, mean-spirited

premise. "Big Tex" is a dimwitted comedy cowboy character whose father despises and tortures him; in "Tales of Tomorrow," a pudgy man of
the future, wearing a '50s-style space outfit, spends his life alone in front
of a TV set that keeps trying to sell him things, as he sucks food from a
tube in the wall.

The nastiest of Ware's gibes are reserved for his "Rusty Brown and
Chalky White" strips—dry runs for the longer "Rusty" novel. Rusty and
Chalky are childhood friends, social outcasts who bond over col-
lectibles and action figures (a world with which Ware seems much too
familiar for his own comfort). As they grow older, Rusty makes collecting his life, to the exclusion of human contact and hygiene; Chalky gets
married, has a daughter who grows to loathe him, drifts into simple-
minded Christianity, and mostly puts aside the childish things that his
old friend still covets. In a typical sequence, Rusty, at a flea market, buys
the "Colonial Warrior in VG or VG+ condition with cloth vest" that
Chalky's been looking for, briefly fantasizes about the woman who sells
it to him, hears her say that her boyfriend "found it in a dumpster last
week," and goes outside and stomps on it: "FUCK YOU! You can't have
it! I won't let you have it! Fuck YOU Chalky White!"

This is a "'joke' format"? What's most obviously missing from Ware's
"gag strips" are gags—they have all the bitterness of pitch-black comedy
without the actual comedy and the acrobatic visual style of his favorite
old newspaper strips without their sense of fun. They're always impressively constructed, and Ware pierces his target through the heart, but he
inevitably plays his form against his content in precisely the same way:
Hey, kids! Torment!

"It's just punchlines," Ware draws himself explaining in his "Apology." "I don't trust them. . . . They don't exist in the real world, so why
should I accommodate them in ART?" That's a specious argument: perfectly geometrical forms don't exist in nature either, but that doesn't
stop Ware from constructing most of his "finished" work from them.
They work for his purposes—he can convey a mountain of information
with two or three lines—but his version of "iconic" often suggests the
sneering remoteness of "ironic."

Why does Ware reject not just punchlines but the entire system of entertainment they're attached to? That emphasized "ART" suggests a reason. More than any other contemporary cartoonist except possibly Robert Crumb, Ware is at home in the gallery-art world, which prefers its manifestations of pleasure-in-looking ironized—or, at least, held at arm's length. Ware understands the mechanics of funny comic strips better than any of his contemporaries; he just refuses to make them. If he did, he wouldn't be able to distance himself from them.

In the early '90s, when they were first published, Ware's anti-humor strips were a lead-lined glove whacked in the face of cliché. Now they're getting to look like a different sort of cliché themselves, as Ware's style has become his formula and he's spawned a small cluster of imitators. Ivan Brunetti, for instance, is another smart, passionate student of comics' history—he edited Yale University Press's *Anthology of Graphic Fiction*—whose own work is similarly formalism-minded, bleak, self-pitying, obsessed with the idea of art-for-pleasure, and biliously dismissive of it anyway. (The most memorable project Brunetti's done on his own is a little book of "horrible, horrible cartoons" called *HAW!*, drawn in the style of elegant old magazine cartoons but with psychotically hateful "jokes." Sample punch line: "You motherfucker . . . did you switch my heroin with Drano again?")

Ware still has it all over his acolytes, though, in part because of his unmatchable, fanatical control and attention to detail—he makes it obvious how much sweat he pours into his comics. The early issues in the *Acme Novelty Library* series were each a different size and shape, and he designed a special rack for stores to display them. ("Have You Them All?" it asked in old-fashioned type.) He doesn't leave a single element of his books' design unexamined—even *Final Report*'s Library of Congress information is the occasion for an extended riff in tiny type. Every panel he draws is stamped into the page by the weight of his ideas about comics and their history. In a minuscule "Ripley's Believe It or Not!"–style box in *Final Report*, he explains that "cartooning is not really DRAWING at all, but a complicated pictographic language intended to be READ, not really SEEN! ALSO, its strongest roots are

NOT in the Academic tradition, but in an arcane system of 19th century PHYSIOGNOMY and RACIAL CARICATURE!" He goes on to
present his personal history of cartooning (in the form of twenty-five
teensy strips on a single page), beginning with a caveman having his
head bashed in as he makes a dirty drawing on a cave wall, touching on
significant early figures like proto-cartoonist Rodolphe Töpffer and
William Randolph Hearst, and taking a few red-clawed swipes at modern "Cheerleaders for the Cause" (unhelpful "friends" of comics): "I
think they're wonderful, because they get people interested in REAL
reading!"

As an incorrigible nostalgic (even though he can't stop mocking nostalgia), Ware is careful to observe the decline of his favorite kinds of personal craft. A tiny strip called "The Letterer in 'Final Insult'" shows a
retired widower who was once a hand-letterer buying a bag of chips
marked "New Look—Same Great Taste!" and realizing that the last ves-
tige of his work has been "usurped by digital vector graphics, bitmap
brickwork, and insolent little computer hobbyists who don't know a
goddamned thing about ascenders and descenders." Then he goes
home and stuffs himself with chips, sitting in front of the TV. The title
panel, naturally, shows him as a young man at his easel, tipping his visor
and grinning.

Still, Ware can't get away from the idea of the artificial pleasures of
childhood for even a few pages at a time. The "Rainy Day Saturday Afternoon Fun Book" in the *Final Report*'s title isn't *entirely* sarcastic —
there are cut-out-and-assemble booklets (along with a little cabinet to
put them on), a "picture scroll," and a "magic moving picture theatre"
to put together. (This last is listed on a "Project Page" along with "Birth
Control Fashioned from the Leavings of the Weekly Slaughter" and "A
Profitable Office Building.")

Ware makes it clear how much he despises Rusty Brown for lusting
after a collectible "Looney Lemon" figurine to complete his set of Pills-
bury premiums, but he draws the vintage toys with the genuine tender-
ness of someone who's bought more than a few himself. And in the title
panels of the "Rusty" strips, he sometimes draws Rusty himself as a

cheerful-looking toy character. (He's also designed an old-fashioned Rusty Brown lunchbox that was mass-produced a few years ago.) There's a struggle visible on almost every page of Ware's comics between his love of "innocent" fun and his attraction to the gristle and reserve expected of an artist of his stature. He distrusts his own fondness for entertainment as something like false consciousness, a regressive attempt to regain simple childhood pleasures. Every so often, he draws a man looking at something amusing, perhaps a newspaper comic strip, and chuckling to himself; the context always makes it look damning.

Ware seems to have done his own share of chuckling. He's a serious collector of "Peanuts"—some of his archival copies of early strips ended up pictured in Chip Kidd's book *Peanuts: The Art of Charles M. Schulz*, and he's described Schulz as his hero. In the last few years, Ware has also been designing reprint volumes of two early-twentieth-century American strips that had an enormous impact on his own work. One of them is Frank King's "Gasoline Alley" (reprinted by Drawn & Quarterly as *Walt & Skeezix*), as humane and sweet a strip as has ever been drawn—the adoptive-father-and-son relationship its early years are built around reads, in retrospect, like a much more warm-hearted variation on *Jimmy Corrigan*'s central plot.

The other series Ware's been designing is Fantagraphics' ongoing *Krazy & Ignatz*, reprinting George Herriman's magnificent full-page "Krazy Kat" strips (as of this writing, there are eight volumes out, with seven more expected to follow). Herriman's work has rarely had more than a small cult following—during the original run of "Krazy Kat," from 1913 to 1944, it supposedly survived largely because William Randolph Hearst was a fan—but within the world of cartoonists, he's a god. Ware is devoted and indebted to Herriman, whose work could scarcely be more different from his own in tone: not precise and "iconic" but scribbly and haphazard, not dour or snarky but pure mystifying delight.

"Krazy Kat" is based on a disarmingly simple premise. Krazy, a cat of no particular gender, loves Ignatz the mouse. Ignatz hates Krazy, but when he demonstrates it by throwing bricks, Krazy takes it as a sign of affection from the "li'l ainjil," and Offissa Pupp, the canine policeman,

George Herriman's November 8, 1931 "Krazy Kat" strip (reprinted in *Krazy & Ignatz: A Kat A'Lilt With Song*).

drags Ignatz off to jail. This formula was repeated in almost every strip for thirty years; it was the setup for the verbal and visual loopiness that was the real substance of "Krazy Kat." Herriman's characters play out their rituals against a crazily abstracted Southwestern landscape, talking in sub-Joycean puns and witty, word-drunk rhetoric ("Ooy-yooy-yooy wot a goldish oak finish—like a swell mihoginny piyenna—l'il dusky dahlink!!!"). The brick becomes a symbol of communication and miscommunication; the love triangle lets Herriman play with every possible angle at which desire and authority meet.

Like Ware, whose work is serialized in Chicago alternative weeklies (first *NewCity*, more recently the *Chicago Reader*), Herriman had a full newspaper page to toy with, and his experiments with layout and page design were bolder than almost anything that can be seen in Sunday comics sections even now, taking their compositional cues from the fine art of his era and throwing in Navajo-inspired patterns. His panels sprawl languorously across the page or subdivide it into crunched-up slivers; the characters are almost always seen at the same tiny size, as if the window we see them through is changing its size and shape but never getting any closer or farther away.

Ware can adopt Herriman's ebullient visual grammar at will—the cat-head-and-mouse games of the *Quimby* material are a refracted variation on its theme. But he's also rarely captured or even aimed for the spontaneity of Herriman's line, at least in his formally "finished" work. If comics are "a pictographic language," as Ware says, then they're meant to be read *fast*. Dominated by simple shapes and "dead," fixed-width lines, Ware's pages zoom along, slowed down only by tricky diagrammatic layouts and occasional indigestible blocks of tiny type. Herriman, conversely, drew some of the slowest-reading comics on record, executed with uneven, scratchy lines; once you get through the crabbed, wobbly handwriting of his dialogue and captions, you still have to figure out what the thick dialect means, and no character or object looks exactly the same two panels in a row.

As it turns out, Ware has published a few direct homages to "Krazy Kat" in the most surprising and frustrating of his books. *The Acme Novelty*

Date Book isn't a date book at all but an anthology of Ware's sketch-books—204 pages selected from the 1986–1995 period. It's almost parod-ically elegant, with a "tab" system to indicate when each page was drawn, a hand-lettered self-effacing timeline of the artist's life ("Discovery that rapidly-thinning hair on top of head may be made to appear fuller by trimming sides shorter to contrast; age 32"), and a gold-and-black-embossed red cloth spine.

It's hard to imagine that any of Ware's just-so, mathematically precise cartoons was ever a sketch. So the raw, frantic energy of the *Date Book* is a pleasant shock: roughed-out comic strips and stories, life drawings, sty-listic exercises, pornographic doodles, self-lacerating self-portraits, quota-tions from writers and teachers, pastiches of his favorite cartoonists, and outdoor scenes, much of the work rendered in delicately observed color and all accompanied by Ware's unforgiving notes on his own work: "Stop imitating yourself!" "Your drawings are becoming much more careless and unobservant—you don't keep this sketchbook just to fill it up!" "LIES! LOOK next time!" "Awful! *Awful!* I can't *draw!*"

As *if*. In the earliest pages of the *Date Book*, from Ware's teenage years, he's still working out his technique (and imitating his favorite comic strips), but he's already observing the subtleties of style beauti-fully, assimilating the work he admires into his own. In 1987, he discov-ers Robert Crumb's sketchbooks and, evidently, decides to try to outdo their spur-of-the-moment translations of the cartoonist's environment into stylistic exercises; by 1991, even Ware's throwaways beat most car-toonists' best work. After he moves to Chicago from Austin, Texas, he starts filling his sketchbook with fully fleshed-out comic strips and a se-ries of remarkable illustrations of buildings. (To paraphrase Henry Miller, when he draws a building, it stays drawn.) And, on page after page, he rips into himself—and makes us watch him ripping into him-self. He did pick the pages we see here, after all; his self-loathing is real, but it's also part of what he's selling.

The second half of the *Date Book* is, in some ways, the most remark-able drawing Ware has published—he's got a gift for representation that his stylized, iconic professional work only hints at. Sketches of people

view from 'Torchlight Cafe' 3/18

man on train 3/23.

A page from Ware's meticulously observed sketchbook, reprinted in *The Acme Novelty Date Book.* ©2007 Chris Ware.

he sees on trains, or coffee cups, or a masturbating robot are more finely observed than he'll ever admit (well, maybe the last is more imagined than observed). When he reproduces images from old comic books, he incorporates a sense of the original printed distortions in their lines and colors. His drawing-not-cartooning is loose and light-hearted, easy to linger over in a way that "pictographic" simplicity resists.

Still, he insists on a hard, formal surface for his "real" work, ruthlessly boiling out the vulnerability and liveliness of his sketchbook drawings. He quotes Goethe's dictum that "architecture is frozen music" and calls it "the aesthetic key to the development of cartoons as an art form" (on a *Date Book* page that also includes some terrific sketches of shoes and cats and a watercolor-tinted twelve-panel doodle about hating his work in progress).

It's a curious double-metaphor to cite, since cartoons usually imply motion and change in a way that architecture doesn't, but it makes sense.
Ware's drawing has music in it, but he chills it into ice for his cartooning.

If all of this reads like an indictment of Ware, it's not meant to be. I'll
read any comic he publishes, because I know I'll be impressed. As easy
as his work is to appreciate, though, it's nearly impossible to enjoy, because it's explicitly meant to write off the kind of "enjoyment" it flirts
with. Ware's rejection of mass-cultural entertainment means more as an
act of will *because* he's a born entertainer; his choice of a sterilized cartooning technique over the lively drawing he's also got a gift for has the
force of a conscious decision too.

That doesn't let him off the hook, because denying the value of enjoyment, and the idea that it can be intimately tied to more complicated reactions to art, also seems like a perverse kind of false
consciousness. "Krazy Kat" is a sad strip—nobody ever gets what they
want, exactly, although nobody seems to mind—and it rarely goes for a
big pratfall laugh. It's still enormously funny, in a way that sneaks up on
you. Read one, and you scratch your head; read ten, and you can't stop
grinning. The Krazy-Ignatz-Pupp triangle hits the sore nerve of endless,
hopeless longing for love from someone who's never going to offer it,
but that only makes its jokes more poignant. There's plenty of subtext
about loneliness and mortality underscoring the good-humored banter
of "Gasoline Alley." And "Peanuts" is entirely driven by heartbreak: the
central conceit of Charles Schulz's strip is that it's kind of hilarious
when children's play anticipates adult agonies.

Even so, every episode of every one of those strips was meant to give
pleasure, if sometimes a perplexing or subtle pleasure—not to dangle it
like a bunch of grapes and then snatch it away as a lesson in the foolish-
ness of hoping for it. Indulging in fun doesn't make Herriman or King
or Schulz a less sophisticated artist; they don't even make a distinction
between whimsical entertainment and desperate wrestling with existen-
tial conundrums. The only thing keeping Ware out of their heights of
accomplishment is that he does.

CHAPTER 23

Alison Bechdel: Reframing Memory

Midway through *Fun Home*, Alison Bechdel's riveting memoir of her family's secrets and love letter to her late, horrifically flawed father, she shows us the earliest entries in the diary she's kept since the age of ten. In its first few months, the young Bechdel started to undergo what she calls "a sort of epistemological crisis"—after every assertion of fact, she'd write "I think" in tiny letters. "I think" was replaced first by a scribble, then by a little symbol that she eventually drew over individual words, and later over entire diary entries, blotting out her own experience with the sign of her uncertainty.

Good thing she got over it. *Fun Home* is a beautiful, assured piece of work, by far the best thing Bechdel has done in more than two decades as a cartoonist. Her language and drawings are impressively sensitive to the details of her physical experience and to the trickier folds of her own self-consciousness; she dives over and over into the cloudy waters of her past, swimming deeper every time. A compulsive self-documenter, she nonetheless glossed over or omitted some of her life's crucial details as they were happening, and now she's gone back to reconstruct them.

Unlike most memoirists, Bechdel doesn't present her family history chronologically. Instead, she spirals around its central incidents repeatedly, approaching them from different angles. Early on in *Fun Home*,

Bechdel lays out her relationship to her father. From *Fun Home: A Family Tragicomic* by Alison Bechdel. ©2006 by Alison Bechdel. Reprinted by permission of Houghton Mifflin Company. All rights reserved.

she lays out most of its narrative landmarks: her father, Bruce Bechdel, a bookish, reserved man who sometimes exploded into fury, ran the local funeral home (whose family nickname provides the book's title), taught high school English, and spent all his free time restoring the family's 1867 house to its high Gothic-revival glory; he died when she was nineteen in an accident she suspects was a suicide; he turned out to have been having sex with teenage boys for years; shortly before her father's death, Bechdel herself had come out to her parents as a lesbian.

This is heavy stuff, in theory, but what Bechdel makes of it is luminous and playful. The book's subtitle is A *Family Tragicomic*, and twenty-three years of producing her biweekly comic strip "Dykes to Watch Out For" have polished her tone's poker-faced hilarity to a burnished gleam. She draws herself and her family and friends as loose caricatures with studiously observed clothing and haircuts and physical settings, and gives the whole thing depth with a watercolorish green wash over her ink lines. The wobble in her line seems like a deliberate gesture to soften the hyper-controlled precision of her drawings, as well as a nod to her first influence, Robert Crumb. Her images flutter forward and backward in time, playing thematically off the narrative captions much more often than they illustrate them. The text is full of double meanings, alliteration, and wryly specific twenty-dollar words. Historical restoration, she writes, was her father's "passion in every sense of the word. Libidinal. Manic. Martyred." (This is accompanied by a drawing of the elder Bechdel, in cut-offs and loafers, carrying a huge, salvaged Victorian wooden post like a cross.)

Bechdel's favorite breed of joke, here as in "Dykes to Watch Out For," comes from unexpected connections. On the story's first page, she shows her childhood self playing airplane with her father as he lies on a Persian carpet and lifts her with his feet, then notes that "in the circus, acrobatics where one person lies on the floor balancing another are called 'Icarian games.'" That kicks off a series of Icarus-and-Daedalus metaphors: her father, she says, "was an alchemist of appearance, a savant of surface, a Daedalus of decor." The chapter is called "Old Father, Old Artificer"—a phrase from James Joyce's "A Portrait of the Artist as a Young Man," whose protagonist is Stephen Dedalus. (When he learned Bechdel was reading "Portrait" for college, her father told her "Good. You damn well better identify with every page.") A later scene riffs off of fifteen-year-old Alison's trip with her father to New York City's West Village, which suddenly looked very gay to her: "It was like the moment the manicurist in the Palmolive commercial informs her client, 'You're soaking in it.' The suspect element is revealed to be not just benign, but beneficial, and in fact, all-pervasive."

In its best moments, *Fun Home* is as airily, intricately choreographed as a grand farce. One chapter, "The Ideal Husband," is mostly concerned with the fallout of an incident in which Bruce Bechdel got into legal trouble for buying a beer for a teenage boy—there may have been more going on, but that was all that ended up on the police report, whose typewritten text his daughter copies by hand. The same weekend, the Bechdel children were staying at the home of family friends ("it was hard to remember to address both parents as 'Dr. Gryglewicz'"). In one image, Alison and her friend Beth, playing police, pull imaginary guns on their siblings: "Spread 'em, punks!" Hanging on the wall in the background, there's a picture of a woman lying naked on a bed with her legs spread, captioned, "One of Dr. Gryglewicz's many interesting paintings of Dr. Gryglewicz."

The chapter's central drama is surrounded by threads about Bechdel's mother performing in *The Importance of Being Earnest*—a panel in which Helen Bechdel is practicing her lines, saying, "An engagement should come on a young girl as a surprise," is accompanied by a caption noting that Alison had just gotten her first period—as well as the arrival of seventeen-year cicadas, Watergate, and her discovery of both masturbation and obfuscatory euphemisms (this was the historical moment when kids learned to call each other "explitive deleted"). It's played for nervous giggles, but it all works in concert to evoke the way the adult world's sexuality and secrecy crept into Bechdel's consciousness over the course of a few months.

It also suggests her drive to understand the larger landscape on which her own experience is only a single window. A chapter that's ostensibly about Bruce Bechdel's funeral also encompasses a discussion of the books he was reading shortly before his death, his fixation with obelisks, Albert Camus's "The Myth of Sisyphus" and accidental death, Alison's teenage experience of seeing a naked cadaver on a prep table, her early childhood confusion of the family in Charles Addams's cartoons with her own, and much more. An artist from a very early age, she's got a deep

Bechdel changes her drawing style to suggest the "reality" of the photographs in *Fun Home*. From *Fun Home: A Family Tragicomic* by Alison Bechdel. ©2006 by Alison Bechdel. Reprinted by permission of Houghton Mifflin Company. All rights reserved.

and intuitive understanding of images and their subtext. In one scene, she draws her hands holding two photographs (all of the book's photos are rendered with meticulous cross-hatching, to contrast them with the clear-line style she uses for everything else). One is a picture of herself, snapped by a girlfriend; the other is a picture of her father at twenty-two. "Was the boy who took it his lover?" she wonders. "The exterior setting, the pained grin, the flexible wrists, even the angle of shadow falling across our faces—it's about as close as a translation can get."

The photograph that comes in for the closest analysis, though, is one she found in a box from 1969—a dimly lit picture her father took of the family's seventeen-year-old baby-sitter, reclining on a hotel bed in his underwear. Was the Bechdels' impeccably and perpetually restored home a sham? Bechdel asks. It was, and it wasn't: "we really were a family, and we really did live in those period rooms." Bit by bit, before and after his death, the truth about Bruce Bechdel emerged, and if we don't learn the details in the same order she did, she still communicates the sense of gradual, inexorable revelation.

But *Fun Home* isn't really about Bechdel's slow discovery of her father's hidden life; it's about her investigation of her own memories of that discovery and the great works of literature through which she's come to understand them. "My parents are most real to me in fictional terms," she writes: she compares them to characters from Henry James, F. Scott Fitzgerald, Oscar Wilde, Marcel Proust, and, in the final chapter, James Joyce's *Ulysses*, which she read around the same time she was coming out, and whose conversation between Stephen and Bloom is echoed by the only real conversation she and her father ever had about their homosexuality.

What ultimately brought her and her father together, in fact, were books. The Bechdels' library was the emotional center of their home, and Alison contextualizes most of her experiences by thinking of them in terms of literature—she even realized she was gay not from an attraction to a specific person but from looking at a book, *Word Is Out: Stories of Some of Our Lives*. Colette's autobiography, Kate Millett's *Flying*, and especially *Ulysses* provided the basis for Bechdel's final discussions and correspondence with her father and pointed her toward some kind of understanding of his death. More than that, though, her family brought her up to live the life of the mind, to understand that observing and refining the wrenching losses of existence through the filter of art and especially writing could turn them into something meaningful and even redemptive. Literature didn't save her father, but Bechdel's cartooning has transmuted his life and death into an extraordinary book, a memorial loving enough to illuminate and even make light of their shared story's most heartbreaking depths.

AFTERWORD: THE ROUGH WAVE AND THE SMOOTH WAVE

The cartoonists I've been writing about, with very few exceptions, are comics' old guard at this point—people who've been drawing for ten or twenty years or more. As I noted earlier, it's very hard to build up a substantial body of work in art comics: they take forever to draw, and it's almost impossible to make any money at them for years. Still, there are always fine new cartoonists turning up. You just have to know where to look for them if you want to know about them before they publish big books of their own.

Very occasionally, cartoonists can make a splash with a debut graphic novel, like R. Kikuo Johnson's semiautobiographical *Night Fisher* or Jeffrey Brown's painfully autobiographical *Clumsy*. A few independent-minded artists have tried to launch a full-size periodical comic book, although serial art comics are almost impossible for little-known cartoonists to pull off, especially now. Anders Nilsen has gotten something of a following through *Big Questions*, and Ben Jones and Frank Santoro recently started serializing *Cold Heat*, but they may be among the last of their kind. Mostly, these days, young cartoonists' first appearances in print tend to be in minicomics or in comics anthologies.

(There are also a whole lot of cartoonists publishing noteworthy work on the Internet, some of them serializing long stories, like Jenn Manley

Lee's "Dicebox" and Dylan Meconis's "Family Man"; Hope Larson's first book-length work, *Salamander Dream*, was initially serialized online too. The one-page-at-a-time rhythm of Web serialization, though, seems to be more appropriate to comic strip–like projects—R. Stevens's "Diesel Sweeties," Chris Baldwin's "Little Dee"—than to extended, punchline-less narratives. And despite early predictions that online cartoonists would change the format of their work along with its medium, not a lot of cartoonists have made particularly clever use of the "infinite canvas." One who has: the Swiss artist Demian 5, with his brilliant "When I Am King.")

Minicomics are the simplest form of print self-publishing: little comics, generally black-and-white, photocopied and assembled by hand. (The godfather of the form is Matt Feazell, who's been publishing his stick-figure *Cynicalman* series since the early '80s.) Usually the only way to get minis is from the artist, and the best way to find those artists is at small conventions: Small Press Expo in Bethesda, Maryland, Alternative Press Expo in San Francisco, MoCCA in New York, Stumptown Comix Fest in Portland, Oregon. Over the last few years, the fare available at small-press comics conventions has drifted from comics alone to aesthetically pleasing cartooning-related objects—paintings, T-shirts, prints, and other things with some kind of handmade element. If you're buying a piece of art of any kind from the person who made it, even if it includes some mechanically reproduced material, you're getting a little bit of "aura," and that's a big selling point if you're paying $2 or $3 for photocopied semi-amateur drawings.

There's actually something of an aesthetic schism developing now among young art cartoonists—not the sort of schism that involves ill will or competitiveness, more like a couple of camps that comics art is starting to organize itself into. On one side are the cartoonists who've been experimenting with styles that are deliberately difficult, going beyond the unpretty cartooning of the '80s and '90s art-comics scene to kinds of drawing that range from obsessive-compulsively detailed (Marc Bell's *Worn Tuff Elbow*) to intentionally amateurish (Anders Nilsen's fat volume of improvised ultra-high-speed scribbles, *Monologues for the Coming Plague*) or even fascinatingly repulsive (Brian Chippendale's

A tiny fragment of Brian Chippendale's frenetic *Ninja* (note that this is only a tenth of the page this is from). ©2007 Brian Chippendale.

enormous, manic *Ninja*), and storytelling techniques that hurl conventional plot dynamics out the window.

It's not an entirely new idea. The godparents of the rough wave's aesthetic are Julie Doucet (the *Dirty Plotte* creator who's now retired from comics) and the underground cartoonist S. Clay Wilson, although ugly drawing is no longer "transgressive" enough to shock anyone—but that's not really the point of it now. What these young artists have in common, ideologically, is the anti-Hollywood narrative, anti-representational, labor-intensive, make-it-nasty tendencies of contemporary visual art. They're the first generation of cartoonists to migrate to comics from the fine art world, attracted by the possibilities for narrative and language in the context of drawing that comics offer and gallery art doesn't.

A lot of their work appears in the descendants of *RAW*: art-comics anthology series whose editors have adventurous tastes. I'd say "anthologies" instead of "anthology series," but there actually aren't many notable stand-alone cartoon anthologies. One-off anthologies are often based around a particular theme and therefore usually include a lot of mediocre stuff that happens to fit that theme. A couple of good volumes of an anthology series, on the other hand, will tend to attract increasingly good work to subsequent volumes, as editors get to be choosier about what they include and can afford more interesting ways of presenting that material.

The book that kicked off the current wave of art-comics anthologies was the fifth and final volume of *Non*, edited by Jordan Crane and published in 2002—the silkscreened cover (in various colors) gave it its aura of handmadeness, the two small tipped-in paperbacks appended to it gave it its sense of artistic superabundance. Since then, *Kramers Ergot* (edited by Sammy Harkham) and *The Ganzfeld* (edited by Dan Nadel) have been leading the pack, each publishing a new issue every year or two and getting bigger and more spectacularly designed and more catholic in their selection of contributors with each one. *Kramers* tends to stick to comics and kinds of illustration derived from cartooning; *The Ganzfeld* extends beyond the boundaries of comics to draw connections with other kinds of visual culture.

I should note that not all of those magazines' contributors belong to the difficult school—Crane and Harkham, in fact, have both included fairly straightforward work of their own in their magazines. There are also a few anthology series published by long-lived art-comics publishers that lean more toward conventionally narrative comics. Drawn & Quarterly's anthology of the same name (edited by Chris Oliveros) hasn't published a new issue in some years; instead, there have been a few volumes of the more low-key *Drawn & Quarterly Showcase*, which features only two or three cartoonists in each volume. *MOME* (edited by Fantagraphics' Gary Groth and Eric Reynolds) is, in some ways, the most ambitious comics anthology series right now: more or less quarterly, it gives a handful of regular contributors, including the excellent

Andrice Arp and Gabrielle Bell, space to experiment with short pieces or serialize longer projects.

The other school that's been appearing over the last few years is young cartoonists with a much smoother, self-consciously pretty style; it includes artists like Vera Brosgol and Hope Larson who've grown up on both American and Japanese animation (and the lush colors and printing techniques of animation books), rather than *Batman* or *Hate*, and often incorporate computer drafting and coloring techniques into their work. If that crew has a godfather, it's probably Jim Woodring, who started out doing wobbly-lined, semiautobiographical comics and adaptations of his nightmares, and gradually shifted to a far easier-on-the-eye, animation-inspired style in the '90s with his "Frank" stories.

The smooth wave first came to public attention with a single book: 2004's surprise hit anthology *Flight*, edited by Kazu Kibuishi. The first volume of what's become another ongoing series, *Flight* compiled short pieces by a bunch of young cartoonists who had initially encountered each other's work on the Web. It's visually lush and dazzling, although its strength is generally more lush, dazzling visuals than compelling stories. (One major exception: Clio Chiang's extraordinary, silent eighteen-page piece, "The Bowl.") In the wake of *Flight*'s success and sequels, a few more anthologies of like-minded cartoonists have featured spectacular full-color artwork (and generally not-so-spectacular writing). They include a handful of showcases for animators trying their hand at motionless drawing (*Afterworks* and *Out of Picture*), a

A sequence from Clio Chiang's silent piece "The Bowl," from *Flight* vol. 1.
©2007 Clio Chiang.

A page from Ron Regé Jr.'s *The Awake Field*: as gnarled
and rough as it is cute and engaging. ©2007 Ron Regé Jr.

book of stories about robots in New York City (*24seven*) and a tribute to
the band Belle and Sebastian (*Put the Book Back on the Shelf*).

There's also a sort of combination of both waves' tendencies in a few
artists like Ron Regé Jr., Kurt Wolfgang, and Brian Ralph: the cartoonist
and publisher Tom Devlin's tongue-in-cheek term for that middle path
is "cute brut." It involves rough linework and wild, reader-resisting distortions paired with some of the signs of cuteness, like big eyes, "cartoony" expressions, and even animal characters, along with whimsy
and emotional openness—deliberate charm to go along with the deliberate ugliness.

All of those groups, though, are more lumped-together convergences
than deliberate movements—no cartoonist among them has actually
come up with a manifesto that anyone else has followed. As I've noted

before, what art comics value more than anything else is the distinctiveness of the cartoonist's work.

Part of the great thing about this particular moment in comics history, in fact, is that there are so many emerging cartoonists who don't fit into any particular paradigm or are taking ideas from the artists who've inspired them in wildly different directions. Vanessa Davis's *Spaniel Rage*, Bryan Lee O'Malley's *Scott Pilgrim* books, Kazimir Strzepek's *The Mourning Star*, Renée French's *The Ticking*, Megan Kelso's *The Squirrel Mother*, John Porcellino's *Diary of a Mosquito Abatement Man*—they've all appeared in the last couple of years, they're all worth shouting about, and the only thing they have in common is that they're not like each other or anything else. Twenty years ago, any of them would have been a shocking leap forward for the comics medium; ten years ago, any of them would have been head and shoulders above virtually all of their contemporaries. Now they're just more really good comics, which may mean that there aren't many more shocking leaps forward left for the comics medium to take. Three cheers for that.

NOTES

Chapter 1

The Best American Comics' first volume was published by Houghton Mifflin in 2006, and edited by Harvey Pekar and Anne Elizabeth Moore.

Showcase #4, DC Comics, 1956, was written by Robert Kanigher and John Broome, and drawn by Carmine Infantino and Joe Kubert. It's been reprinted quite a few times, most recently in *The Flash Archives* vol. 1 (a color hardcover) and *Showcase Presents the Flash* vol. 1 (a black-and-white paperback), from DC Comics.

The Amazing Spider-Man #31, Marvel Comics, 1965, written by Stan Lee and drawn by Steve Ditko, has been reprinted many times, and is currently in print in *Marvel Masterworks: The Amazing Spider-Man* vol. 4, *Marvel Visionaries: Steve Ditko* (both color hardcovers) and *Essential Spider-Man* vol. 2 (a black-and-white paperback). See also chapter 8.

Cerebus #44 by Dave Sim, Aardvark-Vanaheim, 1982, is currently in print in *High Society*. See also chapter 17.

For Frank Miller and Klaus Janson's *Batman: The Dark Knight*, see chapter 9.

For Art Spiegelman's *Maus*, see chapter 21.

For Alan Moore and Dave Gibbons' *Watchmen* (and Moore and Bill Sienkiewicz's *Big Numbers*), see chapter 15.

Bryan Lee O'Malley, *Scott Pilgrim and the Infinite Sadness*, Oni Press, 2006.

For Alison Bechdel's *Fun Home*, see chapter 23.

Grant Morrison and Frank Quitely, *All-Star Superman* #4, DC, 2006, reprinted in *All-Star Superman Vol. 1*. See also chapter 16.

For Kevin Huizenga's *Curses*, see chapter 20.

Sammy Harkham, ed., *Kramers Ergot 6*, Buenaventura Press, 2006.

Ellen Forney, *I Love Led Zeppelin*, Fantagraphics Books, 2006.

Ed Brubaker and Michael Lark, *Daredevil* #86, Marvel, 2006.

David B., *Babel* #2, Coconino Press/Fantagraphics, 2006. See also chapter 6.

Lilli Carré, *Tales of Woodsman Pete*, Top Shelf Productions, 2006.

Megan Kelso, *The Squirrel Mother*, Fantagraphics, 2006.

For Charles Burns' *Black Hole*, see chapter 21.

For Marjane Satrapi's *Persepolis*, see chapter 6.

Classics Illustrated, in its initial incarnation (published by Gilberton), published 171 issues between 1947 and 1971. There have been a few revivals, too.

Lisa Owens and Jennifer Tanner, *Black Beauty*, Stone Arch Books, 2007.

Michael Ford and Penko Gelev, *The Hunchback of Notre Dame*, Barron's Educational Series, 2007.

Paul Auster, David Mazzucchelli, and Paul Karasik, *City of Glass*, 1994, currently published by Picador.

Will Eisner, *Comics and Sequential Art*, 1995, currently published by Poorhouse Press. See also chapter 9.

Scott McCloud, *Understanding Comics: The Invisible Art*, 1994, currently published by HarperPaperbacks.

Samuel R. Delany's "The Politics of Paraliterary Criticism" appears in his *Shorter Views: Queer Thoughts & the Politics of the Paraliterary*, Wesleyan University Press/University Press of New England, 1999.

Denny O'Neil and Neal Adams' *Green Lantern/Green Arrow* stories ran in *Green Lantern* from #76 (April 1970) to #89 (April/May 1972) and are currently in print in two volumes of *Green Lantern/Green Arrow*, DC.

The Gerard Jones–written *Green Lantern: Mosaic* series ran eighteen issues from June 1992 to November 1993, from DC; it's entirely out of print.

Susan Sontag, "Against Interpretation," in *Against Interpretation and Other Essays*, 1966, currently in print from Anchor Books.

Rebecca West, "The Duty of Harsh Criticism," initially published in *The New Republic*, November 1914. Now out of print.

Chapter 2

For Scott McCloud's *Understanding Comics*, see chapter 1.

Peter Bagge, *Buddy Does Seattle*, Fantagraphics, 2005, collecting the first fifteen issues of his series *Hate*, 1990–1994.

For *The Invisibles*, see chapter 16.

The Sandman, written by Neil Gaiman and drawn by a cast of thousands, was published by DC Comics and, later, Vertigo/DC between 1989 and 1996. It's collected in ten volumes from Vertigo/DC.

Andrew Sarris's "Notes on the Auteur Theory in 1962" first appeared in *Film Culture* no. 27 (Winter 1962–1963); it's currently in print in the *Film Culture Reader*, edited by P. Adams Sitney, Cooper Square Press, 2000.

Pauline Kael's "Circles and Squares: Joys and Sarris" first appeared in *Film Quarterly* in 1963. It's currently in print in her book *I Lost It at the Movies* (1965), published by Marion Boyars Publishers.

Gary Panter, *Jimbo in Purgatory*, Fantagraphics, 2004.

Rob Liefeld's run on *X-Force*, published by Marvel, was August 1991–June 1992.

Jack Kirby's *Captain Victory and the Galactic Rangers* (Pacific Comics) ran 1981–1984; he drew at least parts of two *Super Powers* miniseries (DC), published in 1984 and 1985.

Kyle Baker's incarnation of *Plastic Man* (published by DC) ran 2004–2006; most of it is collected in two books, *On the Lam* and *Rubber Bandits*.

Winsor McCay, *Little Nemo in Slumberland: So Many Splendid Sundays!*,

Sunday Press, 2005, collecting strips from the early 1900s.

For Will Eisner's *The Spirit*, see chapter 9.

Harvey Kurtzman's "The Big If" appeared in *Frontline Combat* #5, EC Comics, March/April 1952 and has been reprinted many times since.

Bernard Krigstein's "Master Race" was initially published in *Impact* #1, EC Comics, March/April 1955 and has been reprinted many times since.

Fredric Wertham, *Seduction of the Innocent*, Rinehart and Company, 1954; currently published by Amereon Ltd.

"Howdy Dooit," written by Harvey Kurtzman and drawn by Bill Elder, initially appeared in *MAD* #18, December 1954 (EC Comics). It's currently in print in *MAD About the Fifties* (MAD).

Robert Crumb's "Whiteman" first appeared in *Zap Comix* #1, published by Charles Plymell. It's currently in print in *The Complete Crumb Comics* vol. 4, Fantagraphics, 1989, and elsewhere.

Wendy and Richard Pini's original *Elfquest* series ran twenty issues from 1978 to 1985, published by WaRP Graphics. It had many sequels, and the original series has been reprinted numerous times, most recently as the hardcover *Elfquest Archives* from DC.

For Dave Sim's *Cerebus*, see chapter 17.

American Splendor, written by Harvey Pekar and drawn by a host of artists, has been appearing in one form or another since 1976; there are a handful of collections of it from various publishers.

RAW, edited by Art Spiegelman and Françoise Mouly, published eleven issues between 1980 and 1991; they're all out of print.

Howard Chaykin's *American Flagg!* was published by First Comics from 1983 to 1989. As of this writing, a promised new hardcover edition of the early issues, to be published by Dynamic Forces, is several years overdue.

Bill Sienkiewicz drew *Moon Knight* (written by Doug Moench and published by Marvel) for most of the early '80s; beginning with #15, January 1982, it was sold exclusively through the direct market.

Camelot 3000, written by Mike W. Barr and drawn by Brian Bolland and others, ran twelve issues from 1982 to 1985, published by DC and later collected as a book.

For Gilbert and Jaime Hernandez's *Love and Rockets*, see chapters 10 and 11.

For Will Eisner's *A Contract with God*, see chapter 9.

Teenage Mutant Ninja Turtles, originally by Kevin Eastman and Peter Laird and later written and drawn by dozens of people, has been published in one form or another on and off since 1984; its initial publisher was Eastman and Laird's company Mirage.

Adolescent Radioactive Black Belt Hamsters, initially written and drawn by Don Chin and Christopher Parsonavich, ran nine issues (and a few specials) from 1986 to 1989, published by Eclipse.

Aristocratic Xtraterrestrial Time-Traveling Thieves—later *X-Thieves*—by Henry Vogel and Mark Propst ran twelve issues from 1987 to 1988, published by Comics Interview.

Pre-Teen Dirty-Gene Kung-Fu Kangaroos, by Lee Marrs, ran three issues from 1986 to 1986, published by Blackthorne. This is as good a place as any to mention that I also recalled the existence of *Adult Thermonuclear Samurai Elephants*, which Marvel had planned to publish at one point, but it seems to not have appeared under that name, although it was apparently adapted into the 1989 one-shot *Power Pachyderms*.

Todd McFarlane's *Spider-Man* was launched by Marvel in August, 1990; the first issue was published with at least eleven different covers. McFarlane stayed on the series for a little over a year.

For Frank Miller's *Sin City* et al., see chapter 9.

Dan Clowes serialized *Ghost World* in his series *Eightball* from 1993 to 1993; it was collected as a book in 1997. Both versions were published by Fantagraphics.

For Alan Moore and Eddie Campbell's *From Hell*, see chapter 15.

For Carla Speed McNeil's *Finder*, see chapter 14.

Eric Shanower's *Age of Bronze* has been running since 1998, published by Image. There have been two collections so far, *A Thousand Ships* and *Sacrifice*, co-published by Image and Hungry Tiger Press.

For Craig Thompson's *Blankets*, see chapter 12.

For Chris Ware's *Jimmy Corrigan*, see chapter 22.

For Charles Burns' *Black Hole*, see chapter 21.

Jessica Abel's *La Perdida* (Pantheon, 2006) was originally serialized as a five-issue comic book series (Fantagraphics, 2000–2005).

Jeff Smith's *Bone* originally ran as a comic book from several publishers from 1991 to 2004. Scholastic has been reprinting it as a series of what will eventually be nine volumes; there's also a single-volume edition published by Cartoon Books.

Matt Madden, *99 Ways to Tell a Story*, Chamberlain Brothers, 2006.

Stan Lee and John Buscema, *How to Draw Comics the Marvel Way*, Fireside, first published in 1978.

Neal Adams' story "The Game" was first published in *House of Mystery* #178, DC, 1969, and is currently in print in *Showcase Presents House of Mystery, Vol. 1*.

Mark Millar and Steve McNiven's seven-issue series *Civil War* was published by Marvel in 2006–2007, then reprinted as a collection.

The Fantagraphics retrospective *Comics As Art: We Told You So* is, as of this writing, due to be published sometime in 2007.

Jerry Moriarty, *Jack Survives*, Raw Books & Graphics, 1984.

Mark Beyer's *Amy and Jordan* has appeared in various forms over the years, most recently as an anthology published by Pantheon in 2005.

Peter Bagge's *Neat Stuff* (1985–1990) and *Hate* (1990–1999) were both published by Fantagraphics.

William Messner-Loebs' *Journey* ran from 1983 to 1986, published first by Aardvark-Vanaheim and later by Fantagraphics; it's currently out of print.

For Chris Ware's *Acme Novelty Library*, see chapter 22.

Immanuel Kant's *Critique of Aesthetic Judgement* was first published in 1790. My edition of choice is the James Creed Meredith translation in *The Critique of Judgement*, Oxford University Press, 1952.

Stan Lee wrote and Jack Kirby drew the first 102 issues of *Fantastic Four*, 1961–1970, published by Marvel, as are the many, many forms in which they've been reprinted. The most affordable are the first five volumes of the black-and-white *Essential Fantastic Four*; the nicest is probably *Fantastic Four Omnibus vol. 1*, which reprints the first thirty issues. (The image reprinted in this chapter is from *Fantastic Four* #50, 1966.)

Geoff Johns, Phil Jimenez, et al., *Infinite Crisis*, seven issues, DC, 2005–2006, later collected as a book.

Jim Starlin, George Perez, et al., *The Infinity Gauntlet*, six issues, Marvel, 1991, later collected as a book.

Frank Miller and Geoff Darrow, *Hard Boiled*, three issues, Dark Horse Comics, 1990–1992, later collected as a book.

Chapter 3

For Will Eisner's *A Contract with God*, see chapter 9.

Dave Sim and Gerhard's *Melmoth* was serialized in *Cerebus* from 1990 to 1991, then collected as a book, published by Aardvark-Vanaheim. The "graphic reads" bit reprinted in this chapter is from *Cerebus* #208, July 1996, later reprinted in *Guys*. See also chapter 17.

Ron Wilson's *Super Boxers* (Marvel, 1983) was technically *Marvel Graphic Novel* #8.

Marvel Collector's Item Classics ran twenty-two issues from 1965 to 1969, then changed its title to *Marvel's Greatest Comics* and continued through 1981.

The *Overstreet Comic Book Price Guide*, launched in 1970 and more recently retitled *The Official Overstreet Comic Book Price Guide*, is currently in its thirty-sixth edition, published by Gemstone Publishing.

Lynda Barry, *One!Hundred!Demons!*, Sasquatch Books, 2002.

Gene Luen Yang, *American Born Chinese*, First Second Books, 2006.

Chris Ware's *Rusty Brown* is a work-in-progress, currently being serialized in *The Acme Novelty Library*.

Dan Clowes, *Ice Haven*, Pantheon, 2005.

Seth's *It's a Good Life If You Don't Weaken* was serialized in *Palookaville* #4–9, Drawn & Quarterly, 1995–1996, and later collected as a book.

Dick Lupoff and Don Thompson, eds., *All in Color for a Dime*, Ace Books, 1970.

For *The Sandman*, see chapter 2.

Warren Ellis, Darick Robertson et al, *Transmetropolitan*, 1997–2002, published by Helix and later Vertigo, collected in ten volumes.

Megan Kelso, *The Squirrel Mother*, Fantagraphics Books, 2006.

Brian K. Vaughan, Pia Guerra, et al., *Y: The Last Man*, Vertigo, 2002–present.

"Sidney Mellon" et al., *Sidney Mellon's Thunderskull!*, Slave Labor, 1988.

catherine yronwode, "The Lesser Book of the Vishanti," Alibeck the Egyptian, 1978; now available in part at http://www.luckymojo.com/vishanti.html.

For Howard Chaykin's *American Flagg!*, see chapter 2.

Paul Gambi first appeared in *The Flash* #141, DC Comics, December 1963.

The punctuation-less era in *Thor* (published by Marvel, written in those days by Stan Lee and drawn by John Buscema et al.) was mid-1971.

Don Rosa's "Sun of the Sun" first appeared in *Walt Disney's Uncle Scrooge* #219, published by Gladstone in July 1987; it's been reprinted several times.

Mark Gruenwald et al., *DP7*, Marvel, thirty-two issues from 1986 to 1989.

John MacLeod, *The Mundane Adventures of Dishman*, ten issues self-published beginning in 1985 (and one published by Eclipse).

Fred Hembeck, *Abbott and Costello Meet the Bride of Hembeck*, Fantaco Enterprises, 1980.

Alan Brennert's Batman stories appeared in *Detective Comics* #500, *The Brave and the Bold* #178, 181, 182 and 197, *Batman: Holy Terror* and *Batman: Gotham Knights* #10, all published by DC.

Vanessa Davis's story about the geese appeared in the art exhibition "Cartunnel" at the Queens, New York, gallery Flux Factory in 2004.

Steve Gerber et al.'s *Howard the Duck* #16, Marvel, 1977, is currently in print in *Essential Howard the Duck,* vol. 1.

Stephen Grant and various artists' *Whisper* was published by Capital Comics and First Comics from 1983 to 1990.

Andrew and Roger Langridge, *Art D'Ecco,* Fantagraphics, 1990–1992.

Mike Baron, Steve Rude, et al.'s *Nexus* was published by Capital and First from 1981 to 1991 and intermittently thereafter.

George M. Tarleton, ed., *The Journal of M.O.D.O.K. Studies,* early 2000s, good luck finding it.

For Jack Kirby's "Fourth World" comics, see chapter 16.

Richard McGuire's "Here" first appeared in *RAW,* vol. 2, #1, 1989, and was reprinted in *Comic Art* #8 in 2006.

For Eddie Campbell's *After the Snooter,* see chapter 12.

John Broome and Murphy Anderson's "Atomic Knights" stories first appeared in *Strange Adventures* #117 (DC Comics, 1960), and ran through 1964.

René Goscinny and Albert Uderzo's *Asterix* series first appeared as a serial in 1959; to date, there have been thirty-three volumes, constantly in print.

Sheldon Mayer, *Sugar & Spike,* DC Comics, 1956–1971 and intermittently thereafter.

For William Messner-Loebs' *Journey,* see chapter 2.

The issue of *Planetary* in question is #26, by Warren Ellis and John Cassaday, published in December 2006 by Wild-Storm Comics.

Scott McCloud, *Destroy!!,* Eclipse Comics, 1985.

Max Allan Collins and Terry Beatty's *Ms. Tree* was initially published in 1983 by Eclipse (as *Ms. Tree's Thrilling Detective Adventures*), in color; as of #10, it was published by Aardvark-Vanaheim (and later Renegade Press) and printed in duotone, a technique that continued through the end of the series, #50. There were also ten issues of *Ms. Tree Quarterly* published (in color) by DC in the early '90s.

The death-of-Strontium-Dog story (written by Alan Grant and drawn by Colin MacNeil) appeared in *2000 A.D.* #686, July 7, 1990, published by Fleetway Publications.

Marc Hempel, *Gregory,* Piranha Press, 1989; now reprinted in A *Gregory Treasury* vol. 1 (DC Comics).

Todd McFarlane, *Spider-Man* #1, Marvel, 1990.

Ron Regé Jr.'s "Ouch!" ads appeared in various magazines and comic books circa 2004.

Larry Marder's *Tales of the Beanworld* ran twenty-one issues between 1985 and 1993, published by Beanworld Press and Eclipse Comics.

Mary Fleener's *Slutburger* ran six issues from 1990 to 1994, published by Rip Off Press and Drawn & Quarterly.

"Hypertime" was introduced by Mark Waid in the 1998 DC Comics miniseries *The Kingdom*; some accounts claim that Grant Morrison devised it.

Mike Grell wrote and drew the first fifty issues or so of *The Warlord,* 1976–1981, published by DC. (The series kept going for years after that.)

The issue of *Legion of Super-Heroes* in question is #61, September 1994, written by Mark Waid, drawn by Stuart Immonen and Ron Boyd, and published by DC.

R. Sikoryak's "Hester's Little Pearl" appeared in *Drawn & Quarterly* vol. 4, Drawn & Quarterly, 2001; "Good Ol' Gregor Brown" appeared in *RAW* vol. 2,

#2, Penguin, 1990; "Inferno Joe" appeared in *RAW* vol. 2, #1, Penguin, 1989.

Devin Grayson and Duncan Fegredo's "Photo Finish" appeared in *The Batman Chronicles* #9, DC, 1997.

Flex Mentallo first appeared in Grant Morrison, Kelley Jones, and Mark McKenna's *Doom Patrol* #36, DC, 1990.

Jules Feiffer's *Tantrum* was first published in 1980, and is currently in print from Fantagraphics.

Colleen Coover, *Star of the East*, self-published, 2003.

"Judge Dredd" has appeared in virtually every issue of *2000 A.D.* since 1977; a good selection of the Dredd-vs.-democracy stories appears in the collection *Judge Dredd: The Complete America*, published by Titan Books in 2003.

Chapter 4

Erik Larsen, *Savage Dragon*, Image, 1992–present.

Brian Michael Bendis and Michael Avon Oeming, published by Image and later Icon/Marvel, 2000–present.

Todd McFarlane and many others, *Spawn*, Image, 1992–present.

Jim Lee and innumerable others, *WildC.A.T.S.* a.k.a. *Wildcats*, Image and later Wildstorm, 1992–present, on and off.

Alan Moore, Gene Ha and Zander Cannon, *Top 10*, America's Best Comics, 1999–2001.

Stan Lee and Steve Ditko, *Amazing Adult Fantasy* a.k.a. *Amazing Fantasy*, Marvel, 1961–1962. See also chapter 8.

"Spider-Man No More" was *Amazing Spider-Man* #50, by Stan Lee, John Romita and Mickey Demeo, 1967. "The Night Gwen Stacy Died" was *Amazing Spider-Man* #121, by Gerry Conway, Gil Kane, and John Romita, 1973. "The Death of Jean DeWolff" was *Peter Parker,*

the Spectacular Spider-Man #107–110, by Peter David, Rich Buckler, et al., 1985–1986. All published by Marvel.

Jim Owsley, Mark Bright, and Al Williamson, *Spider-Man Vs. Wolverine*, Marvel, 1987.

For Grant Morrison's *New X-Men*, see chapter 16.

Mark Waid and Barry Kitson, *Legion of Super-Heroes*, DC, 2004–present.

World's Finest Comics, published by DC, featured Superman-Batman team-ups from #71 (1954) to #323 (1986), with a brief pause in the early '70s. There's now an ongoing series called *Superman/ Batman*, which does effectively the same thing.

Lots of '40s-era Wonder Woman stories have been reprinted in DC's *Wonder Woman Archives* hardcover series. For the feminist movement–era version of the series, see especially Samuel R. Delany and Dick Giordano's *Wonder Woman* #203, 1972, cover-blurbed as "Special! Women's Lib Issue." The Greg Rucka–written run on the (relaunched and therefore renumbered) series was #195–226, 2004–2006.

Alan Moore and Brian Bolland, *Batman: The Killing Joke*, DC, 1988.

The first *Sentry* miniseries, by Paul Jenkins and Jae Lee, was published by Marvel in 2000.

Dan Jurgens et al., *Booster Gold*, DC, 1986–1988.

Kurt Busiek et al., *Thunderbolts*, Marvel, 1987–present.

Ed Brubaker and Sean Phillips, *Sleeper*, Wildstorm, 2003–2004, and *Sleeper: Season Two*, Wildstorm, 2004–2005.

Mark Millar et al., *The Authority*, starting with #13, Wildstorm, on and off 2000–2003.

Mark Millar and Bryan Hitch, *The Ultimates* and *The Ultimates 2*, Marvel, 2002–present.

Brad Meltzer, Rags Morales and Michael Bair, *Identity Crisis*, DC, initially published 2004–2005, then collected as a book.

Howard the Duck's presidential run happened in Marvel Comics's *Howard the Duck* series in 1976.

The first issue of *The Badger*, by Mike Baron and Jeffrey Butler, was published by Capital in 1983, and ads for it appeared in other Capital titles (notably *Nexus*) around that time.

For *Miracleman*, see chapter 15.

Mark Gruenwald, Bob Hall, et al., *Squadron Supreme*, Marvel, 1985–1986.

Joss Whedon and John Cassaday, *Astonishing X-Men* #15, Marvel, 2006.

Chris Claremont, John Byrne, and Terry Austin, *Uncanny X-Men* #132, Marvel, 1980.

The Squadron Supreme (or Squadron Sinister) first appeared in Marvel's *Avengers* #70, Marvel Comics, 1969, and reappeared in 1971's *Avengers* #85–86; the Champions of Angor first appeared in DC's *Justice League of America* #87 in 1971.

Dwayne McDuffie, Ernie Colon, et al., *Damage Control*, Marvel, three four-issue miniseries, 1989–1991.

Kurt Busiek and Brent Anderson, *Astro City*, Image and later Homage Comics, 1995–present.

Garth Ennis and Darick Robertson, *The Boys*, Wildstorm and later Dynamite Entertainment, 2006–present.

Warren Ellis and Stuart Immonen, *Nextwave*, Marvel, 2006–2007.

For *Promethea*, see chapter 15.

Warren Ellis and John Cassaday, *Planetary*, Wildstorm, 1999–2007.

The Elite first appeared in *Action Comics* #775, by Joe Kelly and Doug Mahnke, DC, 2001.

Brian Michael Bendis, Michael Gaydos, et al., *Alias*, Marvel, 2001–2004, collected in four books (and the single-volume *Alias Omnibus* hardcover).

Geoff Johns, Grant Morrison, Greg Rucka, Mark Waid, et al., *52*, DC, 2006–2007.

Greg Rucka, Ed Brubaker, et al., *Gotham Central*, DC, 2002–2006.

Keith Giffen, J. M. DeMatteis, Bart Sears, et al., *Justice League Europe*, DC, 1989–1993.

Geoff Johns, Phil Jimenez, et al., *Infinite Crisis*, DC Comics, 2005–2006, collected as a single volume.

Chris Claremont and John Byrne, et al., *Uncanny X-Men* #108–143, Marvel, 1978–1981, reprinted in various forms including *Essential X-Men* volumes 1 and 2.

Steve Englehart and Marshall Rogers, et al., *Detective Comics* #471–476, DC, 1977–1978, reprinted as *Batman: Strange Apparitions*.

Marv Wolfman and George Pérez, et al., *New Teen Titans* #1–40 and *New Teen Titans* vol. 2 #1–5, DC, 1980–1985.

Tom Bierbaum, Mary Bierbaum, Keith Giffen, et al., *Legion of Super-Heroes* #1–38, DC, 1989–1992.

For *Nexus*, see chapter 3.

For O'Neil and Adams's *Green Lantern*, see chapter 1.

Steve Englehart and Marshall Rogers, *Coyote*, initially serialized in *Eclipse Magazine*, Eclipse, 1981–1983, later collected as a book.

Steve Englehart and Marshall Rogers, *Madame Xanadu*, DC, 1981.

Brian Michael Bendis, Alex Maleev, et al., *Daredevil* #26–81, Marvel, 2001–2006, collected in various forms.

For Miller and Janson's *Daredevil*, see chapter 9.

Gail Simone et al., *Birds of Prey: Sensei & Student*, DC, 2005, serialized as *Birds of Prey* #62–68.

Chapter 5

For Scott McCloud's *Understanding Comics*, see chapter 1.

Scott McCloud, *Making Comics*, HarperCollins, 2006.

Joe Sacco, *Palestine*, 1993, now collected by Fantagraphics.

Joe Sacco, *Safe Area Gorazde*, Fantagraphics, 2000.

The Guy Delisle comics I'm thinking of are, especially, *Pyongyang* and *Shenzhen*, originally published in France and published in English by Drawn & Quarterly in 2005 and 2006, respectively.

Chris Claremont, Bob Hall, and Marie Severin, *Marvel Team-Up* #74, Marvel, 1978.

Denny O'Neil, Neal Adams, et al., *Superman Vs. Muhammad Ali*, DC, 1978.

For *Lost Girls* and *V for Vendetta*, see chapter 15.

Hergé's *Tintin* books initially appeared between 1929 and 1986.

C. C. Beck drew Captain Marvel in *Whiz Comics* and *Captain Marvel Adventures* in the '40s.

Carl Barks drew Donald Duck and Uncle Scrooge stories in *Walt Disney's Comics and Stories*, *Uncle $crooge*, and elsewhere in the '40s, '50s, and '60s; they've been reprinted extensively.

Seth, *Clyde Fans Book One*, Drawn & Quarterly, 2004, collecting a story serialized in *Palookaville* beginning in 1997.

Gotthold Ephraim Lessing, *Laocoön*, first published 1766; my edition of choice is Edward Allen McCormick's translation, Johns Hopkins University Press.

Hank Ketcham's *Dennis the Menace* comic strips, 1951–1994, are now being reprinted as a series of books published by Fantagraphics, 2005–present.

For David B.'s *Epileptic*, see chapter 6. For Lee and Ditko's *Dr. Strange*, see chapter 8. For Grant Morrison, see chapter 16.

For Hope Larson, see chapter 13. For Chester Brown, see chapter 7.

A Small Disclaimer

Jim Woodring, *The Frank Book*, Fantagraphics, 2003 (collecting material originally published 1991–2001).

Peter Blegvad, *The Book of Leviathan*, The Overlook Press, 2001 (collecting material originally published 1991–1999).

Chapter 6

David B., *Epileptic*, Pantheon, 2005 (initially published in France in six volumes).

David B., "The Armed Garden," in *MOME* vol. 3, Fantagraphics, 2006.

David B., "The Veiled Prophet," in *MOME* vol. 4, Fantagraphics, 2006.

Joann Sfar, *The Rabbi's Cat*, Pantheon, 2005 (initially published in France in three volumes).

Lewis Trondheim, *Mister O*, NBM, 2004.

Marjane Satrapi, *Persepolis: The Story of a Childhood*, Pantheon, 2003; *Persepolis 2: The Story of a Return*, Pantheon, 2004; *Embroideries*, Pantheon, 2005; *Chicken with Plums*, Pantheon, 2006.

Killoffer, *Six Hundred and Seventy-Six Apparitions of Killoffer*, Typocrat, 2005.

David B., *Babel*, two issues so far from Coconino Press (the first with Drawn & Quarterly, the second with Fantagraphics), 2005 and 2006.

Chapter 7

Chester Brown's *Yummy Fur* had seven issues self-published as mini-comics (1983–1985), then twenty-four more issues published by Vortex (1986–1991), and a final eight issues published by Drawn and Quarterly, who've also published his other work and collections to date: *The Definitive Ed Book* (1992), *Ed the Happy Clown* (nine issues, 2004–2006), *The Playboy* (1992), *I Never Liked You* (1994), *The Little Man* (1998), *Underwater* (1994–1997), and *Louis Riel* (serialized 1999–2003, collected 2003).

Chapter 8

The Steve Ditko–drawn issues of *The Amazing Spider-Man*, written (sometimes scripted from Ditko's plot) by Stan Lee and published by Marvel, are #1–38, 1963–1966; the Ditko Spider-Man canon also includes *Amazing Fantasy* #15, *Amazing Spider-Man Annual* #1 and 2, and *Strange Tales Annual* #2. They've been reprinted many times over; the black-and-white *Essential Spider-Man* volumes 1 and 2 contain all of them.

Jaime Hernandez's "Bob Richardson" is the final story in *Locas*—see chapter 11.

Ditko drew the (mostly Stan Lee–written) Doctor Strange stories in *Strange Tales* #110–111 and 114–146, 1963–1966, published by Marvel and reprinted many times, including *Essential Dr. Strange* vol. 1.

Some of the *Tales to Astonish* and *Amazing Adult Fantasy* Lee/Ditko stories have been reprinted; the hardcover *Steve Ditko: Marvel Visionaries* includes a sampling of them.

Ditko's Question stories appeared in *Blue Beetle* #1–5, 1967–1968, and *Mysterious Suspense* #1, 1968, published by Charlton Comics. They've been most recently reprinted in the hardcover *Action Heroes Archives*, vol. 2 (DC).

The Hawk and the Dove first appeared in *Showcase* #75, 1968 (DC). The Creeper first appeared in *Showcase* #73, 1968 (DC). Shade the Changing Man first appeared in *Shade, the Changing Man* #1, 1977 (DC). The Ditko-drawn Starman (one of many characters by that name) first appeared in *Adventure Comics* #467, 1980 (DC). Static first appeared in *Eclipse Monthly* #1, 1983 (Eclipse). Speedball first appeared in *Amazing Spider-Man Annual* #22, 1988 (Marvel). Ditko's issues of *ROM* were #59–75, 1984–1986 (Marvel).

Ditko's Mr. A. character appeared various places as early as 1968, but the actual Mr. A. comics were published in 1973 and 1974 (by Comic Art Publishers and Bruce Hershenson); Hershenson also published *Avenging World* in 1973 and *..Wha..!?* in 1974.

Strange Avenging Tales's sole issue was published in 1997 by Fantagraphics.

The Ditko Public Service Package was published in 1991 by Robin K. Snyder, who also published *Steve Ditko's 32-Page Package* in 2000.

Peter Bagge, *Startling Stories: The Megalomaniacal Spider-Man*, Marvel, 2002.

Neil Gaiman and Andy Kubert, *1602*, Marvel, eight issues, 2003, reprinted in a single volume.

Chapter 9

Will Eisner, *Will Eisner's New York*, Norton, 2006, collects three books from the '80s and '90s.

Eisner's *The Spirit* ran weekly from 1940 to 1952, and it's been reprinted several times; all but the last couple of years are currently in print as *Will Eisner's The Spirit Archives*, a series of hardcovers from DC. (Note that there are a few patches—during World War II and toward the end of its run—when Eisner wasn't working on it himself, or barely contributed to it.) The paperback *Best of the Spirit* was published by DC in 2005.

Eisner's *A Contract With God and Other Tenement Stories* was first published in 1978 by Baronet Books; it's currently in print from Norton.

Eisner's 1985 *Comics and Sequential Art* is currently in print from Poorhouse Press, as is 1996's *Graphic Storytelling and Visual Narrative*.

Eisner's *The Plot: The Secret Story of the Protocols of the Elders of Zion* was published by Norton in 2005.

Will Eisner and Frank Miller, *Eisner/Miller*, Dark Horse, 2005.

Frank Miller and Klaus Janson drew *Daredevil* (published by Marvel Comics) from #158, May 1979, to #191, February 1983; Miller started writing it with #168, January 1981. The Miller-written issues are collected in the hardcover *Daredevil by Frank Miller Omnibus*, Marvel, 2007.

Frank Miller, *Ronin*, six issues, DC, 1983–1984, later collected as a single volume.

Kazuo Koike and Goseki Kojima's *Lone Wolf and Cub* series began in Japan (as *Kozure Okami*) in 1970; it's currently in print in the U.S. as a series of twenty-eight volumes from Dark Horse, some with covers by Miller.

Frank Miller and Klaus Janson's *Batman: The Dark Knight* was serialized as a four-issue miniseries in 1986, then collected as *Batman: The Dark Knight Returns*; it's still in print on its own, and as part of the fancy hardcover *Absolute Dark Knight* (DC Comics).

For Dave Sim's *Church & State*, see chapter 17.

Miller's *Sin City* first appeared in *Dark Horse Presents* #51, 1991, and has gone on to a number of miniseries, one-shots, and book collections, all published by Dark Horse. The collections, in order, are *The Hard Goodbye, A Dame to Kill For, The Big Fat Kill, That Yellow Bastard, Family Values, Booze, Broads & Bullets,* and *Hell and Back (A Sin City Love Story).*

Frank Miller, *The Dark Knight Strikes Again*, three issues, DC, 2001, later collected as a single volume.

Chapters 10 and 11

Gilbert and Jaime Hernandez are closely entangled bibliographically. Work by both of them has appeared in every issue of *Love & Rockets*. (The first, a magazine-sized series, was fifty issues from 1982 to 1995; the second, a comic-sized series, has been running since 2000.) A lot of it has been reprinted in various formats over the past quarter-century. The hardcover *Palomar* collects Gilbert's stories set in Palomar from the first series (but not stories with the same characters elsewhere); the hardcover *Locas* collects Jaime's stories about Maggie and Hopey from the first series (but not stories about other characters from the Maggie-and-Hopey stories). There's also a recent paperback, *Heartbreak Soup*, collecting Gilbert's early Palomar stories, and another one, *Maggie the Mechanic*, collecting the early stories from *Locas* along with related stories.

Between the first and second series of *Love & Rockets*, each of the brothers did "solo" comics. Jaime wrote and drew *Whoa, Nellie!* (collected in a book with the same title) and *Penny Century* (collected in *Locas in Love* and part of *Dicks and Deedees*); Gilbert wrote and drew *New Love* (collected in *Fear of Comics*). Gilbert's more recent comics also include both *Luba* and *Luba's Comics & Stories* (collected in *Luba in America, Luba: The Book of Ofelia,* and *Luba: Three Daughters*), as well as *New Tales of Old Palomar* and the 2006 graphic novel *Sloth*.

Jaime's *Ghost of Hoppers* collects some of his material from the second *Love & Rockets* series.

All of the above is published by Fantagraphics Books, except Gilbert's *Sloth*, published by DC Comics/Vertigo.

Keven Huizenga's brochure for the Center for Cartoon Studies was published in 2006.

For Scott McCloud's *Making Comics*, see chapter 5.

Gilbert's *Birdland* (four issues, 1990–1994) was published by Eros/Fantagraphics, and later collected as a book.

Measles, 1998–2001, published by Fantagraphics.

Gilbert Hernandez, *Love & Rockets X*, 1993, Fantagraphics.

Chapter 12

For Harvey Pekar et al.'s *American Splendor*, see chapter 2.

Joe Matt's *Peepshow* has appeared intermittently as a comic book since 1992; his autobiographical stories have been collected as *Peepshow—The Cartoon Diary of Joe Matt*, *The Poor Bastard*, *Fair Weather*, and *Spent*, all published by Drawn & Quarterly.

Julie Doucet's *Dirty Plotte* ran twelve issues from 1991 to 1998; it's been collected in books including *My Most Secret Desire* and *Lift Your Leg, My Fish Is Dead!*, published by Drawn & Quarterly.

Eddie Campbell's Alec McGarry stories began to appear in various places in 1981; most of them have been collected in *The King Canute Crowd*, *How to Be an Artist*, *Three Piece Suit*, and *After the Snooter* (all published by Eddie Campbell Comics; the last abandons the pretense of fiction and the pseudonym of Alec McGarry). *The Fate of the Artist*, 2006, First Second, continues some of their threads.

For Dan Clowes' *Ghost World*, see chapter 2.

James Kochalka, *The Cute Manifesto*, Alternative Comics, 2005.

James Kochalka's *American Elf*, www.americanelf.com, has been collected in two volumes published by Top Shelf Productions.

James Kochalka, *Peanutbutter and Jeremy's Best Book Ever*, Alternative Comics, 2004.

James Kochalka, *Monkey Vs. Robot*, Top Shelf Productions, 2000.

Craig Thompson, *Blankets*, Top Shelf Productions, 2003.

Craig Thompson, *Goodbye, Chunky Rice*, originally published 1999, now published by Pantheon.

Craig Thompson, *Carnet de Voyage*, Top Shelf Productions, 2004.

Chapter 13

Hope Larson, *Salamander Dream*, AdHouse Books, 2005.

Hope Larson, *Gray Horses*, Oni Press, 2006.

Chapter 14

Carla Speed McNeil's *Finder* ran thirty-eight issues as a print comic, 1996–2005, and new material is still being serialized on the Web. Its collections, in order: *Sin-Eater* vol. 1, *Sin-Eater* vol. 2, *King of the Cats*, *Talisman*, *Dream Sequence*, *Mystery Date*, *The Rescuers*, and *Five Crazy Women*. All of the above are published by Lightspeed Press.

Chapter 15

Moore drew "The Sounds My Degradation" and a few other things for the

British music magazine *Sounds* as "Curt Vile" between 1979 and 1983, as well as the children's comic strip "Maxwell the Magic Cat" as "Jill de Ray" between 1979 and 1986.

For Eddie Campbell's *After the Snooter*, see chapter 12.

Moore and David Lloyd's *V for Vendetta* began as a serial in the British magazine *Warrior* in 1982, was completed as an American comic book series (published by DC) in 1988–1989, and collected in a book.

Moore and Oscar Zarate's *A Small Killing* was first published in 1991; it's currently in print from Avatar Press.

Moore and Ian Gibson's *The Ballad of Halo Jones*, what there is of it (three of a proposed ten "books"), was initially serialized in the British weekly comic *2000 A.D.* between 1984 and 1986; it's currently in print as a single volume from Titan.

Only two issues of Moore and Bill Sienkiewicz's *Big Numbers* appeared, in 1990, published by Mad Love.

Alan Moore and Dave Gibbons's *Watchmen* was serialized as twelve issues in 1986 and 1987, published by DC, and collected as a single book in 1987; it's still in print, and *Absolute Watchmen* is an oversize hardcover with slightly altered coloring.

Alan Moore and Eddie Campbell's *From Hell* was serialized first in the anthology *Taboo* and later as a series of its own from various publishers between 1989 and 1998. The single-volume edition was published in 1999, and is currently in print from Top Shelf Productions.

Moore and Alan Davis's *D.R. and Quinch* was initially serialized in *2000 A.D.* between 1983 and 1985; it's currently in print as a single volume from Rebellion.

Moore wrote *Supreme* and *Supreme: The Return*, drawn by various artists, from 1996 to 2000; they're currently in print as *The Story of the Year* and *The Return*, published by Checker Book Publishing Group.

Moore and Kevin O'Neill's *The League of Extraordinary Gentlemen* has so far appeared as two miniseries, 1999–2000 and 2002–2003, collected in two volumes, published by America's Best Comics.

The first few chapters of Moore and Melinda Gebbie's *Lost Girls* were serialized in the anthology series *Taboo* in 1991 and 1992; the entire work was finally published in 2006 by Top Shelf Productions.

Moore wrote *The Saga of the Swamp Thing*, later simply *Swamp Thing*, from 1984 to 1987; it was drawn by many artists. His run on the series has been collected in six volumes: *Saga of the Swamp Thing*, *Love & Death*, *The Curse*, *A Murder of Crows*, *Earth to Earth*, and *Reunion*, all published by Vertigo/DC.

Moore, J. H. Williams III, and Mick Gray's *Promethea* ran from 1999 to 2005 and was collected in five volumes, published by America's Best Comics.

A few issues of *ABC A-Z*, by various writers and artists, appeared from America's Best Comics in 2005 and 2006.

Moore and Steve Parkhouse's *The Bojeffries Saga* appeared in various comics, including *Warrior*, *Dalgoda*, *Flesh and Bones*, *A–1*, and *The Complete Bojeffries Saga*, between 1983 and 1992. It's sadly out of print at the moment.

One could write a book about the bibliographical and legal nightmare that is the series variously known as *Marvelman* and *Miracleman*; George Khoury's *Kimota! The Miracleman Companion*, TwoMorrows Publishing, 2001, is just such a book. Let's just say that Moore wrote it between 1982 and 1989 and that it's currently out of print despite a great deal of public demand.

Moore and Scott Clark, *Spawn/WildC.A.T.S.*, Image, 1996.

Moore, Michael Lopez, and Al Rio, *Voodoo*, Image, 1997–1998.

Moore and Ryan Benjamin, *Fire from Heaven*, Image, 1996.

Moore and Brian Denham, *Violator Vs. Badrock*, Image, 1995.

Moore's 1996 prose novel *Voice of the Fire* is currently published in the United States by Top Shelf Productions.

Moore and Dave Gibbons's "Mogo Doesn't Socialize" first appeared in *Green Lantern* #188, 1985, and is now in print in *DC Universe: The Stories of Alan Moore*, published by DC.

Various creators, *Pirates Comics*, Hillman, 1950.

Various creators, *Piracy*, EC Comics, 1954–1955.

Bertolt Brecht and Kurt Weill premiered *Die Dreigroschenoper* in 1928; Marc Blizstein's translation as *The Threepenny Opera* opened in 1954.

Lewis Carroll's *Alice's Adventures in Wonderland* was published in 1865, followed by *Through the Looking-Glass* in 1871.

J. M. Barrie's *Peter Pan* premiered as a play in 1904; he adapted it into the 1911 novel *Peter Pan and Wendy*, also known as *Peter Pan*.

L. Frank Baum's *The Wonderful Wizard of Oz* was published in 1900.

Chapter 16

The Invisibles, written by Grant Morrison and drawn by everyone under the sun, was published by Vertigo/DC Comics as three separately numbered series from 1994 to 2000 (the last of them numbered in reverse, from 12 down to 1). It's collected in seven volumes from Vertigo/DC. In the order the story goes, they're *Say You Want a Revolution* (1996), *Apocalipstick* (2001), *Entropy in the U.K.* (2001), *Bloody Hell in America* (1998), *Counting to None* (1999), *Kissing Mr. Quimper* (2000) and *The Invisible Kingdom* (2002)—and yes, the collections were published out of order.

Morrison wrote and Charles Truog (among others) drew the first twenty-six issues of *Animal Man*, 1988–1990, published by DC. They've been collected as *Animal Man, Origin of the Species*, and *Deus Ex Machina*, all published by Vertigo/DC.

Morrison wrote and Richard Case (among others) drew *Doom Patrol* #19–63, 1989–1993, published by DC Comics. Most of them have been collected as *Crawling from the Wreckage, The Painting That Ate Paris, Down Paradise Way, Musclebound*, and *Magic Bus*, all published by Vertigo/DC; a final volume is forthcoming.

Morrison's *JLA* stories, drawn by Howard Porter and various others, ran in most of the first forty-one issues of *JLA*, 1997–2000, published by DC. It's been collected in six volumes: *New World Order, American Dreams, Rock of Ages, Strength in Numbers, Justice for All*, and *World War III*.

Morrison wrote *New X-Men* #114–154, 2001–2003, drawn by Frank Quitely and many others, and published by Marvel. They're collected in several editions, including the single-volume *New X-Men Omnibus*.

Morrison's stories have appeared in *Batman* intermittently since #655, 2006, DC Comics.

For *All-Star Superman*, see chapter 1.

Leon Battista Alberti's *On Painting* was written in 1435; my edition of choice is the Martin Kemp translation published by Penguin Classics.

For Kant's *Critique of Aesthetic Judgement*, see chapter 2.

Morrison and Frank Quitely's *We3* was a three-issue miniseries, 2004–2005, Vertigo/DC, collected as a single volume.

Morrison wrote and Chris Weston and Gary Erskine drew *The Filth*, a thirteen-issue miniseries, Vertigo/DC, 2002–2003, collected as a single volume.

Seaguy: Morrison writing, Cameron Stewart drawing, three issues, 2004, single-volume collection, Vertigo/DC.

Morrison et al.'s *Seven Soldiers* project, DC, 2005–2006, is a logistical oddity. The short version is that there were two "bookend" issues of *Seven Soldiers of Victory*, #0 and #1; between them were seven more or less simultaneous miniseries: *Shining Knight, Zatanna, The Manhattan Guardian, Klarion the Witch Boy, Mister Miracle, Frankenstein,* and *The Bulleteer.* They're all collected in something close to their original order of release (which is the intended reading order) as *Seven Soldiers of Victory,* volumes 1–4.

Jack Kirby's "Fourth World" comics, published by DC, were similarly chaotically simultaneous. Between 1970 and 1973, he wrote and drew (with some assistance) *Superman's Pal, Jimmy Olsen* #133–139 and 141–148, *New Gods* #1–11, *The Forever People* #1–11, and *Mister Miracle* #1–18, all of which have been reprinted at least once; in 1984 and 1985, he attempted to conclude the "Fourth World" story in a new story in the sixth issue of a new *New Gods* reprint series, followed by a standalone "graphic novel" called *The Hunger Dogs.* As of this writing, there were plans to reprint it all in the order of original publication in a series of volumes of *Jack Kirby's Fourth World.*

Michael Chabon, *The Amazing Adventures of Kavalier & Clay,* 2000, Random House.

Chapter 17

Dave Sim, *Cerebus,* 300 issues and change, Aardvark-Vanaheim, 1977–2004. Most, but not all of it, is collected in sixteen volumes: *Cerebus, High Society, Church & State I, Church & State II, Jaka's Story, Melmoth, Flight, Women, Reads, Minds, Guys, Rick's Story, Going Home, Form and Void, Latter Days,* and *The Last Day.*

Roy Thomas and Barry Windsor-Smith's *Conan* comics, adapting and taking off from Robert E. Howard's fantasy stories of the same name, appeared in the first two dozen issues of Marvel's long-running *Conan the Barbarian* series, which were published 1970–1973. They're currently in print in the first four volumes of *The Chronicles of Conan,* published by Dark Horse.

Chapter 18

Jim Starlin's initial *Warlock* stories, all published by Marvel Comics, appeared in *Strange Tales* 178–181 (1975), *Warlock* #9–15 (1975–1976), *Avengers Annual* #7 (1977), and *Marvel Two-In-One Annual* #2 (1977). They've been reprinted several times, but are not currently in print.

Stan Lee, Jack Kirby, and Joe Sinnott, *Fantastic Four* #66, Marvel, 1967, currently in print in *Essential Fantastic Four* vol. 4.

For the Steve Ditko stuff, see Chapter 8.

Jack Kirby et al., *OMAC,* eight issues published by DC, 1974–1975.

Starlin's *OMAC* stories appeared in *Kamandi* #59, 1978, and *Warlord* #37–39, 1980, published by DC.

Harlan Ellison, ed., *Dangerous Visions,* 1967, currently published by iBooks.

Chapter 19

Michel Houellebecq's *H.P. Lovecraft: Against the World, Against Life*, McSweeney's/Believer Books, 2005; originally published in French in 1999.

Marv Wolfman, Gene Colan, Tom Palmer, et al., *Tomb of Dracula*, Marvel, 1972–1979; collected by Marvel as *Essential Tomb of Dracula*, volumes 1–3.

Various creators, *The Monster of Frankenstein* a.k.a. *The Frankenstein Monster*, Marvel, 1973–1975.

Various creators, *Werewolf by Night*, Marvel, 1972–1977.

Doug Moench, Paul Gulacy, et al., *Master of Kung Fu*, Marvel, 1974–1983; regrettably out of print, thanks to the appearance of licensed character Fu Manchu.

Michael Fleischer et al.'s *Jonah Hex* ran from 1977 to 1985, published by DC. The character first appeared in *All-Star Western* #10 in 1972; the stuffed-and-mounted Hex story appeared in 1978's *Jonah Hex Spectacular*.

Don McGregor, P. Craig Russell, et al.'s episodes of "Killraven" appeared in *Amazing Adventures* #27–39, Marvel, 1974–1976.

Marv Wolfman and Gene Colan wrote and drew *Night Force*, DC, 1982–1983.

Wolfman and Colan's *The Curse of Dracula* was a three-issue Dark Horse miniseries in 1998. Their *Tomb* parody story appeared in *Treehouse of Horror* #11, Bongo Comics, 2005.

Robert Kirkman et al.'s *The Walking Dead* has been running since 2003, published by Image.

Chapter 20

Kevin Huizenga, *Curses*, Drawn & Quarterly, 2006.

Kevin Huizenga, *Supermonster*, self-published minicomics series, dates unclear; ditto for *Untitled*, etc.

Kevin Huizenga, *Or Else*, Drawn & Quarterly, 2004–present.

Kevin Huizenga, *Ganges*, Coconino Press/Fantagraphics, 2006.

For the Center for Cartoon Studies booklet, see chapter 10.

For Hergé's *Tintin*, see chapter 5.

E. C. Segar's comic strip featuring Popeye was actually called *Thimble Theatre*; he wrote and drew it from 1919 until his death in 1938 (although Popeye himself didn't appear until 1929).

Italo Calvino's "The Feathered Ogre" appears in *Italian Folktales*, written in 1956 and currently in print from Harvest Books.

Chapter 21

Charles Burns, *Black Hole*, Pantheon, 2005 (originally serialized in twelve issues published by Kitchen Sink Press and Fantagraphics from 1995 to 2004).

For RAW, see chapter 2.

For Mark Beyer's "Amy and Jordan," see chapter 2.

Ben Katchor, *The Jew of New York*, Pantheon, 1998.

Gary Panter, *Jimbo in Purgatory*, Fantagraphics, 2004; *Jimbo's Inferno*, Fantagraphics, 2006.

Art Spiegelman's *Maus* was serialized in the '80s in RAW, then collected into two volumes (*Maus: A Survivor's Tale*, 1986, and *Maus: A Survivor's Tale II: And Here My Troubles Began*, 1991); there's also a single-volume hardcover. All book editions published by Pantheon.

Miriam Katin, *We Are On Our Own*, Drawn & Quarterly, 2006.

Martin Lemelman, *Mendel's Daughter: A Memoir*, Free Press, 2006.

Art Spiegelman, *Open Me . . . I'm a Dog!*, Joanna Cotler, 1997.

Art Spiegelman and Françoise Mouly edited three volumes of *Little Lit*, 2000–2003, collected in part in *Big Fat Little Lit*, Puffin, 2006.

Art Spiegelman, *In the Shadow of No Towers*, Pantheon, 2004.

Art Spiegelman, "Portrait of the Artist as a Young %@?*!," in *Virginia Quarterly Review*, Fall 2005–present.

Chapter 22

Chris Ware's *Jimmy Corrigan, the Smartest Kid On Earth*, Pantheon, 2000, was initially serialized in different forms in *The Acme Novelty Library*, published by Fantagraphics, and in a weekly newspaper strip.

Chris Ware, *Acme Novelty Library*, 1993–present, initially published by Fantagraphics and more recently self-published.

Chris Ware, *Quimby the Mouse*, Fantagraphics, 2003.

F. C. Ware, *The Acme Novelty Library Final Report to Shareholders* and *Saturday Afternoon Rainy Day Fun Book*, Pantheon, 2005.

Ivan Brunetti, ed., *An Anthology of Graphic Fiction, Cartoons, and True Stories*, Yale University Press, 2006.

Ivan Brunetti, *HAW!*, Fantagraphics, 2001.

Chip Kidd, *Peanuts: The Art of Charles M. Schulz*, Pantheon, 2001.

Frank King, *Walt & Skeezix*, Drawn & Quarterly, 2005–present.

George Herriman, *Krazy & Ignatz*, Fantagraphics, 2002–present. (The first Ware-designed, Fantagraphics-published volume is *Krazy & Ignatz 1925–1926: There Is a Heppy Lend Fur, Fur Awa-a-ay*. There also exists an earlier series of volumes reprinting the earlier years of "Krazy Kat" weekend strips, and various reprints of *Krazy* dailies.)

Chris Ware, *The Acme Novelty Datebook*, Drawn & Quarterly, 2003.

Chapter 23

Alison Bechdel, *Fun Home*, Houghton Mifflin, 2006. Her comic strip "Dykes to Watch Out For" has been collected in eleven volumes (so far) from Firebrand Press.

Afterword

R. Kikuo Johnson, *Night Fisher*, Fantagraphics, 2005.

Jeffrey Brown, *Clumsy*, Top Shelf Productions, 2003.

Anders Nilsen, *Big Questions*, self-published at first and later published by Drawn & Quarterly, 1999–present.

Ben Jones and Frank Santoro, *Cold Heat*, PictureBox Inc., 2006–present.

Jenn Manley Lee's "Dicebox," www.dicebox.net, 2002–present.

Dylan Meconis, "Family Man," www.webcomicsnation.com/dmeconis/familyman/series.php, 2006–present.

R. Stevens, "Diesel Sweeties," www.dieselsweeties.com, 2000–present.

Chris Baldwin, "Little Dee," www.comics.com/comics/littledee/index.html, 2004–present.

Demian 5, "When I Am King," www.demian5.com/king/wiak.htm, 2001.

Matt Feazell, *Cynicalman*, Not Available Comics, 1980–present.

Marc Bell, *Worn Tuff Elbow*, Fantagraphics Books, 2004.

Anders Nilsen, *Monologues for the Coming Plague*, Fantagraphics, 2006.

Brian Chippendale, *Ninja*, PictureBox Inc., 2006.

Jordan Crane, ed., *Non #5* Highwater Books/Red Ink Press, 2002

Sammy Harkham, ed., *Kramers Ergot*, various publishers, 2000–present.

Dan Nadel et al., eds., *The Ganzfeld*, various publishers, 2000–present.

Chris Oliveros, ed., *Drawn & Quarterly*, 1990–2004.

Chris Oliveros, ed., *Drawn & Quarterly Showcase*, Drawn & Quarterly, 2003–present.

Gary Groth and Eric Reynolds, eds., *MOME*, Fantagraphics, 2004–present.

Kazu Kibuishi, ed., *Flight*, Image, 2004.

Various artists, *Afterworks*, vol. 2, Image, 2006.

Various artists, *Out of Picture*, Paquet, 2006.

Ivan Brandon, ed., *24seven*, Image, 2006.

Various artists, *Put the Book Back on the Shelf*, Image, 2006.

Ron Regé Jr., *The Awake Field*, Drawn & Quarterly, 2006.

Vanessa Davis, *Spaniel Rage*, Buenaventura Press, 2006.

Bryan Lee O'Malley's *Scott Pilgrim* books to date are *Scott Pilgrim's Precious Little Life* (2004), *Scott Pilgrim Vs. the World* (2005), and *Scott Pilgrim and the Infinite Sadness* (2006), all published by Oni Press.

Kazimir Strzepek, *The Mourning Star*, Bodega, 2006.

Renée French, *The Ticking*, Top Shelf Productions, 2006.

For Megan Kelso's *The Squirrel Mother*, see chapter 3.

John Porcellino, *Diary of a Mosquito Abatement Man*, La Mano, 2005.

INDEX